MESSAGE TO THE LEVITES
THERE IS AN ORDER TO TRUE WORSHIP!

ELMUS L. HIGH JR.

Copyright © 2013 by Elmus L. High Jr.

Message to the Levites
There is an order to True Worship!
by Elmus L. High Jr.

Printed in the United States of America

ISBN 9781625098856

All rights reserved solely by the author. The author guarantees all contents are original and do not infringe upon the legal rights of any other person or work. No part of this book may be reproduced in any form without the permission of the author. The views expressed in this book are not necessarily those of the publisher.

Unless otherwise indicated, Bible quotations are taken from:

The New King James Version (NKJV). Copyright © 1982 by Thomas Nelson, Inc. Used by permission. All rights reserved.

The New International Version (NIV). Copyright © 1973, 1978, 1984, 2011 by Biblica, Inc.™. Used by permission. All rights reserved.

The English Standard Version (ESV). Copyright © 2001 by Crossway, a publishing ministry of Good News Publishers. Used by permission. All rights reserved.

The Amplified Bible (AMP). Copyright © 1954, 1958, 1962, 1964, 1965, 1987 by The Lockman Foundation. Used by permission. All rights reserved.

The Darby Translation, The American Standard Version and The King James Version, all Public Domain.

Different Bibles were used to get a full scope and clarity of what's being said, and to dispel any questions of what God is actually saying based on the rightly divided Word of Truth.

Information compiled in the Commentary, Study Guide and Levitical References were with the assistance of crosswalk.com ministry study bible

Additional Commentary, Study Guide and Levitical References by Elmus L. High Jr.

www.xulonpress.com

DEDICATION

THIS BOOK IS DEDICATED TO ALL APOSTLES, PROPHETS, EVANGELISTS, PASTORS, TEACHERS, MUSICIANS, SINGERS, DANCERS, WORSHIP & PRAISE LEADERS, USHERS, ATTENDANTS AND ALL WHO SERVE GODS PEOPLE.

THIS IS A BOOK TO TEACH, TRAIN AND INFORM US HOW WE ARE DESIGNED TO OPERATE IN THE HOUSE OF GOD, IN THE MINISTRY OF A LEVITE. TO UNCOVER SATAN'S PLAN TO ATTACK THE HOUSE OF GOD ACROSS THIS NATION & WORLD THRU DECIEPT!

I DEDICATE THIS BOOK AND MANUAL TO THE CAUSE OF SPIRITUAL WARFARE!

IT'S ALL DEDICATED BACK TO GOD.

11/11/17 — Thank you God

ACKNOWLEDGEMENTS

First and foremost I would like to thank my Lord and Savior Jesus Christ, for saving my life and giving me the power to become one of his sons. I thank Him for the vision and understanding to write this book. It's all because of Him that I'm even able to do this. He's the one that makes it all go!

I thank my Pastors, Apostle, Dr. Thomas H. Vinson and Lady Elect, Dr. Carolyn Vinson, whom the Lord has allowed me to be under their spiritual covering for over 28 years. I thank you both for your guidance, love and friendship. You are simply the best Leaders on the face of the earth. I thank the Lord for my natural parents, the late Pastor Elmus L. High Sr. and First Lady Roberta High.

Thank you for the unmatched examples you were of faithfulness and love. You loved me and my siblings all the way to the end. Dad I thank God for the awesome anointing that was on your life that allowed you to pray and believe God until our Mother was raised up from the dead. Mom, (after God bought you back to us and you lived another 24 years after Dads prayer of faith) I thank you for showing us true love to the magnitude that brought junkies, pimps, prostitutes and rejects off the streets and brought them into your home and into the church to be saved and become respectful men and women. I'm thankful for how you trained us in the Word of God and how you made us go to vacation bible school, even though we used to sneak off and run down to Mr. Redding's candy store. I miss the both of you, but I'll carry it from here. To Sheila, Sharon, Edwin and Eric, my brothers and sisters. We have a relationship that can't be broken. Let's stay together and get it done! Also to my church family, Highpoint Christian Tabernacle. If you've never been to an "anointed service," you have to get to, THE POINT! Stop by, we'll love on you real good, but I'd advise you not to come by if you're not ready to hear truth.!

CHARGE IT TO OUR HEADS, NOT OUR HEARTS

In our quest to gather all the information for this manual, and even though the book has been edited several times. There yet may be type o's along the way.

Please don't hold it against us. If you find type errors throughout the book, please let us know, so as more books are printed, we can do so with fewer errors or mistakes as they are found.

We desire to present this work to you with a spirit of excellence.

God Bless You

RECOMMENDATIONS

This manual can be use as a study tool or reference guide in your own personal studies. Its contents can also be applied in your bible studies, ministers meetings, youth explosions, music workshops and symposiums, music classes and much, much, more.

This book is full of scripture references and study guides that will take you through the Word of God. It will provoke you to study and search the scriptures to see if these things are so. For the Word of God tells us to; *"search the scriptures, for in them ye think ye have eternal life."* In other words you don't know if you have eternal life or not unless you read them. My father used to have a saying that says; "If it's not written in the Word, it's not so!"

You will find truth and revelation herein, with a right now prophetic utterance that can only come from the Word of God.

Many of the issues Elder High *covers* or *uncovers* in this book had not yet taken place at the time the Lord began revealing it to him.

This manual will give you total insight on the *anointed* and *separated* call and *ministry* of a **Levite.** It shows you how they operated back in the bible and how we are to conduct ourselves today. God has not changed, but man has!

There are many areas in this book that go into very intricate detail concerning certain religions and beliefs, but it is no way belittling anyone or putting anyone down.

In obedience to Gods commission, we go into detail to give you the actual history or origin of a situation in order to establish and present the information being covered.

This book will *enhance* your understanding of the Word of God and what He is requiring of us who are called by His holy name.

We encourage every preacher, musician, singer, dancer and lay member to get this book into your hands. **It's a must for your library!**

WARNING!!!!!!

There are pictures in chapters 3 and 8 that depict the subjects discussed, that may not be suitable for your children to look at. Understand we're fighting in a spiritual war with our adversary the devil himself and we should take every precaution to protect our seed. If you look throughout scripture, the enemy always sought after the seed and he's hasn't changed his mind today either. In chapter 8 we talk about the *tarot cards* and it's a very *spiritually demonic* subject we cover. Yes, inform your children but you decide whether to expose them to the illustrations used in those chapters.

Please pray and use wisdom in this matter. Our goal is to impart and enhance the people of God, not to tear down or destroy reputations or names. God is not in that!!!

These issues had to be covered in order for God to uncover the plan of the devil against the people of God and his plan to destroy this world through ignorance and deceit!

FOREWORD

BY: APOSTLE, DR. THOMAS H. VINSON PASTOR AND FOUNDER OF HIGHPOINT CHRISTIAN TABERNACLE SMYRNA, GA. 30082

He that hath an ear, let him hear what the Spirit saith unto the churches (Revelations 3:22).

In these days, God speaks to those who have spiritual ears to hear. The Holy Spirit is sending a true word letting the body of Christ know how to truly worship God.

There should be no doubt among believers as to the origin of music and the critical part it plays in our worship experience.

Man was made to worship. Yet, because of man's ignorance and inability to know in and of himself how to worship God as He desires to be worshipped, God has laid down a complete plan in His word as to how, when, where and why we are to worship Him.

John 4:23-24 tells us, "But the hour cometh and now is, when the true worshippers shall worship the Father in Spirit and in truth: for the Father seeketh such to worship Him. God is a Spirit; and they that worship Him must worship Him in spirit and in truth."

For this cause, I feel that this book written by Elder Elmus L. High Jr. is a tool that the body of Christ needs at this critical time in our church history. Elder High has dedicated himself to this particular area of study and has spent countless hours, weeks months and years in preparing this book. With the help of almighty God, he has carried the burden of wanting all believers to know true worship.

Elder High is a true Levite. As an anointed preacher, writer, musician and singer he understands that true worship ushers in the presence of the Lord. As believers, we must realize that it is so important to know that when we assemble ourselves together, we desire true worship so that the Lord's anointing will come into our midst. Yes, God's anointing through true worship will destroy yokes and heal sick bodies. Emotions will be healed and people will be delivered and set free from all types of bondages.

I highly recommend this book for every born again believer. Especially to those of you who want to have a closer understanding of the correlation between music and the worship experience. This book is a must read!

Humbly submitted,
Apostle Thomas H. Vinson

INTRODUCTION

I've been a musician for over 40 years and a minister of God's Word for over 27 years and I've witnessed a lot of things in ministry. One thing I've come to know and understand is the fact that many preachers, teachers, musicians, singers, dancers and ushers, have limited understanding of what a Levite actually is. They've heard it preached by others or they've heard their Sunday school teacher, grandmother or grandfather tell them a story about it. But they really don't have a total grasp of what a Levite is according to scripture.

Levites were set aside and chosen by God to do the work of the priesthood, oversee the worship in the Tabernacle and later on in the Temples. In this book or manual as I like to call it, you will find out who they were and where they came from. Also you will understand why God chose them and what He expected from them.

Even though we are in the New Testament age, we are now God's spiritual Levites that yet have a call and mandate from God to be His chosen ones in the Houses of Worship all across this land. He's still calling for us to be holy and separated for His use; from the presbytery to the musician, singer and dancer, all who are called to lead God's people in Word or in music. You will also experience an in-depth look into the camp and observe the plans of Satan to come against you, but his target is the Church. Meticulous details are given in this book that have uncovered his agenda and will open your eyes to the straight up truth concerning the devils deceit. My brothers and sisters, you are the ones who God called to be on the front lines to fight the enemy. You are the one's who have been anointed of God to pave the way for the Word of God to come forth in free course. You are the ones who have been chosen to take His people into His presence, and for this Satan is mad at you because you now are what he used to be!

This book and teaching manual will help you find out who you are in the eyesight of God, and will give you a better understanding of what God expects from you as a Levite. Not just a preacher or musician but a true Levite.

My beloved, when you discover this key; you will be a good minister, fully nourished in God's Word. This key will catapult you into another anointing from God and you will no longer be ignorant concerning the devil's crafty devices.

The book is sure to open your eye's to things you may have wondered about and wanted to know, and it will open them to some things you may not have wanted to know as well.

But God has revealed His Word to me in a very unusual and powerful way. He has allowed me to look into the deep recesses of His Word and into the dark chambers of the enemy's camp.

I graduated from High school and only attended two years of college. I do not have any of the degrees that many writers have when they write books. But one thing I do have, that's God's Word and His unmistakable anointing resting on my life. I also have His promise that if I would be obedient and write this book; cry loud and spare not; He would cause this writing to go across the globe. He told me because of the vital and serious contents in this, He would give it a international floor and audience. I told the Lord not for my sake, but that His name might be praised and glorified!

My beloved; God has something greater He yet wants to do in your lives. He said that we have not yet tapped in to the place of anointing and power that He's destined for our lives and ministries.

Some people have said that there are no more Levites! Well if this is true, then call all the pastors and tell them to close their bibles and stop preaching the word. Call all the parking lot attendants, ushers, and yes, even call all the musicians, as well. Put your drums sticks away, no more tinkling the ivory, also tape up the mouths of the singer and rapper. There's no need for it right?

Understand that NOW, we are the spiritual Jews and you won't find anywhere in the bible where the actual order stopped. The priest continued in the New Testament, music continued as well. How do we know this? It's because, the whole *levitical order* is based on the worship and order of Heaven!!! So, no, it's not just for the Old Testament, it's for us today.

God is saying that if we would but follow the *order* and the pattern that He has set in place, from the tabernacles of Moses and David, and the Temples of Solomon and Hezekiah to the Centers and Cathedrals of today, then He would bless our ministries and lives.

If we would walk in obedience to His Word, God is going to shift our ministries to the next spiritual realm and He is going to send a word for the nations and he's going to send a word for our local assemblies. He's sending a message to every head and leader; He's sending a **message to the Levites!**

Come let us reason together in the Word of God to find what our place is as Levites.

This book will provoke you to study and get a deeper understanding of God's Word concerning this call. Don't just take my word for it. You search His Word and His heart, to see if these things are so.

God Bless You!
Elder Elmus L. High Jr.

Introduction

TABLE OF CONTENTS

Dedication v
Acknowledgements vii
Recommendations xi
Forward by Apostle Thomas H. Vinson..................................... xiii
Introduction by Elder Elmus L. High Jr.................................... xv

Chapter 1 .... **It's Been My Experience** 25
    Subject
    Prophetic Words from the Author p. 45

Chapter 2 .... **What You Don't Know Can Hurt Others**................ 49

Chapter 3 .... **About the Levites**............................ 55
    Subjects
    What is a Levite? p. 55
    Where did they come from? p.55
    The Book of Exodus and Leviticus p. 56
    What were their Responsibilities? p. 56
    In David's reign, the Levites Served in Rotation p. 57
    David's Internal Tabernacle Issues p. 57
    Many Leaders Deal with Immature Musicians "Naturally and Spiritually" p.57
    The Priest & Levites had to be Holy p.58
    The Priests & Levites had to go through Purifications p. 60
    Moral Standards pg. 61
    What Did they Do? Pg 62
    They were Consecrated by p. 62
    The Instruments p. 62
    The Musician p. 64
    King David's Three "Chief Musicians" p. 66
    Musical Notations & Choreographic Directions/ Movements p. 67
    Their Place in the Ministry p. 70
    The Gift vs. The Anointing p. 70

Sing with an Understanding p. 75
I Never Knew You p. 79
The Song p. 81
Your Gift Works on You First p.84
Bring me a Minstrel p. 85
Psalmists/ Singers/ Worship Leaders p.89
"Psalmist" p. 90
"Singers" p.92
"Worship Leaders" p. 93
Bling, Blings not a New Thing p.95
Hip Hop or Stop? P 101
Goddess Kali, The Thug & My lord the Cars p.103
Rap is not Hip-Hop p. 111

Chapter 4 ... **The Levites Shall Set it Up, Take it Down and Camp** 118
Subjects
The Revelation I received was this p.119
A Song of Degrees of David p. 121

Chapter 5 .... **Vision of the Anointed Cherub, Lucifer** 122
Subjects
Bellows p.132
Process of the Brain p.140

Chapter 6 .... **Asaph, Ethan and Heman** 144
Subjects
David's Musical Organizational Chain of Command p. 147

Chapter 7 .... **Psalms and the Dance** 149
Subjects
Dance in a Worship Form is Totally Original p. 155

Chapter 8 .... **To Mime or not to Mime** 158
Subjects
Mimes description pg 158
Primitive Times of Mime *p. 165*
Ancient Greek and Romans *p. 165*
The Romans p.166
Pantomimes p. 167
"Why am I Uncovering This?" p. 172
Tarot p. 174
Mime, Fool, Jester, Tarot p. 178
Goth Culture p.184 b

What was the question? p.189
So who bought this into the Church? p. 189
Music from the end of the World p. 190 b
It's a mockery! *p. 194 b*
The art of Storytelling p. 195 b
Comedian Spirit p. 197 b
God is Revealing the Comparisons p. 199 b

Chapter 9 ....**Selah**................................ 202

Chapter 10 .... **The Alter** 205

Chapter 11 ....**The Tabernacle**........................ 208

Chapter 12 .... **The Temple** 218

Chapter 13 .... **Satan's Plan in Homosexuality** 225
Subjects
Intro to Satan's Plan in Homosexuality
What God says about it
Prophecy concerning this
We're made in His likeness
Plan to destroy the church
Men, take your Rightful place
God set the Order

Chapter 14 .... **Levites** 240

Chapter 15 ....**Priest, Priesthood** 245
Subjects
Old Testament Priesthood p. 245
A Kingdom of Priests p. 246
The Aaronic Priesthood p. 247
The Administration and Ministry of the Sanctuary p.248
The Custody and Administration of the Mosaic Law p. 249 b
History p.251 a
New Testament Priesthood p. 251
High Priests, Chief Priests and Priests p251 b.
Jesus as Priest and High Priest p. 252
The Priesthood of Believers p. 254 a
The Priesthood Today p. 254 b

Chapter 16 .... **The Worship** 256
   Subjects
   Types of Service in Worship   p. 257

Chapter 17 .... **Cherub/Angles and Seraphim** 260
   Subjects
   Cherub, Cherubim   p.261 a
   Angels   p. 261
   The Old Testament Angel's   p. 261 b
   New Testament Angel's   p. 263 b
   The Cherubim and Seraphim   p. 266
   The Imagery of Revelation 4: 6-9   p. 266 b

Chapter 18 .... **The Amen** 268

Final Note 271

Questions & Answers Discussion Guide and Workbook 273

Commentary 369
   Subjects
   The Musical Men with David   p 371
   Song of the Purpose and the Mercies of God   p 374
   Fallen Lucifer and Those Who Carry Like Spirits   p 377
   Priesthood in Bible History   p 385
   Carnal Pride and Self-Sufficiency   p 391
   Christ's Superior Priesthood   p 395

Study Guide to Know your God 401
   Subjects
   Introduction to Authors Study Guide   p 401
   Ministry, Minister   p 401 b
   Servant, Service   p 404 b
   Words to Study   p 406

Note Pad 408

Bibliography 431

"A Questions & Answers", **"Discussion and Activation Guide"** will accompany this book in the near future" A portion of the "soon to be released workbook" can be found in the back of this book for teaching and learning purposes.

MESSAGE TO THE LEVITES
Contact & Booking Information
Email us at: LEVITEMINISTER@AIM.COM
Or
Contact us at 678 994 5125 or through the church office
Highpoint Christian Tabernacle Church
3269 Old Concord Rd. Smyrna, Ga. 30082 or
770 438-8587
www.highpointlive.org

CHAPTER 1

IT'S BEEN MY EXPERIENCE

It's Been My Experience. When the Lord first spoke to me about writing this book, I responded much in the way Moses did when the Lord told him to go down into Egypt, and tell the Pharaoh to let His people go. I told God how I couldn't spell all that well, when in fact English and Spelling were two of my best subjects in school. Like Moses, who was raised in the ways of the Egyptians, I said, "Well Lord, my speech isn't the best and I'm not all that polished or articulate!" I also told Him how I didn't know enough to write a book on anything. God said, "I know this, but I do!" In other words, He was telling me how it wasn't going to be me anyway. He told me that He would speak through me, and that His Will would be accomplished in this writing.

Furthermore, as I began to think about it, and gain confidence in God, I told myself that this was just the kind of thing I would do. What I mean is, I've always been the type of person who wasn't afraid to try anything, and once I start on something, I'm not going to quit until I have it done! So usually with me, it's a do or die situation, when it comes to trying something that I've never done before.

Some years ago, there was a man of God who came through and preached for our church. In one of the services, he began to stack pieces of paper on the pulpit floor that had a name or a title on them. He had everyone come up and get a sheet of this paper, and to the amazement of most, the paper consisted of a name or some piece of information about their character.

I wasn't there at that service, I was home sick in bed but my wife told my eldest son to get into the line to get one of those sheets of paper for your dad.

When I read the sheet of paper I found the word, **Tarabai** written on it. It is a word that speaks to *tenacity*. I'm not really afraid of much and I will pretty much say whatever needs to be said when it comes down to it. It also means, *"defender of the word."*

I'll go after it even if I don't feel I know it all. I remember applying for a job and the supervisor asked me if I had any experience in that area? I told him, no, but if they were willing to show me I'll know! That's how I am, If God says He'll show me, then I'll know.

So when the Lord began to speak to me and began to confirm it through others, he confirmed it through people I knew had no idea how the Lord was dealing with me concerning this manual. So after much confirmation and prayer, I told Him Yes!

I asked the Lord where do I go, or how do I start? He told me; I already have most of the ingredients to complete it! What was that, I asked? He said, "Your experiences as a musician and minister." He told me to use **my experiences** in the things He'd already taken me through, and it would be a blessing. It's always been a trip to me, *(if I may use that word)* that as people of God, many of the tests and trials we experience in life, aren't just for us. What!!? You mean to tell me that all the praying, fasting and going through trials isn't for me? The answer is No! It helps you, and matures you, but it's not all for you. You see, we go through different trials in life to make us stronger. It makes us better people, and most of all better Christians. Notice I used the words, go through. God never meant for us to stay in our tests, but to go through them. He never allows any test or trial to destroy us. Break us? Yes indeed. Destroy us? No!

You have to understand that when we go through our trials without complaining, He's giving us a testimony so that we can help someone else. You can never have a testimony, without first having a test. Something has to become weak or even die, in order for the will of God to be birthed in us. In other words; we die to ourselves, so that the life of Christ can shine through us.

It's Been My Experience. Didn't Paul say in 2 Corinthians 4:10 – We're always bearing about in the body, the **dying of the Lord Jesus** that the life also of Him might be made manifest in our body?

We are being tried and tested in every area of life, and it's so God can use us and get glory out of our lives. God always wants and deserves the glory! I know you've heard it all before but it's true. How can you minister to someone if you've never gone through anything? Most (if not all) of the people you'll come in contact with will have issues or things they're going through.

You wouldn't have an audience at all, if you've lived a *perfect* and untouchable life.

Who could you talk to, or how could you explain how perfect you've been? You couldn't tell anyone how to come out of a life of sin could you? Who could you tell how God fixed your broken marriage that should have been destroyed years ago, or whom could you tell about the sickness in your body, and how the Lord healed you, if your life were perfect? Probably no one! Understand this, everybody "God" sends you to, will have an issue or a situation they need deliverance from or need strength to endure. That's why He sends you! People, who are well, do not need a physician.

So what does God do then? Who can He send? Who will go for Him? Well my brothers and sisters, He has to send us. Imperfect people, to do a perfect work! Perfect doesn't mean perfection! What do I mean by that? Paul tells us that we are striving for perfection, but total perfection won't come until Jesus returns. Perfection speaks to the condition and intent of the heart. Look in the scriptures. Nearly everyone God ever called to do a work for Him, had some type of issue. David's hands were bloody and unclean, being a man of war and also an adulterer, Moses killed an Egyptian and hid his body in the sand, Abraham was a liar saying, Sarah was his sister, Aaron was in idolatry, **while** God was speaking into his life concerning the priesthood. Peter had a bad temper, cutting a soldiers ear off, and then cursed when put under pressure, Samson and Solomon as strong and wise as they were, had "flesh" issues.

Jacob was a tricky trickster, cheater or supplanter, and even Paul, gave consent to the murder of countless Christians. Need I go on? Now don't misunderstand me. Just because I spoke of imperfections, doesn't mean we have a crutch or a license to sin.

What I'm saying is, we must go through hardship, pain, difficulty, failure, misunderstandings, temptations and persecution to be a well rounded Christian; tried in the fire, and one who is prepared to be used by God. He uses an imperfect people to do a perfect work!

True anointing comes from pain, hardship, trials, temptation and yes even failure.

People need to hear truth. You are cheating people out of a great deliverance when you hold back where you've come from and what God has taken you through.

Your trials are a blessing, because we overcome by the words of our testimonies, and by the blood of the lamb.

When the Lord told me to use the experiences I already had, my mind went all the way back to the time when I was a young boy. From the time I was 5 or 6 years old, I knew I wanted to be a musician and a preacher. When I was around five years old, I traveled to different churches singing. They would stand me on a chair so the people could see me, and I believe the only song I knew was, "*I Know a Man From Galilee.*" I can remember my father building me a small pulpit in the front yard where I would preach and imitate my pastor. (Pastor Justice Morgan) He used to pray, rubbing his hands on either side of his face.

It's Been My Experience. It's something I actually now do to this very day. That let me know that as Priests and Levites, we affect people and the way they live their lives. *(your lifestyle)* I remember when I was about 7 years old, our family used to travel back to my parent's hometown in Wills Point Texas, my cousin, "James Earl Williams" used to let me come up on the stage at his church where many of my relatives attended. My parents bought me a little red plastic guitar, and I used sit in church next to my cousin, and pretend I could play the guitar. By the time I was 9 years old, I could strum a pretty good tune on the guitar and used to play in our organizations district meetings back in Colorado. In the sixth grade my music teacher told my parents she felt that I should play a horn of some sort. In the school bands back then, there weren't any positions for guitar, so they all picked the saxophone!

Now understand, back in those days, there weren't too many sax players in the church. For the most part, you only saw a guitar, a piano, (a little out of tune) and a small drum set. Oh yes, and some of the elderly women would have washboards, and we would just clap our hands until the spirit of the Lord fell. And believe me it did! But back then you didn't hear of many sax players in the church. I used to hear of an awesome saxophonist, by the name of Vernard Johnson, and a good friend of mine by the name of, Louis Brown.

When I finally agreed to play the saxophone, Louis Brown was on his way to college. I remember he taught me two songs, *"Precious Lord"* and *"His Eye's Are on the Sparrow."*

I started playing the saxophone at age 11, and by the time I was 14 years old, I was already playing in studios throughout the state. By the time I was 15, I had already played my horn in several different states across the country and in many churches and major events. I remember getting the opportunity to play with Shirley Caesar at our Civic Center in Colorado Springs. I was invited to come and play as an opening act, and when she heard me play, she asked if I wanted to stay and play along with her band while she was in concert? Of course I said yes. Afterward, she asked for my autograph and prophesied to me, telling me that God was going to take me across this land. At that time, I thought it would be only in music, but God sees much more than we do. He knows the end from the beginning. I always thought signing an autograph for her was special because she's, well. . . . she's Shirley Caesar!!

I was invited to come and play on various local radio stations in Colorado Springs, Colorado, where I grew up. I finally got the chance to play my sax with Venard Johnson. As a matter of fact the way we met was pretty funny. I was invited to come and be an opening act at one of his concerts, and since I studied his style so closely, I could play many of his songs "exactly" the way he played them. So when I started playing, being one of the opening acts, he came out after I completed the song, and began to ask, "who is this out here playing like me?" I told him that I loved his style, and I'd been studying it for the last couple of years. I knew he was amazed at the closeness in our styles, seeing I was only about 15 years old, and he had already made a name for himself in the secular jazz industry and now the gospel industry. I told God at that young age, that if He would anoint me and allow me to be one of the best horn players, and cause me to be a blessing to His people, I would always use the gift for His glory and His alone.

I'm sure you already know, testing time was coming!

It's Been My Experience. I began to play my horn with many choirs and groups, traveling year around in and out of town, recording and making money here and there. But my main focus was always on being a blessing to His people. I've always believed that God anointed me to play with an unusual anointing, because of my desire to be a blessing to His people, even at an early age. As the years began to pass, I had many offers to play secular jazz, and travel with secular bands but I never did. My father used to tell me of times when secular producers would visit our church to hear me play. He never told me about them until I was older, because he knew I couldn't handle that kind of pressure and success that early. He knew that kind of lifestyle would destroy me and my love for the things of God.

Understand that there are so many demands on you in the secular music industry. You are not always your own, you belong to them! Who are them? Record companies, managers or producers. Musicians, I understand the fight you feel, when it comes to your gift and abilities. But no matter what the world is doing, "IF YOU ARE CALLED TO BE A LEVITE"; you can't do everything everybody else does. You can't play secular and sacred music and be all right with God. *(there, somebody said it!)* **Not if you're a Levite!** A Levite is called for the work of the ministry and the ministry alone!! In the OT they were called for the work of the tabernacle and temple. These are some of the areas I'll cover in this manual. I know some feel they're just "giggin" and playing music is just a job. You're just trying to pay the bills. If that's the case, you're a hireling, but such is not the work of a Levite! Let's make this perfectly clear and get an understanding. Many Pastors and ministries won't cry out against this because they need some of you to play in their churches. Not realizing that they're forfeiting the anointing of God that comes from an **anointed** musician. Yes, by contracting *professional musicians*, the music is probably going to be very good. No one appreciates good music more than I do, but there's more to it than that. Is this what God wanted or intended for the church? What really matters when it comes down to it, is true worship. A lot of people are praising Him, but only those who have a relationship with Him can worship. It has to be done in spirit and truth; you must have a relationship, so that you can understand what God wants to **hear** in the midst of worship.

What are we worshipping for? Do we really want to experience a mighty move of God, or do we only want to fill the seats because our band is tight? Yes, I believe in the spirit of excellence in our music, but not at the risk of there being an absence of Gods presence. We need Gods anointing! We have to be so very careful in this day and time, as we usher in a more contemporary style of worship, that we don't usher out the presence of the true and living God. Yes, King David did employ and pay professional musicians to play for their worship in the tabernacle, but understand this; the chief musicians he paid were minstrels, composers, writers and prophets who were in *covenant relationship* with the King. David knew them and grew in ministry with them, they were around him for years, and were proven faithful in the house of God before any residuals were paid out. He didn't make a radio announcement, or fill out any online application, to see if he could find a musician who had the right credentials.

David appointed men who could take them to <u>another level in worship</u>, not just <u>another level in music</u>. I wish I could see the looks on your faces right about now, because this goes against the grain and it doesn't agree with the compromises some ministries are making today. So just what are you saying Elder High? Is it wrong to employ musicians for our houses of worship or not? No it's not wrong! Understand what's being said here. What is God looking for in worship?

It's Been My Experience. Make sure that it is for the right reasons, and that it is an anointed individual who is in *covenant* with the ministry, not just a *contracted* hireling who doesn't always have a heartbeat for the ministry or share in the vision of the leaders. One sure way to find out is; to take a look at the pay.

If it isn't right, you won't see them very long, because they feel they can get what they need and deserve somewhere else. They don't understanding that their true pay comes from God. Most don't understand the concept of covenant. Covenant can be long term, even permanent!

A contract is usually short term and temporal. Just know God has men and women who have a relationship with Him, and are extremely skillful and anointed in what they do. Look for them! Ask God, as a leader of His people, to send you skillful musicians who are saved and have a true relationship with God. You need someone who can see your vision and assist in carrying it out. God knows when your ministry gets to that point, and you feel you must provide finances to bring skillful musicians in. Pray and ask God to direct you. You don't want to risk the move of God, for someone who can enhance the ministry on the surface, but the hearts of the people are still empty on the inside, because they don't have a *ministers of music* who can actually lead them into the presence of the God. Instead we have gifted men and women leading us into a carnal and emotional good time. But nobody's really being ministered to; what happens is, it allows the enemy to insert a spirit of delusion and deception in our praise and worship services. We become spiritually desensitized, where we can no longer discern the difference between gifted ministers of music and anointed ones. We can no longer tell what's truly anointed, or what's a gift in operation. A gifted person is mostly what our *flesh* wants today, but a *holy ghost filled* and anointed person is what our *spirits* need to usher us into the presence of the Lord.

So you're saying our musicians and singers should be saved, and spirit filled before they can truly minister to us and usher us into Gods presence?

Are you kidding? You're kidding right? Yes, they must be filled with the spirit of God!

You can't tell me that a musician or singer, who isn't in touch with God and doesn't have a personal relationship with Him, is effectively able to minister the things of God. You see that's where we make one of our biggest mistakes in the

House of God. We need to hear music that is anointed, with lyrics that can bring deliverance and destroy yokes.

When I was growing up with my brothers and sisters singing and playing instruments in church, I always had a hard time with the church musicians who wouldn't put their all into their instrument. It still bothers me today; my motto was and still is," the world doesn't possess the greatest musicians." God will always reserve; let me say that again! God will ALWAYS, reserve the best for Himself! What's the greatest to you; a gifted musician or an anointed one? What I'm saying is; God can provide us with those who are skilled and anointed all in one package. They're still out there and God is sending them. They may not have the biggest names, or may not have recorded on everyone's album, but they're out there. Pastors if you really desire to have or keep the presence of God in your ministries, God will see to it that He sends you just what the house needs to keep the ministry moving and growing. Therefore, I encourage every musician to learn your instrument, know how to flow with God, be skillful **and** anointed. Don't just get up and depend on the anointing alone! Give God your best in whatever you're called to do! Remember the story of the talents, faithfulness with a few, will cause you to receive more.

It's Been My Experience. If you *invest* in your gift, not only will it grow, but you will receive other giftings as well. Your faithfulness in one or two original gifts can cause your gifts and abilities to multiply. I believe with all of my heart, that because of my earnest plea for God to make me one of His best, He honored that. I'm not bragging or boasting, I'm just trying to point out the fact that if you are sincere and give God your all in the gifts He's already given you, they will explode like a volcano, and the overflow will spill out onto others who will benefit from the giftings God has placed inside you.

Let's look at the secular for a moment. Most of the secular musicians do whatever it takes to become the best at what they do. It is said that the artist Prince, practiced everyday for hours, perfecting his gifts and talents. He took time to balance and enhance each and every one of his gifts, because he plays several instruments. I know, I know, time is always a factor and you don't have his time or his money. He had this harsh regimen of practicing way before he became a big star. The fame was the manifestation and reward of his hard work put in year's prior. It comes down to <u>sacrifice</u> and a <u>love</u> for what you do. (oh that painful word, sacrifice) You might as well get in your mind that anything you do for the Lord is going to require a sacrifice. We want the glory, but we don't want to make any sacrifices for it. We are to present our bodies as living sacrifices in order to be used effectively by Him. I believe that one of the sacrifices we should make; is the perfecting of our gifts. Most of God's people won't invest time and effort in their gifts; instead just throw it all on God to make up the difference. When in fact, God wants and expects YOU to enhance what He gives you. YOU practice, YOU learn how to play in all the keys, YOU take the time to see what God expects of you and your gift. YOU come to rehearsals,

YOU learn how to flow and hear in the spirit, YOU DO IT! Then God, seeing your faithfulness in what He's given you, will enhance the gift and most of all, He'll anoint it. We as a people of God sometimes don't put forth the effort to make ourselves better in the things of God. We want God to do it all as we stand by with a no care attitude. Some will even carry a, "just be glad I'm even here" attitude. Well, we won't stand for it, and God defiantly doesn't have to stand for that type of attitude concerning something that belongs to Him anyway. He'll just pass you by and you'll never reach the potential, God intended for you. It is a privilege and an honor to be used by God. Never forget that! The Bible tells us that the children of darkness are wiser than the children of light! Why is that? It's because sometimes we as the people of God, can be naturally and spiritually lazy and never take our God given talents to their limits or take them serious enough to manage, nor do we invest in the substance that God has placed in our hands. We must become better stewards over everything God places in our hands, whether finances, musical gifts, or ministries. We should consider what a powerful weapon and tool we have in the giftings God has given us, not to mention the anointing of God, which should be treated as a precious stone and guarded at all times.

God gave me an illustration of how we ought to carry His gifts and anointing. He told me to take a cup and fill it to the rim with **hot water**. He told me to walk around the room with the cup. As I walked around the room *softly and carefully*, as not to spill any of the water; God spoke to me and said; *this is how you should carry my anointing, softly, carefully*. As I walked, others came into the room almost bumping into me. I yelled out; watch out, don't you see me carrying this cup? God says; *the anointed* can't have just anyone around them, causing them to waste the anointing. **It's Hot** and can burn you and others if not handled properly! **Am I talking to anyone?**

It's Been My Experience. There were times growing up in the church as musicians, when my siblings and I struggled with our gifts and how we were to use them. There were many expectations people had of us as gifted musicians and as PK's or *pastors kids*. We all were very talented at an early age and God blessed us to sing and play well on our instruments, but at the same time, it put a lot of pressure on us from the church and the secular world. In church we were expected to do NO WRONG, and at the same time, fight off the advances from outside forces, calling us away to do things outside of the church. People would ask me; "Elmus, when are you coming out with an album?" Time passed as, <u>45's and LP's turned into 8-tracks, then those 8-tracks turned into cassettes and CD's</u> , and still no project from me. Now of course here comes Satan adding his two cents saying; "hey man, you know people are waiting on you to do something right?" "Your God STILL hasn't come through, why are you waiting on Him man?" "Why don't you just take some of those offers you've been getting?" *DO YOUR THING! Besides, ain't nothin' happenin' for you on the church scene anyway.*

I'm sure you know by now, when the devil tempts you, it's exactly that! A TEMPTATION! Okay, be honest! You know when "mr. temper" comes to try you, he's coming with something that <u>moves you</u>. If he tempts you with a cigarette and you never smoked, it's not much of a temptation. But he comes with something he knows is going to get next to you or bother your flesh. Understand how the fight works as musicians. Satan used to be who you ARE!

Remember when Lucifer (now Satan) was in the presence of the Lord from the beginning, his *design and responsibility* was to orchestrate the worship before the very face of God.

Can you say that? Or has the tempter come and beguiled you? Does he have you saying the same things he used to say before he was cast out of heaven? Are you lifted up above measure with pride and arrogance?

As time went on the pressure to produce began to ware on me. People constantly asked me when was I coming out with an album, but I had nothing to tell them. Things got worse, after I moved from Colorado to Georgia in 1985. Seemed like I lost job after job, didn't have enough money. . .ever! My wife and I were happy but struggled financially while raising 3 young boys. God did bless us to keep them clothed, fed and in every sport you could imagine.

Still I felt the pressures of going out to do my own thing, but yet remained faithful to the House of God at the same time. Not you Elmus! You're the strong one; the one others come to for their encouragement. Don't get me wrong, I was faithful to my church and I was there nearly every time the doors opened, but you must understand that the devil doesn't care who or what you think you are, he'll tempt you anyway. I mean for real! Didn't he tempt Jesus after he had fasted forty days and nights? Jesus was at a weak fleshly point but at a strong spiritual point after fasting, and the devil still came to try Him. So you see, just because you pray and fast and you go to church every time the doors are open, just because you're gifted and anointed doesn't mean you're exempt from temptation. To be honest, you're actually a bigger mark and target.

As I continued to press on, things just never seem to click for me. I remember getting upset with the Lord and began verbalizing my discontent with Him and the way things were going in my life. I told God; either you move for me or I'm going back home to Colorado. The way I saw it, why should I keep putting up with this non-sense? I had enough talent to go outside of the church and make real money and not have to struggle! I meant it to! I remember taking my wife out to dinner, to explain and justify the way I was feeling. I remember telling her I was tired of being the good guy. Good guys always seemed to finish last!

It's Been My Experience. I was tired of waiting on promises that never ever seemed to come to past. Not understanding that when God makes you a promise, they are conditional. We're waiting on the promises of God but in the midst of our waiting, we continue to mess up, therefore starting the wait cycle over again. We are usually the cause of the hold up.

I went on telling my wife, *(Valerie)* "baby look what's going on, I have no job and no money, I can't even buy suits to make it to ALL the services we're expected to attend!" "God ain't doing nothing for me, ain't no manna fallin'out the sky, so I gotta go make the donuts myself!" "I'm a man, what am I supposed to do?" "Can't call mom or dad, they don't have any ends." "I'm not going to ask the church again for money!" "If God don't do it, I will!"(*can't you hear the influence of the devil in my voice right about now?*)

I began telling her what had happened to me earlier that day. After the devil whipped up on me real good about what I hadn't accomplished in my music. I saw a man driving up my street in a gold 400 LX Lexus; I mean this whip was tight! He saw me working in my yard and parked at the curb in front of my home. As I came up to him, he began to say; "hey bro, don't I know you?" "Yeah, you're that sax player that goes to Highpoint. (*my church, Highpoint Christian Tabernacle)* I said; "yea that's me, how did you know?" He said; "I heard you play the other Sunday at the church and you're the bomb!" (*here it comes!*) "Hey man, we need a horn player for our jazz band. You don't even have to miss your services dude, just come and jamm in California with us from Thursdays thru Saturdays, and we'll fly you back in time for services Sunday morning." (*can you hear the setup?*) "I mean it's cool, we play a little *churchy style* music too." "You know, **it's all just music right?**" At that point he pulled out a wad of money, ($50ties and $100dreds) and said; "you can make this money just like me and drive what I drive." "Who needs that; I was broke and waited on God testimony anyway?" "God didn't mean for you to be broke my brotha, here's my god, this wad supplies all my need, and heals me of all my disease, and look at you; you don't even have a job." "You have all that talent and ain't doing anything with it, man don't waste all your good talent inside the four walls of a church."

Now you have to understand, the *state of mind* I was in at that time. I had allowed the devil to feed my mind and my spirit with so much negative garbage and complaint that I couldn't even think straight. Can anyone relate? Here I was, saved, sanctified, filled with the Holy Ghost *(and that with a mighty burning fire)*, no money, no job, no self esteem but always trying to encourage someone else while my own situation was totally jacked up. Now here comes this brother who's serving the devil, pimpin' a phat ride, sportin' the nice shoes and don't forget about that wad of cheddar in his pocket. How can I witness to this brother while he's looking at the pitiful state I'm in?

I finished by telling my wife at dinner, that I was leaving to go to California with this band for about six months and I would be back. I told her that I would send her money every week and that she could spend money on her and the boys and get whatever they wanted. She could pay off all the bills and catch the mortgage up. I continued saying; "Can't you see my point baby?" "What do I have now, nothing?" "I see guys out there that I taught how to play, making it better than I am." "That bothers me baby, where's mine?" "I've been faithful,

I've tried to do the right things, I've tried to help people and now I want some stuff!" "I WANT MY STUFF!!"

I remember my wife telling me to talk to my Pastor about it to see what he says. NOT!! So I went on to church the next morning, determined to leave out that Monday morning.

It's Been My Experience. We got to church the next morning and I had enough nerve to tell God that I could pay better tithes if I had this money and opportunity. God told me; "just give what you owe me, along with what you have and I'll bless you." *(that's a message right there, did you hear that?)* As church let out, I was just trying to get out the doors fast so I could do my thing, when a mother of our church, *(Mother Shaw)* called for me to come over and talk with her. Man! I really didn't want to talk to her. She's like a female Jesus, or that's the way I looked at her. *(God knew how much I respected her)* Anyway, she called me over and began to tell me not to go. I acted as if I didn't know what she was talking about. She said; "God said don't go,"

I asked her "why?" "Nothings going right and I'm tired of trying."

She told me that if I went away from God, the devil would give me everything I wanted, cars, houses, money and fame, but at what cost?

I don't have to tell you all that the devil doesn't give you anything for free! **It will cost you**! Everything the devil has looks good, smells good, talks a good game, sounds good, but there's a price you have to pay for it. Are you willing to pay that price? Don't buy into anything before you find out how much it cost first. From my own experiences, it's more than you want to pay!

I began to think about, "so called", successful musicians who are out there in the secular world doing their thing and making lots of money and *seemingly* needing nothing, nothing materialistic that is. I began to think about some of the musicians I knew and used to listen to, how they are millionaires and can get anything they want but they're miserable, how is that? How is it that you can pay all of your bills, buy anything your heart desires, have the best this life has to offer and yet be miserable?

Well dear hearts it's not about the bling at all. God was just keeping me from destroying myself. He knows what's best for us even when we don't know ourselves. First of all, God didn't want me to record lots of albums, and run all over the country playing my sax in His name, and had not yet learned to live holy from day to day. God wanted to teach me something first.

I appreciate Him for that. He saw my heart at an early age how I purposely missed out on a lot of different sporting events in order to learn how to play the sax and be good, and better yet, be anointed. I always wanted to be used by God in some way or another. He had to first teach me how to be a saved young man and not just another musician running around playing before His people, but one living the life I played and sang about. He wanted me to be different than the others. God didn't want the same ole, same ole from me.

I remember a good friend of mine told me I was the first musician he had ever met who actually carried a bible. He said, not only did I carry one, but I knew the Word that was inside of it as well. I was totally amazed at what he said. All I know is I didn't want to be like everybody else, but at the same time I wanted to do something with what He gave me. Have you ever felt like that? Be honest! You don't want to really leave God or anything like that, but you have this tug on the inside that's pressing you to do something more with your gifts. You struggle with using your gifts, only in the confines of the four walls of your local church, then what Satan does is takes occasion against you while you're going through this struggle and begins to corner you off in much of the same way he cornered off the fallen angels. He tells you that you are better than the four walls of the church and you need to be heard. He plays on words, like he did Eve in the garden. Yes, your gifts will take you outside the WALLS OF THE CHURCH, BUT NOT OUTSIDE OF THE CHURCH!! Understand the devil aims to set you up, he knows the power of an anointed gift, and sets out to pervert the way you think.

It's Been My Experience. If he can get another musician to leave the church, he'll continue by compromising and prostituting your gifts, causing you to leave your place of worship.

By leaving your place of worship, I mean your consecrated life to God. Your place of worship!

I began to realize that the devil was trying to trick me, and God was trying to mature me. Gods plan wasn't at all to hold His blessings from me. He was going to perform everything He ever told me but He had to take me through some things to make me what He wanted me to be. He wanted to make sure that I could handle the things He would eventually do in my life. It was about character and integrity! God doesn't want us traveling the country using His name and not living the life we play, sing and preach about. It's time out for that! It's been time out actually!

All things work together for our good. He wanted my word ministry to walk hand in hand with my music ministry. Both had to be at the same level so He could use me the way He intended.

A couple of weeks had gone by after I changed my mind about going to California. I went to my church one Sunday evening to pray alone and empty out all my garbage and to be honest with God about the way I was yet feeling. I remember apologizing to God for entertaining the possibility of leaving Him to play secular music, because I had promised Him from a child that I would only use this gift for Him. I've been criticized for this, talked about, made fun of, and told that I was making a big mistake for making such a promise. But it didn't and still doesn't matter to me anymore. As I began to let it all go in prayer, the music, the money, the missed, *(or what I thought were missed)* opportunities, the fame and all that came with it. When I got to the place in my walk with God that those things were no longer important or the center of my attention and joy, that's when God started to move for me. I've learned over the years it's all about ministry. Many musicians will never be satisfied in their gifts until they develop a true relationship with Christ and understand the importance of the call on their life. I'm not saying God won't allow you to have fame and notoriety or be blessed financially with the gifts He's given you, but it shouldn't be the single most important reason why you do it. Ask yourself; what is your gift for, really? Is it to make a name for myself? Is it just a job or a gig to make ends meet? Or is it to give God glory? When ministry became my main focus, there arose a peaceful satisfaction that the worlds, fame or fortune could **never** give me. I remember how my Pastors wife called me up to pray for me during a service, and began to prophesy and tell me. "God said tell you, He hears your *horns on high*." That became the most important thing that, He was pleased with the music ministry He had put in me. God told me the playing of my horn came up to Him as a sweet savor and a pleasant sound in His ear." He told me He was pleased with the way I ministered to Him on my instrument. **WOW**! You'll never understand how much that meant to me. "<u>Horns on High</u>" was the name of a music demo I recorded in 1995.

I've since recorded another project titled, "Expression of Worship," which I released back in 2003. Neither recording were on a national scale but the recordings have blessed many people and God yet has greater things for me, like this Levites manual. . . . .

When my First lady *(my co-pastor)* spoke those words to me, it was like medicine to me, and just made everything alright. I had a better understanding of what God wanted from me and the gifts He had entrusted me with. I knew my First lady could identify with me. She's a very gifted songwriter and author. Even though she has national recordings out, *(which I'm proud to say I was a part)*, I knew she understood what I was going through and was there for me.

It's Been My Experience. Now in order to further substantiate and establish myself. Please allow me to digress and rewind in time for a few moments.

I remember back in the mid 70's, playing for a band by the name of; "Sounds of Joy." We were really tight in those days, with a full horn section, percussionists, a true left handed drummer, a Spanish bass guitarist and really good vocalists. I was only 14 years old when I met all the members of that band and after three years of traveling, picture taking and what seemed like never ending bus rides, hours of rehearsals and studio sessions, we split up. It was all in the plan of God though. In 1977 I met a pastor by the name of; Apostle Ruben Beechum in Denver, Colorado. I met him by way of the group I played in for three years. I also met Apostle Beechums son, Ralph Beechum who is presently the Pastor of that church. *(The House of Joy Miracle Deliverance Church)* Now I grew up in another denomination *(C.O.G.I.C.)* than the one Apostle Beechum pastured, and I was to say it lightly; ridiculed, scorned, talked about and misunderstood for visiting the Apostolic church and playing with their musicians, because they weren't of the same denomination. I must say this, that I've got to make it to heaven, because I want to see if there's going to be different signs up there on the streets of gold saying; "alright, your denomination over here, your group over there!" There are people all over this world who are receiving Christ with signs following that don't know a thing about our denominations and they are saved and filled with His Holy Spirit! No matter what the sign says on the front of your church, the main requirement for making heaven is living by the sign that says, "Holy" on the front of your Bible! Ok, I digressed for a moment but I'm back.

I was able to spend quality time with Apostle Beechum, but some people didn't like him but that didn't matter to him. He knew God and walked in the power of God!

My father, *(who was a pastor and minister in the Church of God in Christ for some 40 plus years)* allowed me to go and visit Apostle Beechum's church, even though he was a pastor of a church as well in another city about 120 mile away. Although I was just a young teen, my father allowed me to catch the bus and go minister at Beechums church for several years. I learned how to walk humbly from my father, *(Elder Elmus L. High Sr.)* and from Apostle Beechum, in which I saw perform great miracles by the power of God. In my eyes these men were two of the most anointed men I knew. I was blessed to grow up around great leadership in my young days.

I would see my father pray for hours at a time and witnessed the power of God in his life when he prayed for my mother after she had died from a massive heart attack. My father went into the hospital room and asked everyone to leave the room so he could pray. The priest had already come in to perform the last rights on her. After putting everyone out of the hospital room, he began to tell the Lord how he needed my mother and the kids did also, he began to pray.

He told God that he knew 7 represented completion and perfection, and that he would take four steps to the left and three to the right and after taking that seventh step he told us that he commanded God according to the scriptures and she came back to life after being dead for some time there in the hospital room. **"I know it sounds like I'm wandering but I'm not, I'm coming to a point."** When I would visit Apostle Beechum's church I would see him pray for the sick and watch them recover. That spoke volumes to me because you can allow yourself to be deceived by the traditions of men, thinking your church or denomination is the only one that has the power of God manifesting in it. I've been all over and believe me it's not true. God is pouring out of His spirit upon ALL FLESH, boys, girls, women and men. Show me in the scriptures where you're the only ones that God will use or call. Find it in the Word!

It's Been My Experience. Check the Word of God again, it's not in the bible! The bible teaches us that we are to; <u>search the scriptures, for in them ye think ye have eternal life</u>! God has been pouring out of His spirit upon all flesh, sons and daughters are prophesying, God is moving upon all that will call upon His name out of a pure heart.

Back in those years, I saw God use Apostle Beechum, and I have to say it, there were *some* preachers in that same city that prayed for us and preached to us who didn't possess enough power to pray a headache away. They could preach *(gift)*, but lacked power. *(anointing)* As they say; the proofs in the pudding. I'm mentioning this because I'm making the point that God has a plan for our lives and God was teaching me back in my early days to, "know Him" and how to hear and recognize **His** voice for myself. But how could I hear, without a preacher? What was God trying to show me? Many things the Lord allowed me to see and experience back then, were precious nuggets that were preparing me for what I would do in ministry here today. God really taught me how to discern people.

About five years passed and I knew God had a different plan for my life, different from the one I had mapped out for myself, but I didn't know what it was. By this time I was in college in 1980. I remember going out of town to a church service in Colorado Springs at Progressive C.O.G.I.C. There was an evangelist ministering there by the name of Donald Curry who was conducting a revival that week. As the service approached its end, the evangelist called me out of the crowd and began to prophesy to me. He began to tell me that God had a new direction for my life, and that it wasn't the one I'd planned for myself at all. He began to tell me that God was going to direct me and show me His will in the next few days to come. More specifically, he went on to say that I would meet **two people**, and after meeting these people, God said, to stick with them. Now can you imagine what I was thinking? Here I am in college, barely making it spiritually and now God says that His hand is on me and He would show me His will for my life in the next few days? To be honest with you, I didn't understand at all what the minister was talking about, I just took him at his word that he was a man of God and that whatever he said would come to pass. Well it did! Two weeks had passed and I received a call from Ralph Beechum, *(Apostle Beechum's son)* who told me that his church was having a musical and he wanted me to come play my horn and meet his sister and her husband, who had moved from Ohio to Colorado. I told him I would try and make it. Remember I had met Ralph about six year's earlier at his fathers church. He was a gifted singer and bass player.

Anyway the Saturday night of the musical came and I was late getting there. When I arrived there stood Ralph and this young lady looking at me as if she already knew me. Her first words to me were, "you're late!" I said; "I know this, but do you see the amount of snow out here on the ground?" I thought to myself; she doesn't even know me, telling me I'm late. Doesn't she know who I am around here? Then to top it all off she asked me if I could actually play that thing, meaning my sax? I was about to say; where have you been sister? "Of course I can play, just wait and see." I was thinking to myself that Ralph got me all the way up here in the snow, just for some out of towner to ask me if I could play? She introduced herself and said, "my name is Carolyn Vinson, it's nice to meet you." I thought she was a little too *"up in my business"* for my taste at first, but she had such a pleasant voice with a "hi pitched" infectious laugh that I had to at least hear the rest of what she had to say. At the concert I remember playing, "Pass Me Not Oh Gentle Savior", because that was one of the songs Apostle Beechum (*Carolyn's father*) liked for me to play.

It's Been My Experience. Well this Sister Vinson had a children's choir who could really sing and they were one of the only recording choirs there in Denver at the time. After the concert I met her husband, a quiet humble man, who also had a wonderful laugh, he was just a nice guy, who talked to me as if he had always known me. He made it so easy to talk to him.

As I began to come around them more while they were at her father's church there in Denver, Carolyn Vinson played the organ and sang, while her husband would watch the children with two of them sitting on his lap in the front row. They had six beautiful daughters and three of them were in their mother's children's choir. Her husband's name was, Brother Thomas Vinson, he was really a nice man. *(did I say that already?)* He had a great smile and became the men's chairman there at the church, he sported a thick black afro with a mustache to match. You could just feel the love of God in both of them and their children were very well mannered and just hung around me and talked to me. I was so impressed and overwhelmed I said to myself, "man!, is this whole family saved?," From the Dad, down to little 2 year old, Shelly. I thought they all had the Holy Ghost. They were just so NICE!!!

Well after that first night at the musical, and then spending the next couple of Sundays there at the church with them, I had to go back to school in Pueblo, Colorado about 120 miles away. As time went on while at school, I couldn't stop thinking about Thomas and Carolyn and the wonderful time I had meeting them that night at the concert. I began to ask myself, what was it about those people that I couldn't stop thinking about them? I just wanted to go back to Denver and see them or at least talk to them on the phone. As I began to ponder over all the things in my mind concerning meeting the Vinson's, the Lord suddenly spoke to me and brought back to my remembrance what the prophet had spoke to me a few weeks prior. **The Lord said these were the two people I would meet, and they were the one's I was to stick with**.

Needless to say I was in a state of shock, it had happened exactly like the man of God said. I met Thomas and Carolyn exactly to weeks after the prophecy.

But I wondered what my role with them would be? Would it be playing with her children's choir, which I did? Was it to travel and record songs with her, which I did? That was just a part of it. She was a really gifted and anointed woman of God. She was also an anointed songwriter. She's written songs like; **"Peanut Butter & Jelly"** later recorded by the Truthettes out of Oklahoma. **"I Feel Jesus,"** recorded by Vanessa Bell Armstrong. She was also a DJ at KDKO radio in Denver, Colorado, a wife and mother of six girls. Yeah, she was anointed!

Well to finish out this story, we began to play together, travel and record, and in January of 1984, I got married to a beautiful young lady I met in college *(my wife, Valerie)*. And as soon as it seemed I was fulfilling my purpose and doing what God had intended for me to do, Carolyn's husband's job was moving him out of state. IBM gave him the ultimatum of moving to San Diego or Atlanta, Georgia. I remember Sister Carolyn calling me to tell me that they were moving to Georgia. I could feel my heart in my throat and my posture dropped and I could actually feel the pain from the thought of loosing such wonderful people that I had spent the last 3 years with. The Lord seemed to knit my heart and spirit to Sister Vinson like David and Jonathon. It was a *genuine* Godly love that I could not explain and can't until this day. I also loved brother Tommy and the six girls so much. All I knew at that time was, God had spoken a word in my life and it seemed as if He was taking His word back. I remember not even wanting to go to the *going away service* they were having for their family at her father's church, there at the House of Joy Miracle Deliverance Church. I was confused, hurt and didn't understand.

It's Been My Experience. Well the Vinson's had moved down to Georgia in September of 1984, and I continued in Colorado playing and doing what I always did. It wasn't the same, it seemed as if my musical gift was enhancing but my spiritual life seemed to be in regression. I remember going back to Pueblo, Colorado to help my mother and father in the ministry. People were already treating me kind of strange because I had actually spent most of my time for the last 3 years with people that were from another denomination. So here I am feeling all alone because the ones God told me to stick with were in another state, and now many of the saints I grew up with didn't really understand what was happening to me. Have you ever received a word from the Lord, and just as it seems His word is going to come to pass, your blessing seems to move to another state? Mine did! They were down there in Georgia visiting other ministries for a few months, looking for a church home. Meanwhile I'm helping my father in ministry and working to take care of my new wife and two baby boys. Then all of a sudden, I began to hear the Lord's voice speaking to me, telling me to move to Georgia. Now understand, I loved the Vinson's and all, but to leave my family, friends and the place where I was comfortable and grew up? I couldn't do that. Besides where would I go to church? The Vinson's hadn't yet found a church home. That didn't stop God from speaking though. His timing is perfect, putting things in order and setting things up for us. He's moving even when we don't know He's moving. Well, it was about four or five months since the Vinson's had moved and the Lord was now telling me to move as well. I was so afraid to tell anyone what the Lord was saying to me. You have to understand the pressure I was under in obeying what the Lord was placing on my heart and in my spirit to do. People were already calling my mother and father, asking them why was I even playing my sax for those people over there at that, "*other church?*" They are not of the same denomination, as if ours was the **only one** God had called in the whole world.

(I better get off of that!)

So imagine how I was feeling, how could I tell people I was leaving? I really didn't know what God was doing, all I know is He said move. I began to get a little sarcastic saying that God would just change His mind again, if I move down to Georgia. He'll probably move the Vinson's to Africa or something! As I went to work one morning, God continued to speak to me, telling me to move. I remember telling God that if I was supposed to move, allow Sister Vinson to send me a letter that day. Well, when I returned home from work that evening, my wife met me at the door smiling saying, "hey we got a letter from Sister Vinson and the family." I just kind of laughed it off saying, "yeah, how are they doing?" The letter was one of those, how are you all doing, we miss you type of letters. But I downplayed the fact that God did this.

Another week passed and once again I told the Lord; "if I'm supposed to move away from my family, take the two babies away from their grandparents, uncles and aunts, then let Sister Vinson send me another letter." *(as if my sarcasm would change God's mind)* Once again, about two weeks later when I came in from work, my wife met me at the door and said; "you got another letter from Carolyn but read this." This time the letter was more direct. Sister Vinson wrote in the letter saying that she had perceived that the Lord was speaking to me about moving to Georgia. She said, pray and be obedient to the voice of the Lord, for obedience is better than sacrifice. I had been fasting from the first time God spoke, but it wasn't time to fast, it was time to obey Gods voice.

It's Been My Experience. By this time, the Lord was speaking to the Vinson's, leading and instructing them that He had called them to Georgia to start a ministry there. They start having services in their home, inviting neighbors and co-workers from Brother Tommy's job. Meanwhile back home, I met with my parents and told them all that the Lord was saying, and I thank God for speaking to their hearts. I began to tell them that they had taught me from a child, how to listen and hear the Lord's voice. I told them that I didn't understand or know why He was saying go, but that He was in fact saying go! My father told me that when I said; "the Lord said go," he had already observed my actions of prayer and fasting and released me to do what I felt the Lord said to do. I know they didn't fully understand why, but when you train up your children in the way that they should go, you shouldn't be surprised when they actually go the way you train them. So I packed up my wife, my two baby boys, who were 17 and 2 months old, and put them in the car and started off to a land I knew nothing about. I felt like Abraham, when the Lord told him to get away from his kindred to a place where God would show him.

We arrived in Georgia on a Friday night and the Vinson's were going to be having service in their home on Sunday morning. I remember all of us singing, I played my sax and Tommy, now Pastor Vinson, was preaching the word on an old blue metal clothes trunk. The spirit of the Lord met us right there in their home. Just a few months passed and we all moved into a small office building which held around 60 people. God blessed, and filled that place to capacity in no time. From there God blessed us to move into a church building, which held around 300 people packed in like sardines, and the church floors shook up and down when we shouted. You shouted whether you wanted to or not because those old wooden floors shook when everyone started to dance.

Now I grew up in church, but God did things in that old building that I had never seen Him do before. The presence of God was so real in that place, you didn't want to enter the building any kind of way, or with known sin in your life. God really revealed Himself in that place! From that anointed building we moved to our present location, at 3269 Old Concord Rd. in Smyrna, Ga. which held close to 700 people or more. We were in that sanctuary for ten years or more and have since built a new sanctuary, adjacent to the old one, which holds nearly 1300. My wife and I have now been with the ministry for some 28 years, with my wife working in the drama department and on the usher board and prophets team. I'm now an ordained Elder, sound engineer, a care group leader, altar worker and musician in the ministry and will serve under their leadership until the Lord says different. It's so wonderful to see how the Lord works and how He has your life mapped out from the foundation of the world. Our footsteps are ordered by God and I'm glad I followed Him.

Now, that I'm in their ministry at Highpoint Christian Tabernacle, I have a ministry, and yes there are things God is yet going to do through me and for me. But it's all going to come through obedience to leadership. Yes, I said obedience to leadership!

God has taught me so much through my experiences with my pastors. I'm a living testimony that if you remain faithful to God and faithful to where God has placed you, you will see God's glory, power and blessings manifested in your life by your obedience and faithfulness to His leaders. You can't be a great leader unless you've been a good follower. How can God trust you with your own, if you're not faithful in that which belongs to another man?

It's Been My Experience. Now these are the same *"two people"* I met at the musical, years ago, not knowing that God had it all mapped out and thought out in His awesome mind.

Gods plan was for us to be together in ministry. The things I learned from my natural Father and Apostle Beechum, were preparing me to work in the ministry with Pastors Vinson. With my father, I was a Sunday school superintendent and musician, and with Apostle Beechum, I used to go with him many Saturdays to the hospital or out on the streets to do outreach.

Now although I've known the Vinson's as friends for years, I respect them more as my pastors.

I know them in the spirit, and for what God has ordained them to be. I know and understand my place. They are an absolute Godsend in my life and I don't know what I would have done or where I would be without their impartation in my life. God has called them to a higher calling and they have answered the call of God which has taught me to move out when God says move. They are a blessing in my life and the life of my family. Thank you Pastor Vinson, thank you <u>First Lady</u>, *(which by the way is the name of her first book)* much respect!! She also now has another book titled; *"This Poor Tit."* I'll let her explain that to you! It's a wonderful book.

There's a promise I made First Lady Vinson years ago back in Colorado. She probably doesn't remember, but I remember telling her that if I made it, she makes it. In other words, whatever God allows me to accomplish in this life, I will include her because God put us together and now they are my pastors, they are my covering and God gave them to me. You should always want the *covering* and the *authority* that comes with your leaders blessing when you go away from your church home to minister. There's an anointing that follows you when you're ministering under an anointed covering. Always have your pastors blessing before going out to minister!

I understand *covenant* and *commitment* in this relationship God put together. I'm not a *hireling* but I'm in **covenant** with my pastors. I will be there with them until the Lord says different. It doesn't matter if you agree or disagree with what's being said or done, always remember that they are human *just like you*, allow them to make mistakes, *just like you.* You see when you're in covenant, you can disagree, get upset and pout, you can have misunderstandings, laugh and then turn around and cry, but you won't leave, you'll be right there, "no matter what." It's a true test of your character, it's how you know that you're in covenant with your pastors, not in contract with them. You'll stay until the end, you'll be willing and obedient. That's how you'll be blessed in your own ministry and gift, by being faithful to another mans.

In my pastors ministry I've seen many come and go, and I've seen how God continues to bless the work of their hands. I absolutely don't know of anyone else I would trust more than these two God given people, with the care of my soul. My father and mother entrusted my very spiritual life into their hands and I can only pray that God gives me at least a drop of the anointing He has placed on their life. I thank God for putting us together!

I love you all very much *(you too my six)* and I'm here in any way you need me.

Thank you for being in my life.

<u>Some Pastors just go; you were sent!</u>
<u>. . . . . .Thank you Lord!!!</u>

PROPHETIC WORDS FROM THE AUTHOR

God is sending forth many people from all over the country and the world to join with powerful and anointed deliverance ministries, whose leaders are in tune with the move of God.

God is now sending in anointed Levite ministers who will answer the call of God and operate in the power and authority that comes with the call. They will team up with Pastors all over this world. There is going to be a greater outpouring of God's spirit because they will be willing, obedient and submissive to leadership and they will operate with skill and understanding.

It's not time for us to fight one another in the body of Christ. It is time to join forces against the attack of the enemy, but it will not happen for many of us if we don't operate in the fashion God commanded us to as Levites. We must pay attention to God's detail in ministry, or run the great risk of missing out with God because of doctrines of men that are dividing the Body of Christ. A prophetic move of God has already begun to infiltrate this world and the church world as well; no more business a usual. It's time to stand up and walk in obedience, so we can see the mighty move of God in this final hour. It's an obedience which will cause us to walk in total favor with God. In these last days, the ministries who'll put the program of God first and not their own agendas will begin to see a change in their church services. And the ones who chose to walk in their own way will miss a true move of God in their own homes, and in the houses of worship. For NOW is the time when God is looking for *"true worship"*, true *"holy living"*, and *"true praise"* from His people. No more meeting just to be meeting, no more shouting just to be shouting, and no more jealousy in Gods house. God is going to stand against many who will not come to this new realm of obedience in worship. We must come higher in worship!

There have been thousands of meetings and calls to worship in our churches, but out of those thousands of gatherings, how many has **_God actually accepted as true worship_**?

There's a job that must be done. People all over this planet are dying by the hundreds and even thousands in many instances at one time, and we as God's people are sitting around our local churches worrying about who will be the greatest in the kingdom. There's none great but God!! We should all desire to be used by God and walk in His anointed power, but after we are used, we should continue to walk humbly and with a sober spirit so we don't get puffed up by the mighty things God is going to do at our hands. God wants us to have His agenda on our minds. He doesn't want us to pursue the fame of preaching and teaching, prostituting our gifts and making our anointed call a scheme to make money, thus making the call of God as common as a 9 to 5 job.

Levites, God has a plan for your life, be patient and listen to the voice of God. Even if you don't understand what He's saying at the time, wait on Him, for He doesn't want His will for you to be a mystery. Don't run out in this last move of God unprepared, making shipwreck of your ministry. God is calling us to come to stability in Him, a maturity that only comes from a consistent obedient walk with Him. Only then can He use us to the capacity He desires to, but He needs us to be obedient to Him. Even if you slip and fall God says get back up and run knowing that you don't have to fall and get up, fall and get back up again. Now unto Jesus, who is able to keep us from falling through the power of His Holy Ghost.

I personally took longer than I had to, to get where God wanted me to be, but everyday I find myself trying to improve in areas He wants me to improve in, even if it seems small.

I'm a living testimony that God can use you through the experiences He's taken you through.

All the ups and downs, faults, failures and imperfections, have helped make me who I am today. He can still use you to carry out His plan.

I can tell you that He's a healer because He healed me of severe asthma at a young age. He healed me while I was playing a saxophone solo under an anointing that caused a healing to work in me first. I can tell you that He can restore your marriages, because He restored mine when it should have been totally destroyed. He can take you from the pit to the palace with just one word!

After losing jobs and possessions, Gods been faithful, but you "must" trust Him in every situation you face. There is a name that is above ALL names. That name is JESUS!

I can't stand here and say that I've been perfect in all of my ways. I can't even say that I've been perfect in most of them, but one thing I do know, is how to give my self over to a perfect God who is able to make me the man He wants me to be. He's able to keep me from falling.

I want to thank God for all of the great clouds of witnesses He's placed throughout my whole life. It has made me the man that I am today and I'm still growing.

This is a book to stir up the Levites throughout the body of Christ to begin to take your "rightful" place and watch the mighty works of God in your life.

God spoke to me and told me that many of you have desired a tool like this book to enhance your ministries, but you didn't know where to find it. Some of you want to know and understand the call of God on your life and how you are to *properly* operate in your gifts. I believe that God is answering your prayers through the powerful and vital information in this book.

If we begin to walk in the spirit and obey the call on our lives, we are going to be a sure blessing to the House of God.

Being a true Levite is not the most comfortable walk. Many times it's a lonely walk, it's not always the most popular way, but it's a separated walk that's ordained and highly needed in the body.

Get ready! God is raising up troops of "new" spiritual Levites in the earth who are obedient to the call on their lives. They will not succumb to the pressures of this world nor the temptations thereof. They will be a blessing to the Houses of God and the Body of Christ everywhere. They are going to cry out against compromise and mediocrity in ministry and what should be anointed and separated. They will have great wisdom and understanding in the things of God, and shall carry the Word of God in their mouths like a sword, crying out in the wilderness and in the House of God with a prophetic word. Gods anointing shall rest highly upon them and His word from their mouths shall not be stopped! All of us are Levites who work in the house of God. From the parking lot attendant, to the usher and deacons, to minister and Elder, to the musicians, singers and song writers, to the choir director and praise leaders and to the Sheppard of the flock. We all have a work to do for the Lord and in the Body of Christ.

"He that hath an ear to hear, let him hear what the spirit is saying to the church."

God is sending a "MESSAGE TO THE LEVITES."

YOUR THOUGHTS

CHAPTER 2

WHAT YOU DON'T KNOW CAN HURT OTHERS

What You Don't Know Can Hurt Others. The passage here further substantiates what this manual is all about. We perish as people of God for lack of knowledge. Not only that, but it stifles and retards our total effectiveness as Levitical ministers of Jesus Christ. No longer should the lack of knowledge be an excuse in non-effective ministry.

2 Timothy 2:15 tells us to; *study, to show yourself approved unto God, a workman that needeth not to be ashamed, rightly dividing the word of truth.* Before you can tell others anything, you should know what you are talking about first. More importantly, you must understand what the Word of God is talking about. How would it look if you were on a job for twenty years, and never took the time to learn all you could about your job or read up on the benefit package it offered? Before going into battle, the military is briefed and given all the information needed to be successful in its quest. So it is with us as spiritual soldiers of God, we should learn all we can in order to fight and conquer all the forces of the enemy, who is well versed, trained, equipped, ready to fight, and has been doing so for centuries. This is why we need the knowledge and power of God's Word in our lives. We need to arm ourselves likewise and train ourselves to be the ministers of Christ. Verse 16 says; **But shun** or as it states in the Amplified Bible; **But avoid** all empty *(vain, useless, idle)* talk, or **vain babblings,** *for it will lead people into more and more ungodliness.* In other words if you don't know the truth of what God is saying, you can be misleading to others and be mislead yourself. Example: 2 Timothy 2:17 in the Amplified Bible says; *and their teaching [will devour; it]* **the truth** *it will eat its way like cancer or spread like gangrene.*

You always want to be prepared for what may come your way. There are so many people today who have different beliefs and understanding. So many divers doctrines of man. They can be in error as well because they don't take the time to look in God's Word, and seek Him to see what the Word of God is actually saying. People have come from so many diverse spiritual backgrounds, and have their own ideas of what truth actually is. But even having their own ideas, they have an excuse or a theory as to why they believe the way they do.

The Jehovah's Witness can explain the things they believe in without blinking. Even those who are a part of the Nation of Islam are very *well versed* in the Koran and even in the Bible, that many of us as Christians scarcely read.

We too must be ready to give an answer to a dying world, which is void of understanding and lacking in truth. What is truth? The Bible lets us know that His Word is truth!

We must give people the truth of the Word of God. It's the only thing that is going to stand in the midst of all the false doctrine that's in the world today. Heaven and earth are going to pass away, but it's only the Word of God that is going to stand the test of all time.

There are many who are falling away from the faith, because they're in error of the truth that has already been established through the ministry of Jesus Christ. Many of God's people are falling away because the plain truth doesn't seem popular or catchy enough. We feel we have to add gimmicks and entertainment to it for people to accept it. But don't be in error my friends, for many are missing the mark because they don't want to live according to God's Holy Word. So it was with **Hymenaeus** and **Philetus**, who **erred,** missed the mark, and swerved from the truth by arguing that the resurrection had already taken place. They are **overthrowing** or undermining the faith of some.

HYMENAEUS [high muh NEE uhs], an early Christian who denied the faith (1 Tim. 1:19-20; 2 Tim. 2: 16-17).

What You Don't Know Can Hurt Others. His message was heretical because he claimed the resurrection of the dead was already past. His profane and vain babblings, spread like cancer and destroyed the true faith in some of the believers. You can have the best intention of ministering the right word, but if you don't understand or believe what the word is saying, you can really harm and confuse others, and they can walk through life in error because you failed as a minister to read and study God's Word for yourself. <u>Good news can travel fast but the problem is that bad news travels even faster</u>.

Does this mean you have to know every scripture and verse? No, but when you study (*not just read*) God's Word, He brings it back to your remembrance. But He can't pull out what you don't put in!

Now those of you who have been ministering for a while, *(or not)* know that God may not speak to you at all, until it's almost time to deliver. The Lord has done me that way on several occasions, but at the same time when He gives me something to say, I know it's God because His Word dwells on the inside of me, which makes preaching a little easier.

Now we know that the anointing can make preaching easier, but it's sure good to know that when He speaks, you at least know what the Lord is talking about!! Right? God wants you to know as much about Him as you can and develop a relationship with Him so He can share Himself with you, and tell you intimate things about Himself. Praise and Worship God in your private time. People are waiting on what God has given you, whether by preaching, singing, or whatever God has called you to do. Give it out! There are souls at stake and many lives depend on your obedience to His call. Will you be that sacrificial lamb and feed God's people? Or because of your disobedience, will there be an empty spread with missing bread from the table? The table of Christ, which is spread freely to mankind? God is giving you the ingredients and the recipe to minister to His people. He's given you His Word. You are being sent out to a troubled world and a stiff-necked people who don't necessarily want to be ministered to.

They want to be entertained. What the church and the world needs is truth when we're ministering. They don't need to hear a tickling message or a funky sound. They need to hear the truth in the word so they can be delivered. There are enough false prophets already in the land, both priest and minstrel. God has need of His true men and women to stand up in boldness and call right, right and wrong, wrong! 1Timothy 4: 1; *Now the spirit speaketh expressly, that in the latter times some shall depart from the faith, giving heed to seducing spirits, and doctrine of devils.*

Note: The Holy Spirit has explicitly revealed that in the latter times, there will be a great falling away, both from personal faith in Jesus Christ and from Scriptural truth.

(2 Thessalonians 2:3; Jude 3-4)

There will appear within the church, ministers who are highly gifted and mightily anointed by God. Some will accomplish great things for God and preach gospel truths effectively, but they will depart from the faith and gradually turn to seducing spirits and false doctrines. But because of the former anointing and zeal for God, they will mislead many people.

What You Don't Know Can Hurt Others. Many believers will fall away from the faith because they will fail to love the truth *(2 Thes.2:10-12)* and fail to resist the sinful trends of the last days. *(Mat. 24:5,10-12; 2 Tim. 3:2-3)* Thus the distorted gospel of compromising ministers and educators will find little resistance in many churches. *(see 2 Cor. 11: 13-15)* Ministers, it is a serious time we're living in, and the need for sold out ministers is a must in order for the church to come to the full stature of Christ.

The popularity of unbiblical teaching will be primarily the results of Satan's directing his demonic hosts in a more intensified opposition to God's work. The second coming of Christ will be preceded by a greater intensity of Satanism, spiritism, the occult, demon possession, and demonic deception in the world and in the church *(Eph. 6:11-12)*.

The believer's protection against such deception involves utter loyalty to God and His inspired Word, and the knowledge that men of great charisma and anointing can be deceived and then deceive others with their mixture of truth and error. This awareness must be accompanied by a true desire within the believer's heart to do the will of God *(John 7:17)* and to walk in righteousness and the fear of God. *(Ps. 25:4-5, 12-15)*

My brothers and sisters, don't think that because apostasy is prevalent within Christianity during the last days, that authentic revival cannot occur or evangelism according to the New Testament pattern cannot be successful. God has promised that during the "last days" He will save all who call upon His Name and separate themselves from this perverse generation, *(Acts 2:16-21, 33, 38-40; 3:19)* and He will pour forth His Spirit on them. Levites be different, walk in and out among God's people and, BE THOU AN EXAMPLE. *(2 Tim. 4:12)* This is one of the most important qualifications for the Levitical Priesthood. Example: *(Gk. Tupos)* translated means "model, image, ideal, or pattern." If you are going to be used by God with power, anointing, and signs following, you must walk as an example before God's people.

God is watching our every move, and just because He hasn't come and struck us with leprosy or sent fire down from heaven, doesn't mean He doesn't see. Judgment delayed IS NOT judgment denied! Can you see how important it is for you to be truly prepared? *1Timothy 4: 6 says; If thou put the brethren in remembrance of these things, thou shalt be a good minister of Jesus Christ, nourished up in the words of faith and of good doctrine, whereunto thou hast attained.*

It doesn't matter whether you feel you have all the tools or not, just be obedient to what you hear the Lord tell you. Don't let anyone tell you that you're too young to be called of God. One sure way to know is to stay under the covering and the authority of your pastors. You can't afford to be out here ministering without the covering and blessing of your leaders. You can get yourself in a lot of trouble, not to mention that the devil will not be subject to anyone who isn't walking in accordance to the Word of God, and the authority of headship. Why should he? You're not subject to authority and thus you are not covered. Furthermore, you are an open target for the enemy's attacks.

Understand that the blessing and authority that comes from your leaders, is a type of mantle placed on you while you're out ministering. You should be a reflection of your leaders and the anointing that's placed on them. My pastor says it all the time; "You don't have authority, unless you're under or subject to authority." This is important, because the devil understands the concept and power of authority. That's why he wanted to be in authority above God.

What You Don't Know Can Hurt Others. 1Timothy 4:12-16 says; *(Amplified Bible) 12. Let no one despise or think less of you because of your youth, but be an example (pattern) for the believers, in speech, in conduct, in love, in faith and in purity. 13. Till I come, devote yourself to (public and private) reading, to exhortation-preaching and personal appeals-and to teaching and instilling doctrine. 14. Do not neglect the gift, which is in you, (that special inward endowment) which was directly imparted to you (by the Holy Spirit) by prophetic utterance* *when the elders (or presbytery, KJV) laid their hands on you (at your ordination). 15. Practice and cultivate and meditate upon these duties, throw yourself wholly into them (your ministry), so that your progress may be evident to everybody. 16. Look well to yourself (to your own personality) and to (your) teaching; persevere in these things-hold to them; for by so doing you will save both yourself and those who hear you. (Amplified)*

Therefore, prepare yourselves and be well equipped ye ministers, preachers, teachers, singers, dancers, minstrels, prophets, evangelists, and all saints of God. We should all be ready to give an answer to the reason why we believe the way we do. No one should be able to throw us off track. Be prepared in your home life as well as your public life. See to it that home is taken care of. God wants us to have a spirit of excellence in "*everything*" we do, from our jobs to our households, to our finances, and our faithfulness to our own local ministries. So the preparing of yourself isn't just in Bible knowledge, but in every facet of life. Holy living everyday is a must. It's a lifestyle, not just the way you act on Sunday morning. Enlist into this army now! God is moving His people into their positions, and we are now attacking the enemy's camp with praise, which always confuses the enemy. What do I mean? If I bless the Lord at all times as Psalms 34:1 says, then the devil gets confused. Let me further explain; I always say, "praise is an act of faith," Why? Because praise tells my situation that it doesn't care what I'm going through or what it looks like, I'm yet going to give God His due praise.

You see the devil feels that he can steal your praise through tough circumstances, setbacks and even failures. But if you keep on praising God through all those things, the devil gets frustrated and rattled. If he can't get to you, he'll try the kids, the car, the bills, your job and yes, even saints and friends. But oh! Levites, oh! Saints of God, bless the Lord and give Him praise in all situations, and the devil will be discouraged and upset, not you.

Yes he's going to come again, but you keep right on blessing God, until your praise becomes perpetual and continual, which will always defeat the enemy. Now I know it sounds like I got off track as far as preparing, but I really didn't. This is involved in preparing yourself to be used by God. How could I even attempt to write this book if I hadn't gone through anything, or if I don't give Him all praise? I know that I have to give Him praise, because it keeps me sane. It keeps me encouraged and strengthened. For the joy of the Lord IS my strength. One of my favorite ways of preparing myself is playing my sax in my room. Sometimes I go into the bathroom with the lights out and begin to play my instrument without interruption. Remember, the gifts God gave you, work on you *first*, before it can truly be effective on others. Many times I've had to play myself into a victory or out of an oppressing situation. What a wonderful tool God has given all of us. He's given us the garment of praise for the spirit of heaviness. Put it on sometime. It looks good on you.

What You Don't Know Can Hurt Others. Now go! Prepare, read, learn of Him.

Pray and get an understanding of what God wants out of your life. Please don't head out there without being prepared or without the blessing from headship. While you're waiting on your ministry, get all you can and can all you get. Know what is going on in the world and know what God is saying to you, because, **what you don't know can hurt you and others.**

CHAPTER 3

ABOUT THE LEVITES

What is a Levite?

A Levite was a descendant of Levi, one of the sons of Jacob, later called Israel. Aaron and his sons were charged by God with the responsibility of the *priesthood* and offering up *burnt offerings and sacrifices*, and *leading the people* in *Worship and Confession.*

All who were not direct descendants of Aaron, were to serve as the *priest assistants*, taking care of the *tabernacle* and *temple* and many other duties found in; (Num. 8:5-26).

Aaron and his sons were consecrated to the priesthood to serve in the tabernacle, (Lev. 8:1-14).

Where did they come from?

Aaron was chosen as a priest, the son of two Levites. His father was Amram and his mother Jochebed. Aaron's wife Elisheba, who was *"out of the house of Judah."*

Notice: *"God gave him a wife out of a people that praised, worshipped and sang songs."* (Ex. 6:23)

He was three years older than his brother Moses and quite a few years younger than Miriam their sister. They were chosen because of their willingness to come back to God, after Moses came down from off Mt. Sinai and found the children of Israel in idolatry, Moses began to question, *"who is on the Lords side?"* (Ex. 32 26-28) It was the tribe of Levi who first came and repented for their idolatry and God in return considered their hearts to repent and chose the children of Levi *(the Levites)* for His service in priestly duties and offices.

The Book of Exodus and Leviticus.

These books are closely related in the fact that both records show how the Israelites were:

1. **Delivered out of Egypt.** 2. **Received Gods law.** 3. **Built the Tabernacle.**
2. This is in parallel to the church today, 1. Represents God bringing us out of sin. 2. We hear the word of God through our leaders. 3. We as Levites are to help BUILD the church. NOT THE PASTORS ALONE! We are to work directly with our leaders in ministry. We are a gift to the leadership and to the Body of Christ at large. When we are in our proper place, the glory of the Lord will come in and dwell or *"tabernacle,"* with us, Exodus 40: 34-38. The Glory of the Lord showing up and filling the room was God's approval on what the "Levites" were doing.
3. The setting up of the tabernacle and putting all things in order, established "God's Descent" on the tabernacle, representing his approval. When things are in order, the Lord will show up in the camp of our church buildings and structures and do mighty, wonderful works.

What were their responsibilities?

1. They served as, *Doorkeepers, Members of the Temple Orchestra, Administration, Porters* and *Moved the Tabernacle Furniture as God's glory and presence moved from place to place.*
2. From age 25 and up, they worked many times as musicians and at the age of 50, they moved on into other areas of ministry, and many of them became instructors in the house of God.

The Book of Exodus and Leviticus.

3. They guarded the tabernacle, cleaned it, and took care of the furniture therein, (Num. 1:50-53, 3; 6-9 and 4:1-33). After the age of 50, the more experienced Levites also served as *"overseers"* to the younger musicians and singers. They also gave assistance to all of them in the musical or priestly tasks. (Numbers 8: 5-26)
4. Numbers 18; 24, explains the tithe process. The Levites were paid tithe from the first fruits of the children of Israel. Out of the tithes *they* received, they were required to pay a tenth themselves out of the first fruits they received. (Numbers 18: 21-32)

In David's reign, the Levites served in rotation.

The musicians of his time were anointed and would prophesy on their instruments. (1 Chronicles 24 & 25 and, Ezra 6: 18-22) The musicians would prophesy and play under the influence of the Holy Ghost, so understand that you need to be *saved* **and** *filled with the Holy Ghost* in order to accomplish this feat in the spirit realm.

There was plenty of room for all to *work* and *exercise* their *gifts*. When David was old, he numbered the Levites so he would know how to use them. I will cover his count of the Levites, later in the chapter. But if you can't wait, you can find out how he numbered them in, (1 Chronicles chapter 23, 1Chronicles 16: 4-6). They also *cast lots,* (1 Chronicles 26: 12-19).

David's internal tabernacle issues.

I found that David had many of the selfish issues we have in our houses of worship today. David had so many musicians and singers that he had to use them in rotation based on their level of skill. Back then they even resorted to *casting of lots,* because some of the musicians were arguing over who would minister first upon the instruments. (sound familiar?)

Many times in the Old Testament, the use of casting lots was one of the ways God allowed them to make a decision or to determine what action to take. It was like what we call *pulling straws,* or even *rolling dice.* Remember, not much of the Bible or law was really known at that time, and God apparently allowed this method to determine His will. But ONLY ONCE, DID THIS HAPPEN IN THE NEW TESTAMENT. With God's approval, Matthias was chosen to take the place of Judas in Acts 1: 26 *(some say, the exact nature of casting lots is unsure!)*

Many leaders deal with immature musicians naturally and spiritually.

1Cor. 3:1-9 speaks of, *carnal babes.* Many times in our church settings, we deal with people from diverse backgrounds and spiritual levels. Some of you have to be pumped and primed to give God your service, and others act as if they are doing you a favor by even showing up.

These are just a few of the many forms of immaturity we experience in ministry.

We can only pray that our musicians today would take on the humble spirit of David. In Psalms 84: 1-12 it says:

¹How amiable are thy tabernacles, O LORD of hosts!

²My soul longeth, yea, even fainteth for the courts of the LORD: my heart and my flesh crieth out for the living God.

³Yea, the sparrow hath found an house, and the swallow a nest for herself, where she may lay her young, even thine altars, O LORD of hosts, my King, and my God.

⁴Blessed are they that dwell in thy house: they will be still praising thee. Selah.

⁵Blessed is the man whose strength is in thee; in whose heart are the ways of them.

⁶Who passing through the valley of Baca make it a well; the rain also filleth the pools.

⁷They go from strength to strength, every one of them in Zion appeareth before God.

⁸O LORD God of hosts, hear my prayer: give ear, O God of Jacob. Selah.

⁹Behold, O God our shield, and look upon the face of thine anointed.

¹⁰For a day in thy courts is better than a thousand. I had rather be a doorkeeper in the house of my God, than to dwell in the tents of wickedness.

¹¹For the LORD God is a sun and shield: the LORD will give grace and glory: no good thing will he withhold from them that walk uprightly.

¹²O LORD of hosts, blessed is the man that trusteth in thee. KJV. In this passage, David was just glad to minister to the Lord. He longed to be in God's presence.

Just from David's excitement and earnest desire to be in God's presence, God gave him a song. In other words, David didn't need a beat or a secular influence to write a song to the Lord, God gave him the songs out of His heavenly songbook. You see, David was mature in his thinking toward the house of God. He didn't have time for many of the petty things we do in today's music ministry. You must understand that David probably had more musicians, singers, and dancers to deal with than any church you know of today.

Hezekiah had a shortage of priests, and some of those priests were allowing themselves to be *hired out* for secular events for other nations. For example, they took on *motivational speaking*, and other *secular festivals*, instead of ministering unto God in the Temple. So the Levites had to help out until the younger upcoming priests sanctified themselves, and became ready for service. . . . . **(how sad!)**

Take note that 2 Chronicles 29:34, speaks of the *priests being too few*. What was happening back then was some of the priests during that time were unhappy with the amount of tithe that was being paid to them of the Temple, and many of the Levites had to step in and help in the priestly duties.

The Priests, Levites & People had to be Holy.

It is a given to say preachers, and musicians should be holy. But I learned from my father years ago, never assume anything! But in case you're questioning, whether the Priests and Levites back then and now, need to be holy, the answer is YES! You must be holy to walk in the anointing of a Levite. Daily worship was a part of life in those days, and should be now. (Lev. 23: 1-24).

Many *feasts* were made to God as a *form of worship*. These weekly and annual feasts were for redemption, consecration and to let Israel know that they were people of the Almighty God. **The feast tied worship in with their daily lives, and caused the people of Israel to understand that worship was to be part of their DAILY LIVES.**

Worship doesn't start when you get to church. It should be an extension of what you do in your own home, or the way you live each day. Worship is your life, *prostrate* before God in total *obedience* and *submission* to Him. It's not just something you do on a Sunday, and then live they way you want to the rest of the week. Ask yourself, can you act in church, the way you act at home or at work? Would we recognize who you are? If you bought a visitor to your church or ministry, would they be able to identify you, based on your daily actions?

God wanted Israel to understand that Holy living was not just for temple worship, but should now become a part of their new *lifestyle*.

If you pay attention to the main theme of the book of Leviticus, you'll find that God was establishing **Holy living**. When God established the working of His *power* in the book of Exodus, He had already given Israel *commandments* and *instructions* on how to **get** Him in their presence. He now begins the book of Leviticus, by giving them meaningful *rituals* to and *feast*, to teach them how to **keep** His presence in their midst. God was now demanding that His people become more like Him, or more *excepting* to Him. I'll explain what I mean by more excepting to Him. God's **holiness** is not a *singular* or *separate attribute*, but rather is the result of the *sum total of ALL His Attributes!!* All of His attributes equal the totality of His holiness.

Understand that at this time in biblical history, **sacrifices** were used more so, to remove the **effect of sin**, from the presence of God, than to actually remove sin from the people. It was more important that they obeyed the rituals in order to keep the presence of God in their midst.

Therefore God accepted various sacrifices, to remove the effects of sin from His presence. So when the priest went in to offer up sacrifices for himself, and then the sins of the people, *once a year*, God showing mercy, allowed these sacrifices to be enough. Understand that this offering did not actually remove sin from the people because Christ had not yet come to sacrifice Himself on the Cross for all men, *once and for all*. (Hebrews 7:26, 27) So what God is asking us to do today, is really just to give Him our *reasonable service*, (Romans 12:1) seeing that in comparison to His holiness, the best we can actually offer Him today is as *filthy rags*. (Isaiah 64:6) And just like the days of old, God allows our sacrifices and reasonable service to be enough.

Therefore, God gave instructions for feasts, to commemorate His goodness to them as a nation.

The Passover Feast: This feast was held in early spring. This was a mandated feast for Israel to remember what God did for them in Egypt, when He caused the death angel to pass through the land and smite the firstborn child of all Egypt, even the firstlings of their cattle.

The Feast of Weeks or Pentecost: So called, because this festival took place seven weeks or 50 days after Passover. This was a continued celebration of God's goodness, so they never forget.

The Feast of Tabernacles or Sukkot: This feast was an autumn celebration feast, which purpose was to remind them of His provision, and protection of them in the wilderness. At least four other feasts developed probably after their Babylonian exile.

The Feast of Trumpets: Was a feast and ritual of *blowing* the *trumpets* to call the people to a *fast* at the end of the summer, before the beginning of the New Year, Rosh Hashanah. This feast ended on the seventh day with the, *Day of Atonement, or Yom Kippur* as it was so called. This date was considered one of the most important days on the Jewish Calendar. It was held on the final day of the feast, when *Repentance and Forgiveness* took place throughout the nation.

Sabbath Feast: Later on in Jewish history, there was an additional weekly feast called the *Sabbath*. This began at sundown on Friday evenings, with a family meal. It marked the division between *work* and *rest*, and highlighted the people's dependency upon God alone to always provide for them.

Feast of Unleavened Bread: This feast later became part of the Passover Feast, and is also described as a *thank offering* to God for His provision throughout the year. All of the feasts had distinct instructions with them, and were used in Israel to commemorate what God had done for them, starting with the exodus out of Egypt.

Actually, there are many other feasts that you can look up and see their whole description and purpose. There are also many post-biblical feasts that are used by the Jewish population today, for example, Hanukkuh.

The Priests & Levites had to go through purifications.

Purifications happened in the time of Moses, Solomon, and also in Hezekiah's reform of rebuilding the Temple just to mention a few. In Hezekiah's reform of the Temple, he made sure that the Priest and Levites didn't make any sacrifices unto God on any of the old defiled vessels of the Temple. The old vessels had to be burned and new vessels had to be bought in. (2 Chronicles 35:1) Can you imagine in our churches today, if we had to trash all the instruments in the houses of God, every time sinful hands touched the instruments? How much money would your audio, video, and music department have to spend in a year's time? WOW!!!

Moral Standards.

The moral standards for the Priests and Levites were very high. (Lev. 18: 1-22)

God wanted them to be a people above reproach. He wanted all His people to be men and women of moral character and integrity. But the standards of the Priests and Levites were on a much higher scale. You will read throughout the book of Leviticus, the standards that God set for His people, to be holy unto Him.

The root meaning of the word holiness is the word, *separation*. God's people were to be separated from, and different than, the surrounding pagan nations. God put great emphasis on moral sins. This could cause for swift judgment for the Priests and Levites. Moral sins were something that could totally dismiss or disqualify one from the priesthood or any other tabernacle or temple duties. This would cause one to lose his inheritance in Israel, his land, but furthermore, no common priest in his right mind would have tried to enter the holy of holies with sin in his life.

Needless to say, in view of these, and other sacred duties, all priests were to be men of good character with **holiness** being their first priority. Holiness is often confused with meekness, kindness or a sacred bearing. Holiness doubtless encompasses these things, but is much more. **Holiness is spiritual purity, dedication, total commitment and a setting apart for God, His Son and His cause.** They were to be set apart for sacred use, so that the Spirit of the Most High would always and consistently be overwhelmingly present with them.

Mor·al:

1. pertaining to, or concerned with the principles or rules of right conduct or the distinction between right and wrong; ethical: moral attitudes.

2. expressing or conveying truths or counsel as to right conduct, as a speaker or a literary work; moralizing: a moral novel.

3. founded on the fundamental principles of right conduct rather than on legalities, enactment, or custom: moral obligations.
4. capable of conforming to the rules of right conduct: a moral being.

4. conforming to the rules of right conduct (opposed to immoral): a moral man.

What did they do?

The Levites were chosen as the first fruits, after God spared the firstborn in Egypt. The firstborn were to be dedicated to God in all the families of Israel. It was the Levite tribe that came back to God after the *Golden Calf* incident. God then chose the Levites to be separated unto Him. God saw the condition of their heart to repent. (Numbers 3: 12-13) The service of God with the Levites started at about age 20 to 25 years old. They were groomed how to serve God and the people.

They were consecrated by.

1. Sprinkling *the waters of purification.* (Numbers 8:7) The hair of the men had to be shaven off the body and they had to change their clothes. Then sacrifices were made of two young bulls. The Levites were taken to the door of the tabernacle and set apart by the laying on of hands by the elders of Israel. (Numbers 8: 1-26)

2. Young Levites began as assistants to the priest. Older Levites moved on through the ranks to higher duties in the ministry.

3. They learned to write or **sing songs.** Every time God wrought a victory among them, someone would stop and write a song. Moses and his sister Miriam had the first recorded songs in the bible. (Exodus 15)

4. The Levites were given *48 cities* and *6* of them were called the *Cities of Refuge.* (Numbers 35: 1-8, 9-34) Note, their cities were spread throughout the land of Israel for ministry. This signified that God wants us as Levites, to be *in our proper place* to minister and *serve* the people. God wants us to put ourselves in the way of people and be accessible to them. God didn't want the Levites to be apart or act distant from the people. He wanted them to be in position to minister to the people whenever needed. God wants us today to consecrate ourselves and place ourselves in position to minister. That position is a position of servitude. Just like the Levites who were sent through a series of sacrifices, they were putting themselves in a position with God to be made available to be used by Him. Ministry in that day was not the glamorous thing we've made it today. Jesus told his disciples, whoever wanted to be greatest among them, let him become a servant. To minister is to *serve.*

Their Instruments.

HARPS: Lyre, Lute, Psaltery, Sackbut, Trigon (*in old times*)

Note: A man by the name of Jubal, the 4th great grandson of Cain was considered the FATHER of those who played the Harp. *Zither*, a type of triangle harp played mostly by the Canaanites used around 2700 B.C. The *harp* was the larger of the *harped stringed* instruments, which David played. But the

Lyre was considered the most *noble* of all the instruments, used both in *sacred* (2Chron.29: 25), and *secular* music. (Isa. 23; 16)

TRUMPETS: *Rams Horn, Shophar, Bugle*, and *Cornet horn*.

(Blow the Trumpet with a **long blast**!). (Josh. 6; 1-5) Look up the words, Trump & Trumpet in the dictionary. You can also look it up in, (1Chron. 15: 28).

FLUTES: Organ, Pipes.

In Nebuchadnezzar's day. (Flutes were used as a secular instrument in Nebuchadnezzar's time for example in the case of Shadrach-Meshach and Abednego). The *Fife* was another name for flute or, *Dulcimer*.

ISTRUM: Shaker or Rattler.

(Used by some women in mourning or funerals).

DULCIMER: Was a type of *Bagpipe*. A Babylonian instrument mentioned in Daniel 3; 5-7.

BELLS: Not really used as a musical instrument, but were used as part of the *High Priestly Garment* of Israel. Now commonly used in Palestine unto this very day.

GONG: Usually played at weddings, happy occasions or the entering of a *notable person*.

TABRET: Timbrel, Tambourine, played primarily by women in the early days. (Ps. 68:25) Read; *"Music of the Bible" (In Nelsons Bible Dictionary)* There were some instruments known to be used by heathen nations and **were not** used in the worship of God. There were also instruments that were normal for use in the worship of God. They were hand picked by David the King.

Note: *(The musicians in Babylon played the sackbut and the dulcimer to taunt the three Hebrew boys when they were put into the fiery furnace)*.

The SACKBUT: Back in the Old Testament, was a *type of harp*, not the woodwind instrument of latter days.

HUMAN VOICE: The *voice* is also an instrument, *lift up your voice like a trumpet*. (Isaiah 58:1) You don't have to play an instrument, just use the natural one God gave you. You can make a *joyful noise* unto the Lord and lift up your voice giving God praise. That's what it's for!

SING/ SINGER: Many times the singers, who sang under the anointing, would flow into prophecy by *word* or *song*. Such a one would be called a ***"Prophet-Minstrel" or "Prophetic-Minstrel."***

Nehemiah 12: 27-35, Singers and Trumpeters. Webster Dictionary says; **Sing**: is to proclaim or to extol something in verse.

Note: In verse 35, Zechariah was the 5th generation grandson of Asaph, the *chief musician* of David.

"A Greek geographer by the name Strabo, of the late first century B.C. and the early first century A.D. once said the female vocalists of Palestine were considered some of the most skilled and talented singers in the world during the periods between the Old and New Testament writings." "A span that covered some 400 plus years."

The Musician.

Here is an interesting question posed to the musician. **Should church musicians demand to be paid?** If so, **why?** Don't hate on me, just hear me out. You will hear many musicians and singers say that the laborer is worthy of his hire. What does that mean musicians? Well, the fact is, the biblical statement was for the priests, not the musician. Furthermore, most musicians won't be able to tell you where that passage of scripture actually is. (Read: Matt. 10:10, 1 Tim. 5:18, Luke 10: 1-7 and 1 Cor. 9:9)

Now don't get all bent out of shape with this. I want you to understand that some musicians are hired to do a specific job in the church, and if money is agreed to by both parties, then it may be ok. But it's not to be a demand by any musician, the bible doesn't mean it that way. Now I know in the church world today, the whole mindset of our musicians is different than it was in David's time, but God is the same today as he was back then. The call of a Levite or musician has become more of a job position rather than a call of God. As I said before, there are some who are employed to do a specific job in the church. It may be a musician or the head of a tape or video ministry, but as I stated earlier, whatever duties we are performing in the church, it should not be a demand put on the ministry to financially compensate for something that should be part of your *reasonable service* to God.

I know I won't get many Amen's for this, but you need to ask God is He pleased with your attitude and demands towards payment before you'll serve? You've prostituting your gift and you're like a slot machine. Just put money in the pocket and I'll work for you. I know you don't understand yet where I'm going with all of this, but just stay along for the ride and you will.

It all started in 1Chronicles 29, David started the actual *paid or paying,* of the musicians in the tabernacle. But it wasn't so in Moses' day. Now don't get this confused with the *paying of tithes* the 11 tribes of Israel were instructed by God to give the Levite tribe. This was because the Levites did not receive a portion of land like the other 11 tribes of Israel did. Their duties and responsibilities were in and around the tabernacle, in the house of the Lord. Their work was to minister to the Lord, so they did not have other regular jobs or duties. However, they were granted 48 cities which were scattered throughout the lands of the other 11 tribes to dwell in. So King David started the *paying* of the musicians for their services. Again, this was not the case in Moses' time. (Numbers 18 and 35th chapters) David may have been influenced by other pagan nations who paid their musicians for their services. It is said that David may have gotten the idea from Assyria and Egypt, though it wasn't David's intention to have Israel take any methods of worship or culture from any other nation or people. They were to always be a *separated people*, not like any other nation, but obedient to God. In spite of God's command to avoid the religions and cultures of other nations, the musicians of Israel were now being paid in addition to the tithe for their services, and thus brought about a *non spontaneously* played music in the worship. This had now birthed *carnal minded* musicians who were no longer totally *spirit led*. Instead the musicians were no longer playing for their love of the music and devotion to God, but were now concentrating on **a paycheck**. Sounds like some of the musicians of today doesn't it? Now as it was back then, so it is today. The musicians now had and do have an ungodly attitude, that if you don't pay, I won't play!

What will we say on the Day of Judgment, if God Himself ask us why we had to have compensation first, before performing our duty or using our gifts which were *freely* given to us? Are we going to tell God that a laborer was worthy of his hire? For the most part, when you hire someone to perform a certain duty, they usually perform that task first, and then get the pay. But many of us today are demanding the pay first, before a *word* is *spoken* or *a note* is *played*. Be real, God can't be pleased with that method and that's **not** what the Word of God meant at all!

I suppose people will have to be in a certain *financial bracket* in order to hear anointed music, or to hear a word from the Lord! I guess salvation is free, but to hear a word from the Lord today, there's defiantly a *price to pay*. So, what we're saying is, if a person can't afford to pay that price, I guess they won't get to hear that word from their favorite preacher or a song from their favorite musician either. Have we actually convinced ourselves that God is ok with this?

Let's go back to the time of King David, where the musicians were not to play their instruments in clubs or in *secular* environments. (Isaiah 5: 11-14).

Now this didn't mean celebrations, weddings or holy feasts. You have to understand I'm talking about the **Levites**, and the responsibilities of that separated office.

There were many times in Old Testament history, where the Levite musicians waxed *hot and cold, then hot,* just like the whole nation of Israel did, time after time. But the Levites should have been different. God called them to be separated, even from the rest of the Israelite tribes in order to minister to Him, but it always seemed as if the ways of God were not enough for them. There is a passage in the book of Judges, where a Levite agreed to hire out his priestly services to a man who was a known worshipper of false gods. (Judges 17: 8-13) Does that sound familiar to you? We are also hiring ourselves out to secular events, to people who DO NOT worship the **True and Living God**. The secular world is able to give God a praise of thanksgiving, but they can not worship Him because they do not have the spirit of God down on the inside, therefore preventing them from worshiping in spirit and in truth. (John 4: 23-24).

Study about the man by the name of Micah, who thought he could do his own thing by worshiping other gods, and still have the blessings of God on his life. *He did what was right in his own eyes,* and would not submit himself to the laws of God. He was a man from the hills of Ephraim who **would not submit to authority**! The bible lets us know that, for *those who would use their gifts in any other way, but for the worship of God, He would soon reject.* Matthew 21: 33-44. *(parable of the tenants)* The musicians and priest of that time had many of the same struggles we have today. They struggled with using their God given gifts and talents for God and God alone, and began to make excuses for why they used their gifts in the House of God, and for secular and ungodly occasions. But just as it was then, it is now; God is not pleased with that.

Man was created to worship, and can only serve one of two masters. You will either love the one, and hate the other, or hold to one, and despise the other. You can't have both! (Matt. 6:24)

King David's three Chief Musicians.

Read about these three men in more detail in Chapter 6 of this manual. King David had three *Chief Musicians* by the names of, **Asaph**, **Heman** and **Jeduthun** or (Ethan). All three of these anointed men had sons and daughters who wrote songs, and even had a hand in many of the hymns and songs in the book of Psalms. Each of these men led choirs of 4000+ members, and in them there were 288 musicians under their direction, whom they worked in *rotation*.

They would have the *higher skilled* musicians instruct the *lesser skilled*, and the more skilled you were, you became responsible for training the younger musicians how to **minister and flow** upon their instruments in the tabernacle. They were divided into **24 courses** which had 12 musicians in each of them. This included the orchestra and singers as well. (1 Chronicles 16: 4-6).

David then started the preparation of the Temple, (1 Chronicles 22) and began the organizing of the Levites in chapter 23. But his son Solomon would be the one who God chose to finish the Temple and become David's successor as King. David would not be allowed to complete the Temple because he had the blood of men on his hands, being a man of war. (1 Chronicles 29) Solomon, David's son would have the knowledge, the wisdom, and the favor of God to complete the Temple in his dad's stead. He was a man of wisdom and knowledge, with the gift to write poetry, a gift that was handed down from his talented father.

Musical Notations & Choreographic Directions/Movements

ALAMOTH: This was a direction or notation for the flutes to play or for the soprano vocals to sing. It meant to sing in a *high-pitched tone*. Psalms 46, 1Chronicles 15: 20.

SHEMINITH: An octave down from the **Alamoth**. *Tenor or Bass voices* to sound off. Psalms 6: 12 and 1 Chronicles 15: 21.

NEGINOTH: Some traditions say this was a notation for an *8 stringed instrument to play*. Other translations like the NKJV, say it simply means a song. (Ps. 4; 6 54, 55, 61, 67, 76). You'll find this word in Psalms 54 and in some other headings in your Bible. This direction gives the instruction, **On Neginoth,** which means there will be a musician who will play the *lead* musical part on a stringed instrument.

For example; the title heading in the, "*Greek Hebrew Key Study Bible*" by Zodiates, says; "To the chief musician on "neginoth,"Maschil. A psalm of David when Ziphim came and said to Saul, *"Doth not David hide himself with us?"* This neginoth heading is telling the reader that this psalm of David was written or arranged by one of the chief musicians. On neginoth, is to say that this psalm will be the *lead musical part* on an *8 stringed instrument*. This was also a musical term.

In the headings in Psalms, you will also see that it says; **Machil**, which means, the song that is to be the *lead instrument* on an 8 stringed, is in the form of an **anthem**. That meant it could be played at various ceremonies, special occasions or usually some type of feasts.

MUSICAL ORIGINATORS, NOT IMITATORS: Many songs were *birthed* after a great event or *victory* of some sort that had taken place within the nation of Israel. Once again, remember that Israel always wrote a *new song* about present events or victories God had bought them through. They were **originators**, not imitators of other nation's music.

MASCHIL: A Hebrew term, **Maschil**, used alone was mentioned at least 13 times in the *titles* of songs in Psalms. (Ps.32,42,44,45,52,53,54,55,74,78,88,89 and 142.) The song was used only at special occasions or festivals accompanied by a special kind of music. *(a type of anthem or opening ceremonial music)*

MAHALATH: This was the name of a choreographer, and **Mahalath** was also the name or a choreographic motion as well. Mahalath was a choreographer for David. (Ps. 53) He directed the anointed dancers. Many times in the book of Psalms you will see in the chapter heading, statements like; *"To the chief musician, a song of David"* or *"To the chief musician* upon *"Mahalath, Maschil"* a Psalm of David. So when you see this in your bible, many times it's giving musical notations, credits on who wrote the song or what instrument is playing and or musical instructions on how the song is to be played or sung.

Mahalath also meant *dance or sickness.* 1. Mahalath was also the granddaughter of Abraham and the daughter of Ishmael who married Esau. (Gen. 28:9) 2. The granddaughter of David and wife of King Rehoboam. (2 Chron. 11:18)

MAHALATH AND LEONNOTH: In Psalms 88, these groups were song writers and choreographers who wrote in such a way that instructed the singers how to sing a particular song. **Antiphonally**, which means to *sing responsively* to the music or in a *resounding manner* in *echoes* or a *repeating effect.* Catholics in their Mass Ceremonies use this method of singing to this day.

SHIGGAION: Found in Psalms 7, to sing *enthusiastically* or *erratically* or in the form of a *lamentation.* A song David sang.

HIGGAYON: To sing in a *solemn manner* or to sing it *softly* with *soft music.* (Psalms 9) If you read to the end of verse 16, you will see the words, **Higgaion Selah**, which means to play the *music only, very softly,* verses 5, 15 and 16. This is interesting because, in this softly spoken song, David was actually *prophesying* what was to come. This particular song he sang, was telling of events that had not yet come to pass. He was speaking those things that were not, as though they were. In Psalms 92: 3 and Lamentations 3: 62, music was played *softly on the harp* by David.

MUTH-LABBEN: In the chapter heading of many study bibles, at the start of Psalms 9, you may see the heading; "To the chief musician upon, **Muth-Labben.**" This may also mean to sing in *hi pitched* tones and notes.

A TYPE OF HYMNOLOGY: The practice of using *Cue Words.* This was the practice of setting *new words to old songs.* Today it would be called a *re-arrangement.* Songs that sound alike in melody but had different lyrics. This leads us to the word, **Shoshannim Eduth**.

SHOSHANNIM EDUTH: This may have meant, *The Melody* to which the songs were to be sung. This would be musically noticed today as the *main part, chorus, or the hook* to a song.

About The Levites

HYMN OF TAUNTING: *O LUCIFER,* son of the morning. **Light Bearer,** Isaiah 14: 1-11. Verse 12 starts with; *how art thou fallen from heaven, O Lucifer!* This verse was actually a **prophetic song**, that spoke of the soon coming downfall of the King of Babylon at that time. This passage had a two-fold meaning, it also spoke of Lucifer himself, and the fact that the King of Babylon had taken on the same spirit Lucifer had, by being lifted up in pride. Included also in this prophetic song, was the King of Tyres, who exalted himself as a deity in pride. Ezek. 28:11-19 But Isaiah 14:15, actually starts the *taunting prophetic song* that sang of the downfall of the King of Babylon. This prophesy was sung out loud.

So in Isaiah 14 starting with vs. 12, was a two-fold message to the King of Babylon and to Lucifer. In chapter 13, the prophet Isaiah prophesies the overthrow of Babylon just like God destroyed Sodom and Gomorrah before time. Babylon was the center of pagan culture, opposing God and His ways very early in human history. (Gen. 11: 1-9)

(this also references to the fall of the world system and the end time anti-christ rule) Rev.17; 1-3.

SELAH: A break in the singing to allow the music to play under the anointing of God. It occurs 71 times in the book of Psalms, also in Habakkuk 3: 3, 9,13. So when you read any passage of scripture in the book of Psalms, you don't have to actually say, *selah!* It's a musical notation for the singers to stop singing and allow the musicians to continue playing. **Selah** actually has many meanings, but this is the description I wanted to point out. It also means to *pause*, or to be in *silence*.

GITTITH: "*O Lord our Lord, how excellent is thy name in all the earth.*" This was a song, sung by David himself in Psalms 8: 1-9. A song about God's Glory and Man's Honor.

There are many songs today that were birthed from this scripture. **Gittith** or **Gittite** is said to actually be a musical instrument used or manufactured in Gath.

Gath was a Philistine city where Goliath lived, along with a race of other giants called the Anakims. (Josh. 11; 22)

It is said that three different meanings or descriptions of the word **Gittith** may be possible:

1. Gittith, an instrument of Gath used as an *accompaniment* to the singing of Psalms 8, 81& 84.
2. A *vintage song*, whose tune was to be followed in the Temple music.
3. The *tune* of a *military march* used by the Gittite Warriors. *(Warriors of the city of Gath)*

It is thought that David may have come across this instrument in his encounter with Goliath and the Philistines. It may have been an instrument the Philistine warriors used in battle.

Their place in the ministry.

As I mentioned earlier in this chapter, there was room for all the Levites to work. God spread the Levites throughout 48 cities in their own land and space. Six of those cities were, *cities of refuge*. The Levites cities were geographically spread throughout the land of Israel. This was a symbol that God intended for the Levites to be *accessible to all the people* of Israel. Always remember, when you're called to ministry, you are called to **SERVE!** *That's what the word minister means, to serve or to become a servant.*

Gifts vs Anointing.

There is a difference between *giftings and* ***anointing***. There's a definite danger in not being able to discern the difference between the two. You're born with certain gifts and abilities that mature and begin the manifest themselves as you get older. Some are gifted to write, some are gifted to sing or play an instrument. Some have gifts to paint pictures or even preach. It's all done according to our *several or different abilities.* (Matt. 25:15)

There are people who can sing a song, or preach a sermon to the point where it seems like your hair is going to stand up on the top of your head in excitement. Some have the "*gift*" or "*ability*" to tap into the *emotions* of people. They know what to do, and how to do, but their *lifestyle*s are raggedy. Yet, people flock to them because of their gift. Some live like *devils*, yet can sing like an *angel*! It's because you don't actually have to have a relationship with G*o*d *to b*e gifted. **Not so, with the *anointing*!** The anointing is the *supernatural ability* and *grace* of God to perform or minister a spiritual task. In order be anointed, you must present a godly lifestyle! The anointing demands it! Furthermore, you don't have to necessarily pay a large price to be gifted, but to have the anointing of God on your life, <u>YOU WILL</u>, pay a price! It's cost your time, it involves making sacrifices, it costs you being talked about, and lied on. It takes you suffering loss, and being in discomfort. It cost you pain in one way or another, along with a few tears. It takes a YES TO THE LORD, unconditionally!

One great thing about the anointing is, it enhances the gifts and abilities you have. I wrote a song that says; "<u>the anointing destroys the yoke, and your gifts it will invoke</u>, *so don't give me the fake, I need the real deal."* In other words, don't just settle with being gifted, but be anointed. It's the only way people will be delivered and made free from any bondage.

Our churches don't need gifts alone, but the anointing that will ***destroy yokes*** and change lives, it's imperative. As the body of Christ, we can't afford to take on a secular world mentality of how we treat our gifted individuals, to the extent that we can not tell the difference between a gifted person and an anointed one. Even in our music, we must keep our *sacred music* just that. . . . . SACRED!!! It's important to have music that will change your very life, simply because it's anointed. There must be a difference between *clean, unclean, holy* and *unholy*. There can be no **confusion** of whether it's a song from the Lord, or a song you just wrote. The shame of it is, there are people who don't know Christ that can tell there is some type of difference. They may not understand what that difference is, but they know there is one. Those of us, who understand spiritual "*godly*" music, can also tell because there's a godly change that takes place inside. <u>It ministers to us, and most of all it ministers to God</u>. Most churches today are filled with gifted individuals who know how to move a crowd and make them jump and shout. I personally know many singers and musicians who can sing and play until you can hardly take it, and at the same time they lead sinful and immoral lives. Where are the minstrels, where are the anointed psalmists, where are the preachers and teachers? Are you still here? Have you <u>ALL</u> gone out from the church and from the presence of God to give your gifts to swine? Have you prostituted your gift for filthy lucre? Is God no longer the center of your joy? Has **fame** and **fortune** now become the **new lover** to whom you sing, and the god to whom you serve?

I facilitated a praise and worship symposium at our church, and I remember telling the congregation how King David actually started the compensation or **paying** of *professional musicians* in their worship. But God didn't intend for that to be so. The focus should have stayed on **ministering** to God and ushering in the people into His presence.

Let's take a look at that word *minister* or *ministering* shall we? It means to, *serve* someone or something, or to be in *submission to*. It means that our *ministering gifts* are to be in *submission to something* or *someone*.

Now I'm sure you could go the dictionary to describe the word, serve as being; *a means to provide a <u>service</u> or to <u>be employed</u>*. But the *serve* the bible speaks of, is the fact that we are submitted to God and slaves of Jesus Christ, who gave us our gifts to serve Him and His people. Understand that we were all bought with a price, paid for on the cross. We are not our own, we were purchased by the shedding of Jesus' precious blood. In history, most slaves weren't paid at all. Some slave owners did get to the point where they began to pay wages out of appreciation, but the slaves would dare not demand or require it!

I also explained to the congregation that a slave had no rights or say so in what they were told to do. They just did it whenever instructed. They did it whether they felt like it or not. Likewise, as slaves to Jesus Christ, should always be ready to work, and minister to the needs of people, instant in season and out of season, whether we get a paycheck or not.

So, ask yourself this question, that if there was no money to be made, would you yet be willing to be a blessing to God's people? Would you give your all to the Lord, if you knew there was no financial gain or reward? Could you be like the Apostle Paul who said; *we are always bearing about in the body the dying of the Lord Jesus, so that the life of Him might be manifested in our bodies?* Are you willing to become weak, that others through your ministering may become strong? Are you willing to be a living sacrifice, or do we have to wait until you get paid, manicured, pedicures and put in the finest hotels? Do you have to have all flavors of water, juice, warm milk, tea, coffee, steak or lobster, with a glass of wine? Yeah, I said it, a glass of wine! Do all these accommodations have to be in place first, before you give out? Believe me; this goes on in many of our "so called", Christian and Gospel circles!

So tell me whose gifts are these anyway? How can you **demand** payment for something you received for free? I've heard may people say, that they paid a price for their gift, and should be compensated. You're yet missing this simple but profound point!

As I mentioned earlier in this book, there are situations where you may be *employed* in ministry to do a certain job or service, but to say that you won't minister unless X amount of dollars are on the table? You can't make me believe that God is pleased with that attitude and mentality! You may not think this is going on in the body of Christ, but just send for some of our "**leading**" Apostles, Bishops, Pastors, Prophets, Teachers, and Musical Artists. You may have to take out a second mortgage on your church to get them to minister to your crowd. What ever happened to, *whosoever will let them come and drink of the waters of life, freely* or *freely ye have received freely give?*

Now I already know some of you may be getting a little tight jawed at what I'm saying, but just chill out, and if you're allowing yourself to get upset, just calm down so you can hear what God is trying to say to your spirit.

I do understand that it takes finances to accomplish just about any and everything in today's society. But I do not believe that when the scriptures talk about a *laborer being worthy of his hire*, that it meant I can only minister with the gifts God gave me, only if the a church has over 200 members or you have the means to raise a twenty-thousand dollar offering before you come. What would it be like if we had to pay God, to speak a word into our lives? If you were broke, I guess you'd never get to hear from Him, right? I guess you'd have to find a way to get the videotape or the CD man, cause you won't get some of these musicians and ministers to come and minister to a financially deficient house!

Please understand what I'm saying. I know that money does play a big part of what we can accomplish in ministry.

We have to have finance to run ministries and make them go, and there are ministers out there *full time*, who depend on the support of our churches to continue ministry and the furtherance of the gospel. I'm not talking about those people, because they already understand what it takes to minister and reach out the lost and the hurting. We should **pay** and **pray** for them who have a heart for God's people and are out there ministering to their natural and spiritual needs. But it also takes faith to believe in what God has called you to do. It takes faith and hearing from God to understand how your gifts are to be used and in what capacity. It takes total obedience to His will for your gifts and talents. It's ALL for His glory!

If God told you to minister for 1 year without the comforts of money, and totally depend on Him, could you do it? Could you depend on Him to feed and take care of you like He did Elijah? God is the same today as He was back in the Bible days. The time is coming and is already here, where God is going to call some away from the four corners of the church, to minister to the masses. You won't always have the comforts of having all the finances upfront, or of all the amenities you may have been used to having before you minister. God is going to provide for you as you go. It will be a total walk of faith in these final hours. Your gift alone won't be enough to get you by. It's going to take the ANOINTING along with your GIFTS to sustain you and cause you to continue. You will need to be spiritually mature enough to totally trust God and know that He will not fail you!

This is the reason why I went back in history to show you how it was all done, originally during the time of David. The minstrels played their instruments and the singers sang for the love of the worship, until the King incorporated the professional musician. From that point on, the mindset of the musician changed, and the priest's attitudes soon followed suit.

As I stated earlier, the *professional* musician in worship was pioneered by King David. God did not introduce this to him. He picked up the idea from other pagan nations who were paying musicians to render their services at *secular* gatherings.

I remember talking about this same thing at another symposium I was having in Columbus, Ga. When I mentioned the fact that David started this, the congregation at that church became silent. All of a sudden a drunken man came off the street and stood in the back of the church and said; *well thank God for David.* Well as we all know, David did some good things in his lifetime and he also did a few not so good things. Bringing in compensated musicians was not really one of the good things. Why? Well, as years passed by and the nation of Israel was again going through one of its many instances of disobedience, that King Hezekiah came on the scene at a time when their temple was now in ruin through the nations folly and sin.

Hezekiah came to bring reform to the House of God. Look at what the scriptures talk about in, 2 Chronicles 29:25-36, where *Hezekiah cleansed the temple.*

The Amplified Bible says; *25Hezekiah stationed the Levites in the Lord's house with cymbals, harps, and lyres, as David [his forefather] and Gad the king's seer and Nathan the prophet had commanded; for the commandment was from the Lord through His prophets.*

²⁶The Levites stood with the instruments of David, and the priests with the trumpets.

²⁷Hezekiah commanded to offer the burnt offering upon the altar. And when the burnt offering began, the song of the Lord began also with the trumpets and with the instruments ordained by King David of Israel. ²⁸And all the congregation worshiped, the singers sang, and the trumpeters sounded; all this continued until the burnt offering was finished.

²⁹When they had stopped offering, the king and all present with him bowed themselves and worshiped.

³⁰Also King Hezekiah and the princes ordered the Levites to sing praises to the Lord with the words of David and of Asaph the seer. And they sang praises with gladness and bowed themselves and worshiped.

³¹Then Hezekiah said, now you have consecrated yourselves to the Lord; come near and bring sacrifices and thank offerings into the house of the Lord. And the assembly brought in sacrifices and thank offerings, and as many as were of a willing heart brought burnt offerings.

³²And the number of the burnt offerings which the assembly brought was 70 bulls, 100 rams, and 200 lambs. All these were for a burnt offering to the Lord.

³³And the consecrated things were 600 oxen and 3,000 sheep.

*³⁴"**But the priests were too few**" and could not skin all the burnt offerings. So until the other priests had sanctified themselves, their Levite kinsmen helped them until the work was done, for the Levites were more upright in heart than the priests in sanctifying themselves.*

³⁵Also the burnt offerings were in abundance, with the fat of the peace offerings, and the drink offerings for every burnt offering. So the service of the Lord's house was set in order.

³⁶Thus Hezekiah rejoiced, and all the people, because of what God had prepared for the people, for "it was done suddenly".

In this passage of scripture King Hezekiah made some calls to his church members, especially his Levites and Priests. He also had Nathan the prophet along side of him. He called for the priest to do their duty. Now notice the Levite Priests were to blow on the trumpets along side of the singers and dancers. They all were to make *sacrifices* that I'm sure, called for a lot of work in order to consecrate all of those animals. Well verse 34 says; "*But the priest were too few.*" I did further research as to the reason why, the priest were too few. Well, remember in David's time, **before** the paid musician was inserted into the worship? The musician's main concern was the move of God, and the flowing anointing in which they played upon their instruments. They concentrated on the ***spontaneous*** anointed music during their worship services. Now that they've come years later during the rule of King Hezekiah, there **was not enough priests** or musicians to do the job of the temple. Why? I'm glad you asked!

The reason why they were too few was because some of them had left the service of the temple to play in secular venues. Some of the priest had polluted their gifts by allowing pagan nations to hire them out to do their weddings and social events or _motivational speaking engagements_ if you will. They were no longer only doing the work of the priesthood; they were now selling their gifts and talents to do secular jobs outside of the Temple. They became _greedy_ and _unsatisfied_ with their pay and _provision_ God had established for them!

Remember, the Levites were paid tithes from the rest of the tribes of Israel. You would think that was enough.

But somewhere down the line they felt they were no longer being paid _enough money_ from the tithes of the church if you will, and started hiring their services to people and nations that did not serve God.

This was in direct disobedience to God's Word. God let them know that they were not to mix and mingle or take on any ideas or rituals from any other pagan nations. They were to be set apart and separated, _sanctified_.

No longer were the priests concerned about the move of God in the Temple, they were about making enough money to take care of their families, instead trusting in God. They were out prostituting their gifts for money and favors. This had become their mind set now.

In verse 34b it says; _their brethren (the Levites) helped until the work had ended_. Since the younger priests had to wait until completing their sanctification process before they could help out. This caused many of the older priests and Levites to be overloaded with duties of the temple, because others had left their posts in the House of God to search out the _all mighty dollar_.

Many priests would not return because they wanted to make more money than what was being paid to them by the tithe. Does that sound like something that's going on today? Many pastors are leaving their pulpits and from preaching the whole truth of God, to preaching a **sad, watered down, no anointed version of the gospel**. No ones telling you how to make it to heaven, they're just telling you that you can prosper in this present world. Preachers are not willing now to tell men and women about their sins, and the fact that we must come out from among sin and be separated. No, we've reverted to _motivational, inspirational preaching_ that tickles the ear and draws the large crowds. Some of our priests today are now doing everything but preaching the Gospel. It's the spirit of this _new age movement_ which is full of deception. Its gifts and paths are full of darkness, but appear as a guiding light! Don't be fooled by the gifts and _fancy speeches_ of men and women. (Romans 16: 17-19)

Discern the gift verses the anointing! God's anointing!

Sing with an understanding.

Proverbs 4:7, _Wisdom is the principal thing; therefore get wisdom: and with all thy getting get_ **understanding**. KJV.

Psalms 47:7, _For God is the King of all the earth: sing ye praises with_ **understanding**. KJV.

What is it that we are to understand? Well, we are to understand how to operate in the gifts God has given us.

"now i'm going to add my own little wrinkle to this, but not to take it out of biblical context!" One of the first things to understand and realize is, that your gifts do not *supersede* that of your spiritual *leaders* or the set authority in the house of God. Secondarily, one of the fastest ways to cause God to discipline you is to disobey, disrespect or overstep your boundaries as a Levite. You must learn to submit your gifts to leadership, and commit to being under spiritual authority and covering, not running around like a vagabond, prostituting your gifts and being spiritual bastards, with no spiritual parents. Thirdly, you are not to be *subject to the gift*, but the *gift is subject to you*.

When you understand how to possess your vessel in holiness and control your spirit, then you're on your way to understanding Gods order, and how to operate with understanding.

We learn how to be used by God through our pain and suffering, through our moments of being on the mountain, and times of being down in a valley. We learn through our mistakes, failures, trials, and yes, even our temptations. It's through all of these things that we become well-balanced ministers of Christ. Romans 8:28 says; *and we know that all things work together for the good of them who love God, to them who are* **the called** *according to His purpose*. KJV. Good things, bad things, things we don't understand, and things we do understand. It takes all of these ingredients to become a minister of great *understanding* and *anointing*.

If you learn how to use all of these things in your ministry, you will be much more effective in how you minister. There is an anointing for you, but it comes through conflict, humility, pain, being misunderstood, talked about, forgot about, left out, not invited and separation from, just to name a few.

Hebrews 5:7-8 says; *who in the days of his flesh, when he had offered up prayers and supplications with strong crying and tears unto Him that was able to save him from death, and was heard in that he feared.* verse 8; *though he were a Son, yet learned he obedience by the things which he suffered."* KJV.

Even Jesus had to go through pain and was subject not only to earthly authority, but even unto His Heavenly Father and the death of the cross. Are you willing to die out to your own will and desires to be used by God? Even if it means dying to the ambitions you have for your own ministry? Your first duty as a Levite is to be subject to the vision of your own church or local ministry. That's how you enlarge your own ministry, by being faithful to another's. You also must understand that all of you are not called to a national or international ministry. Some of you will never have thousands or even hundreds know about your ministry.

Can you handle that? Will you be happy and satisfied in the fact that God himself has called some of you to minister at a local or personal level? Remember, it's not about you or your gifts, whether you minister to tens, hundreds, thousands, or even millions. It's God that's working in us, both to will and to do of His good pleasure. If you're obedient to the call of God on your own life, you will receive the same reward in heaven. Is that enough for you? Think about it!! Many times we get caught up in the gifts and not the one who gave the gift. It's all about ministry, it's all about the message of Christ.

Can you be satisfied once you *understand* where God has placed you in the body of Christ? You will only be blessed to the fullest when you operate in the absolute will of God. There are only two wills. I know some of you have been taught about a *permissive will*, but that can't be backed by scripture. No, there are only two wills, your own will, and the will of God. There's a song Twinkie Clark used to sing that says; t*he safest place in the whole wide world is in the will of God.*

Don't you know you can spend your whole life doing the Works of God, but not the Will of God, and be lost at the end? Doesn't Matthew 7: 21-22, tell us that there will be many in that day who will say to him, vs. 22; *Lord lord, have we not prophesied in thy name? And in thy name have cast out devils, in thy name done many* **wonderful works**? Verse 23 goes on to say; *and then will I profess unto them, I never knew you: depart from me, ye that work, iniquity.* KJV. Do you understand that you can go through life doing the works of God, and God not even acknowledge or count what you have done? I NEVER KNEW YOU, YE THAT WORK INIQUITY? I don't want to be on earth all this time and end up hearing that word, *iniquity*. Iniquity is what was found in Lucifer before he was sentenced and kicked out of heaven. One of the descriptions of iniquity is; *LAWLESSNESS!* Man, just like some of you who are running around without headship or covering. Moving from place to place, church to church, ministry to ministry, walking in disobedience, and not willing to submit your gift to anyone in authority. But just as Lucifer was cast down, if we don't become subject to authority, and submit ourselves, we will also find ourselves, cast down and judged just the way he was, and not able to get back to our place of worship with Him, losing out on all the benefits that He has for us.

Matthew 7:21 says; *Not everyone that will say unto me, Lord lord, shall enter into the kingdom of heaven; but he that doeth the WILL OF MY FATHER, which is in heaven.* KJV. Know where God has placed you in the body. You will only be effective where God has placed, anointed and appointed you to be. Some of you, God has called to preach, and you are somewhere trying to be a recording artist. Others, God has called to minister in song, and you are somewhere trying to preach. Just because people jump and shout when you get up doesn't mean you're anointed or doing what He's called you to do. It sadly means that many Christians aren't in tune enough with the spirit of God to know when gifts mingled with flesh are on display, or when the gift is operating under the anointing of God. Our flesh is tingled and satisfied but our spirit is the same and not edified. We leave out of our church or worship services the same way we came in.

Don't misunderstand me when I say; some are preachers trying to sing, and some are singers attempting to preach. I'm aware that God has called some to do both and more. I'm trying to get you to see that you must be sure of what area of ministry God has called and anointed you to. If you do this, you're guaranteed success. Not the success as the world sees it, but the success as in the **approval of God** of your ministry, which will produce *grace* and *favor* on your life. It's so important to run *your race*, in the lane that's assigned to you. It's not a speed race or one you're required to finish first. Just run at the pace God gives you, and *see it to the end*. Walk in *your own* anointing, and you'll be blessed, and can be a blessing to someone else also. Some have one, five and even nine gifts, but when you're faithful and operate properly in those gifts, we will witness the **fruits** of that gift! The *fruits* are the anointing that destroys yokes, changes lives, delivers captives, and sets people free from all types of bondages. Having this understanding of your gifts or ministry will make you so much more effective, and will allow you to always accomplish what God uses you to do.

So when I say; **sing with an understanding**, I want you to realize that when you're obedient to God, and operate where He's placed you, when you understand there's a *blessing* in *submitting* your gifts to *spiritual authority*, when you've learned how to *wait* on your ministering, and while waiting, adding *necessary ingredients* to your ministry. You'll begin to realize that there's more to this than you originally thought.

You'll begin to notice that there's a **spiritual calling** required of you first, before you can truly be used in the **calling** that is recognized as your gift. What do I mean by necessary ingredients and spiritual calling? There's a calling that's spiritual, and there's a calling that's natural. The natural calling is in the realm of your gifting and talents, but they'll only be effective when you've added the ingredients of the spiritual calling mentioned in, 2 Peter 1:3-10, which says;

³ seeing that his divine power hath granted unto us all things that pertain unto life and godliness, through the knowledge of him that called us by his own glory and virtue; ⁴ whereby he hath granted unto us his precious and exceeding great promises; that through these ye may become partakers of the divine nature, having escaped from the corruption that is in that world by lust. ⁵ Yea, and for this very cause adding on your part all diligence, in your faith supply virtue; and in your virtue knowledge; ⁶ and in your knowledge self-control; and in your self-control patience; and in your patience godliness; ⁷ and in your godliness brotherly kindness; and in your brotherly kindness love. ⁸ For if these things are yours and abound, they make you to be not idle nor unfruitful unto the knowledge of our Lord Jesus Christ. ⁹ For he that lacketh these things is blind, seeing only what is near, having forgotten the cleansing from his old sins. ¹⁰ Wherefore, brethren, give the more diligence to make your **calling and election sure***: for if ye do these things, ye shall never stumble.* ASV

What is the scripture saying to us? It speaks of the **call of God to salvation**. Our faith and salvation must not be taken for granted. We can continue faithful to God until the end, only if we sincerely endeavor to add to our ministry, the necessary ingredients listed in this passage.

Verse 10 says to make our **calling** and **election sure**. It speaks to us answering the call of God to salvation and sanctification. Notice, that the calling is first in order; then the *election* comes when we accept the call. Making the call and election *sure,* requires effort on our part. It means to *stand firm* in our salvation, (*spiritual call*) being *strong* and *secure* in the call and operation of our gifts. (*natural call*)

If you do this, the Bible ensures us that we will never fall. (kjv) We won't come up short in our fellowship with God, while operating in a long lasting relationship with our gift. Having this godly wisdom and understanding will give you longevity in ministry, and prevent you from being a **public success**, but a **private failure**!

God will then honor you, and allow your gift to make room for you, and bring your before *great men!*

One revelation the Lord shared with me concerning bringing us before great men is; that if you *humble yourself,* and be obedient to Him, He will lift you *higher* and bring **YOU before** those who won't obeyed him, or those who have *considered themselves* great. He also showed me that He would bring us before **great men**, great meaning; before a **multitude or masses of people**, not just those who are considered to be great in this world!

Finally, when you've come to the realization of what *type of song* this is of which I speak. You'll understand that; <u>sing with an understanding</u>, is a song of your *character, integrity, willingness* and *obedience*. It's a *song* that *has a look of,* the anointing resting on your life. It's your *ministry* that sings this song and has the *sound* of a well oiled machine. It's a song that has the *vibe* of a highly complex composition! So go ahead and sing your song, but sing with an understanding that. . . . .***Your life is that song**!!!*

I never knew you.

*"I keep going over this because it's so important for us to operate in the area God called us to. I don't want anyone to miss the mark by walking in disobedience, or perish for the lack of knowledge, because of spending years doing something God never called you to do. Only to have it all end up for naught. That would be totally messed up to stand before God after doing the **works** of God for years, to hear Him say; I didn't even recognize what you did, because you spent all your time doing your own thing. . . . . . . .therefore I have no reward for that!*

I Never Knew You. These words of Christ make it unmistakably clear that a preacher may proclaim the gospel in the name of Christ; cast out devils, and perform miracles while he himself has no genuine saving faith in Christ. (Matthew 7: 23)

Scripture teaches that fervent gospel preaching; an apparent *zeal* for righteousness, and the occurrence of miracles can be performed in this age under the influence and power of Satan. *Yes I said Satan!* Didn't Paul warn that Satan himself is transformed into an angel of light? *Therefore it is no great thing if his ministers also be transformed as the ministers of righteousness.* (2 Corinthians 11:13, **14**-15; cf. Matt. 24:24).

Paul makes it clear that an *apparent* powerful anointing can be nothing more than the *working of Satan,* (see 2 Thes. 2:9-10; Rev. 13:3, 12-15.)

(Read the scriptures on False Teachers)

Many times God overrides the activity of Satan in false preachers in order to bring salvation or healing to those who sincerely respond to Gods Word. (see Phil. 1: 15-18). It is always Gods desire that those who proclaim the gospel be righteous. (see 1 Tim. 3: 1-7) *Yet* when an evil or immoral person preaches His Word, God can still work in the hearts of those who receive His Word with commitment to Christ.

How does this happen? It happens because the Word of God is a living mechanism. It is spirit and life; it's the power of God which brings to us the way of salvation. Therefore it carries the ability to tear down, uproot, cut away, devour, consume, deliver and make free within its immeasurable contents.

God does **not** endorse any unrighteous preacher of the gospel, but He will endorse Biblical truth and those who accept it in faith, because God will *honor* and is bound by His Own Word!

It doesn't matter who you are, it is vital that you be in the will of God where your ministry is concerned. God is looking for ministers, *(whatever your ministry is)* who will talk the talk and walk the walk. He wants us to be who we profess we are. While we preach to others, we need to make sure that the Word of God is living in us, and that we're walking by the words, we tell others to live by. The world has seen enough of the fake and powerless in Christian ministry. It's time to walk up right before the Lord and minister in the power of His Word and in spiritual demonstration. Not fleshly demonstration, we're getting enough of that now. We need demonstration in the power that His anointing produces in us. It can not be imitated or duplicated, although many try!

Wouldn't you hate the fact that you worked on a job for twenty years just to find out that it didn't count? No retirement plan or benefits, zero pensions, no vacation time, no gold watch at the end? It really doesn't matter what our opinions are about it, the Word of God is just and true. If we're not going to operate in your gifts and abide in your call and do it according to God's word, we might as well pack it all up, get out and do our own thing, but remember, God will still have the last say so. It would be awful to think I was doing the will of God and wake up to find out that it was all for nothing, God forbid!!

The Lord gave me a sermon entitled; ***I don't want God to use me.*** Now don't get nervous, here's what I mean.

One evening I came in from work and I turned on the television to unwind before going to bed. I turned to a station that had a known preacher that had been on the air for years preaching prosperity oriented scriptures, biblical principals and *partial truths,* in order to get the people in his church and those watching his program, to give offering and money to the ministry. Doesn't it sound like what that old serpent did to Eve? He told her *partial truths* and played on words? (see Gen. 3: 1-6)

Now there's nothing wrong with giving but you should even consult God on what and to whom to give, amen? Now this particular preacher is very wealthy because people took the Word of God at face value and believed on it, and therefore gave their money. People grabbed a hold to the Word of God in faith, and were obedient in giving to this minister.

So, you can actually be living like a devil and your gift will yet operate in you. Remember the Bible says in Romans 11:29, *the gifts and callings of God are without repentance.* That's because of Gods covenant with man.

(study gifts and callings without repentance, when you have time)

Anyway, I asked the Lord, how can a person who isn't living right, <u>appear</u> to be so blessed? The Lord told me; His Word has power and the words He speaks are spirit and life. *I will honor My Word for My Own namesake. I will bless the people because they have believed on my Word, so at the end when judgment comes, those people who have been preached to,* **can be saved**, *but those persons who preached* **will be lost**. He also told me, He would allow ministers to continue bringing thousands to the Kingdom by *using their gifts,* but in judgment they will be **eternally punished!** (see Romans 1:18; *holding the truth in unrighteousness*)

After the Lord revealed that to me, He asked me; *what happened to that false preacher?*

I replied. . .**you just used him**.

So in that manner, **I don't want God to use me**, but I want God to **use me**!!! Do you want God to use you, or ***do you want God to use you***? <u>The choice is yours!</u>

The Song. New College Edition / The American Heritage Dictionary song; is defined: *1. A brief musical composition written or adapted for singing. 2. The act or art of singing. 3. A melodious utterance, such as a bird call. 4. Poetry; verse, a lyric, poem or ballad.*

There is just not enough time or space to share with you all the aspects of a song. So we'll just give you a brief synopsis of what the Word of God says about **the song**.

Understand that you don't have to be a; **"quote"- "un-quote"** songwriter, in order to write a song. There are times when God will give you a song in times of happiness or sadness, and in times of temptation or trials. Have you ever gone through a hard time in your life and God gives you just the right song to make it through? Sometimes He'll give you a song you may know of, or know the words to, and sometimes He'll give you a song fresh from His Throne.

Now I don't consider myself a great song writer, but God has given me many songs to write. One of those songs was in the form of an instrumental on my CD, *"Expression of Worship."* I was going through a really hard time, and I remember praying in my room and crying out to God, asking Him questions, why things were as bad as they were. As I asked, I heard Him reply back to me, but His reply was not in the form of *verbal words*, but **a melody**. As I cried out, He told me to pick up my saxophone and begin to play. As I picked up my horn, I began to hear this *lovely melody*, and in the melody I could hear **my cry** and **His reply** within the sounds of the melody. I decided to record this melody and when I did, the Lord said to me; *No words, only music on the recording.* Of course I asked Him why? He said; *when people hear the melody that I gave you out of your pain, they will also hear this anointed melody when they're going through their own struggles, and hear their own expressions of worship. They would have their own* **words** *of* **expression** *to God, coming from within this melody.* He said *the melody would bring forth a cry of worship out of their own spirits.* I simply said to myself, "God you're awesome!"

To further confirm what God told me about this song, I introduced it at one of my Pastors Anniversaries a few years ago. After I finished ministering the song, one of the sisters of my church came up to me and said; *brother Elmus while you were playing that song, I heard words coming from your horn.* She then handed me a piece of paper that was full of words she heard while I was playing that same melody. I told her; *these are beautiful words sister, but they're not for me, they came out of your spirit, they're for you.* Just as God had told me earlier, the words were *her expression to God* out of her own spirit. That's just so awesome to me!!!

Sometimes God will give me actual lyrics to an instrumental song. There's a little praise God gives me when I'm going through and it just seems to pull me through, it simply says; **hallelujah, thank you Jesus, Lord we maaag-nify your name, hallelujah, thank you Jesus, Lord we magnify your name.**

So you don't have to be a Kirk Franklin or Richard Smallwood (*writers*) in order to write a song. As a matter of fact Moses and his sister Miriam had the first songs recorded in the Bible. Miriam was a prophetess and Moses was a Pastor, if you will. You'll find in scripture when God gave the children of Israel victory over their enemies, or some other triumph, they would name that place where the event happened, build an altar or write a song about it. Understand that these were not songs already written because the events they sang about had not always happened yet. Now these were real prophetic gospel songs. The reason why I say *gospel* is because the songs were directed at, or sung about Him! The word gospel is not limited to any one culture!

What is gospel anyway? It's the Word or good news of Jesus Christ. You can't call it; gospel rap, gospel jazz, or gospel whatever, if it doesn't point to Him or is about Him. It may be a nice song with a tight beat but; you know what I'm gonna say........*IT AIN'T GOSPEL!*

Now does this mean your songs have to say; Jesus, Jesus, Jesus, Jesus, written throughout? No, but it shouldn't be a question at the end of it as to what you meant either. Even an instrumental that doesn't have any verbal words or lyrics can yet be so anointed, that words can actually be heard by the carnal or spiritual ear. Songs prophesy, they speak to us the Word of God through melody. I have to say that **God isn't saying** many of the things <u>we're saying</u> in our songs. Did God give you your song? You'll even hear some people say that God made all music. Wrong! God created music originally for the worship of Himself. There is music that came and originated straight from the devil himself. God created music; true, but as far as the different ways it's presented, God didn't do that!! Lucifer from the beginning ministered music in the presence of God, but has now *perverted the music* since being cast out of heaven. I'll cover that in the, **Vision of Lucifer** segment of the book.

God can and will give you songs that minister to our spirits and not just tickle our flesh. He has *songs of deliverance* and melodies that will promote and perpetuate righteousness in the earth. Understand that music **carries the spirit** of its **original author**. Since this is the case, what is the name of the *spirit* that comes from your song? What would its intentions be or what assignment is carried out once listened to? A song is a long lasting *statement* in the *atmosphere*. What spirits are you releasing when your song is introduced in the heavens? Are we getting the right message, or are we receiving *error* or *mixed* messages when we listen to your tune? Are people hearing your unhealed pain, or unresolved anger? Or are they hearing about God's love and delivering power? That's the kind of lyrics they wrote in scripture. Even the love songs and poetry of Solomon, spoke of a woman, but the contents spoke of the perfection God created when He made her. What is the *undertone* message, when we listen to your songs? Is it like King Solomon who had *fleshly issues*, which issues could be heard in many of his writings?

A song lasts throughout the ages and can affect the way people live their lives. Don't you know that people *talk, dress and act out*, based on songs they've heard? When the group, "Kris Kross" came out wearing their pants backwards, how many young people, (*older ones to*) start wearing pants the same way? People start talking the way they hear **artists** talk on their albums, and you know I'm telling the truth, *for rizal!* Why do some secular Hip Hop artists wear what they wear? I'll cover that later but, it all has to do with **spirits** that are **coming from the music.** Songs can change the way a person looks at themselves and others. The **music media** has the ability to change the very course of life. A song has the power to fulfill every dream and aspiration, and a song can pick you up in victory, or put you down in the dumps. Songs carry the spirit and attitudes of the persons who birth them. Just like a mother who brings forth a child, that child can carry her traits throughout its life. So it is when you birth a song; when that song is born, it will live throughout the ages, even if it's **not** a huge top seller, the spirit that is attached to it, will always follow that song. It will carry the spirit of the one who birthed it. That's why we just can't sing any kind of song saints of God, or listen to it either for that fact!

Levites, give us songs that tell us the way, songs that tell us who the truth and light is!! Let's give God the praise because He has given us all a song that not even the angels in heaven can sing. We've been washed in the blood of the Lamb, the Crucified One!

Notable Mention: *It is said by some theologians that, Ps. 115 & 117, were songs actually sang at the Lord's Supper.*

Your gift works on you first.

I remember talking to a sister on one of the praise teams at our church; she began to ask me questions about a word the Lord gave me for her. She reminded me what the Lord said to her through a word of prophecy. He told her to *sing, sing and come forth*. Now the Lord spoke other things to her as well but her question was on the words, sing and coming forth.

She also reminded me that I'd given her the same word of prophecy on other occasions. She wanted to know exactly what the Lord was requiring of her by telling her to sing, sing and come forth. Sometimes I remember what the Lord speaks through me on occasions and sometimes I don't, but in this case I did. Really listen to this because I feel this will minister to many individuals who have struggles in your life and the enemy tries to come in and bind you up with guilt, fear or inferiority complexes. You may have sickness in your body and need a healing, or you may need deliverance in your life in one area or another. Understand that the devil especially has it in for the Levite, and would love nothing more than to stop us, or discourage us in any way he can. He strives to keep us from using our anointed gifts and from being a blessing in someone's life.

I began to tell this sister that, *the answer lies within her* and *God already gave her the power to overcome*. You see when you have a gifting from God, that brings deliverance or healing to the body of Christ, that same gift **works on you first.** I told her that whenever she gets down or needs deliverance in any area of her life; then *sing*. Her deliverance was in her own mouth through her singing. She's anointed, and as I'll continue to say throughout this book; it's the anointing that destroys the yoke, even if the yoke is on you!

If you need a healing and you have the gift of healing, don't you know you can pray for yourself and see the results of the gift that lies within you? It's only when you're delivered and free, that you can be used of God to deliver and free someone else.

I use this spiritual benefit all the time. Many times when I'm going through a trial that tries to weight me down, I'll pick up my sax and begin to play until I sense a difference or change in the spirit realm, or a breaking or shift in the atmosphere. That's when I know everything is all right! Well, after hearing this, she had a better understanding of what the Lord wanted from her. She now understood that no matter what she goes through, she didn't have to stay in it long or wait until the Pastors Sunday morning sermon to get free, she could simply sing. God has given her an anointing of deliverance when she sings to his people, so now she understands that she can use that same gift in her own everyday situations.

Isn't it strange how we always have a ready and **right now word** for everybody else, but have the hardest time hearing God for our own lives? Use all your gifts on you first, and you will be free to minister those same gifts to someone else in need of deliverance. God's anointing operating through a clean and free vessel is as a sweet smelling savor in His nostrils.

Bring me a Minstrel. (Musician)

In this segment I'd like to briefly talk about the importance of the **anointed musician** that has the ability to play well.

Understand that it is vital to ministry, or a church, that the musicians be anointed and skillful, with a character lifestyle that matches the gift. A *minstrel* is a musician, whether their instrument is an actual musical instrument, or the human voice. Both can be used to usher in the presence of Lord, when the persons ministering are under the anointing of God.

Let's go to the scriptures for a moment to validate what I'm saying to you.

2 Kings 3:15-19, shows how Elisha the prophet, made an anointed request for a minstrel to play upon the harp. If you read in the earlier verses of this chapter, you find that the prophet Elisha was visited by Jehoshaphat the king of Judah, and two other kings of Israel and Edom, to prophecy.

Upon their arrival, they inquired of Elisha, a word from the Lord. But before he uttered a *prophetic word*, he requested a minstrel to play upon their instrument. Verse 15 goes on to say that, as the minstrel played, the hand of the LORD came upon Elisha and he began to prophesy. Understand what was happening here. The musician actually **set the prophetic tone** or **atmosphere** by ushering in the presence of the Lord, so that the prophet could begin speaking the Word of the Lord.

Ask any preacher, evangelist or pastor, who ministers under the anointing of God, how important an anointed musician or anointed music is, **before** or *while* they minister. I know you may have thought they just wanted to have a musician there so they could, squawk and moan if you will. But the fact is, that anointed music and musicians can provoke a prophetic word from the man or woman of God. Just having any ole musician who can play well will not do!!!

There are several passages in the bible that can give us examples of how important it is for musicians to be ready, and anointed. How would it have looked if the prophet called for the musician and the minstrel had excuses for not being able to play under the anointing? *"Well Umm, I was at the club last night, so therefore the anointing is not flowing through me at the moment,"* or *"I was in bed with Jack or Sue last week and I'm not able to minister at this time."* The whole outcome for the kings and that nation could have been totally messed up because the minstrel was not found in their proper place at the proper time to be used to usher in the presence of the Lord. Understand that it's not your gift that ushers Gods presence; it's the anointing that must be upon you that energizes the gift in you to minister.

Here's another example in, 2 Chronicles 5; 11-14, *"¹¹And it came to pass, when the priests were come out of the holy place: (for all the priests that were present were sanctified, and did not then wait by course: ¹²Also the **Levites which were the singers**, all of them of **Asaph**, of **Heman**, of **Jeduthun**, with their sons and their brethren, being arrayed in white linen, having cymbals and psalteries and harps, stood at the east end of the altar, and with them an **hundred and twenty priests sounding with trumpets**:) ¹³It came even to pass, as the trumpeters and singers were as one, to make one sound to be heard in praising and thanking the LORD; and when they lifted up their voice with the trumpets and cymbals and instruments of musick, and praised the LORD, saying, For he is good; for his mercy endureth for ever: that then **the house was filled with a cloud**, even the **house of the LORD**; ¹⁴So that the priests could not stand to minister by reason of the cloud: for **the glory of the LORD had filled the house of God**."* KJV

This passage of scripture in 2 Chronicles, shows the Levite and Priests, singing, playing and praising God upon their instruments, under such an anointing, that the Priests themselves could not stand to minister.

Wow!!! Wow!! In my own mind, I can see the music and singing coming forth in that service in 2 Chronicles; to the point where the musicians were with one accord, the ministers and priests were also playing instruments and singing, The Chief musicians and directors; Asaph, Heman and Jeduthun were directing the music and the choir. The priest weren't just standing there with their arms folded, looking deep. They all were praising God, and as the music began to play and prophecy, even the priest in vs.15 could not stand. I see them staggering around under the influence of the Holy Spirit to the point that there was no need for them to *stand and minister* because the *anointed music* was already prophesying the Word of the Lord, and speaking what God wanted to say at that particular moment!

Can you see how important it is, when you're asked to play or sing, that you do it with an anointing, and that you give God your all, not ministering half heartedly and timid or not prepared? We don't need a display of flesh or carnality when it's time to warfare in the spirit realm. We need ministers who are ready and available to be used at any given time. Ready to minister in season and out of season.

There are times when my Pastor will ask someone to come up and give a sermonic solo, or play their instrument before he ministers. Now when he does this, you have to understand that he's not always doing this just to hear how well you can sing or to see how talented you are. Many times he's doing this to set the tone before the Word of God comes forth. He'll also call you to minister a song, knowing full well that the song has the ability to deliver even the one ministering it. See; as I said earlier that your anointed gift has the ability to work on you first, before it ministers to someone else. That's the importance of anointed music, it heals and delivers and eases the troubled spirit, just ask King Saul.

Bring me a Minstrel (Musician) cont'd "This segment comes from the book entitled' *The Ministry Anointing of the* Prophet Minstrel, by David L. Brown. . . . . .used by permission

You must understand that there is an anointing that destroys yokes off of the lives of people, and declares warfare against Satan and his imps in the heavenlies or atmosphere. The ministry of a prophetic or prophet-minstrel is one that is very fruitful and needed in the local assembly, and in the body of Christ at large. Satan tries to build spiritual walls between individuals in the body and in the local church and many times the call for a minstrel is needed to bring those "Jericho" spiritual walls down before the "preached" Word of God comes. **Prophetic-Minstrels** are musicians and or singers who have a "prophetic gift," but do not necessarily walk in the "office of a prophet." When they play or sing, the "song" may flow into a song of prophetic utterance or the song may cease, and a word of prophecy may come forth from the minstrel. **Prophet-Minstrels** are also musicians and or singers who walk in the "office of prophet." They flow the same way but they are also prophets in the house as well. In this anointed call, the prophet-minstrels primary place of operation is in or during a time of "praise and worship." They can flow in prophecy during a song, or even sing a prophetic song while ministering. They also carry a prophetic word in their mouth because they walk in the "office" of prophet. What are some of the functions of the prophet? Prophets impart, they stir up, exhort, edify and build up a body of believers. (1 Tim. 1:6; 1 Cor. 14:29-32)

The New Testament minstrels are linked together with leadership or the set authority in the ministry. The leaders depend on dependable minstrels to help in ushering the people of God into the presence of the Lord. by David L. Brown

There's a sister at my church; well I call her one of my younger close sisters in the Lord. I've known her since she was about twelve years old or so. She's my pastor's eldest daughter, Lisa Harper. She's one of our many praise team singers, and she's also one of the prophetesses in the house. Many times when she's leading a song, and the spirit of the Lord is high, she will begin to flow into the prophetic. Sometimes she prophesies in the midst of the song, and sometimes as the Holy Ghost moves, the song will pause, and she will give a word of prophecy for the house. I've told her on a couple of occasions, that there is a sound in the midst of the sound. When the spirit of the Lord is moving, there's a sound in the spirit realm that you can hear. Sometimes the sound may be a call to warfare. I told Lisa, there are times when she sings and the anointing comes, that there's a *hi-pitched note* she hits when the spirit is high. That hi-pitched note is actually waging war in the atmosphere. I didn't know if she noticed or understood when this happened, but I recognized it in the spirit. There are times during our services when I'm in the sound booth mixing the sound, and the Lord will speak to me and tell me to get on my horn and begin to play. Now I'm way past playing my sax just so people can hear me play, but I play to help do my part in the warfare against the demonic forces that may be present in given service. I noticed that when I hear a certain sound in the spirit, I begin to play a very *hi-pitched note*, and I can feel the very atmosphere change; and you can just hear and feel God gaining the victory in the midst of the service and defeating the plan of the enemy to hinder His move.

These are demonic forces pastors have to fight <u>themselves</u> when they get up to preach or teach if the minstrels aren't in their rightful place, or fail to understand what's going on in the spirit. You must flow with the anointing! You must do it with an understanding!

I began to understand more why David used terms like, **Muth-Labben,** in the book of Psalms. It meant to play or sing, *"hi-pitched"* notes. They too were playing and singing under an anointing to fight off and warfare against the enemy in the spirit realm.

I also told Lisa that she didn't have to worry about being technically sound in order for God to move through her. What do I mean? Well there are some, who may know how to run the scales and use various techniques with their voices, but some don't know how or they're yet learning how to flow in the spirit. They may want to complete the song because, *"that's how we rehearsed it."* But when the anointing comes and the spirit of the Lord begins to move, you must use *wisdom and understand* how to *move with the spirit*. Let me make that clear, I'm talking about the **spirit of God**. There are a lot of spirits floating around out there and even in our churches, but I'm talking about the spirit of the **living God!!**

I understand this may be difficult for some, but when you walk in the anointing of a prophetic or prophet-minstrel, this is almost second nature to you. At the same time, when you are used in the area of praise and worship, you must know when the spirit of the Lord is **shifting** in another direction. Speaking personally, I would rather have someone who can flow with the spirit, even if they don't possess all of the technical skills, than someone who can sing like an angel, but doesn't have an understanding of how to usher us into the presence of the Lord and declare warfare in the spirit.

Now you may say; "Elmus, isn't that in conflict with 1 Samuel 16:17?" which says; *"and Saul said unto his servants, provide me now a man that can **Play Well** and bring him to me.* The *play well* actually has two different meanings. (1) Not only could David **play** his harp **well** and with great skill, (2) He also understood how to ***flow well*** with the spirit of God. In other words, whatever giftings God has allowed you to operate in, do it to the best of your God given ability. And it will all be **Well**. So playing or singing well, goes a lot deeper than how **well** you can *mechanically* flow through the notes and scales. Can you flow with the spirit and move when God moves, change when He changes or modulate when God modulates in the spirit? See, there's more to playing your instrument or to singing on Sunday mornings than you thought huh? There's a responsibility to be not only available, but warfare ready!

My younger brother, Elder Eric High is another who operates in the prophetic-minstrel area. He's an organist a Chief Musician and one of the praise and worship leaders at our church. There are services where the praise team is ministering, and the spirit of God starts flowing and Eric may begin to sing a song they rehearsed, but then as the spirit *shifts*, he will begin to sing a completely *different song.* I'm not talking about a song that has already been written, but a **new song**, a **prophetic song** just for that moment! Just for that appointed time. It is what the Lord is saying or wants to hear in the midst of worship at **that time**! That's how they flowed in scripture, as the spirit moved on the musicians, they began to minister in song and dance and began to play upon their instruments and sing praises unto God, many times **un-rehearsed**.

It's what God wants to hear about Himself, in the midst of the worship, or it's the *right now* word or song for the house. In David's time, they knew how to flow with God. The instruments prophesied and began to sound off ***mysteries*** (Psalms 49:4) and the praise and worship of Almighty God took place in spirit and truth. Psalms 49:4, ***I will incline mine ear to a parable; I will open my dark sayings upon the harp."*** KJV. It's so needed in our churches today!

Psalmists/ Singers/ Worship Leaders.

I want to shed a little more light on this subject and make it clearer concerning the diverse anointed ministries of these three callings.

I know I mentioned the fact that a minstrel is a musician, and how the ministry of a prophetic or prophet-minstrel operates. Many who were called minstrels, played upon a harp in the Old Testament. There is a natural meaning and a spiritual one I see in this. The minstrel as I said, were mainly known to be a musician upon a harp. I introduced my brother Eric and my sister Lisa as *prophet-minstrels* because *the voice* is an instrument as well. Although my brother Eric plays an instrument, he also sings prophetically. It is possible for *one person* to walk in the anointing of each of these musical ministries. Are we clear so far?

Psalmist.

One on the best ways I know to describe a Psalmist is a, **songwriter/spontaneous composer,** who has the ability to compose a song that flows directly for the *heart of God.* The song can be a melody that is meant to be sung directly to the Lord, or a melody that articulates the present emotional state of God's heart toward his people at any given time. A psalmist can hear what God wants to say at that moment. He or she begins to minister what God wants to hear in the midst of worship or praise. They have a special ear to hear what God wants us to say to Him. A psalmist is not only called to minister to people from God's heart, they are also anointed with the *ability* to minister to God Himself. So their main objective is to discern what God wants, and not what the people want to hear.

The song of a psalmist can range from a simple one-line melody to a very complex orchestration that would require great *skill* and *ability* to arrange." "Handel was a Psalmist who wrote *"The Messiah"* and the classic, *"Hallelujah Chorus."* He also states; Andre Crouch walked in the anointing of a true Psalmist with a simple song called, *"Alleluia."* With that simple song he was able to tap into the *heart of God* and come away with a wonderful worship melody still used in many places of worship today.

So then we find, it's not always the complexity of a song that gets the job done, but the ability to find God's heart and mind. Many times a psalmist is given a song in personal prayer or it can be a song of an **extemporaneous nature**. Many times in the context of the worship moment, a psalmist will sense the heart of God and compose a song and flow in it **spontaneously**.

(from the book ,"The Ministry Anointing of the Prophet-Minstrels") David L. Brown

It can be praise, it can be edification, or exhortation, and it can also be a lament or a declaration. King David was also known as *the sweet psalmist of Israel*, because of the anointing that was upon the many songs he composed. He was credited to have written and composed many of the songs or psalms in the Book of Psalms.

Many people confuse Christian songwriters and singers with the calling and anointing of a Psalmist. First of all, it is important to understand that just because one has the ability to compose, and or sing songs and minister with a great anointing, doesn't make them a psalmist. A psalmist is one who has *access* to the heart of God and can compose a song on a whim, from the very heart of God, or minister it to God. God gives them songs that will minister to His people, and songs that will minister to Him alone. Now all of you true psalmists that possess this anointing know exactly what I'm talking about. You may not have understood what is was, but what I'm saying to you is starting to make sense because it's what you've been doing all along. One of the key words or phrases I mentioned was, **access** and **Heart of God.** One of the descriptions or attributes of the psalmist is, *one who will minister to or from the heart of God.* I know I keep mentioning this but it's a key factor. Anointed singers will sing what's in their heart or whatever seems fitting for that particular situation. And that's ok, but the psalmists anointing doesn't operate in that manner. They may start out singing one song and in the midst of that song, they may sense the heart of God moving in another direction and they flow that way. You might say, well doesn't everyone do that? No, the psalmist is used by God for that very purpose. Not only will they sense the Lord moving in another direction, but they may even hear a totally brand new unrehearsed song that flows directly from the heart and mind of God. They're anointing allows them to compose a song right on the spot, to fit the spiritual cause and purpose.

The Heart of God, can you imagine that? Knowing the heart of God in a song?

Do you understand or can you fathom what it is to begin to get to *know* the heart of God?

Well for starters, it involves a deep and intimate relationship with God. Not only that, it also involves God Himself trusting you enough to open up and reveal His heart to you. That is what *access* is all about. We can sing songs that we know or have rehearsed, and God appreciates that, however it is a whole different level of intimacy for God to open up His heart to us, so we can minister to Him. This level of worship can not be selfish, just how intimate relationships should be. It's not only about you, but also the one you're in love with.

That's what the psalmist ministry is all about, discerning God's heart and serving and ministering unto Him. To truly discern the heart of God, He has to give you access to it. A psalmist must be clear that their first priority is to minister to God! Ministering to the people is secondary. *(I'll explain that in the" singer" segment)*

The psalmist must realize that their *first function* is not to minister to the flesh, emotions and needs of the people; but firstly to minister to the spontaneous will of God. We need to hear what He wants, and even God's musical taste changes, isn't that something?

(from the book ,"The Ministry Anointing of the Prophet-Minstrels") David L. Brown

A true psalmist doesn't care whether the worship and praise of God happens corporately or not. What I mean by that is, they can discern what Gods heart is saying or wanting at any given time, and if it doesn't happen corporately in worship and praise for whatever reason, the psalmist will make sure that Gods heart is carried out whether they carry it out in a corporate setting, or in their own private time. They are trained to hear what God wants to hear, and their hearts beat as one. The song will be sung even if the psalmist has to sing it *mono-e-mono* with the Lord.

Singers.

All who are *anointed* to sing fall into this category. There were many in scripture that sang and played instruments. There were those who were singers in the temple choir, and those who sang professionally. So singing in and of itself was not the total gift. Do you follow me? Singers had their own place in ministry just like a prophet or a musician on a musical instrument. Heman, one of David's chief musicians, was a choir director, worship leader, a great singer and a prophet as well. Most of the singers in the Old Testament usually read music by way of hymnals or some type of musical notation book. Many of the musical notations that I mentioned earlier were found in hymnals or music books for the musicians and singers to read in the midst of their worship services.

Even if your ministry is more charismatic, don't look down your nose at those who read out of hymnals during the course of their worship services. And at the same time, you who do not operate in a charismatic fashion, don't turn yours up at their style of worship, as if to say they've lost their minds or seems like something barbaric. Actually both methods were used in the Old Testament and later on in the New Testament.

Singers were used in many functions from weddings to funerals and from parades to victory celebrations, from various annual feasts, and political gatherings to, even sporting events. Habakkuk 3:19b says; *to the chief singer on my stringed instruments*, or it would be seen in their hymnals or music charts (*if you will*), a Hebrew word, **Neginoth**, which meant to play upon a stringed instrument. But remember Habakkuk 3:19 also says; *to the chief singer,* which tells me that not only does the person in this verse, play a *stringed instrument,* but is a *singer* as well. So it's not very complex at all to understand that many of the musicians were singers and composers and there were those who were employed to only sing. When I say employed, I don't mean paid! They were simply bought in to sing the praises of God in the tabernacle during David's time and years later in the temple. There were also those who sang songs in the local assembly and those who sang professionally. Many of these men and women in scripture were trained singers and knew the *mechanics of singing*; not only that, but they were anointed to do it. The point I'm making is; they sang *skillfully*, with *understanding* and they were *anointed*. That's a powerful combination.

Now the word, *skillful* goes further than just how well their voices sounded. It also speaks to how skillful they were in *flowing* with the spirit of God as well.

They knew when to sing and when to **Selah.** *(pause or be silent)* They carried an anointing to deliver a song that would bless and uplift the people of God.

There's nothing like the anointing of God on a singer, especially one who knows and understands how to sing from the depths of their very soul. One who can sing about all the experiences they've had in life and how God has bought them out.

No matter how special the talent is, I can always tell someone who is just singing because they know how, and one who is singing from their *experiences* and walk with God. There's just a whole different level that you can actually hear. You can hear the pain, the struggle, the victories but most of all you can hear the anointing that all those experiences exhibit in their voice. You remember how I talked about the character anointing of the psalmist? Well all of you anointed singers should carry the characteristic that an anointed singer carries. They are anointed to hear from God as to what should be sung, and then their anointing is to bless and bring deliverance to the people who are hearing or listening to the song.

So therefore, one of the differences between a singer and a psalmist, is the fact that the characteristics of a <u>psalmist anointing</u> is firstly concerned with *ministering to God,* and then sharing God's heart and mind with the people. The <u>singers anointing</u> is to inquire of God, and to obtain what to *minister to the people*. Understanding this cuts out envy or jealousy because they both work together hand in hand for the purpose of God.

Worship Leaders.

When you say worship leaders that includes praise as well. These are they who lead the people of God into *praise* and *worship*. They should also be lead of the spirit of God by an inquiring sensitivity of His will, and then they move forward by directing the order of the praise and worship through singing or with music, instrumentation, congregation participation, declarations or any demonstration form of biblical or spiritual based expression that will lead us into the presence of God. The goal for a worship or praise leader should be; getting God Himself to come, manifest Himself and to *tabernacle* with us. We need praise and worship leaders who are **Holy Ghost filled** who can tap into the hearts of God's people and direct them to give God His due praise. If you are timid and fearful, you'll have a hard time properly doing what a true praise and worship leader is anointed to do.

Worship leaders have an ability to exhort the people in the spirit realm and get them to a point of *true praise* and *worship*, and then the minstrels do their part along with the singers and dancers. . . . .Oh my! A worship and praise leader must be one who like David, has the ability to bless the Lord at all times. Every time you see them, no matter what they're going through, you will always hear praise, not a complaint coming out of their mouth. They have the ability to pull that praise out of you even when you're experiencing your worst day, a worship leader will have you praising God at the end of the day. When this is accomplished by the leader, then we all can experience the presence of the Lord in the area of worship because now, the Lord has come down in the *Tehellah Praise*, the type of praise God *inhabits* or *sits upon*.

Now we're entering into sweet and true worship. When all of these anointed gifts are in operation, can you see how power packed our churches would be? It would make for a wonderful Sunday morning service don't you think?

A worship leader must be just that, a worshipper! As I said before, you can't lead anyone into true worship if you don't spend any time in worship yourself. You can't lead me into a room you've never visited. Worship takes you into a different room than praise. Anyone can show up and crash a praise party, but you must be invited to a worship party. You must intimately know the one who's throwing it, or you can't come in. *(RSVP!)* **R**eally **S**tarts w/ **V**ictorious **P**raise.

So I suppose worship doesn't start when you get behind a microphone. Worship starts with your life, *prostrated* before God in total surrender to him. It's your lifestyle everyday 24/7/365. I can hear some of you saying; *Well, I lead my church last week in worship service and the Lord just came right on in.* Yes, that might be true but believe me it wasn't because of you and your worshipless sacrifice. God who sees the needs of His people will come in and bless the people but many times it's a struggle in the spirit to arrive there, when in fact, if the worship and praise leaders lived a life of worship and praise to God, they could actually get the congregation there with ease because they operate as I said before, with **the spirit of inquiry.** What do I mean by inquiry? I mean they are in contact with God and are inquiring of Him as to what should be done or what direction He wants them to move in. They inquire and find what God wants to do at a particular congregational setting, and then begin to relay that information to the body, and then coupled with congregational participation; we can follow their leading and flow in the spirit with ease. There's just a certain sound you can hear in the spirit realm and you can hear when it's right on, and you can also hear when no sacrifices have been made to get into the presence of the Lord. It just sounds off! Does anyone know what I'm talking about?

I thank God for all of the gifts I see much of the times in my own church. I want them to understand that many of these gifts are already in operation there and if we understand how to flow in the gifts God gave each and every one and then we will see ourselves moving even higher into a whole new *dimension* of praise and worship. It starts with the **Musicians/Levites** and the **Priesthood.**

That's what this book is about; to shed some light on what God is requiring out of His people. We are striving for excellence in God and why shouldn't we? We serve an excellent God and God has given my church EXCELLENT leaders who allow us to exercise our gifts. Many churches don't allow their ministers to minister at all. So if you are in a ministry that doesn't allow you to exercise your gifts, you may want to seek God concerning His will for your life. Now I'm not telling you to leave your church because you don't get to minister enough; too many are doing that now. But when God has given you a gift as I've stated in this book, you should always submit your gift to the authority of that house first, and if he or she is spirit lead, they will know what God has placed inside of you concerning your gifts and anointing.

God is going to use us in a mighty way when we learn to use these giftings the way He intended. Let's step up to the plate and come out swinging. Not only that, but when you do get up to bat, HIT THE BALL!!

To the worship and praise leaders, to the singers and dancers, (see *Dancers in the Study Notes portion of the book)* minstrels, prophet and prophetic minstrels, to the psalmists and preachers, teachers, prophets and evangelists, let's do our part in the area that God has called us to, and we'll see the mighty works and manifestations of God's awesome power and deliverance that is so badly needed in our homes and churches and in our local communities. With all of this knowledge and understanding, we can be a powerful force in this world. Men and women everywhere are looking for something to turn to. We have the answer and God has given us a strategic part to play in the in gathering of the harvest. You see that's what all of this really boils down to. That's why all the gifts, that's why all of the talents and anointing, that's why we have the spiritual gifts, that's why He's calling Apostles and some, prophets, evangelists, some, pastors and teachers. He's calling us to a higher place of praise, a higher place of holy living. He's calling us to go into the highways and hedges and compel men/women to come and sup with Him. He's given us all the tools we need to get the job done, all of us can praise, all of us can worship, all of us can experience the presence of God when we are *directed properly* by those who are called and anointed to take us into the presence of the Lord.

Psalmist, Singers and Worship and Praise leaders; It's time to come forth with power!

Bling, Blings not a new thing.

This seems like a strange place in the book to put this title, but I just felt led to do it this way. Once I actually started researching this as the Lord gave it to me, it actually made a lot of sense to place it right in the midst of talking about the gifts we posses and how we are to use them along with the anointing. We are to always be mindful and careful how we carry the anointing of God and not get caught with the cares of this life and lust after the same things the world lusts after, which is fame and fortune. Everybody wants to be rich and famous. Everybody wants to be a star. Even Christians have found themselves caught up with the pomp and glitter that the lifestyle of fame *seems* to offer.

We as Christians are not to take on the same mindsets the world has when it comes to riches and fame. You may not agree with this, but riches, (*if not possessed soberly*) has a way of changing a person's spirit to where they feel they are above others. It can introduce a *lofty spirit* that you may not have otherwise had, if you didn't posses it. That's why the Word warns us not to *love* it or to set our *affections* on the things or riches of this world. We as ministers of Christ's, have to be particularly careful that greed or the pursuit of money doesn't consume us, especially when it comes to understanding its rightful place in our ministries. That, although it's needed to operate ministry, we don't make it the focal point of our ministry, thus falling into the snares the enemy has set up, through ancient old demonic spirits.

The Bible tells us that the **love of money** is the root of ALL EVIL that is in the world. Did you understand what I just said? The *LOVE* of it is the very root, of every evil that's in the world today!

I know you all want to know what this segment is all about! It is an interesting but very serious thing that's been going on for centuries. **Bling** or of course is a term or slang used now by many of our young people, and old ones too for that fact. It's really interesting how we come up with these *slang words* or *terminologies*, that are usually introduced to us by the media and musical artist, but really don't know where they came from or why they're actually being used. What I'm about to tell you comes from a combination of my years of observance and nuggets the Lord has shared with me in my personal time with Him. *(revelation!)* I know you've heard the term, *bling bling*. Well it's a new word being used, but not at all new in its context or background. Bling actually speaks to having or possessing *material things* if you really look at it. It's one of the main desires of the day; **money**, cars, **money**, silver and gold, **money,** and shiny things like *ice (diamonds)* that cost lots of **money** or have great dollar value. Today, *gold* is almost played out and may not be sufficient by itself. You now must progress to *platinum* and Lord knows what else. Did I mention *money, paper, chedda, bengies, stacks..etc?* Again, 1 Timothy 6:10 says the **love** of money, not money in and of itself, but the love of it is the **root** of ALL evil. It's the **spirit of the day** but it's not a new spirit at all. **You do realize it's a spirit right?** It's because of the love of money that every evil work has a foundation to build on. Take a look at the big corporate companies now in trouble because of shady dealings and downright breaking of the laws.

It's the cause of robberies and many murders, car jackings, games of chance, prostitution, drugs and gangs, should I go on? In almost all cases, the undercurrent cause for all of these evil works is; yes, money! I know the Bible says that money answers all things, but God didn't intend for us to use ungodly methods to acquire it either. I know you're asking yourself; where is he going with all of this? I'm going to tell you but first let's see what 1Timothy says through the rest of this passage for better understanding.

1 Timothy 6:3-14 says; 3 *If any man teach otherwise, and consent not to wholesome words, even the words of our Lord Jesus Christ, and to the doctrine which is according to godliness;* ⁴ **He is proud**, *knowing nothing, but doting about questions and strifes of words, whereof cometh envy, strife, railings,* **evil surmisings**, ⁵ *Perverse disputings of men of* **corrupt minds**, *and destitute of the truth,* **supposing that gain is godliness**: *from such* **withdraw thyself**. ⁶

But godliness with contentment is great gain. ⁷ For we brought nothing into this world and it is certain we can carry nothing out. ⁸ And having food and raiment let us be therewith content. ⁹ **But they that will be rich fall into temptation and a snare, and into many foolish and hurtful lusts, which drown men in destruction and perdition.** *¹⁰ For the* **love of money** *is the root of all evil: which while some coveted after, they have* **erred from the faith**, *and pierced themselves through with many sorrows. ¹¹ But thou, O man of God, flee these things; and follow after righteousness, godliness, faith, love, patience, meekness. ¹² Fight the good fight of faith, lay hold on eternal life, whereunto thou art also called, and hast professed a good profession before many witnesses. ¹³ I give thee charge in the sight of God, who quickeneth all things, and before Christ Jesus, who before Pontius Pilate witnessed a good confession; ¹⁴ That thou keep this commandment without spot, unrebukable, until the appearing of our Lord Jesus Christ.* KJV.

In a nutshell this passage is instructing us that because of the lust of the flesh and the pride of life, which are the main contributing factors to the reason why many are destroyed and many are constantly destroying themselves. Mankind wanting more and more never satisfied but striving for unattainable goals, always desiring more or better that they might possess it upon their own lusts. Having a strong pride about themselves, acting as if others don't measure up if they don't possess the material things they themselves do. There's something God hates so much, that He tells us not to even walk around with the look or appearance of it. It's pride!

1 John 2:14-16 says; *¹⁴ I have written unto you, fathers, because ye have known him that is from the beginning. I have written unto you, young men, because ye are strong, and the word of God abideth in you, and ye have overcome the wicked one. ¹⁵* **Love not the world**, *neither the things that are in the world.* **If any man love the world, the love of the Father is not in him**. *¹⁶ For all that is in the world, the* **lust of the flesh, and the lust of the eyes, and the pride of life, is not of the Father, but is of the world.** *¹⁷ And the world passeth away, and the lust thereof: but he that doeth the will of God abideth for ever. ¹⁸ Little children, it is the last time: and as ye have heard that antichrist shall come, even now are there many antichrists; whereby we know that it is the last time.* Now we're ready to get into it. This is probably going to bring controversy but that's ok, because the spirit of understanding is usually birthed out of conflict!

Earlier I said that the love of money <u>is a spirit right</u>? It's been around a long time, and just like the Word of God just told us in 1 John 2, that we are not to love the world and its lusts. Where am I headed with this? Well, there was one who carried this lustful spirit in the days of old, and is now re-introducing this same spirit in the world today, and sadly in the church as well. Many people believe, <u>ALL music came from God</u>. If you search the scriptures, you'll find that it's not so. Even though God is the creator of all things, there's another who has taken the original purpose of God's creation and has **perverted** it for the purpose of *greedy gain*, lust, *immorality,* and to make a **mockery** of the sacred sacraments in worship toward a Holy God. Music is no different! Some of you are going to get upset because we as humans are routinely programmed to fight against what we don't understand or haven't heard of. It is a fact that Lucifer was a worshipper of God, but now a worshipper of himself. He's just a mere **counterfeit** of the great God Jehovah. So the only thing he can do now is **mimic** the ways of God with things that seem good and real, but are false, phony and deceptively evil in nature. Everything the devil does is backed or supported by a lie. It has to be because that's all that comes out of him are lies because, HE IS A LIE! He's no longer a worshipper, but a liar, a deceiver and an accuser of the brethren, out to steal, kill and destroy. He's going to and fro, seeking whom he may devour. He's trying to bring his lies into the house of God, and the worse part about it is, we as Christians are *willingly* taking on the lies and supporting them as well. Don't forget what we read in 1Timothy and 1 John earlier! We **cannot** do everything like the world, whether it is it's fashions or styles its thoughts and ways and even it's **music. . . . .ouch!** Be careful saints of God, just because it sounds good, looks good and has a tight beat, doesn't mean it belongs in the house of God or in your own home for that matter. Now you'll hear many people say that their music isn't for the church walls. Well what does that mean exactly? Think about it, if your music came from God, how can it not be for the house? Even if it's style is different than what some people *think* should be in the house. . .if it's anointed, God will accept it! Let's dig deeper! Now it's a very sensitive situation, but I have three sons and my oldest son Anthony is a rapper, and a very good writer of *rhyme* and *poetry*, and can freestyle like crazy. Many times we have discussions on this very subject and probably some things he agrees on and some he doesn't, but he's starting to get an understanding of what *God expects* from his music. I began to tell my son that the bling, bling as we call it, is no new thing at all. Remember Lucifer had many precious stones embedded in his bodily vesture and garment. Only the finest was invested when God created him. He was beautiful, he was all that! The problem was, he knew it. Lets take a look at many of the Hip-Hop artist of today, the way they operate, the things they're saying and the message they're sending out to our communities. They all carry much of the same spirits or attitudes as Lucifer did. If you don't think so, maybe you should take a peek at MTV, BET, 106 n Park or some of the other popular hip hop videos. The gold, the money flying around, the phat whips *(cars)* and the fine women tryin' to *get upon it*. In other words you have to have it like them in order to roll with them. Gotta' have the dubs and rims and now bigger than that, tippin on 4-4's, the bling on the ring, treating women like objects and calling them hoes, riding them like ponies, and grindin' on them and other things I won't write down!

Smokin' drolls, burnin' trees and blunts and acting like or actually being a gangsta out here on the streets, layin' down with as many as you can peep. Pimpin' rides, pimpin hoes, cars and clothes, that's how all these pawtnas roll.

Yeah you know the stuff that your kids are listening to? And some parents to! It's all about gain, gain and more gain. Get what you can, while you can, as much as you can or die tryin! Everything that I just mentioned, God speaks to us all through the scriptures, telling us to stay away and not to love, or have fellowship or dealings with those who do such.

You better realize that Satan has a plan for the world and the church. There are different genres and styles of music that are being used in the church, and God has given many of us creative talents to reach people. But understand that when we in the church, try to **mimic** the way the world does things we are allowing Satan to take advantage of us and furthermore he's trying to make **no difference** between his perverted music and Gods Holy music in the minds of people. Now we are dressing and acting like the world in order to make our shows and gospel events go over successfully. We are now **entertaining** and ***not ministering***. I hear many Christian artists say that they mix secular and Christian music to get the young peoples attention. I used to go for that until the Lord rebuked me and taught me how He's actually NOT PLEASED WITH IT! After one of my Levite Symposiums, I was approached by a young teenager asking me why gospel and Christian artists think they have to use *gimmicks* and copy secular music to win the youth over. I was shocked! You would think he thought it was cool or ok! He went on to say, when artists do that, they lack understanding themselves. They're telling me that they're not concerned about the ministry of God's music at all. They're sending a message to the young people that there's no power in the Word of God within the songs or there's just not enough power in the Word at all. <u>The young man told me that he's talked to many of his friends who say they actually don't need the *secular similarities or samples*</u> in order to be won to Christ. He said; that's the reason I came *out of the world*, to find something **different** and **real**. He went on to say that he remembers the **demonic spirits** that would *oppress* and *taunt* him when he listened to those **same beats** and **samples**, some of our *so called* Christian/Gospel artists are using in their music today. It's going to get worse, but some artists have already let you know that in the intros of their songs and on their CDs! I don't actually want to mention any names because they might be some of your favorites! I wasn't *called* to name bash, I was called to *teach the truth!* Now days you don't even have to buy the secular artist anymore, just pick up some of our leading artists and musicians in the church world. You'll hear, Prince, "Ooo, hoo, hoo hoo!" You can hear Michael Jackson, Bar-Kays, Earth Wind & Fire, the list goes on. You nam'em we got'em in there! But we yet want to call it, and convince people that it's true worship?

I'm going to stop right here; the Lord just spoke this to me as I was writing this segment. I'm prophesying now, and it will come to pass during or before the release of this book! "*The devils plan is to make all of the music,* **one music!** *His plan is to take away the sacredness of holy music and make it* *like all the other music. Satan understands the power of anointed music. He used to do it. I know it's already started, but you watch in the next 3 years."*

*"It's going to be nothing to see Christian music in the secular clubs, **on a regular**, and secular music creeping more and more into the houses of God as a norm. God is not going to hold the artist and musicians responsible alone for bringing ungodly music into His house. God is going to visit the Leaders and Pastors who He called. He's going to hold you accountable for disregarding and polluting His House."*

You don't have to believe me, just watch God's Word come to pass, and you'll know this is God! *"You're also going to see our Christian or Gospel artists, promote **more and more** of the secular, giving alms and thanks to them for inspiring them as if God had nothing to do with it! What's happing is, Satan is introducing an ANYTHING GOES type of spirit throughout the land. This anything goes message will show up in the clubs, it will involve the **music, sex and drugs.** You're also going to see more secular artists give thanks to God for the sinful things they're currently doing, saying it's alright and already covered under his blood. IT'S A LIE!!!* The really sad part about this prophecy is the fact that the devil is not going to accomplish it through the power of the secular artist, but through the influence of the Christian Musicians and Artist who have sold out and compromised the pure message of Jesus Christ. The good thing about it is, God does see it and IS going to judge it!!! That may be a sad thing as well. . . . .

Ok, I stepped away but I had to say it while the spirit of the Lord was dealing with me. Let's go back now. Remember I said the young man told me that he left the worldly music to find something that was **different** and real? He wanted to know why some of the gospel artists mix their music with the secular stuff. Isn't that an oxymoron? He wanted to know what's up with that or what's the problem? The problem is that it's not **different** at all. I actually tried to cover some of our artists and make excuses for them, so that he and the other young people wouldn't be hurt or confused. I told him that when you are in the "business of music", sometimes you have to make decisions you don't want to make. Some have compromised, some have chosen to chase the all mighty dollar, and some don't know what they want. You can't stay in the music industry race if you don't sell units or records. Some have sold themselves out to fame; fortune and success in this life, but risk hearing God tell them; what did it profit you to gain the world, and now losing your soul? Some have become prideful, arrogant and unapproachable. It's **no new thing**; people have been selling themselves out to compromise and have actually weakened their ministry *without realizing it,* thinking they're still anointed, but they **stick out** like a **sore thumb!** Why do I say, without realizing it? Well, first of all, many have now taken on the same, *it's about me spirit* Lucifer had just before he was cast down. Second, don't you think God being *omni-present, (everywhere at the same time)* heard him when he began to parley about himself and how wonderful he was, and how he wanted to be like the Most High? The problem was that Ole Lou didn't *realize* he had already messed up while he was in the middle of speaking highly of himself. God was already making plans to kick him out of his spot. Don't let God kick you out of your place of ministering. Don't lose your spot in the Kingdom. We don't have to be like the world to get the message across. God doesn't need your help with His already powerful anointed message. But Satan's plan is to make all things common.

Besides. . .there shouldn't be any difference in the music right? It's all just music anyway, right? Hey, come on over and sing songs in our strange land. *Come and be on my program and let us be on yours, and let's just make it all one big ol' holy. . . . .well, one big party.* No matter what people are doing, God still has a people who will not bow to the images and gods of this world. Yes we are in the world but not of it. God is tired of the same old excuses as to why we do the things we do. *(we have to take the gospel to the world and show love)* Yes, take the gospel which is the good news of Jesus Christ to them, but that doesn't mean to mix and mingle it in a way where no one comes away asking for Jesus or what should they do to be saved. No, they go back doing what they always do because there was no real godly seed planted in them.

Common, common, make all things the same, that's what we've got to do, says Satan. *We gotta get'em looking like us, acting like us, singing like us, entertaining like us and after a while we'll be able to infiltrate their camp and take captive their entire ministries. There will be no <u>anointing, no deliverance and healing power in their</u> **music**. **It will be, just. . .like. . .ours!**

So understand it's no new thing to him. He's dressed for the part. The riches, power, pride, the stones which were his covering, every precious stone, the greed and evil surmisings, corrupting minds, but the error and fall from truth is his reward. Now he's trying to bring the same spirit into the Body of Christ. Be watchful; be wise, for God has not called us to be like the world but that we should be living examples to the world. James 4:4 explains that; *friendship with the world is (enmity) enemy with God!* God so loved the world, yes, but He sent His Son to die for the world, and to separate the world from its sins, which He hates. That should be your message to the world.

An age-old trick of the devil is to make people think that they have to compromise in some way in order to obtain wealth and riches in this life. How Absurd! Psalms 24:1 says; *the earth is the LORD'S, and the fulness thereof; the world, and they that dwell therein.* KJV.

We as Christians can not be ignorant concerning the devils devices. His tricks are old, his lies are to. All of his bling, bling is no new thing!

Hip Hop or Stop?

Here's a special note I wanted to insert before moving on. I want you to totally understand about the music and the culture we call hip-hop. You must understand how they think and the message they're pushing into the minds and hearts of our youth and adults as well. Pay attention people, they are operating in a spirit that originates from *pride, lust* and *greed*. Lucifer carried the same damnable spirit. This is the message of their religion. Oh yea! Hip-Hop is not about the music, it's a legal religion that's on the rise! They have their own *Apostles, Prophets, Evangelists, Pastors, Teachers, Bishops* and *Disciples* and they're **not** teaching you about Christ. You don't believe me? Just talk to most of the youth in America today. They know more about Hip-Hop than Jesus Christ? Over 48% of the youth in America know of Jay Z more than Christ.

Some of the Hip-Hop artists are now telling the kids that the Illuminati is good, and Jesus Christ is actually the devil. Your 6 year old can tell you that they've already heard about the anti-christ in the songs they listen to. Should I go on? Ok I will. You can see it in the eyes of your children. You can see young people walking around like zombies memorized by what the music and the artists are feeding them. You know it has to be demonic, because many Hip Hop rappers are now defaming the name of Jesus in their songs. If it's only about the music, why blaspheme His name? They're feeding your kids the same spirit of Lucifer, of pride and arrogance. They make you feel like you don't have a good life if you don't have stuff! You have to have all the bling and things that go along with it. They pray to their gods, they fast, many of them say that they'd rather serve this lifestyle than serve Christ!!!!!

So you still think hip-hop is about the music?

Because of its origin and what Hip Hop originally represented in its earlier stages, we cannot embrace it as Christians. There can be no Holy Hip Hoppers or any Christian Hip Hop because the culture cannot lend itself to the direction of the Holy Spirit. Yes, we do have very powerful Christian rap groups that preach the Word of God through rap, but we must not get confused and call what they are doing Hip Hop. You have to understand that God does not embrace anything that has a *corrupt origin*. The very word "Hip Hop" was created by **Afrikka Bambatta**, the pioneer of the culture and professed Zulu Nation god. He created the term to describe the parties that he was hosting in clubs across New York in the early 70's. Since then, he has developed a religion that rested upon the Hip Hop culture. The term is not from God; therefore, it should not be used to describe anything from God!

People, please understand that Hip Hop is a way of governing your life. Therefore, it cannot be exploited as a Christian way of living.

KRS-ONE and **Afrika Bambaata** have used the term Hip Hop to describe emceeing, deejaying, break dancing, and other forms of entertainment, but Hip Hop is also, to them, **a religion** and a way of *worshipping themselves* instead of the Lord Jesus Christ. How can we as believers hold on to this culture when its origin is *rooted* in witchcraft and voodoo?

"How can we call ourselves Holy Hip Hoppers when this move of the enemy is influential enough to persuade Christians to protect it and defend it as a culture that should be embraced by the church even though its founders don't embrace Jesus Christ? God forbid! My people search the Word of God for yourself."

Insert from: Elder G. Craige Lewis and EX Ministries.

I understand that many of you have formed your own opinions bout this, but all I can do is tell you what is actually going on in our world today. God is soon to come, and Satan understands that he only has a short time left, so he's using the *main weapon* he has, which is his music.

He's a deceiver and has been doing so for centuries. He has the ability to introduce to a nation his way of thinking and is now sending out HIS disciples into the world to convince you that all music is ok, and that it's actually the church that is in rebellion and doesn't understand. He's an ancient liar, and nothing he does is new, it's the same old bag of tricks he tried to use in heaven.

Let's keep moving on. I have much more I want to tell and show you. Let's start with the Word of God in Corinthians that tells us that we can have a new life in Christ, and don't have to settle for the ways of this corrupt world. . . . . . .

(2 Co 5:17) *Therefore if any man be in Christ, he is a* **new creature**: *old things are passed away; behold, all things are become new*. KJV.

There's no way for the church to move on into the land of promises, when we're always looking back into Egypt. We have to press toward the mark for the prize of the high calling, which is in Christ Jesus and Him alone. Let's take what God has given us and change the world. God NEVER needed any help from Satan, to redeem the world. He's God all by Himself and there **IS NO OTHER BESIDE HIM!**

I hope and pray you see the urgency of this. It's the last day and the devils pulling out all the stops and he's not going to quit just because we expose him. But know that when we sound the alarm, many people will hear it and begin to pay more attention to what he's trying to do. If we choose to ignore him, we are condoning it and are therefore guilty, having a hand in the destruction of millions.

Goddess Kali, The Thug, Siva & My lord of Cars.

In this section of the chapter, and in the entire book, God is trying to get you to understand that everything we offer up to Him **must** be **holy**, or He will not accept it! It may be accepted in the eyesight of men, but not with God Himself. He's trying to get us to see that Satan is not concerned about his place in the world. He wants his place back with God, through the church. Satan is using any means necessary to get his agenda in the house of God.

When we as saints of God finally realize that the devil is not playing with us, maybe we'll take it more serious about what he's trying to accomplish in the body of Christ today.

We're dealing with issues we've never dealt with before; pressures, satanic oppression and attacks that have not been seen or understood. There are **ancient old spirits** and **demons** that have been re-assigned to infiltrate the house of God. And we as Christians are standing by idle watching and making excuses for the ungodly things *we see* and *allow* to go on in God's house. You better believe that there is a worldwide attack on our young people and our children, and it's being done **through the music**. There are old spirits that have been on this earth for centuries, who are now assigned to get into the hearts and minds of all men, women, boys and girls through the media.

Not only do you see young men all thugged out, you see the older one's also, trying to do their thing. The older widow mothers of Zion are not praying and guiding the young women much anymore because they still want a man themselves. There is a sneaky attack whether you know it or not against Christians, and it's having a negative effect on the church today. Demons have been assigned to specific regions of the world to wreak havoc on the Churches of the living God.

I'm going to show you a *stunning comparison* in the Hip Hop culture today, that *strangely* compares to old idol worship back in the 19<u>th</u> century and *earlier*.

What we don't seem understand is that we're dealing with ancients spirits that have been around for thousands of years. They destroyed and deceived people back then, and their doing the same today. Let's see how your spiritual discernment is working these days. Or has the compromising ways of this world erased the spiritual sensitivity you once had?

Take note of the *heading* in this segment. **Goddess Kali, The Thug, Siva and My lord of Cars.** In my study of the music in its diver's cultures; I saw something very interesting and applicable to what I've been talking about. In the segment, <u>Bling is not a New Thing</u>; I found out how true that statement actually was when the Lord directed me to **this** segment. In the Hip Hop culture, we can see it all in today's society how the respect for one another has fallen. We see the mind set of our youth, is to get what you can, as much as you can, and as quick as you can get it. Start from the top and go higher! No one wants to start from the bottom and work their way up anymore. The mindset is, I want what I want, how I want it, when I want it, as often as I want it, and I don't want to work too hard to get, and I want it right now! Movies are telling people, to get rich or die trying, and that's just what they're doing. Murders, robbery and the disrespect for others are the norm in the Hip Hop culture. Get all you can get is what they'll tell you. Get the gold and diamonds, make **idols** out of **rap stars,** and sport only the finest cars. But again, all that *bling* is not a new thing. Back in the early 19th century in the Hindu culture, there was a Hindu goddess by the name of **Kali.** She was considered to be the *goddess of death and destruction?* You may ask why anyone would worship a god that is known to be a goddess of death and destruction. Well first you must understand the faiths and beliefs of Hinduism. Allow me to set this all up for you. You'll find this information very interesting. There are several *branches* that stem from the Hindu religion that I will not cover at this time. But Hinduism came into importance around 2000 B.C. when the *Aryans* brought their religion with them. It was a religion of *hymns, prayers* and *chants* which in time, were written down in what is called; *Vedic Literature.* Some say the origin of Hinduism can be traced back to around 1500 B.C in what is now India.

It began as a *polytheistic* and *ritualistic* religion. At first, the rituals were easy enough to be performed by all the heads of households. But as hundreds of years passed, the rituals became increasingly complex.

As a result of this; priests were appointed to train other priests how to perform the new rituals correctly.

This is when the **Vedas** were written to give the priest instructions on how to perform the Hindu rituals. The *Hindu Priests* became increasingly more and more powerful and became as lords and mediators between the people, and the Hindu gods. Stay with me, this is going to get good!

As hundreds of years passed, many inserts into the *Vedas* were written. The Vedas are thought to be *revealed wisdom* and are sacred laws and rituals that are as sacred to the Hindu, as the Bible is to the Christian. It is their equivalent to the New Testament Bible. Many gods populate out of the pages of the Vedas. They are similar to the gods and goddesses of Greek, and Roman mythology. Like many other ancient history religions, the Hindu people believed that the gods could cause *death and destruction,* so much of the object of their religion involved, **keeping the gods happy**, which is bringing me closer to the point I want to make. There arose a group in the Hindu religion called the **Brahmans,** who performed much of the priestly duties. They added more and more entries into the *Vedas* and called it the **Brahmanas.** This *new entry* into the Vedas installed **sacrificial rituals**. Hindus now see ultimate Reality, or Brahman, as being an *impersonal oneness,* that is beyond all distinctions, including *personal* and *moral distinctions*. **Brahman** has developed as a type of *god* or *force* and *existence.* The universe is seen by most Hindus as being continuous with and extended from the **Being of Brahman**. Most people in the Hindu faith believe that they are in their true selves, extended from and *one* with *Brahman.* They are taught that this *earthly body* is nothing and that <u>gold, diamonds and riches</u> are of <u>little value</u>. They are told to detach their inner self from their outer self which is full of pride and ego.

They believe in the law of **Karma,** which teaches them that they reap what they sow. They feel that what you do in this present life follows you from lifetime to lifetime, which is why they teach *reincarnation.* Brahman is now considered as the (Creator god) of the universe. With Brahman, unlike our God Jehovah,

Karma with them can not affect your relationship with Brahman as long as you stay in oneness with your *inner self* which is an *extension of Brahman god*. In short, you pray to your inner self because you within yourselves are god.

Sidebar: There are now **New Age** movements increasing in these last days, that take on this same, **self god** doctrine. But again it's nothing more than the same ancient spirits that are working in them as well.

It is important that I lay the Hindu foundation, because as I started digging into the history of the Hindu goddess Kali, I began to ask myself why people would worship someone or something that represented death and destruction. One reason was they did it out of fear for the gods. They felt like they had to keep the gods happy, therefore they did things they felt would make the gods satisfied and approachable, like bringing them **gold** or *fine jewelry* as one of their sacrifices.

Now here's where the comparison came in between the hip hop culture and this Hindu goddess. The goddess Kali had followers that worshipped her statue. This statue is shown in different forms, but one of the forms I've seen of the statue was a *pale woman* with two legs and four arms with a necklace of *skull & crossbones* around her neck. A *pitchfork* in one hand, a *axe* in another, one hand holding a mans *chopped off head* with the *blood running* out of the bottom of his neck and with the other hand holding a *bowl* that's catching the blood coming from the man's head.

When followers would come into the temple to worship the statue of Kali, there were men disguised as temple officials in those days that would hide out and lye in wait inside the temple, and when the worshipers would come in to make sacrifices, these men would jump out from hiding and would rob, and even kill the followers for their money and jewelry. Hears where it got creepy for me! These men who robbed and murdered the worshippers were called. . . . . .**THUGS.** That's right these men back in the 10th century were called Thugs!

Webster's Dictionary; Thug; *one of a former group of professional robbers and murderers in* **India** *who strangled their victims; > a professional band of assassins from northern India/; to cover or hide.* . . . .

Not only that, but I found out that when they would rob the people, they would hide the money on their person, and they were known to hide the gold and jewelry **in their mouths.** I'll say it again; these **Thugs** would hide the **gold** and **diamonds** in their mouth!

Does that sound like some of the thug mentality of today? These young men and women don't have a clue in the world that when they subject themselves to this music, they are actually channeling in these ancient old spirits! The artists **have to** show you their bling and sport the gold and diamonds in their mouths, it's a spirit their portraying. The comparison of these **ancient spirits** goes a little further. When I studied and did much reading on the Hindu history and the goddess Kali; I also found there's another god they worship presently.

They honor this god by *restoring* guess what? **CARS!** There is a ritual now that honors one of the Hindu gods through *material sacrifice* and worship. They honor the god **Siva**, aka **Shiva**, by *fixing up* and **restoring old automobiles** to **mint condition,** as if to say that this god is responsible for their own soul's restoration. Shiva [shee-vuh], *"the destroyer" third member of the Trimurti, along with Brahma "the Creator" and Vishnu "the Perserver."*

So let's sum this up. There were people who would come to the Temple Kalighat, to worship this Hindu goddess, and there were men who would hide in the temple where people worshipped? They would rise up to kill the worshippers and these brute robbers were called thugs, who would hide the gold and diamonds in their mouths? And now there's a sacrificial ritual called, **"my lord of cars"**, where they worship and give honor to a Hindu god by **restoring "old cars"** back to mint condition? Humm. . .sounds like the rollin' 60's to me. And you think that when you see people out here on the streets with their nice rides, bumping their music, worshipping whatever artist they're listening to, and rockin' a mouth full of gold and diamonds, that it just started with the hip hop movement? No baby, what they've done is taken on the same *characteristics* as those thugs back in that day. The bible calls it ***familiar spirits***.

I wasn't amazed at all to also find out that the Hindus used the word **"Vehicles"** to describe the beasts their gods supposedly road upon. Many of the statues show their gods riding on animals, which they called, vehicles. They believed that since their gods were deity, they should not be **low to the ground,** so they placed them **high** upon the, **vehicles.** Humm!

Sooooo. . . . .they placed their gods on **vehicles that rode up high?** The *riding high* speaks to a form of *pride* and *invincibility*. Does all this seem familiar to you?

During the 10th-12th century in India a movement arose called *Virasaivism*, which means; *heroic worship, (kinda like what we do with our artist today)* but in this case it is the worship of *Siva*. The Virasaivites were wandering ascetics who adored the god **Siva**. They would perform all manner of strange feats and would typically act a little crazy. They wrote poetry, actually considered to have written the first *blank verse* in history. (*look up blank verse*)

The reason for writing in blank verse style was that Siva, as the god of chaos and destruction, would not like tightly rhymed verse. These Virasivite poems were called, *vacanas,* a word which comes from the same root as the English word; *vacant,* as in "blank" verse.

I thought it was interesting that they actually wrote in a manner where the words did not rhyme, much like many of the songs of today.

The beauty of poetry in the lyrics is diminishing, and is being replaced with shout outs or beefs with someone. The so called rap isn't hardly rhyming either because they're too busy feeding us their own garbage about sex, drugs and money. So maybe the music is going to pot, because like the Virasaivites, they're also serving a god of chaos. So in this blank verse style of poetry and music, I also found out that not only did they write in a manner where their words didn't rhyme. I also learned that the beat or the tempo of their music had a *sluggish* or a *delayed effect* to it. If you actually pay attention to the some of the secular music, the *off tempo* or *delayed beat* is very popular in some of today's music. Wow! Another strange but similar comparison was the fact that each of the Virasaivite poets had *signature names* for Siva. That is, each of them addressed their entire output of poetry to him in a name that only he or she used. To one he was, "*my lord of meeting rivers,*" to another he was, "*my lord of caves.*" So some of the poets are only known by the signature name they gave themselves for god, Siva.

So to make this clearer, each writer who wrote poetry to this god, gave up their own names and took on signature names as a way of worshiping their god by not using their birth, or God given name.

So in their *heroic worship*, they didn't use their own names as a way of honoring their god.

In other words, they actually had stage or performance names they used. So then, by the poets changing their names, to **names that gave worship to their god**, the people who listened to, and loved their music, would not actually be giving honor to **them**; but by approving of their music, would be giving honor to the **g**od they served! Ask your self, which superstar hero are you giving honor to?

We keep telling ourselves its ok to allow the hip hop movement and culture in the churches for the sake of our youth, not understanding that we're giving the enemy a license to attack the minds and hearts of our youth. We are fighting a spiritual warfare against principalities and powers, demonic forces that have been introduced to us through these ancient rituals, and pagan worship. Ancient but demonically infested worship from hundreds of years ago have now resurfaced with striking resemblances to the culture we call hip hop today.

But why? Why the gold? Why the diamonds and ice? Why the cars in the air that seems to breed a sense of arrogance and pride? Why is the cultures music filled with verses of murder, hatred and disrespect?

Go ahead, keep opening the door to allow the *ancient demons* to come in, and wonder why you can hardly control your children. You can hardly speak to them because they've got the devil in them, literally!

Many youth are no longer talking to us or singing sweet songs of Godly poetry and worship. They're now listening to music that is *chaotic* from a *false god* who causes nothing but confusion, and has now caused the speech and reasoning of many to be off beat, delayed and blank!

I wanted to add a little dialog to the previous segment on, bling, bling. When I mentioned about the dress of those performing Hip-Hop or Rock n Roll, etc, it was not a slam on any particular race or background by any means. The point being made here is the fact that Satan has an overall plan to destroy the very fabric of Holy living and make mockery of a sanctified lifestyle. The fact is that people have various reasons for the way they dress. Some are trying to make a particular statement, some dress provocative and seductive, their trying to make a statement as well. What I'm talking about is the spirit behind it all, that we may not recognize. What is the motive behind what we're doing? Have you asked some questions? Why the gold, platinum and diamonds and why is such emphasis put on it in the videos our children watch? Most young people don't have a sense of setting realistic goals anymore. They want everything yesterday without much sweat, tears or effort. The television tells them to get what you can get, as much as you can get and as fast as you can get it. There are rappers with movies out telling you to *get rich or die tryin.'* And since real life doesn't always allow such fortunes; they do what they feel they must do in order to attain these unrealistic goals.

There were shows on television like, "Cribs" and other rising programs that show what most entertainers possess, namely hip hop and movie stars. But what they don't tell you is at what price? What's being done undercover or out of the sight of the public? What *sacrifices* or *compromises* are being made? Understand that it's a form of worship, so some type of sacrifices are being made! Believe that!!

It's all about the lust of the flesh, the lust of the eye and the pride of life. When you see these videos the kids watch today, they are being enticed whether they know it or not, to attain riches in this life by any means necessary. They're telling your youth that material possessions mean success.

Now we have some young rappers in our ministries that don't fully understand what it truly means to rap for the Lord. But they see all of the bling, bling and the money being made by the secular artists, not realizing that they may never reach these material goals in Christian oriented music. So what do they do? They leave out of our Churches not understanding that they are a fresh new creative blessing to the Body of Christ, but they go out into the world to chase that *golden dream*. Oh excuse me, *platinum!* Imagine how many musicians and singers out there singing secular music, used to sing or minister in the church?

Then they come back and try and sing songs to us telling, us that God will make a way for you just wait on Him. But yet they couldn't wait on the Lord to bless their own ministries. This may sound a little harsh but, how can someone living a ungodly life, tell me they know what I'm going through when they don't serve the God I serve? How can they tell me spiritual things when they don't have a spiritual walk with God? You can't know what I'm going through and you aren't able to *minister* the things of God to me, because you MUST have a true walk with God to hear the words ONLY an anointed Levite can hear. If you do sing or play to me at all, it'll sound good, but wouldn't have that delivering power to refresh me like an anointed song from a minstrel would.

I refuse to take away from the God given, anointed power that comes from a musician who sets themselves apart from the attractions and temptations of the world. We need minstrels and singers who are not afraid to sing a true **love**

song. The Lord is saying, don't leave Him out of your song; don't deprive the world of a true love song. If you need help writing one, want to hear it, hear it go.. . . . (John 3:16) **Now that's a true love song!**

I tell young people all the time as I've always told my three sons, there's nothing wrong with being cool and saved at the same time. What you should understand is; the way you dress becomes a matter of the heart. If you're striving to be saved, I feel the Holy Spirit will begin to speak to a person concerning the way they dress. The Bible gives instruction on it but we must be obedient to what we hear the Word telling us, without concerning ourselves with how the world will look at us. Fashions and styles will always be, and I'm not saying that we should go around dressed like monks or something out of the dark ages, but by now I think you get the picture. People of God, there must be a difference somewhere, both outwardly and inwardly. I encourage you *Ministers of Music* to allow God to do a new and wonderful thing in your lives concerning your music. God is going to use us in a new and unusual way, and we won't have to mimic the world to accomplish it. God has already given us the ability to be creative innovators with the gifts He's placed in us. I believe the world will begin to look over at us for a change.

The world is supposed to be able to look to us and see Christ, but too many times all they see is Christians looking back into Egypt themselves for their inspirations. God can bless you with the things you need for your ministry without compromising your gift. The Lord wants me to stress that, and I feel this so strongly how much He wants to bless you with success in your ministry, but understand that success in ministry **isn't** *fame* and *fortune*. Is that enough for you?

There are people leaving this life everyday that will never truly be ministered to, because we as Levites have so many worldly hang-ups and selfish desires. I believe God is going to hold us responsible if we don't do what we were called to do, and not just what we wanted to do.

Step out on God in your ministry. See what He'll do if you live right and trust him wholly! Many times in my ministry, I've had to step out of faith and just trust what God said He would do. Even the writing of this book was a long hard journey, but God has promised me that this would be a blessing to me as well as others. I'm not worried about the material gain, because the Word of God lets me know in, Psalms 84:11, F*or the LORD God is a sun and shield: the LORD will give grace and glory:* **no good thing** *will he withhold from them that walk uprightly.* KJV.

God wants to know that you can be good stewards over what He gives you. Because He desires to present His ministers to the world, He needs to be able to bless you materially. But you must learn and strive to be faithful stewards in every area of your life. That in itself is a full time job! Understand that whether you have much or little, it ALL belongs to God.

He that is faithful in that which is least is faithful also in much: and he that is unjust in the least is unjust also in much. If therefore ye have not been faithful in the unrighteous mammon, who will commit to your trust the true riches? Luke 16:10-11. KJV.

What this is telling us is? Whether you have more or less, see that you are faithful as well as wise stewards. He that is faithful in what is least of all, *worldly substance*, is also faithful in things of a higher nature; and he that uses these lowest gifts unfaithfully, is likewise unfaithful in spiritual things.

John Wesley's Explanatory notes

If you are not faithful in the small matters pertaining to this world, if you do not use aright your property and influence, you cannot expect that God will commit to you the true riches of his grace.

Albert Barnes' Notes of the Bible

So when we don't treat the small things of God as precious, and can only see or look to the greater, you will miss all the special nuggets along the way that will help your ministry down the road.

And though thy beginning was small, Yet thy latter end would greatly increase. Job 8:7 KJV.

No, bling is not a new thing, but understand that all good riches belong to the Lord!

Additional information by the Author

Rap is not Hip-Hop.

As I began to dig deeper into this subject and began to understand more about the music and the culture of hip hop. I have to admit that I had to repent and change some of my own philosophies towards this music.

Don't get the different *styles* of music confused with hip hop. Hip-hop isn't a style of music at all; it's a culture or a way of life. Its mind controlling, and a smooth manipulative way for Satan to introduce a CULTIC LIFESTYLE!! Don't even let anyone tell you anything otherwise.

Anything that can control the way you think, dress and act, and has the ability to adjust your very lifestyle, has the aurora of witchcraft written all over it. We have to call it just like it is!

We've become so *accustomed* to its ways that we find it hard to see the harm in it.

We allow it and treat it as if it's just another fad, but baby it's far from any fad or fashion!

After I began to reveal this information in one of my Levite Symposiums, some of the young rappers I knew began asking me what they should do about their music and rhymes. I told them, for those of you who are writing Gospel or

Christian oriented rap, it's ok! **Rap isn't hip hop!** Rap speaks to a *style* or the *art* of, setting poetry to music. You can write your lyrics the way God gave it to you in the form of a rap or rhyme. If you study the book of Psalms, you'll find that David's musicians and writers had already mastered this style.

Hip hop speaks to a way of life or a self-worship customs or culture. So like me, if you've used the word hip-hop to describe your music, you're belittling yourself and buying into their way of life which is ungodly and has *idol worship beginnings and origins.*

I had to get a clearer understanding of all this myself. On my former website there used to be a write-up where I said I was developing a sound called, *JAZZOP*. The style would be a mixture of *jazz and hip hop*, or what I thought was hip hop. Therefore coming up with the word jazzop! While developing this sound, the Lord started rebuking me for using this term and I wondered why? My intention was not to glorify the hip hop way of life at all, but before I studied this culture, I thought the way so many people still think, that hip-hop was a sound or a style of music, when in fact it is a cultic way of life, promoted by Satan himself. So needless to say, there will be a retraction of that statement even if I didn't intend any harm, I don't want anything I do or say to be a stumbling block to anyone.

When we come into the knowledge that something is wrong or ungodly, the Holy Spirit should rise up on the inside of us and give us a mind to change and turn away from any ungodliness. That's an issue in the church world, we're trying to mix and mingle, and instead of the **church affecting the world, the world is infecting the church!**

When the young rappers at our church got an understanding of what God was saying to them, they told me something very profound. My eldest son who raps, told me that now he can see how important it is for the church to have **ITS OWN** music, which is a point I'm trying to hammer into the minds of our church musicians and singers. Just like the musicians did in the bible, that's the same spirit our musicians should operate in today. God inspired the men and women of the bible to write *spontaneous songs* of praise and worship to Him. That IS what we're doing all of this for isn't it? For Him?

On Christmas morning, 2004, I was listening to the radio with my family, enjoying the Lord, and all that was going on around the house, when I heard something come on the radio that absolutely disturbed my spirit. Now you have to understand that I'm a musician also, and I absolutely love music, and it took God to tear me away from a lot of different ungodly styles and genres of music.

But when this particular song came on, it made my spirit jump up, and rise in righteous indignation. As the song began to play, there was a narration at the beginning of this song, and you could hear someone say; *what's up? check it out; we have here, the best of both worlds.*

So I began to listen closer and I said to myself, ok cool the best of both worlds but what is he talking about? At that point, the narrator begins to name the name of two musical artists now starting to sing on the song. The issue was that one was *secular* and the other a *gospel* artist. Yea, yea, I know many of you don't have an issue with it. But you're missing the point here of what God wants out of us as Levites! You may already be *desensitized* to what Gods *holy music* is actually all about. Did I say holy?

Okay then here's the problem. In the song they were singing that, they have some *angels following them*. Now on the surface that sounds ok right? Thank God for the angels watching over us, right? *(keep reading!)* The secular artist began to say that these *invisible beings* are his friends, and that there are angels following and watching over him.

The gospel artist who was singing as well begins to say to the other artist saying; *go ahead and do your thing*. Right at that point the Holy Spirit spoke to me and said; *Elmus, he's right!* I said, to the Lord; what do you mean, *how can he be right?* The Lord said; *he does have angels following and watching him*. But then the Lord said; **but they are not my angels.**

Oh Lord, somebody please let these artists know that God isn't pleased with them mixing and mingling His music! Who's the song for, or who's getting the glory out of this, God or Satan?

I know the enemy has come up with a good excuse for you to give us, by telling us that you have to go to where they are in order to reach them. *(you know. . . the highways and hedges scripture?)* **Yes, the scripture does say to go out, but in the second half of that same verse it also says; (and compel them to come in) not, (and stay out there with'em!)**

God is going to allow you to be heard across this nation and world, but He's going to do it without you having to put your music on secular projects and vice versa. **God forbad it in the scriptures and He hasn't changed today!** Actually, Luke 14:23 says to; *go out into the highways and hedges and compel them to come in*, so **His House could be filled.**

Many are going out there, but because of there lack of commitment to God and holiness, there's no consistency in their Godly witness, therefore many aren't *coming in* are they? Some come near for a while and then have to go back out to their way of life to serve the god they *must serve,* because it is impossible to serve two masters at the same time. The sad part about this is many of our musicians, singers and yes even preachers are going out there with them with no condemnation at all. It's now become hard to witness to a dying world and tell them truth, because we've now become best friends with the world and it's sometimes hard to tell a friend the absolute truth as you should, depriving them of a new life that would ultimately lead them to eternal life with Christ.

Therefore, true worship of God isn't taking place many times in the Christian and Gospel music arenas because you cannot mix evil, and good, sinfulness and holiness, sweet and bitter, then offer it up to God, and expect God to lower His holy standards to receive a tainted sacrifice. We're offering God *our own versions* of worship, and calling it true worship. Check the scriptures people of

God; it's not true worship at all! At least not the worship of the true and living God of heaven. I'll go further than that! Just because someone calls themselves a Gospel or Christian artist, doesn't mean that God is accepting their sacrifice.

You must produce a holy life along with your song and message. It doesn't matter if it's rap or traditional music. God is longsuffering but He's going to judge us for everything we do and the motives for which we do them. Then we have the nerve to call ourselves doing it all in the name of Jesus. Really?

I heard a preacher ask; what's a gospel music award, and who's the judge; God? Then to top it all off, we get someone who doesn't even have a relationship with God, who's music totally points to and glorifies the devil, and we ask them to present *us* with an award for singing songs that are supposed to glorify God. How is the sinner supposed to be won by that? He or she thinks they're ok! Hey, it must be alright, because I'm presenting their awards and I even have some of my music and lyrics in their worship songs. Tell me again, how we're winning the world for Christ but we're just like them? Again, the Levite priests, musicians and singers tried this already in Hezekiah's day and it didn't work, and God was not well please with it at all!!!

Can you just imagine David getting up to get an award for one of his psalms? *"And now the winner is; King David for, I Will Bless The Lord at all Times."* Then David gets up to receive his award saying; **thanks ye to all whom thoust didst vote for me to win the Israelian Jamfest Philistinian Award!** How confusing would that be? About as confusing as it is now to get an award for a song God gave you. Now I'll be honest with you and run to the defense of those who are in the Gospel or Christian Music Industry. If you are *honestly* recognized by your peers with <u>NO POLITICS</u> involved, and you receive an award for your work, then **God bless you and congratulations!** Even I would like to receive an award from my everyday job for doing good work. What I am saying to you is, keep your integrity in all you do. What I've found is that even in the workplace, when there's an award to be obtained, many will stoop or lower their standards, and even cheat to receive the awards and accolades from peers and constituents.

Keep your name as precious as gold for the bible says a good name is priceless and nothing is more important than your Christian witness when God has allowed you such a large platform.

In the Bible, the music that God *accepted* and *was moved by*; were the times when the *psalmists* of King David **ministered it to Him**. It was not tainted by that of pagan musicians and singers or their traditions. <u>The highly trained musicians of Egypt and the skillful singers of Babylon were not invited to this party man</u>! **GOD IS HOLY**, and He wants **holiness** and **holy music** coming from **holy musicians**, and He's not going to settle for anything less!! Holy, Holy, Holy!!!

Darkness and Light never mix well. That's what is happening in the music industry today. When you mix the blackness of sin, with the brightness of His glory, you get *gray.*

This is what's happening to the sacred music; It's operating in gray areas, and the message isn't very clear.

The message I'm talking about now has nothing to do with the words you're singing. I'm talking about the message that's speaking of your lifestyle.

You remember. . .it's being that living sacrifice holy and *acceptable* unto God? Some of the things we're doing is acceptable to us, but not to God. It is with Him we all have to do. It is with Him that you will give an account for every deed done in your body.

But for those of you who understand what God is calling you to do in your ministry. Go ahead and be obedient as long as it's done according to His Word.

Go ahead young men and young women, write your rap songs and give God the glory. Use His Word and His Name to the tightest beats GOD gives you. USE YOUR TRACKS! Don't sample them from worldly and ungodly mixes that have ABSOLUTELY NOTHING to do with praise and worshipping God. Please don't confuse the people or the kids any longer by giving all the excuses that are now being given for doing so. It's a lame excuse, and not only that, it's a lie! Don't let anyone tell you that David got half of his music and beats from the Philistines. Just let them know they need to go back and study the bible again to see what David actually got from the Philistines.

Take your matchless and anointed gifts, and blow the power of *hip hop's weak message* of *compromise* and *self gratification* right out of the water. God is with you all young ministers, and we support you. Just know that you must have a *true relationship* with the Savior and don't depend solely on a *beat* to keep you saved and walking up right. God just wants you to have a clear understanding of what you're **not to do as musicians and ministers of Christ!**

He's going to cause you all to take your rightful places in this world and you are going to make an *impact.* It's going to be a quick work!

Many of the artists who will not listen and obey the voice of God, will begin to take a back seat and God is going to bring YOU, the *obedient ones* to the forefront so you can shout out the name of the Lord in the world, and declare His name among the nations, letting them know that they **must stop,** and turn to **truth**!

Please let them know that it's Jesus Christ and that He is the only way and truth. Let them know that they can't ride both sides of the fence and make it into the pearly gates.

Many of you are going to be *street preachers*, but you must first know God and *rightly divide* His Word. Don't divide it according to the way you want to live; don't even divide it according to what you think the Word of God is saying. Pray and ask God, and He will give you wisdom. Even King David inquired of the Lord before going into battle. Pray earnestly, and if the answer you get back in return has anything to do with you sending out *mixed messages* or ministry that doesn't glorify God, and God alone; then get back down on your knees and pray again until you hear from God Himself. Pray for all who are beginning to rise up and take the Word of God to the streets and nations. God is going to bring them forth right under the devils nose, and under the noses of those who choose to be friends to the world.

This new breed of ministers will understand how to show themselves friendly, but **will not compromise** with the world, in order to show and demonstrate the power and anointing of God. By doing so, they will actually be able to ***minister and win*** many souls to Christ. All excuses from compromising ministers will be done away with, and their own ministries will be for naught.

God spoke to me that Christmas morning in 2004, when I heard that "angels song" on the radio, and told me a change was coming and is already taking place. God **will not share** His glory with Baal! A new crop of Levite is on the rise for this last day move of God. God told me starting in 2007 you will hear of new groups and singers, you will hear of new bands and preachers, new choirs and praise teams. They may **not** record albums or sing in auditoriums or be on national television, but their voices **will** be heard across this nation and world. They will be in it to give God glory and bring honor to His name. **Rap groups** will begin to operate with a ***new understanding*** of who they are, and what their purpose is concerning the youth of this nation and world.

LISTEN!!! ***The Lord showed me*** **that many would rise in this time and in the years to come, before His return, who would sing and minister under a** ***peculiar anointing,*** **and in such a fashion, that even the music world and industry would not know what** ***genre*** **to put their music in. They will understand the** ***Godly Message,*** **but as far as the** ***style,*** **they will not be able to understand or pinpoint what style of music it is. For there will be a** ***new move*** **and anointing on it. Not just anyone will be able to sing it, because in order to even obtain this sound, you will have to have a** ***true worship relationship*** **and a** ***lifestyle*** **of worship with God.**

Those who don't worship God in spirit and in truth WILL NOT sound right singing this anointed last day music, because it will be totally prophetic. The music will not give glory to *flesh*, but only to God. It will not speak of itself; it will only speak of Gods greatness and the return of our soon coming Savior.

The music industry will not be able to stop you! Not even those "*secret societies*" who actually believe their running things! No, this will be the work of God Himself, the creator of the music. It will be His doing!

To be perfectly honest with you, those who have a true spirit of discernment have been able to tell for years, what's anointed and what just sounds good. This music will sound good and it will be anointed, and able to ***destroy yokes*** and not only ***bob heads!***

*****EXTRA, EXTRA, READ ALL ABOUT IT!!!*****

I can't wait to hear and be a part of this God given sound that's on the rise. None can sing it but those who mean to give God His glory. Sorry, a raggedy spiritual lifestyle won't work with this. It won't even matter if you have all your degrees in music; you won't be able to duplicate this sound because it's coming straight from the heartbeat and throne room of God.

You haven't a clue about this, because this category of music will have favor with God. Only true worshippers will be able to play it, and only true worshippers will be able to understand it. It will have the power to reach out to the sinner, and to the ears of the lost.

Thank God for that! Thank God that not just any ole somebody will be able to do this.

It means that we'll hear songs again that only say what God is saying in the music that will give Him glory, and not what some are saying in their music that many times gives them all the glory, and just gives God thanks!!!!

**As far as the origin of Rap oriented music;
you might want to study up on some
of King David's boys!**

So go ahead rappers, do your thing. Just know that Rap ain't Hip-Hop!

CHAPTER 4

THE LEVITES SHALL SET IT UP, TAKE IT DOWN AND CAMP

Numbers 1:47-54. Verse *47. But the Levites were not numbered among them by their fathers tribe; 48. for the Lord had spoken to Moses, saying: 49. "Only the tribe of Levi you shall not number, nor take a census of them among the children of Israel; 50. but you shall appoint the Levites over the tabernacle of the Testimony, over all its **furnishings**, and over all things that belong to it; **they shall carry** the tabernacle and all its furnishings; they shall attend to it and **camp around** the tabernacle. 51. And when the tabernacle is to go forward, **<u>the Levites shall take it down; and when the tabernacle is to be set up, the Levites shall set it up</u>**. The outsider who comes near shall be put to death. 52. The children of Israel shall pitch their tents, everyone by his own camp, everyone by his own standard, according to their armies; 53. **<u>but the Levites shall camp around the tabernacle of the Testimony,</u>** that there may be no wrath on the congregation of the children of Israel; and the Levites shall keep charge of the tabernacle of the Testimony." 54. Thus the children of Israel did; according to all that the Lord commanded Moses, so they did.* KJV.

No one can ever say they don't have enough to do in the kingdom. Just look at what the Levites did here in scripture. First of all, they were separated for the use of the tabernacle. The same goes for us today. God will cause us to be separated from people, friends and yes even family, when He wants to call us away to do a work for Him. In this passage the Levites were given their own space and land for the service of the tabernacle.

Verse 51 sys; *the Levites shall take it down; and when the tabernacle is to be set up, the Levites shall set it up.*

Yes, there's plenty to do. You say you want to minister? You want to be anointed? You want to get busy working in the ministry? Alright then, I need you to move some church furniture.

This passage of scripture reminds me of something similar I went through. At one point and time I was feeling a little down, frustrated and a little burned out to be perfectly honest with you. I'm a sound engineer in my church. I'm also a minister of the gospel as well. Now I'm not one who has to be out front all the time, so I don't have that struggle, if you know what I mean. But I didn't feel like I was doing what I was called to do, being a preacher or minister of Gods Word. I thank God because He's so mindful of us. He's always teaching us things even when we don't realize we're being taught.

It seemed like all the other ministers in my church were doing what God had called them to do, and I was somewhere sitting behind a mixing board, running the audio. One evening our church was having an anniversary service for our wonderful Pastors; Drs. Thomas and Carolyn Vinson. *(I had to slide that in there)*

We were having our banquet at another location in Atlanta Ga. Now understand that when we traveled to other locations, it usually meant, *loading all of the sound equipment* in the cargo van. Mixing boards, microphones, cables and snakes, amps, recorders, mic stands etc. . . .

(audio people, can you feel me?)

We would *break the equipment down* at the church, *pack it up* in the van, drive down to the spot, *unload the equipment, set it up*, and when service was over, *break it down*, drive back to the church that night, have it all *set back up* and working properly by Sunday morning service.

The Levites shall set it up, take it down and camp. I actually felt like I wasn't doing anything as a minister. I didn't understand that God was actually teaching me ministry all along. The Lord began to show me real ministry even more. He took me to Numbers 1:51 and showed me what the Levites did as stated in the book of Numbers. He said; *son, you're already doing ministry when you set up, break down and move the equipment around. That's what the Levites job was as ministers even back then.*

That gave me a whole new outlook on what ministry was in Gods eyesight, and not mans. So ministers, be encouraged and understand that whatever duties you're called upon to do in the church, remember you are walking in the will of God, and in obedience to the order He has set up in His Word. You're operating in the ministry of a true Levite!

I realized that *moving* the audio equipment was in parallel to what the Levites did in scripture. Do you remember in the book of Numbers, when the *cloud* or the *presence of God* moved from one place to another? It was the Levites job to gather up all the furniture of the tabernacle and *move it* to wherever the presence of God was.

The revelation I received of God was this.

When my Pastors preach in one place or another, they represent *the presence of God*. We would follow them wherever they traveled, *set up* the equipment so they could minister, and *brake it all down* when they were finished. Now that's ministry in its truest form! You see my idea of ministering wasn't what I thought at all. What the Lord was showing me, was the spirit of humility, servitude and obedience. This is how you become an anointed minister of Christ.

If you ever want to be blessed by God and anointed. Learn how to serve, that's what ministry is all about. You can't be a great leader until you learn how to be a good follower. Learn how to follow your leaders, just like the children of Israel followed the cloud of God, and they were looked after, blessed, and there was guidance and protection for them. So it is with your leaders. They're your covering, so learn to stay under their umbrella and you'll have the blessings and protection of God in your life. By submitting willfully to headship, you're actually honoring God, and He can't help but to bless you in everything you do. My father used to say, the way up is down and the way down is up! God has a *divine order* for the Levites, whether you're a musician, usher, porter or priest, to serve faithfully under a High Priest.

Numbers 1: 53; *But the Levites shall pitch round about the tabernacle of testimony, that there be no wrath upon the congregation of the children of Israel.* Now I like this verse!

What this means in, Numbers 1: 52- 54, is the *camp of Israelites* were organized with an inner circle of Levites. Someone say; *inner circle?* Yes, an inner circle of Levites were camped around the tabernacle and an outer circle of the twelve tribes, with three tribes on each side of the tabernacle. Marching lines were also organized so that when the cloud of God lifted, they could move quickly, and when the cloud settled, they could find their places, someone say; *their places?* Yes, they could find their places in the camp without confusion. The tabernacle set in the *center of the camp* symbolized that the life of the nation (*church*) revolved around the Lord, and the worship of Him as their Redeemer.

The Levites shall set it up, take it down and camp. The Levites *pitching around about the tabernacle,* speaks to *unity* in the priesthood. Protecting one another and guarding the house of God, so that no harm comes to the ministry, whether by natural or spiritual forces of the enemy. It's also a symbol of the priesthood protecting and working together with leadership to get the job done. No matter what the task, as long as God is the center of what we're trying to accomplish, we shall be more than conquerors in our quest to do the Lords will in ministry.

We are to guard our **leaders** and under gird them in intercessory prayer. We are to keep them up before God, so that the enemy is not successful in destroying the vision of the house.

There are many attacks on the local church and the body of Christ at large. If we pull together the devils attacks will always be defeated. Where we make the mistake is, we pull against one another. Who's going to preach or lead the song, who's going to play the drums this Sunday?

We cannot be divided in the body and expect God to do the miraculous in our midst.

There are individual blessings we can receive, but there is a *corporate blessing* that God has for us when we dwell together in unity. How can we be a strong and mighty army for God if we're fighting and devouring one another on the battlefield? Let's come together Levites and win the war. If we don't, God's going to draft new soldiers who'll fight the enemy, and not each other, in order to get the job done!

A Song of Degrees of David.

Psalms 133:1-3 *1. Behold, how good and pleasant it is for brethren to dwell together in unity! 2. It is like the precious ointment upon the beard, even Aaron's beard: that went down to the skirts of his garments; 3. As the dew of Hermon and as the dew that descended upon the mountains of Zion: for there the Lord commanded the blessing even life forevermore.* KJV.

This will also happen to us today, when we all come together in one place having the same goal and the same mind with no one having their own hidden agenda. When we come together as a body of believers, God can then command a blessing on his people. Everyone must be in their place, doing what God called each and every one of us to do, and then a corporate blessing comes into play where *everyone's* need it met. I could use a corporate blessing right about now! When the blessing of the Lord comes; it starts with the *head* or the high priest, and then it runs down to the *beard*, which is the priesthood and then to the *skirts* of the garment which is the rest of the body or the church.

If your head is blessed the rest of the body is going to follow as long as everyone stays in their proper place in the ministry, and walking in obedience. God will send his blessing to every household, and all will experience the corporate blessing from the Lord.

That's the kind of blessing I'm waiting for. My Pastor speaks of this kind of blessing often and it's a blessing we all need, but it's going to take all of us coming together with no schisms and divisions in the body so God can perform His word. He cannot lie, but His blessings are conditional. If we meet the conditions He'll supply the blessings. God is bound by His own word, and if we get our acts together and do what His Word says, we will see the blessing Malachi 3:10 speak of. The type of blessing we won't have room to receive. I still have some room don't you?

CHAPTER 5
VISION OF THE ANOINTED CHERUB; LUCIFER

(LOU SEE FUR) (MORNING STAR)

Vision of the Anointed Cherub; Lucifer. First let me start by saying, there is knowledge you receive by studying or researching and there is knowledge you receive by revelation, fresh from the throne of God. I've studied the Word of God and have used many study tools and resources to compile some of the information that I'm sharing with you. The Bible tells us in 2 Timothy 2:15 to, *15Study to shew thyself approved unto God, a workman that needeth not to be ashamed, rightly dividing the word of truth.* KJV. The thing about the Word of God is; you can't understand it with a carnal mind. The Word of God must be spiritually discerned, it's not just the black letters on a page like other books, but the Word of God is *spirit and life.* In other words, if you apply the Word of God and it's principles to your life, you'll experience the life changing power and spiritual demonstration of the book. 2 Corinthians 3:6 speaks of how *the letter kills, but the spirit gives life.* It's not only in the reading of the book, but it's the power of God that endows us with wisdom and understanding to discern His voice and walk in faith enough to act upon His word. So the *letter* of the law can't provide this, but the spirit can.

There are many symbols, revelations and mysteries in the Bible, and you should pray even before reading, asking God to give you *divine understanding* of His Word. Though you may not always understand all of the passages of the Bible, God will send revelation in His Word just because you ask of Him, and you dare to spend time searching for Him. God desires to reveal Himself to us, for he who seeks will find, and he who knocks, God will open the door. He is a rewarder of them who *diligently* seek Him. (Heb.11:6) Like natural relationships, you get to know the one you love by spending time with them, and you learn and recognize their voice.

Although many things have been written and spoken about this angel, his creation and who he was remains somewhat of a mystery in the minds of many people. What do we know about this creature God created? Well, we know he was kicked out of heaven for wanting to exalt himself up above God. Yes, he wanted to do that, and yes he was removed from the presence of God! (Isaiah 14:12) What else is known of him? We know a third of the angelic host followed him when he was cast down. Yes, this is true also; they did side with him and were cast out of heaven along with him. (2Pet. 2:4, Judges 1:6)

Although this book talks about the Levites, most of my concentration was upon the *musicians* and not the *priesthood*. But I had to realize that there are many people called to both a word ministry, as well as a music ministry. The ministry of a Levite is so broad in its perspective that I had to put it all together, because both ministries walk hand in hand for the purpose of God. When you actually look at it, we are all Levites working in the church from the parking lot attendant to the ushers and from the user to the pulpit. We all have a work in the church to do.

Now I want to share some things about this being God created. When I first made mentioned of the vision the Lord gave me, many approached me asking where I obtained this information, or what book I studied to acquire it. I simply told them the Lord showed me this in a vision and explained what it was. You know most looked at me as if I were from another planet. I guess it was strange to them that God would show someone a vision of this magnitude, but why? Didn't God say in the last days he would pour out of His spirit on all flesh? Your sons and daughters would prophesy? It also says that the *old men* would dream dreams and the *young men* would see visions. I must be a *middle aged man* because some of the illustration I saw in an *open vision* and the rest I saw in a dream. . ."That was a joke!!! Ha!"

Vision of the Anointed Cherub; Lucifer. When the Lord showed me this vision of Lucifer it blew my mind. I said to myself; *if I share this, people will think I'm just another crazy preacher or musician trying to get attention with gimmicks or just trying to make a name for himself.* But quite the opposite, the Lord told me that if I shared this with His people, it would be a blessing to all, it would cause many to dig into the origin of who this being actually was and what his purpose was in heaven, and what his hidden purpose is in the world and church world today. This will actually give you an understanding of the purpose and writing of this book.

So in obedience to the word God spoke to me, here it is:

In one of my **_praise and worship symposiums_**, I mentioned the fact that Lucifer was *the anointed cherub that covered.* In other words, he was head over the *atmosphere* and *worship* in heaven. He was over the music and directed the heavenly choir if you will. He stood in the very presence of God and worshipped God face to face. In a sense that's what we do when we worship God. We deal with him face to face, naked and open before Him. Worship is a time of closeness, a time of intimacy with God. God always desires to be worshipped. John 4: 23-24, tells us; *the hour cometh, and now is, when the true worshippers shall* *worship the Father in spirit and in truth, for the Father seeketh such to worship him.* Verse 24 goes on to say, *"God is spirit and they that worship Him must worship Him in spirit and in truth. KJV*

"**Truth**" *(Gk. Aletheia)* is a characteristic of God. *(Ps. 31: 5; Rom. 1:25; 3:7; 15:8)*, incarnate in Christ, *(14:6; 2 Cor. 11:10; Eph. 4:21)*, intrinsic to the Holy Spirit *(14:17; 15:26; 16:13)*, and at the heart of the gospel *(8:32; Gal. 2:5; Eph. 1:13)*.

Therefore worship must take place according to the truth of the Father that is revealed in the Son and received through the Spirit, into the hearts of man. Those who advocate a worship that sets aside the *truth* and *doctrines* of the Word of God have in reality set aside the only foundation for *true worship.*

The English word *worship* is derived from an Old English word *worth-ship*; in other words you are agreeing that worship constitutes the actions and attitudes that revere and honor the *worthiness* of God Jehovah, the Great Almighty God of heaven and earth. Therefore worship must be **God-centered and not man-centered or self-centered.**

This is where O Lucifer messed up. The angel God himself called *"perfect in beauty"* got beside himself with pride and wickedness. He wanted to be worshipped!

You are the full measure and pattern of exactness [giving the finishing touch to all that constitutes completeness], full of wisdom and perfect in beauty. [13]You were in Eden, the garden of God; every precious stone was your covering, the carnelian, topaz, jasper, chrysolite, beryl, onyx, sapphire, carbuncle, and emerald; and your settings and your sockets and engravings were wrought in gold. On the day that you were created they were prepared. [14]You were the anointed cherub that covers with overshadowing [wings], and I set you so. You were upon the holy mountain of God; you walked up and down in the midst of the stones of fire [like the paved work of gleaming sapphire stone upon which the God of Israel walked on Mount Sinai]. [15]You were blameless in your ways from the day you were created until iniquity and guilt were found in you. (Ezekiel 28:12b-15, 16-19) KJV. *(study the words, "iniquity, wickedness and lawlessness, in a good bible dictionary and reference guide and commentary")* We must understand that all we have and possess belongs to and came from God. It is not by our own power or might.

Vision of the Anointed Cherub; Lucifer. We have to be careful not to get lifted up above measure, thinking that we're more than we actually are. It doesn't matter if we can sing melodiously like a bird, or preach cunning persuasive words. We are nothing without God, and God hates the spirit of pride. He hates pride so much that he tells us not to even carry the *look of pride* on our faces. Proverbs 16:18 tells us; *pride goeth before destruction, and a haughty spirit before a fall.* Proverbs 29:23[a] says; *a man's pride shall bring him low.* KJV. The effects of pride always result in a downfall of some sort, and eventually death and destruction to one's life or ministry. What you're actually doing when you take on the spirit of pride, you're taking on the very same sinful attributes Lucifer carried when he decided to come against Gods authority.

Pride and a spirit of lawlessness and wickedness were in him, and the bible tells of his downfall when he became lifted up within himself, and disdained set authority.

Lucifer was the head-honcho in heaven over the worship. He understood the original purpose for music, and how it was created by God for the worship of God alone. Lucifer realized through his own worship of God, how the anointed music that came from his own body affected him, and also how it affected the other worshipping angels. The anointed music was so powerful that it even *aroused* God Himself.

a•rouse, [uh-rouz] verb, *a•roused, a•rous•ing. verb (used with object) 1. to stir to action or strong response; excite: to arouse a crowd.*

The perfect sounds that came from the pipes, strings and tibrels, always created a sound of perfect harmony in **major chord progressions**. So crisp and clear, that you could actually hear the **frequencies** of **perfect pitch** in the heavenly host. *(those of you who tune instruments or master music, can understand what I'm talking about when I say; "frequencies of perfect pitch")* When God created the *music*, and set Lucifer to oversee it, Lucifer became the anointed cherub that covered or oversaw the heavenly musical department if you will. He began to see himself as greater than the one who created him. Now understand that God a sovereign God already knew what He had created. It was yet all a part of His plan. God knew what Lucifer would do before iniquity would pry its way into this perfectly built creation. Since Lucifer has been relieved of his duties in heaven, he's now using his gift as a weapon in the earth today. **The weapon of music!** He knows all about music, the structure of its sounds, and how the musical tones, and frequencies can be used to manipulate the mind and control human emotions, causing people to conform to any sinful passions he pleases.

I've learned from my own experiences how powerful music is. Can you remember before you received Christ, (*sometimes even now if you aren't careful*) how you've heard a certain *song* from *back in the day,* and how it took your **mind back** to the first time you heard it? It may have been a time when you were doing God knows what, with God knows whom! But the tune took you to the beginning, or back to the *first time* you heard it. It's been a proven medical fact that the left side of your brain reasons with the information it receives and *decides* which information it will process and *keep* and which piece of data it will *reject*. The information it keeps then becomes stored in memory on the right side of your brain. But hold up! The only piece of data the left side of the brain cannot stop or *deny entry* and processing of information, is music! Music can *by-past* the reasoning sessions of the left side of your brain and go into memory storage on the right side of the brain without your permission and knowledge.

"Heard that song that you can't seem to get off your mind lately?"

Vision of the Anointed Cherub; Lucifer. Understand that, **music will always carry *the spirit* of its *original author.*** No matter how it's *re-arranged or re-mixed*; it carries the authority of its writer or creator. When you copyright a song, it doesn't matter who else sings that song, the original writer gets the credit for that song. Be mindful that, what comes from the *heart* of one has the ability to reach the *heart* of *another*. Luke 6:45 which says; *a good man out of the good treasure of his heart bringeth forth that which is good; and an evil man out of the evil treasure of his heart bringeth forth that which is evil: for of the abundance of the heart his mouth speaketh.*

Heart: *According to the Bible*, the heart is the center not only of *spiritual activity*, but of all the operations of human life. "Heart" and "soul" are often used interchangeably (Deuteronomy 6:5 ; 26:16 ; Compare Matthew 22:37 ; Mark 12:30 Mark 12:33), The heart is the "home of the personal life," and hence a man is designated, according to his heart, wise (1 Kings 3:12 , etc.), In these and such passages the word "soul" could not be substituted for "heart."

The heart is also the seat of the conscience (Romans 2:15). It is naturally wicked (Genesis 8:2), and hence it contaminates the whole life and character (Matthew 12:34 ; 15:18 ; the process of salvation begins in the heart by the believing reception of the testimony of God, while the rejection of that testimony hardens the heart (Psalms 95:8 ; Proverbs 28:14 ; 2 Chr. 36:13).

M.G. Easton M.A., D.D., Illustrated Bible Dictionary, Third Edition

If you do a biblical study of the *heart,* you'll also find that it speaks of the *spirit of a man.* So in other words; that which comes from the *spirit* of one person, can enter the spirit of another person. What am I saying? A persons spirit follows or is forever connected to their music. It's how Satan uses the music in his ultimate plan of destruction. He can literally transfer his message into the hearts and minds of men and women by playing the music. Thus passing on the *spirit of the author* of that particular piece or music. Realize that since he can no longer play his music in worship, he's going to take his gift and use it for his own glory.

Follow me; if you take someone who has a *lustful spirit*; that lustful spirit can be *discerned* in the frequency and sound of their music. Let me bring it closer to home! No matter how you try to change the words of a secular song and add the name of **Jesus** to it; when you hear the song, notice that your mind *goes back* to the *first time* you heard that song. Your mind does not originally pay attention to the, *"Jesus"* that is presently added in the new lyrics. This is because the spirit of the original author is *still* attached to that song!! Music is a perfect *conduit* for *spirits to travel* through, that's why your emotions change when you hear that **certain song**.

You're being affected by *supernatural spiritual influences* that reside in the invisible precincts of the music. Whether a good influence by the Holy Spirit, or a bad one by the forces of Satan.

It's enough that as Christians we have to guard our hearts and war in the spirit against the demonic principalities found in the world's music. But it's an absolute shame to have the same struggles listening to a Gospel/Christian song, because our minds are battling against the former demonic oppressed music we were once delivered from. For some of us, it was a struggle to tare away from the dark passions of secular music. Now we have our artists bringing the struggle right back to us, and calling it worship music. You have to almost cut the music off just to stay delivered in your mind, because your mind goes back to the time when you first heard the song.

Vision of the Anointed Cherub; Lucifer. I know some of you may say that our minds should already be renewed and it shouldn't bother you. But it seems like our minds have to be renewed after every *so called* gospel song. . . . .Sorry for not being as strong as you want me to be. But the strong ought to bear the infirmity of the weak as well. Some things aren't good to do because it misrepresents Christ, and may throw a weaker or younger *would be* Christian off track.

Have you ever put a thought to the fact that you're now doing what Satan now does in his presently perverted music? His music is no longer Holy or consecrated, but is now unholy and in most cases carries sensual connotations. And like him, you yet want to call your music, worship!

Again, let's establish the fact that music carries the spirit of its author. Many of you as musicians spend years perfecting and creating a sound of your own, or an identity in your music.

When other people hear your music, you would like for them to be able to recognize that it's you they hear. People can immediately identify you by a *certain sound* that represents you.

Where do you think you get your total sound or style from? I'll tell you where. It comes from your life's *influences*, your *experiences* and many of the *heart felt* situations you've gone through or deal with. You relay those situations and experiences in your music or song, and when you write a song out of the *abundance of your heart*, that song reaches out and touches someone who can identify with what you're saying or what you've been through. In short, it carries *your spirit* with it! What comes from the heart reaches another's heart or spirit, remember? That's how music works, it can reach your heart or spirit without you actually giving it your permission. *(study this and you'll find out it's true)*

So can you understand how powerful the Word of God can be through an anointed, *God inspired song*? Music, like the Word of God can go into the hearts of men and plant a seed in them that they didn't even know was there. Some will *plant*, some will *water* and God will give the increase. Just like a farmer who has to plant the *correct seed* to get a harvest, it's imperative that we sing the right type of songs, first of all that minister to the Lord, and then to His people.

Years ago, back when Jazz music was introduced, there weren't any saxophones used with that style of music. But today, the sax is probably one of the most, if not the most widely used and most romantic instrument there is. If played correctly, it is one of the most sensual instruments of all time. Some say it's the closest thing to the human voice, and can be played in such a manner where you can almost hear words coming from its tones.

Most musicians, who play this instrument, usually have a decent voice or understand the theory of singing as well. They can actually sing the song in their mind, while playing it on the instrument. Then when you hear them sing, you'll find that their style of singing is close to the way they actually play their instrument. Now I'm a saxophonist, and I've actually seen this in other horn players as well.

Well, producers began to recognize the fact that the saxophone could move you in a way that no other instrument could. So what did they do? They began to record their jazz compositions more and more with saxophones in them, to create the emotion or atmosphere they desired. But the sax wasn't originally used in jazz music. Let's look at the *smooth jazz* scene of today. It seems like every other artist in the smooth jazz industry is a sax player, or the sax is used on most of its recordings.

Vision of the Anointed Cherub; Lucifer. The enemy can use rock, rap, jazz, country, blues, reggae, r&b, heavy metal, electronica, dance, classical, and sad to say, even gospel forms of music to communicate his messages. *Notice* I didn't use the term *hip-hop*. That's because the phrase hip-hop, is not a style of music, it's a way of life, a mind set or culture, which is now registered as a religion.

There have been surveys across the country asking young kids what do they believe in the most? Hip hop or Jesus Christ? What kind of question is that if hip hop is just music? How are they matching this up, what is the comparison here? What does that question have to do with music? The sad part about it all is 43% of the youth when asked this question stated, they believe more in hip hop than they do Jesus Christ. Wow! I know I may have made many of you upset, but we need to take a second look and see what the devils plan is. He's on his job, we better get on ours. The bible teaches that Satan is going to *cause many* to be deceived. He's not just going to walk right up to you and tell you what he's going to try and do to you. Remember, he's a lie!!!

Now I know many of you are saying God can use any form of music to bring people to Christ. Well that has some truth to it, but for the most part is fiction. The scriptures tell us how we are to sing *psalms, hymns and spiritual songs to ourselves, making melody in our hearts toward God.* (Eph. 5:19, Col. 3:16) Now can you honestly say that if you heard the song; *More Bounce to the Once,* or one of your old favorite secular songs, **and then add**, *in Jesus name,* to the lyrics of that song; that your mind would concentrate on the, *in Jesus name* part of the song? I beg to differ. Your mind and brain are a memory chip, and computer hard drive that records and stores every piece of information you put into it. Your mind will *automatically go back* to the day when you were doing your thing, dancing to "More Bounce to the Ounce," because that's the song your brain was first introduced to. *(there's a danger in the power of introduction)*

Then your mind tries to justify itself by adding; *in Jesus name,* in the lyric to the song. But if you were to hear your favorite or any other tune, and then attempt to *re-arrange* that song or tune with different lyrics, your mind will go back to the **origin** first.

(I used the song," More Bounce to the Ounce" because that was one of many, Zapp or Roger Troutman songs I used to mix when I d-jayed)

I'm telling you that I've heard plenty of gospel artists over the years, use those same beats in their music, and when I heard their *quote-unquote,* gospel song, my mind actually paid NO ATTENTION to their *Christian lyrics* for a good amount of time, because my mind instantly went back to, not only the original song, but also the wrong I was doing at the time the song came out! Do you think those are the *images* God wants us to have when we sing our *so-called* worship songs?

This *same practice* was used back in the bible by many *pagan nations* who *did not worship* the true and living God. They practiced putting their own *perverted words* to the *melodies of Zion.*

It was really a **mockery** of the people of God and our belief in Him.

(also study Psalms 137: 1-9, where the Babylonians mocked and made fun of the children of Israel, asking them to sing some of their Zion songs of victory before the barbarous people of that country, who held them in captivity!)

How is it that we have convinced ourselves of conforming to the world's way of doing things with its pride, glamour and fads? *(lusts)*

Vision of the Anointed Cherub; Lucifer. Now we're *mimicking* the world with Christian dance clubs with the teens and adults, actually doing secular dances to holy music together on a dance floor. Really! Don't be fooled though; many of the gospel/Christian recordings are geared aimed for this type of setting, and not for the purpose for which Gods music was intended. There's enough pressure on our young and our singles as it is, without us helping the devil out with some of these so called Christian social events which aren't spiritual at all. Now I'm as *"that's whuss up"* as the next man, but I know that the devil has taken occasion with every little chance he gets. He's an accuser of the brethren. Now we've come up with all kinds of compromising excuses and reasonings, saying that we're just trying to win the young people to Christ and give them an *alternative.* Alternative speaks to *choices.* But the choices should be *different than,* not *just like!*

Let's look further, because it's so serious now, we can't afford to be like the world in any way, shape or fashion. I know many of you disagree but we had better start discerning Satan's subtle but strong tactics of deception he's transporting right into the church, and stop helping him out!

Isn't it strange that we haven't seen any worldly clubs having testimony or church services?

You don't hear them say; *hey no drinking or partying tonight, we're going to have worship service and altar call tonight!* Can we please stand up and make a difference? Why can't they look on this side of the fence and see what we are doing? The truth is, they don't need to because the, *supposed to be separated people of God,* are all up in *their* kool-aid, mixing! God teaches in His Word that *bitter* and *sweet* cannot come from the same fountain. I'm not passing judgment on people, so I rebuke that spirit now! We can be *fruit inspectors.* We know what type of tree it is by inspecting the fruit it bares or yields. If it's an apple tree, we shouldn't see almond growing out of it. The same goes for the fruit our lives are supposed to yield. We can't yield righteousness and unrighteousness on the same tree. That's part of our problem today. Where there should be a harvest of fruit in the body of Christ, we're producing a bunch of nuts!!

We try so hard to be like the world, not really understanding what's going on behind the scenes.

First hand, I know of secular groups that you and I've danced and partied to; fall down on their knees in the studio before a recording session or a concert and *chant* out words in *different tongues, (not holy tongues)* or they've shot up on heroin or other drugs before performing, praying and asking Satan to bless them and make them **successful in this life**, *in Satan's name amen!* Then you wonder why some secular groups can release an album one day and it turns multi-platinum the next? They've sold their souls to the prince of darkness, the prince and power of the air or *atmosphere.* Now here WE come, as saints of the Most High God, **re-mixing and sampling the same songs that were prayed over and anointed by Satan himself**, and we try to use them as a tool of righteousness *to draw our young people?* This is what so many of our musicians will tell you! So tell me, if God told you right now to stop it, could you? Would it mess with your goals, your vision or your money? What our young people need today is truth! Gods *saving power* has not changed, and He's the same yesterday, today and forever more. God is not intimidated by a tight beat or a funky hook to a groove! God can give you, *O Levite,* a fresh new sound that no one has ever tapped into. That's one reason I call my music production, *Sound of the Timez.* God can give you the *right sound for the right time baby!*

Vision of the Anointed Cherub; Lucifer. I'm trying to encourage us, not rebuke us. But we need to know that God is *not pleased* with the fact that we as musical Levites don't have enough confidence in our God to pray to Him and ask for a song straight from His throne. The world does it; they asked their god when they pray, and he gives'em hits that *not only* the secular world hears and listens to but you hear and listen to it also! *Oops* did I say that? So why can't the only wise God, the only true and living God of heaven give you the same and better? Music was created and intended for the worship of God alone, and Satan knows that. Our priorities are in the wrong place. Our prayer to Him shouldn't be, God make us successful in this world. For the Bible tells us to love not the world neither the things of the world with its lusts and sinful passions.

Your first concern as a Levite is to minister to Him, so He can minister to you, and in return, you can minister to the people.

Now doesn't that make better sense? Stop prostituting the gift that came from God to be used for His purpose, not your own selfish one! I'm sorry; *the preacher came out in me, I went off for a moment but I'm back now!*

Let's get back to the anointed cherub who was called Lucifer. Believe it or not, I had to say what I did over the last few pages of this chapter for the very purpose of what I'm about to say. There is an undercurrent plan by Satan to taint the worship of God with an injection of his own music.

Here's the vision God gave me, and I didn't believe it myself until God lead me into a very in-depth research on it. I really had to pay close attention to what God was telling and showing me.

You must understand that this creature has been around for a long time and knows how to operate in his musical gifting. He was an angel, but a musical instrument wrapped up in one!

One night while lying in the bed not yet asleep, I began to think about music, and how Satan is using it as his *major weapon* to deceive the church and the nations. While lying in the dark of my room, I began to see this figure. Not just any figure but a wide and unusual figure in this open vision I was having. *I'm getting chills just writing this*; anyway, he was this absolutely beautiful archangel with huge wings of multiple colors. Now I spent many years in the printing industry, and one of my duties was mixing ink. We mixed colors that didn't even have names to them, so we just gave them numbers. I was introduced to colors I hadn't seen before with my natural eye, so in seeing the *colors* of this *angelic being*, makes it impossible to describe the colors illuminating in his wings. Tall and majestic he stood there in front of me, he was more beautiful than any being I had ever laid eyes upon. He had an aura and presence about him that suggested excellence and perfection! He looked wonderful!

The bible explains that he stood in the very presence of Almighty God and walked among stones of fire. It is vital to remember that Lucifer was in and of himself, was a *living musical instrument*. God made him for worship and God didn't hold anything back when He created him. In this vision I couldn't see his face because it was covered up by a pair of wings. But it was the rest of his body that intrigued me. He began to move and spin around slowly like he was on a revolving carousel, and when he turned his back to me I saw these *huge pipes* coming out of his *back* and *sides*. Each one of the pipes were different sizes. They were what looked like a *silver transparent color,* if you can imagine that. Not only that, but he had what looked like *timbrels* or *tambourines* hanging off his sides and his wings.

(here's where it started to get deep to me)

Vision of the Anointed Cherub; Lucifer. As he turned back to face me, he lifted up his pair of wings which were connected to larger wings. When he lifted up his wings, he had what looked to me like a *pleated bag (if you will),* underneath either side of his wings. Now days later as I began to dream about this creature, I remember asking God, what were the *pleated bags* underneath both of his wings? The Lord said; *they're bellows.* "Bellows," I asked? It didn't dawn on me what a bellow was until the Lord instructed me to look up the word in the dictionary.

When I read it in the dictionary, it absolutely blew my mind because I then understood what I was looking at when I saw the *pleated bags* under his wings; it was absolutely astonishing to me! Remember the pipes of all different sizes I saw in his back? They were *organ pipes!*

Organ pipes you say? Organ pipes I say! "You telling me Ole Lou played the organ?" No, I'm telling you Ole Lou was the organ!

Lets go back to the word bellow(s). As I looked in the *American Heritage Dictionary*, it blew me away again; the description was this; bel-*lows (bel'l^oz)* 1. An apparatus for producing a strong current of air, as for **sounding a "pipe organ"** or **increasing the draft to a fire.**

Bel-lows *(bel'l^oz) It consists of a flexible, valve air chamber that is contracted and expanded by a* **pumping force** *or* **pumping to force the air through a nozzle.** STOP RIGHT THERE!! Folks, this is what I saw on Lucifer's body. The bellows under his wings were *pleated flexible tissue like* fabric, *(I'm not sure)* connected to his body that contracted air throughout his body *every time he moved.* Hummm! **Every time he moved?**

Hold on to your seat, it gets deeper!

Webster's Dictionary; 2. *(bel-lows), something resembling a bellows, such as a"pleated windbag" of an accordion.*

I digress; Let me remind you that I saw all of this on Lucifer's body **before** I even knew what the dictionary was going to describe to me. So the dictionary actually served as confirmation of what God was showing me in the body of this beautiful archangel.

Wait, there's more!

3. *(bel-low)* **"The Lungs"** *[Middle English- belwes, bellows, plural of "belu", or* **below**, *probably from Old English word, "belga" plural of* **bell**. *g. belig, meaning,"* **bag**" *or (see "belly")* **"Belly"** *4. The part of the body between the* **rib cage** *and the pelvis. The underside of the body such as* **snakes** *or fish. (snakes or fish, is there a revelation right there?)*

5. *the front part of the body of a"***stringed musical instrument**.*" (wow, more revelation!)*

The reason I pointed out **"the lungs,"** is because I could see the insides of his body as well.

He had what looked like, *one lung* like a *bellowed bag* with a horn coming out from his mouth.

Even though I couldn't see his face, I knew the horn like stem came from out of his mouth.

Notice in the *fifth description* mentioned earlier, the *bel-low* was the front part of the body of a *stringed instrument*. These strings were also connected to the front part of his body like a guitar, violin or harp. I can't explain to you how they were connected, I just knew they were.

After looking at the *bellows description*, I also looked up the word organ. Why? Well in my searching out of the scriptures, and tracing the history of the organ, I found that when the organ was mentioned in scripture, especially during King David's time, the organ consisted of pipes.

Vision of the Anointed Cherub; Lucifer. Psalms 150 verse 4 tells us to praise God with the <u>*stringed instruments and organs*</u>. Now David didn't have a band with an *organ player* like we have today. As a matter of fact, when the mention of the organ was made in scripture, it wasn't a **keyboard** type instrument at all. Back then they were pipes that were powered *if you will*, by bellows or pleated sacks. In other words, the bellow bags were connected to the pipes, and the **force of the air** would cause the *pipes* to **sound off**. It would remind you of an *accordion* or *bag pipe* in today's instruments. Therefore in the Old Testament, I learned that the organ was part of the *flute* family! The flute is an instrument mentioned in Psalms 150: 4. However, the Hebrew word, *nihility* or *nehiloth* in the title of Psalms 5 means; **with flutes.** Some flutes were made of silver and some were made of reed and wood. Again, another word used for flute in other translations of the Bible is, **organ;** *(Gen. 4:21, KJV);* ***fife*** in *(1 Sam.10:5, NEB);* **pipe,** in *Job 21:11, RSV).*

Not to get off track, but understand that the *organ* developed through the process *of time*, and when the 150th division of Psalms mentions it in the 4th verse, it's speaking of praising with the pipes. *(organ)* KJV.

As centuries passed, by the *1800's*, the organ had now developed into a *keyboard operated* instrument, that was yet powered by, guess what? You got it; bellows! The instrument was actually introduced to society as the *piped organ*, now used in many of the Catholic Churches and Cathedrals across the world even today.

Focusing back in on Lucifer; he had all of these instruments built in his body and the pipes coming out of his back and the bellows coming out from under his wings and mouth.

Understand that the *rituals* of *godly worship* here on earth are *shadows*, *types* and *symbols* of things that go on in the *worship* of God in heaven. Also recognize that the **dance** is part of worship. It's backed throughout scripture.

In my vision, after I observed Lucifer worshiping in the presence and face of God. I now had a greater understanding of what we are supposed to do in the midst of worship.

Hear this! In this vision, Lucifer would move his body and flap his wings, and the force of his movements would cause the sounds to come out of his body and out of the pipes in his back. In other words, he had to <u>move</u> in order for the sounds to expel out of his body or spiritual being.

So if anyone tells you that you can't express yourself with dance in a church service, just tell them that it was already done in the *heavenly worship* of God from the very beginning.

As I kept my eye on this cherub, he finally opened up his mouth and when he did, it was like the sound of a million synthetic trumpets and synthesizers playing in *perfect harmony* all at the same time. Can you imagine a million part harmony? Directors, how would you like to teach those harmony parts to your choir?

Motion and movement are a part of worship, just ask King David. Since this is the case, how could you just sit there and not move when the spirit of the Lord comes and sits among us? There's something about the move of God that should make you move. . . . . . .it's like fire!! If I took a match and set you on fire, there's no way you could just sit in one place and not move.

The same goes for our God, who is a consuming fire. When He moves, it should move you!!!! The prophet Joel said the presence of God is like fire, shut up in his bones. If that's what it felt like to him, I guarantee he started to move and *dance* when the fire of the Lord came down.

1 Peter 2:5 says that we as His people are lively stones in the house while offering up sacrifices.

Vision of the Anointed Cherub; Lucifer. Now what I thought was wonderful and special, was the relationship I could sense between God Almighty and this *creature* He allowed to worship right in his presence, face to face. If you remember earlier in the description, the mechanism I saw attached to either side of his body, were *bellows*. The bellows were attached under two of his wings on either side of him, and they had what looked to be some type of *tubing or hose (for lack of a better word)* attached to them, that went out and up to the organ pipes built in his back. As he moved his wings it would seem to create a flow of air that would start from the bellows continuing through the tube passage and up to the pipes, thus creating sound in much of the same manner an old pipe organ operated. The faster the movements he made, the higher the sound pitch would be. The slower the movements, the lower the pitch would be. It was absolutely incredible to see how he moved, pumping the bellows almost like an accordion and raising his wings, which had timbrels attached to them.

As I continued in this vision of him, I began to see **fire**. I understood the *fire* represented the presence of God. As Lucifer began to move, the sound producing bellows built in him would blow on the fire and cause a flame to enlarge itself. As Lucifer stood in Gods presence during worship, he would turn and open his mouth in worship to God, and the draft from his body would blow towards the throne of God, and the worship towards the throne would excite God.

After the draft from Lucifer's body would blow towards the throne of God, in return, Gods presence would overshadow and move upon the anointed cherub, thus causing Lucifer to move even the more. That was awesome to me! It was a symbol of them *ministering* to one another in worship. Isn't that how it's supposed to work? We minister to God in worship and in return He comes down and overshadows us with His marvelous presence?

So when Lucifer breathed and moved towards the throne, God would move back on him causing him to move even more, and remember every time the anointed cherub moved, music came out of his body. **This signified that anointed music in worship moves God!**

He used all the instruments to worship God. All the instruments mentioned in Psalms 150:3-5, were attached to the body of Lucifer! You may be saying, what's the significance of this?

Well look at it in this manner, he used <u>everything he had,</u> to worship the true and living God.

He had a special place with God but lost it because he got caught up in his own gift and splendor. Be watchful Levites! He knows all about your kind. You are one of his main targets! Musicians are a breed all their own, we think different, we understand different, we talk the same language, we process things in a different manner. Satan understands all of your muses, creativity and inspirations, because God once inspired him.

In the vision, he opened his mouth and spoke out in praise to God. He was quiet and then he was loud again as he moved about. How do I know this? Remember the pipes in his back were different sizes, and the *less* he moved, the *lower* the *pitch* coming from the pipes and the *more* he moved the *higher* the pitch! It was awesome to behold and something I'll never ever forget!

I thank God for showing me this, but I asked why did he pick me to witness this? As one who God had seen fit to anoint for His service, I've gone through many struggles as a musician. Many of you struggle with your gifts as well saying, *where do I go from here and what do I do with my gift?* Many of you are not satisfied where God has placed you in the body of Christ, or you struggle with using your gifts *for the Lord ONLY*!!

Vision of the Anointed Cherub; Lucifer. Some of you have become lifted in pride and want more and more and have no concept of true Levitical service and ministry.

Lucifer, who is now that old serpent called **Satan,** knows what makes the musician tick. He's mad at you because, **he used to be who you are!**

God showed me the vision so I would **sound an alarm** to let you know that Satan wants you to end up just like him, in total anger and misery. Misery loves company. You have to be extra careful and *guard your heart* when you're really *gifted* from God. The same *struggles* Lucifer had, *you have*. And without knowledge and understanding of Satan's plan to destroy you and ultimately the church, we will perish and be defeated.

Understand that he wanted to be more than what he was. He should have known that he couldn't be equal or more than the one who created him. Now he's trying to get into the minds of the musicians, singers and priesthood; telling them that they don't have to wait on God. He'll tell you; *you're talented, go and do your thing, it doesn't matter what your Pastor says, he doesn't understand that you're gifted and you have do your own thing. You don't need any man telling you how to use your gift anyway.* Once you allow Satan to lie to you, he begins to plant a *seed of discord* in you, and a *spirit* of *iniquity* follows. *(the spirit of wickedness and lawlessness)*

Then all of a sudden, you start having issues with **anyone in authority**, because you don't think anyone is good enough to tell you what to do.

What happens to an individual who is having problems or issues with *leadership* or *authority?* They begin to **talk** about their issues to others. They always have a problem or an issue with something that's going on in the church or ministry. They always seem to strike out on their own, and they always have to **tell someone else** how wonderful they are. The **prideful spirit** within them will not allow them to keep **their own wonderfulness** to themselves. I mean what's the use of being great and wonderful, if no one else knows about it, right?

When someone in your church starts sowing discord or talking about leadership, many times they start by saying things like; *I could have thought of that* or *I could do that too.* They always have a better idea or a better way of doing things, but the problem with that is, they're usually never around when it comes time to doing it. They always have a problem with someone else in the church that's been **delegated authority** by the pastor. They usually start by being late for church or choir rehearsals. Their *attitude* changes and they become *distant* and hard to talk to. **Pride** usually sets in, and you can't tell them anything, because they already know it all. No one sings or plays better, no one preaches as good, and if their gift is *prophetic*, wow, watch out because **no one** hears from God as well as they do. Do you see any similarities in some of the people you know, or in the way you're acting yourself?

Lucifer started talking about himself more and more and how he would raise himself up above the throne of God. The same throne where he once truly worshipped the true and living God.

Now when Lucifer started *noising* the fact of how *wonderful* he was, and how *marvelous* he looked, who do you think **he** was talking to?

Notice, that when someone in the church starts acting in a similar fashion; he or she **always** wants an *audience*. Lucifer also needed an audience. He began to *communicate with the angels,* cornering them off saying; *(paraphrasing)* "hey man, God ain't all that!" "Look at me, I'm wonderful and beautiful, let's communicate to some of the other angels and we can start our own thing, we can have private prayer meetings, and start our own praise and worship group."

Vision of the Anointed Cherub; Lucifer. "See, I've already got all the instruments right here on me." "We'll start our own ministry right in the face of God." *(or authority)* "And if he don't like it, we'll move our congregation over to the north side!" *(or was it the sides of the north?)*

See Isaiah 14:13. . . . humm!!

Have you ever seen this kind of rebellion in your church? They can never do it on their own, they **always** have to have a *following* or some *weak folk* that look up to them. But be warned; just like Ole Lou was cast out and *punished*; so will we if we take on the same prideful spirit.

Be careful oh gifted Levites; God still has an order for us to follow. Yes, you should know who you are in Christ, and yes, be all you can be and strive for the *spirit of excellence.* But understand that no matter how gifted and anointed you are, you don't possess the same *anointing* and *grace*, that God gives His leaders or set authority. I've seen it many times in my days, where there were gifted and anointed preachers or elders and ministers of music who could preach play or exhort well. I've also seen where other elders in a church, could probably out *preach* the pastor, or had better preaching techniques. But does that mean God has changed his approval of the *set man* or *woman* of the house?

No matter how well can hear from God, or how sensitive you think you are in the spirit. Just like God spoke to His servant Moses *face to face* and before the children of Israel, He'll always speak to His leaders first!.. . . . . .remember that!!!

Where there is more than one vision, you'll usually find division!

Vision of the Anointed Cherub; Lucifer. It doesn't matter how well you do what you do, God does not, and will not speak to you in the same manner he speaks to His leaders.

Read (Exodus 19: 1-25 and 20:1-26). God spoke to Moses *directly*, and he relayed the information to the people of Israel. There were times when the people wanted to hear God for themselves and when they attempted to do so, they became afraid when they heard and saw the thundering and lightening from the mount and quaking of the ground. They quickly changed their minds and requested Moses to go up for them, and they would hear him.

Just be what God called you to be, walk in the anointing that is yours. Be found in your own place and God can truly use you. God made you who you are, and He wants to use you in a greater way. Can you be satisfied in whatever area or capacity God places you in?

As Levites we have an awesome responsibly not only to God, but to the people of God as well.

He thought enough of you and me to put His special anointing and gifts inside us, and called us to a *holy calling.* You are a soldier and a vital part in the army of Christ, and He doesn't want you to waist time with endeavors that will lead you everywhere, but to of the will of God. Be what God called you to be and you'll have good success.

All Lucifer had to do was be content in the place God had given him. But he wanted more, he wanted the glory for himself. No one can have or deserves any glory, but God!! He's the creator of the whole universe, the one who gave this ungrateful creature the beauty and the gifts to be used for Gods good pleasure.

He saw himself as more than he was actually created to be. And for that, it eternally destroyed him and a **third** of the **angelic host** who were **persuaded** by Lucifer to follow him.

As Lucifer began to lift himself up in pride, he started to persuade the other angels to side with him. How did he do it? Now I know we've read in scripture, where it describes events when **Satan** spoke in a **verbal language**, so don't get confused on what I'm about to say here. This is just some of my own creative thinking, but it was something I feel the Lord pointed out to me that further substantiates the fact of how powerful the *unspoken* or *subliminal language of music* actually is, and how spirits can *conduit* through its *melodic sounds* and *frequencies*. In the natural, there are sounds that can not be heard by the human ear. For example, dog whistles sound off frequencies the human ear can not pick up. So imagine *in the spirit realm,* the possibilities of *hidden messages within the music*. This is a technique that's even been used by studio engineers over the last three or four decades. It is possible to put an undertone message or sound in the music that *only* your subconscious picks up, but your ears don't always hear it.

What you have to realize is there were times in scripture where Satan spoke and said *he was going to and fro, throughout the earth, seeking whom he may devour*. But remember he wasn't in his *heavenly form* when he spoke those words to God. Now I know the scriptures shows *dialogue* when he spoke of himself while he was yet in heaven in the presence of God and the other angels. But work with me for a moment. This is a little nugget the Lord shared with me and I thought it would be *very interesting* to share it with you.

Remember when I said earlier that I saw Lucifer *open his mouth,* and when he did, I heard *music come out of it?* He began to use the gift God gave him, and that gift was music!

Vision of the Anointed Cherub; Lucifer. When *iniquity* was found in Lucifer, his *gift* in heaven had now become his *weapon,* as he was being cast down to the earth's atmosphere. (Ezekiel. 28:15)

Remember Lucifer was both **cherub**, *(angel)* and **musical instrument.** *(Organ)* When I saw him speak out of his mouth, only music came out of it. Now don't trip on this, but as I did a really in-depth study of **cherubim** and **seraphims**, I found out that cherubims were *quieter* in their nature. Seraphim's were *more vocal* as you can read about them in the book of Revelation. They were the angelic beings crying out, *"holy, holy to the Lord."* But the cherubims carried a different attitude because their assignments were different and more direct. *(I can imagine millions of you looking at this page really strange now!)* Well, that's why this book is actually a training manual. Its purpose is to provoke you to *study* and *search* the scriptures to see that these things are so. *(use as many study helps as you can and God will reveal the rest to you)*

Moving on! I seen the creature open his mouth as I said before, that music came out of the horn like tube I saw coming out of his mouth. *(now here's the nugget)* The Lord enlightened me to the fact that Lucifer didn't have to speak a **verbal language** in order to persuade a third of the angels to follow him. I'm not saying he didn't speak a verbal language to convince them, but since he had the ability to *communicate through music* that exuded from his body, he didn't have to *speak* a word to the angels to get his prideful point across to them.

You mean to tell me Lucifer could have used **music alone** *to persuade the angels to do something they had not intended to do?* **Yes**; isn't music a weapon he's using today? God told me he could have actually **played music to the angels** to relay his intentions of an impossible heavenly overthrow. *(I wish I could see the look you have on your faces right now!)*

I was also amazed when I realized the fact that the *unspoken language* in music was a form of communication that could have actually been used, even in heaven. Interesting huh? Let's bring it up to today's music. When is the last time you've heard that certain song that just does something to you? *(tell the truth and shame the devil)*

You know, that one song you heard and couldn't get off your mind? Once you've entertained a piece of music in your *ear gate*, it can enter the realm of your **sub-conscience without your permission**, or you realizing it. Music has the ability to penetrate, and enter at will. There have been psychological studies that have proven this fact, and it can actually be backed in scripture, that music has the ability to enter a man and sooth or affect his spirit. Just ask King Saul about the anointed musician, David.

Music can get into your mind and **habitat** without your consent. It can war against your thoughts and emotions at will. Music doesn't need your permission to enter into your sub-conscience, that's why advertisers use **subliminal messages** coupled with music to get their point across. They know something the average consumer doesn't understand. It's also been proven that it only takes a total of 15 seconds for the brain to recognize, record and store information based on what **the eyes see**, *(storing images)* and **what the ears hear**. *(altering & storing emotions)* There's a book out called, **Thought Particles** by doctor Roy H. Williams, who explains how the left and right side of the brain process and store information, thought patterns and how the brain functions in relation to music. He shows how information partnered with music can enter certain areas of your brain **without** your consent. Sounds like what I've been saying for years now.

(take a look at the diagram of the brain process)

Vision of the Anointed Cherub; Lucifer. This is why you have to be careful of the things you **watch** and **listen** to. Lucifer very well could have used the very gift God gave him, pervert it, and use it to pressure the angels who knew it was wrong, but because of the **power of persuasion** music possesses, it could have caused them to rebel against Almighty God, to follow a former anointed musician. Now what was used for the worship of a holy God, is now a perverted sound of persuasion and wickedness by the same God given gift. But in Gods ears is now a sounding of brass and tinkling cymbals. . . . . .

The brain maps you have seen thus far have been of the left hemisphere only. Frankly it's pretty hard to find a map of the right brain, although I've known that the "sylvian fissure" angles more sharply upward to the right hemisphere compared to the left. The sylvian fissure is the line that separates the left auditory association area from the areas above it.

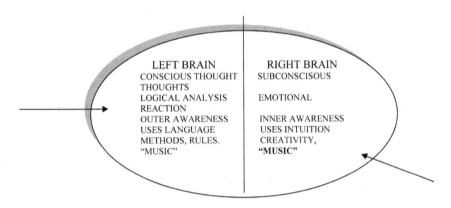

Information enters here

Study by,
Dr. Roy H. Williams

Information stores here

Read the book *"Thought Particles"* binary codes of the mind.

After beholding the vision of the angel God created, I understood how powerful this cherub actually was. He was created to stand in the presence of God and should have kept his focus on Him. But he took his eyes off God and bought attention upon himself. That was and always will be a mistake! When we start worshipping the creation more than the **Creator**, we're headed on a sure path to destruction.

After seeing all of this in the vision, it took about a year for me to understand all that I had seen. I actually began to see this same prideful spirit manifest itself in different people I knew. I understand why they were acting that way, and where it came from. I began to understand all of the things God invested in this creature, and how we are no different. God put His very best ingredients together when He made you and I. But woe to us, if we repeat the same thing Lucifer did by **rebelling against Gods authority**, by being full of pride! Many of you out there are talented and gifted by God. The talents He's given you are second to none. But I warn you today; please don't take on that awful spirit of *pride* and *rebellion*. For rebellion is a form of witchcraft. There are actually witches and warlocks sitting in our churches today. Yes, witches and warlocks sitting right in the church because they've taken on the same **spirit of rebellion!**

Vision of the Anointed Cherub; Lucifer. They're on our instruments; they're on our usher boards, and even in our pulpits.

If you have a spirit of rebellion, you are operating in the spirit of **witchcraft.** 1 Samuel 15:23 tells us that, *rebellion, is as the sin of witchcraft.* Why do I keep mentioning this? Because it's the very spirit that worked in Lucifer. He's mad at you preachers, because he was in the presence, and dwelt with **The Word.** He's angry at you musicians because, **he used to be who you are!**

Now he's still a musician, but he's not a musician who plays under a *holy anointing* or one who can still feel the presence of God when he performs. Don't you see why he's after you man and woman of God? When the anointing comes upon you in the midst of your sermon or song; can't you feel the awesome presence of God resting on you? Don't you just love how the anointing makes you feel? I'm not talking about showing off or performing in your flesh, I'm talking about moving in the Holy Ghost and the anointing of God overshadowing you. There's no better feeling in the world, than being used by God, it's an absolute pleasure! Thank you Lord!

Satan used to be in a position where he felt the presence of the Lord. He used to commune with God *making melody* and worshiping the true and living God. It's like someone leaving a church or ministry where the presence of the Lord was, and going to a place where there's an absolute *void* of the presence of God. It's like seeing someone sitting in a seat you used to sit in. Like a runaway person looking through the window of the home they left, seeing everybody enjoying each other's company. It's like hearing others singing songs you used to sing, and preaching sermons you used to preach. That's how Satan feels now, he's full of hatred and regret at the fact that he knew God! He saw God move! He heard God speak! He played all the instruments before God. Now God has other musicians playing the same instruments he used to play. Feeling the same anointing he used to feel. Now he's wroth at any gifted or anointed person who is allowing God to use them. He's trying to get you off track! Musicians, pay attention! He's trying to work through **you** to destroy the church and the body of Christ!

He's trying to get you to play music that sounds good, but **has no power.** He wants you to take the name of Jesus out of your songs. Instead of singing about the power that's in **the name**, he just wants you to talk around the name with inspirational type music that talks about **angels** but won't point anyone to **Jesus Christ**. He wants you to mention *your name*, more than the name of **Jesus,** because there's NO POWER in your name! It'll be pleasing to the flesh, but won't pack any anointed power. Preachers, he's trying to change your message. Instead of instructing people how to *come out of their sins* and teaching them how they must *live holy* in order to make it to heaven. He's telling you to teach them *faith and prosperity* as if that's all God has to say. **Better preach the whole book!**

He's telling you to move the church into more compromises, by having meetings and conferences, with invitations to carnal people who try to teach us how to lead a spiritual life. God has no shortage of; *writers, producers, motivational speakers, artists, painters, window washers, carpet layers, doctors, lawyers, comedians, politicians, preachers, teachers, evangelists, prophets, pastor's. . .etc.* Get the picture? It's all in the body of Christ! God never needs Satan and his imps to help promote holy things! He replaced Lucifer with the true praise of his people, and told us to **come out** from among them and **BE SEPARATE!** Study that!

Vision of the Anointed Cherub; Lucifer. God's people have replaced the third of the angelic host that fell from heaven, and we are commanded to give God **praise** and **true worship,** which He is seeking such to do so. Don't loose your place or your anointing because of selfish gain in this life.

Now upon completing this chapter, the Lord dropped this word in my spirit.

God told me that He would take some ministers down, and raise others up, to do what He called them to do. Now when the Lord said this to me, He showed me how He would allow some to continue their ministry, and that it may not *negatively affect* the thousands of people they may actually minister to. He told me it may not affect the amount of CD's they're able to sell. It may not even affect how their gift operates in the house of God. But the one thing God said it would *affect,* was their place with Him and in the Lambs book of life. What He means by that is; what you do **now** will be your reward! He won't acknowledge or recognize what you have done.

You can go around the country singing, preaching and teaching in His name, but it won't be recognized, and you won't receive a crown for the labor! Just like Lucifer, he still has the skills, but he has no place of honor with God. What will it profit you though? To gain all of this world and its riches, and loose the one and only soul you have?

God told me to cry out! I knew going in that this would not be a popular message to preach because it deals with **where we are,** in comparison to where God actually **wants us to be.**

I'm not some disgruntled musician or preacher who's lashing out because things haven't happened in my ministry as it's happened in some others. I'm very happy and content with where God has me and what He has me doing. I want only to be in Gods will, it's the safest place for me.

A shifting is already taking place in the realm of the spirit. God is raising up His chosen vessels in this last day, and nothing will be more important to them than ministry. Obeying God, will mean more to them than money, fame or notoriety. They have been grooming for years now and are on the rise in the world today. They have not been seen as the most popular, or the most gifted, but they are the ones God has chosen and you will soon know who they are because they will begin to operate in the kingdom with POWER and DEMONSTRATION of the HOLY SPIRIT!!!

You know who you are Levites! God has begun to speak to you already, and His Word and purpose are now stirring in your belly, and the time in now approaching for you to deliver and bring forth those babies into the earth. The world doesn't know you, but they are waiting on you to bring Gods Word to them whether it come by song, or by preaching the Word. It's all about the assignment God has given you to carry out. Some it will be the ability to love others and draw them into the kingdom. Others will be to attack the very touchy areas of Satan's camp and cry out that there is only ONE GOD, and He has a name!!!!

Don't change! Don't take down! Don't give up or quit! Don't lose your identity. God will have a people who are after **His heart**, and are just glad that their **names** are written in heaven! They just want the will of God to be done in the earth. Don't lose your name over in heaven over pride. . . . . . .*Lucifer did!!!*

CHAPTER 6

ASAPH, ETHAN & HEMAN

Asaph, Ethan and Heman.

Asaph

"who gathers together"

- Father of Joah
- 2 Kings 18:18; Isaiah 36:3, 22
- Son of Berachiah. One of the three leaders of music in David's organization of the tabernacle service
- 1 Chronicles 15:16-19; 16:5-7; 25:1-9; 2 Chronicles 5:12; 35:15; Nehemiah 12:46

Appointed to sound the cymbals in the temple choir
1 Chronicles 15:17, 19; 16:5, 7

A composer of sacred lyrics
2 Chronicles 29:13-30
See title of
Psalms 50; 73; 74; 75; 76; 77; 78; 79; 80; 81; 82; 83

Descendants of, in the temple choir
1 Chronicles 25:1-9; 2 Chronicles 20:14; 29:13; Ezra 2:41; 3:10; Nehemiah 7:44; 11:22

- A Levite, whose descendants lived in Jerusalem after the exile
- 1 Chronicles 9:15
- A Kohath Levite
- 1 Chronicles 26:1
- Keeper of forests

- Nehemiah 2:8
- A Levite; one of the leaders of David's choir (1 Chronicles 6:39). Psalms 50 and 73-83 inclusive are attributed to him. He is mentioned along with David as "skilled in music", and a "seer" (2 Chronicles 29:30). The "sons of Asaph," mentioned in 1 Chronicles 20:14, and Ezra 2:41, were his descendants, or more probably a class of poets or singers who recognized him as their musical master.
- The "recorder" in the time of Hezekiah (2 Kings 18:18, 37).
- The "keeper of the king's forest," to whom Nehemiah requested from Artaxerxes a "letter" that he might give him timber for the temple at Jerusalem (Nehemiah 2:8).

1. A Levite, son of Berechiah, one of the leaders of David's choir. (1 Chronicles 6:39) Psalms 50 and 73-83 are attributed to him; and he was in after times celebrated as a seer as well as a musical composer. (2 Chronicles 29:30; Nehemiah 12:46) (B.C. 1050.)
2. The father or ancestor of Joah, the chronicler to the kingdom of Judah in the reign of Hezekiah, (2 Kings 18:18, 37; Isaiah 36:3, 22) probably the same as the preceding.
3. The keeper of the royal forest or "paradise" of Artaxerxes, (Nehemiah 2:8) a Jew, in high office at the court of Persia. (B.C. 536.)
4. Ancestor of Mattaniah, the conductor of the temple-choir after the return from Babylon. (1 Chronicles 9:16; Nehemiah 11:17) Most probably the same as 1 and 2.

Ethan

"The Ezrahite," distinguished for his wisdom (1 Kings 4:31). He is named as the author of the 89th Psalm. He was of the tribe of Levi. A Levite of the family of Merari, one of the leaders of the temple music (1 Chronicles 6:44; 15:17, 19). He was probably the same as Jeduthun.

E'than

"enduring"

1. Ethan the Ezrahite, one of the four sons of Mahol, whose wisdom was excelled by Solomon. (1 Kings 4:31; 1 Chronicles 2:6) His name is in the title of (Psalms 89:1)
2. Son of Kishi or Kushaiah; a Merarite Levite, head of that family in the time of King David, (1 Chronicles 6:44) and spoken of as a "singer." With Heman and Asaph, the heads of the other two families of Levites, Ethan was appointed to sound with cymbals. (1 Chronicles 15:17, 19)

3. A Gershonite Levite, one of the ancestors of Asaph the singer. (1 Chronicles 6:42) Heb. 27. (B.C. 1420.)

The same is Jeduthan

A Levite of the family of Merari, and one of the three masters of music appointed by David (1 Chronicles 16:41, 42; 25:1-6). He is called in 2 Chronicles 35:15 "the king's seer." His descendants are mentioned as singers and players on instruments (Nehemiah 11:17). He was probably the same as Ethan (1 Chronicles 15:17, 19). In the superscriptions to Psalms chapters 39, 62 and 77, the words "upon Jeduthun" probably denote a musical instrument; or they may denote the style or tune invented or introduced by Jeduthun, or that the psalm was to be sung by his choir. KJV.

- A musician of the temple
- 1 Chronicles 16:41; 25:1
- Called **ETHAN**
- 1 Chronicles 6:44; 15:17
- See title of
- Psalms 39; 62; 77

Note: when you see the name Ethan, it's short for the Chief Musician, Jeduthun, he's the same person.

He'man

"faithful"

1. Son of Zerah. (1 Chronicles 2:6; 1 Kings 4:31)
2. Son of Joel and grandson of Samuel the prophet, a Kohathite. He is called "the singer," rather than musician, (1 Chronicles 6:33) and was the first of the three Levites to whom was committed the vocal and instrumental music of the temple service in the reign of David. (1 Chronicles 15:16-22) The 88th Psalm is ascribed to him. (B.C. 1014.)

- "The singer," a chief Levite, and musician
- 1 Chronicles 6:33; 15:17, 19; 16:41

The king's seer
1 Chronicles 25:5

His sons and daughters temple musicians
1 Chronicles 6:33; 25:1-6

"Maschil of," title of
Psalms 88

Remember, King David was a prudent man and wise in his business. He was a man of order. He set up the music department (if you will) like a corporation. Understand that he was setting up order in the House of God. This is what we need in our Churches today, we need natural and spiritual order among the musicians. David had everyone in their proper place based on their anointed gift or ability. No one was operating in another one's place and **if two had the same gift, there was no jealousy allowed or you were not to participate.** How many of us would be disqualified already before the King set everything up? He had total order and obedience among the musicians, dancers and singers. Wouldn't that be wonderful in today's church?

Asaph, Ethan and Heman. David's musical organizational chain of command was as follows:

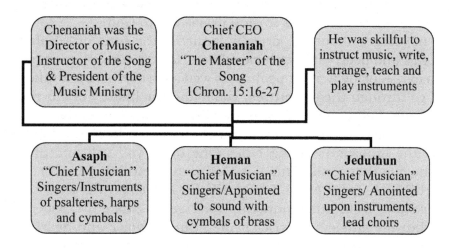

Ranks of "Second Degree" under the Chief Musicians based on their talent & musical skill

These were musicians and singetrs under the Chief Musicians	Zechariah	Ben	Jaaziel	Shemiramoth
Jehiel	Unni	Eliab	Benaiah	Maaseiah
Mattithiah	Elipheleh	Mikneiah	** Obed-edom	**Jeiel

They were musicians and singers, but many of them also had other duties like, porters and gatekeepers.

(this would be like your own church having "security" and "parking lot attendants!)

Asaph, Ethan and Heman. In 1 Chronicles 25:1, the sons of the Chief Musicians were separated or chosen for service, prophesying on harps, with psalteries and with cymbals. Heman was not only a musician but he was also a *seer* or a prophet who God gave fourteen sons and three daughters who served under his hand. You can find out more information and scripture concerning this in chapter 3, *"About the Levites."* These three men were anointed and separated to do service in the house of God. Their sons and daughters followed them in the music ministry and as you will find out in the pages of this book, they also did other duties in the ministry. King David left the music ministry in anointed capable hands. **He did not bring in musicians less skillful than himself,** but brought in men and women of God who were ***skilled and anointed*** upon their instruments and in their voices to sing praises unto God.

Let us not forget about the priestly family of the sons of Korah who wrote psalms, songs and poetry for centuries. Even David's son Solomon continued in his fathers footsteps by writing psalms as well as proverbs. Just take your time, study and go through the scriptures, you'll find the history of our musicians is very interesting. I admonish all who are singers, musicians, dancers, choreographers, music directors and even prophets to take a look into the fascinating ministry of the musicians of the bible. One thing you will find and I'll say it again for the one thousandth time, is God wants and intended for ALL MUSIC TO WORSHIP HIM, TALK ABOUT HIM, BE ABOUT HIM AND HIM ALONE, with no pagan *mixture* from other nations. Don't get it twisted, David had outside influences but his music and lyrics came from the voice and heart of God, not *samples,* uh huh, from any other nations. Study the bible right!!

CHAPTER 7

PSALMS & THE DANCE

Psalms & the Dance. The Psalms are the production of various authors. Only a portion of the Book of Psalms claims **David** as its author. Other inspired poets in successive generations added songs and made contributions to the sacred collection, and thus in the wisdom of Providence it more completely reflects every phase of *human emotion* and circumstances than it otherwise could. But it is especially to David and his contemporaries that we owe this precious book.

In the *titles* of the Psalms, the genuineness of which there is no sufficient reason to doubt, 73 are ascribed to David. Peter and John in Acts 4:25 ascribe to him also the second Psalm, which is one of the 48 that are anonymous. Approximately two-thirds of the whole collections have been ascribed to David.

Psalms 39, 62, and 77 are addressed to **Jeduthun**, to be *sung* after his manner or in his choir. Psalms 50, and 73-83 are addressed to **Asaph**, as the master of his choir, to be sung in the worship of God. The **sons of Korah**, who formed a leading part of the Kohathite singers (2 Chronicles 20:19), were entrusted with the arranging and singing of Psalms 44-49, 84, 85, 87, and 88. In Luke 24:44 the word *psalms* means, the *Hagiographa*, i.e., the holy writings, one of the sections into which the Jews divided the Old Testament. None of the Psalms can be proved to have been of a later date than the time of Ezra and Nehemiah, hence the whole collection extends over a period of about 990 to 1,000 years.

There are in the New Testament 116 direct quotations from the Psalter. The Psalter is divided, after the analogy of the Pentateuch, into five books, each closing with a doxology or benediction. The first book comprises the first 41 psalms, all of which are ascribed to David except 1, 2, 10, and 33, which though anonymous, may also be ascribed to him.

The second consists of the next 31 psalms, 18 of which are ascribed to David and 1 to **Solomon** (the 72nd). The remaining ones are anonymous.

The third contains 17 psalms (73-89), of which the 86th is ascribed to **David**, the 88th to **Heman** the Ezrahite, and the 89th to **Ethan** the Ezrahite.

The fourth also contains 17 psalms (90-106), of which the 90th is ascribed to **Moses**, and the 101st and 103rd to David.

The fifth contains the remaining psalms, 44 in number. Of these, 15 are ascribed to David, and the 127th to Solomon.

Psalms 136 is generally called *the great hallel*. But the Talmud includes also Psalms 120,135. Psalms 113 & 118, inclusive, constitute the *hallel* recited at the three great feasts, at the new moon, and on the eight days of the *Feast of Dedication*.

It is presumed that these several collections were made at times of high religious life: the first, probably, near the close of David's life; the second in the days of Solomon; the third by the singers of Jehoshaphat (2 Chronicles 20:19); the fourth by the men of Hezekiah (29, 30, 31); and the fifth in the days of Ezra.

The Mosaic ritual makes no provision for the service of song in the worship of God.

David first taught the church to sing the praises of the Lord. He first introduced it into the rituals of the tabernacle music and song. Various names are given to the *psalms* or songs. Some bear the Hebrew designation **shir** (Greek ode, a song). Thirteen have this title; it means **the flow of speech**, as it were, in a straight line or in a regular strain. . . .i.e., *(like rap oriented music today)*. This title includes **secular** as well as **sacred** songs.

Psalms & the Dance. Fifty-eight psalms bear the designation (Hebrew) **mitsmor** (Greek psalmos, a psalm), **a lyric** ode, or **a song or poem set to music; a sacred song accompanied with a musical instrument.** Psalms 145, and many others have the designation (Hebrew) **tehillah** (Greek hymnos, a hymn), meaning, **a song of praise**; a song the prominent thought of which is the praise of God. Six psalms (16, 56-60) have the title (Hebrew) **michtam**, may be a **musical notation** or some suggestions include a title for Psalms connected with **expiation of sin**. At Isaiah 38; 9 Hezekiah's *writing* (Hebrew *Miktav*) should perhaps be Miktam. Psalms 7 and Habakkuk 3 bear the title (Hebrew) **shiggaion**, translations suggest to mean, **a frenzied or emotional style**: as in a wandering musical fashion or an expression of a song of lament.

Songs are very powerful and they carry spirits. As I've mentioned before, we must be careful as to the *type of song* we allow into our spirits. Understand that **music carries the spirit of its original author.** I'll say that again! Music carries the spirit of its *original author*, therefore it doesn't matter how you **change the words** of a *secular* song; it carries the *emotion* and *spirit* of its writer. So when you take a song of a secular origin and mix it with Godly oriented lyrics, it becomes a perverted work. Though your natural ear may hear the *newly worded song*, your brain and your spirit pick up the *original spiritual* undertones that lie within the *tempo* and *beat frequency* of the music. Thus storing it in your brains memory bank and ultimately affecting your spirit.

What do I mean when I say, *ultimately affecting your spirit?*

The bible teaches us in Luke 6:45, *a good **man** out of the good treasure of his **heart** bringeth forth that which is good; and an evil **man** out of the evil treasure of his **heart** bringeth forth that which is evil: for of the abundance of the **heart** his mouth speaketh.* KJV.

In other words, that which comes from the heart, reaches the heart. When you study that, it also speaks to the *spirit of a man*. So in essence; that which *comes from* the spirit of one man, *can transfer* and *enter* the spirit of another man. So if an original writer of a song has a bad or perverted spirit, it translates or transfers in his or her music. Think about it; have you ever heard a song or listened to a CD or the radio and say, *hey that sounds like so and so?* Their music is identified by a certain sound. Well my friend, that sound comes from the abundance of that writer or performer's heart or spirit. So when you recognize a certain sound of a person's music, you're also recognizing that person's spirit. So whatever spirit the originator is of, that spirit will always follow his or her music. So it doesn't matter how you *re-mix it, revamp it,* or *change the lyrics* into a Christian oriented message, the original author has the *spiritual copyrights* to that tune. It will always carry the spirit of the original author. Now if you understand how that works; then what kind of songs are we offering up to the Lord, seeing that back in Moses and David's day, they always wrote *original psalms* to the Lord? They were always singing unto the Lord, *new songs.* Singing *spiritual songs* and *making melodies* in their *hearts towards God*; something God wants us to do today as well. Can someone please present God with something fresh and original? I'm sure He would like to hear what His investment in you sounds like. Untainted I pray! Ephesians 5:19, *speaking to yourselves in psalms and hymns and **spiritual songs**, singing and making melody in your heart to the Lord.*

Colossians 3:16 says; *let the word of Christ dwell in you richly in all wisdom; teaching and admonishing one another in psalms and hymns and **spiritual songs**, singing with grace in your hearts to the Lord.* KJV.

Psalms & the Dance. Just as God commanded Moses and David not to take any ways, customs or cultures from any other nation, we don't have to *mimic* the world's styles or ideologies and bring them to God as worship. It's not the true worship that's mentioned in John 4:23-24 at all.

We take songs and music from other nations and say; *hey world, give us some of your musical beats and songs;* **this stuff God has is whack!** As if God needed your help with creating a song, being the creator of all things! There's power in His name alone to save the world from sin.

He doesn't need you, your name or your compromising gift to reconcile the world back to Himself. There's enough power and anointing in His music to get the job done!

When you attempt to mix *secular* music with *sacred*, you're actually taking the place of God. What do I mean when I say that? You're taking on that Luciferian spirit by saying, *there's more power in my gifts, than there is in the original anointed psalms of God.* Now instead of the deliverance that anointed music births, we add our own two cents to it, and just come up with a good sounding song! Then we act as if it were us, who made the changes in people's lives.

As if it were by our musical power and might. It's like saying the anointed music that God gives us, needs our aid and assistance to make it sound good. **Now that's whack!!!!**

The dance is spoken of in Holy Scripture universally as *symbolic of rejoicing,* and is often coupled for the sake of contrast with mourning, as in Ecclesiastes 3:4, Psalm 30:11; Matt 11:17. In the earlier period it is found combined with some song or refrain, (Exodus 15:20; 32:18, 19; 1 Samuel 21:11) and with the tambourine *timbrel* more especially in those impulsive outbursts of popular feeling which cannot find sufficient vent in voice or in gesture singly. Dancing formed a part of the *religious ceremonies* of the Egyptians, and was also common in private entertainments. But for the most part *dancing was carried on by the women, the two sexes seldom and not customarily intermingling.* In the Eastern cultures, men and women didn't dance together for sensual or social purposes. Usually the men danced on one side of the room and the women on the other. **So dancing among Gods people, was not a social occurrence. Dancing was the result of divine spiritual victories or rejoicings.**

Let me share some revelation with you that the Lord gave me concerning the *dance* and or *choreography.* In my Levite Symposiums I facilitate, I often mention the fact that, people who have an anointed gift of a **dancer/choreographer**, have the ability to **see** the music, and can actually **visualize the motions of dance,** *caused* by *the music.*

This is one of the *characteristics* of that gift. Those of you who have the *gift of dance* can understand what I'm saying. When you hear **anointed** music or any music for that fact; you have a hard time keeping still; **you must move!** Why? Is it that internal rhythm clock you have on the inside of you? No, that's not it. Is it because it's your favorite song playing? No, that's not it either. **A dancer has the ability to see the motions of music and portray them to us in a visual display.** Yes, a dancer or choreographer can actually see the music that's being played. They have a gift from God to put music into *actual motion.* Therefore, those of us standing by are able to *observe* the anointed music through the dancer who is being used as a *conduit* for the music to flow through. With that being said; we should dance to music that is **God inspired.**

When they danced in the days of David, they were inspired by *spontaneous* praise and worship to God, and had skills to visualize the anointed music played by the musicians and could exemplify the actual **movements of worship.** Our dancers carry the same anointed gifts today. I know before this, some of you dancers thought you were strange, but you're not. It's your gift!

Psalms & the Dance. You don't have to borrow any motions or dance moves from anyone else. God will give you *spontaneous moves* that give Him glory and you won't be the one responsible for offering up, **strange fire** or something you took from a worldly system, and offer it up to God as worship. God wants it to be *pure* and *original*. It should be what He wants at any given time, a spontaneous *gesture* of worship. Those of us who walk in the spirit can **hear** the **worship sound.** But the dancer or choreographer can **see the worship** and visually portray it to the rest of the body of Christ, through dance.

Thus we are all able to see and hear what God is saying to us. Therefore having a total worship experience, understanding what God is saying and doing at any given moment. A *visual ramah word* if you will. In the earlier period of the Judges, the dances of the virgins of Shiloh were certainly part of a religious festivity. (Judges 21:19-23) Dancing also had its place among merely festive amusements, *apart from any religious character*. (Jeremiah 31:4, 13; Mark 6:22)

Dancing found in Judges 21:21, 23; Psalms 30:11; 149:3; 150:4 and Jeremiah 31:4, 13, etc., as the translation of *hul*, which points to the **whirling motion** of Oriental sacred dances. It is the rendering of a word **rakad'** which means to *skip* or *leap* for joy, in Ecclesiastes 3:4; Job 21:11; Isaiah 13:21, etc. In the New Testament it is in like manner the translation of different Greek words, *circular motion* (Luke 15:25); **leaping up and down in concert** (Matthew 11:17), and by a single person. (Matthew 14:6) Dance is also spoken of as symbolic of **rejoicing.** (Ecclesiastes 3:4) Compare Psalms 30:11; Matthew 11: 17. The Hebrews had their sacred dances expressive of joy and thanksgiving, when the performers were usually females. (Exodus 15:20; 1 Samuel 18:6) **Eastern ancient dance was very different from that which was common among Western nations.** It was usually the part of the women only. (Exodus 15:20; Judges 11:34)

Hence the peculiarity of David's conduct in dancing before the ark of the Lord, was something not normally done by men. (2 Samuel 6:14) The women took part in it with their timbrels, and Michal should, in accordance with the example of Miriam and others, have herself led the *female choir*, instead of keeping aloof on the occasion and looking through the window.

David led the choir *uncovered*, i.e., *wearing only the ephod or linen tunic*. He thought only of the honour of God, and forgot himself. David put praising God before his own personal needs and desires. He used the dance to express the victory that God had given the nation of Israel in the return of the Ark of the Covenant back to the nation. King David understood that praising God through the dance was a powerful weapon as well. It has the ability to change the atmosphere, and make it conducive for God to move by His spirit, and destroy yokes of bondage, which in return, will produce an environment of spiritual liberty.

Dance, was also known to be a *musical instrument of percussion*, supposed to have been used by the Hebrews at an early period of their history. **Dancer/Dancing Rhythmic movement** of the body, usually done to musical accompaniment. Among the Jews, dancing generally occurred among women, either singly or in groups. It was a way of celebrating joyous occasions. In the scriptures, dance was used as a way of making it known that a **victory** of some sort had indeed taken place.

Psalms & the Dance. Indeed, dancing became a symbol of joy, the opposite of mourning (Psalms 30:11-12) *¹¹ Thou hast turned for me my mourning into dancing: thou hast put off my sackcloth, and girded me with gladness; ¹² To the end that my glory may sing praise to thee, and not be silent. O LORD my God, I will give thanks unto thee for ever.* KJV.

(Ecclesiastes 3:4) *¹ To every thing there is a season, and a time to every purpose under the heaven: ² A time to be born, and a time to die; a time to plant, and a time to pluck up that which is planted; ³ A time to kill, and a time to heal; a time to break down, and a time to build up; ⁴ A time to weep, and a time to laugh; a time to mourn, and a time to dance.* KJV.

The Bible gives several examples of dancing. Groups of women danced at celebrations of military victories (1 Samuel. 18:16). Occasionally, children imitated the dance in their play. (Job 21:11; Matthew 11:37)

David danced before the Lord with all his might (2 Samuel 6:14) when the **ARK OF THE COVENANT** was brought up to Jerusalem from the house of Obed-Edom.

Dancing by the Israelites was usually accompanied by the rhythmic beating of timbrels-or tambourines. (Judges 11:34)

On great national occasions, Israel also praised the Lord with stringed instruments, flutes, and cymbals (Psalms 150:4). **Men and women never danced together.**

I know this hurts some of your feelings, but the fact of the matter is, Gods people didn't have separate events where they **danced together socially.** *(Christian Night Club Dancing?) Humm!*

Even on those occasions where both sexes participated in the sacred professional dances, they always danced separately (Psalms 68:25; Jer. 31:13). The *together* mentioned in Jeremiah 31:13 means the *young men* and the *old* shall rejoice *together* in the dance, also the women would dance but in their own separate space. *(You will find this fact in most Bible History Books or Commentaries)* Dancing for entertainment was unheard of among the Hebrews.

Salome's infamous dance, which gained her the head of John the Baptist on a platter, was in the tradition of *Greek dancing*, a sensual art form rather than an act of worship (Matthew 14:6). In Matthew 14 verse 6, the public dancing of an ungodly young girl before men led to the death of John the Baptist. Worldly parties, dancing, and ungodly films lead to a forgetfulness of Gods laws, an inciting of passion, and a hardening of one's ability to discern sin, righteousness, or judgment. In these things the *true* children of God *will not* participate. According to scripture spontaneous dancing by Hebrew women and girls was done on exceptionally joyful occasions (Jeremiah 31:4), and especially after victory in battle as they sang to the Lord. (Exodus 15:19 21) There is no Scriptural record that Jewish men danced with women, nor is there any indication that Jewish women ever danced publicly with or before men or an audience. The dancing of the daughter of Herodias before men was a **pagan practice.**

As you can see, the dance is and has been used for various situations. Today's dances or dancing for the most part, usually have sexual innuendos and connotations. Some of the dances you'll see on many of the television programs and videos suggest sexual encounters. You don't have to use your imagination much any more, because the dances demand that you get so close that it leaves very little to the imagination. But I'm not talking about that type of dance at all! As I mention in other parts of the book, Satan has now perverted the sacraments of God, and has attempted to make a mockery *(mimic)* of Holy things. The problem is; much of the mocking is coming from those who are within the house of God.

Psalms & the Dance. Dance in a worship form is totally original. Even though there were many choreographic instructors in scripture who taught and trained others to flow in dance. They moved under the unction and anointing of God. Their movements in worship weren't always rehearsed before time. That's the beauty of it all. It's a total and absolute *expression of worship* through movement. Are you feeling what I'm feeling here? Those of you, who feel the presence of God, and express yourself through the *ministry of motion*, understand what I'm saying here. In the spirit realm, you can actually discern how you should move, and you're able to sense what God is doing and saying. You're able to relay that to us by way of *motion* and *spontaneous movement*.

There's a special anointing that comes from the *visual ministry*. Of course it's necessary to hear the Word of Truth; it's also wonderful to hear the sound of anointed music and preaching.

But there's just something awesome and powerful in the *ministry of demonstration.*

Think about this for a minute. We've read the story of how our Lord and Savior tortuously died on that dirty tree. **But could you fathom being there to witness the nails being harshly driven between the tender bones of his wrists/palms? The rusty early railroad type spikes in the small bone of His feet, the blood and water coming out of His side, and the pain of wearing a thorn pressed crown? Not only that! The robe that was placed on his bloody torn up back, and blood that had dried up on his back, formed a scab like appearance, and then it was ripped off His back and skin, causing the bleeding to start all over again. I can feel you cringing, as your mind sets up a visual image of Jesus on the cross.** You see? There's just something about the visual when you can *see* or *picture* the very thing that is happening. It has a different but lasting effect to it. So it is with the ministry of dance, it ministers to God, and to the ones who have the privilege of viewing this anointed demonstrative ministry. I imagine in my mind that God loves to see it too.

Let's take it a step further; there are *anointed dancers*, and there are those who *dance prophetically*. There are also prophets/prophetesses who prophesy through the visual expression of dance. I'll give you an example of what I'm talking about. . . .

There's a sister in our church who is a prophetess. Now I've often seen her dance or shout as the Spirit of the Lord begins to move on her. But on this particular Sunday, her dance was different than someone shouting because they feel good or because the music sounds good. This dance was a *prophetic visual utterance*! Let me explain what I mean. Some of you may think this is strange but it's really not at all.

The name of the sister who was dancing that Sunday is; Dorothy Williams. Now she may or may not have realized what God was doing and saying through her at that time, but on that particular Sunday morning, the spirit was really high at our church, and there was a spirit of prophecy in the building. **Yet no one uttered a word, not one!** Humm! But I could hear the *music prophesying* in the atmosphere. I could hear the music declaring *victory over the enemy*. I could hear *prophetic notes and sounds* coming from the instruments.

As the service progressed, the Lord instructed me to pick up my horn and play. As I began to play, I could hear a sound and melody of victory coming from my saxophone. My eyes were closed at first but as I opened them, behold the prophetess began to do a dance across the front of the sanctuary. It wasn't the same shout we occasionally saw her do, this was a *dance of victory,* with a *skipping motion. (which is totally biblical)* As I watched her dance, the Lord allowed me to see and understand what was taking place in the spirit realm.

Psalms & the Dance. You see, we may not always know what God is doing at a particular time, but it is important to obey and yield to the spirit of God at the moment He speaks. If we obey His voice, we will see many more manifestations of God in our midst.

As Sister Williams continued to move in what looked like a light *leaping, dancing motion*. The dance was revealing that God had bought us the victory over what the whole church was battling through at that time. It was a time when it seemed like the enemy was attacking our health and finances specifically. God was letting us know that the victory over sickness and poverty were on its way. He spoke to us that Sunday just like He did the nation of Israel of old.

Don't say this can't be! Sure it can! Just look in the book of Exodus 15:20-21. Verse twenty says, *then* **Miriam the prophetess**, *Aaron's sister, took a tambourine in her hand, and all the women followed her, with tambourines and dancing.* Verse twenty-one says, *Miriam sang to them; sing unto the Lord, for he is highly exalted. The horse and it's rider he has hurled into the sea.* NIV.

Of course this spoke of the time when God delivered the children of Israel out of the hands of Pharaoh, and opened the Red Sea for them and swallowed up Pharaoh's army in the midst. Yes, after that victory, Mariam *the prophetess* just like Dorothy *the prophetess,* sang, danced and played the *tambourine* to commemorate the victory God gave them at the Red Sea.

Now Sister Dorothy didn't have a tambourine, but she does play a mean *scrub board.*

Victory over health and finances was our Red Sea crossing on that Sunday. *"Sister Williams you might want to pull that ole board out again."* We could use a few more Red Sea victories!!!

Can you understand the **power** of the **dance** in praise and worship? We must find ourselves moving away from the norm, or business as usual when it comes to the *true* worship of God.

God is trying to take our worship and praise to a whole new realm and sphere. There will be times when *prophetic dancing* will take place in our worship, and it will sound the alarm for **warfare** or **declare victory** in a battle that has already been, or about to be won. Don't frown upon it or laugh, without understanding what it is, and how it can actually benefit us in the midst. It's a vital part of praise and worship, and it's awesome to know that God can *speak* to us without *uttering* a single word. God uses whatever weapons are necessary to get the job done! **He's using *dance*, to call His people to worship.**

God uses music to call us to worship and even to battle. He used the horn of a wild ox (Deuteronomy 33:17), rams horns (Genesis 22:13), and *curved horns called SHOPARS* to call the Israelites together for religious occasions and signal them during battle. (2 Chron. 15:14)

He can do anything, or use anyone, anytime He chooses. All He needs is a humble willing, obedient and holy vessel to work through. It doesn't matter about your background or where you came from. It doesn't even matter what you've been into. He's God all by Himself and desires to use us to get the job done. He wants us to replace the *third* of worship and praise that departed heavens atmosphere when Lucifer wanted the praise and worship to be given to Himself.

So therefore, God created man for the purpose of worshipping and giving Him all praises due His name, because He's worthy of it. **He's Awesome!!** So sing your songs and do your dance! **But do it unto the Lord!!!**

CHAPTER 8

TO MIME OR NOT TO MIME

To **Mime or not to Mime. Mime,** *(mim) n.* **1. a.** *A form of ancient Greek and Roman drama in which realistic characters and situations were farcically portrayed and actual persons mimicked on the stage.* **b.** *A performance of, or dialogue for, such a comic drama.* **c.** *An actor in such a drama.* **2.** *A modern actor or comedian who specializes in comic mimicry; buffoon; clown.*

3. a. *The art of* **pantomime or the art of storytelling.** *(see)* **b.** *A performance of pantomime.* **c.** *An actor skilled in pantomime.* –v. **mimed, miming, mimes.** –tr. **1.** *To ridicule by imitation; mimic; ape.* **2.** *To portray in pantomime; act out in gesture and body movement.* –intr. *[Latin mimus, from Greek mimos, imitator. See* **mimos** *in dictionary Appendix. *]* -**mim'er n** . *The American Heritage Dictionary, of the English Language. (College Edition)*

Now that the dictionary has given its general description of the mime. I have somewhat more to say on this subject. I know you may be wondering why I didn't include this subject in the last chapter, *Psalms and Dance*. Let's dig deeper into the history of this art form for the answer.

I must admit, when I started writing about the mime in this chapter my total understanding of the art form, I understood to be the mime, was limited. But since I talked about the dance in the previous chapter, it seemed fitting to talk about the mime or pantomime as well. As I began to write about the mime in this book, I gave my understanding of it based on what I had read about it. I found in my studies that there was a man who was considered one of the greatest mimes ever, a man by the name of; Marcel Marceau. I read up on the history of this talented mime. I've also had the pleasure of being personal friends with some of the most anointed *dancers* I've ever seen. Therefore the mime I had witnessed in the past, was based on what I had read, and the mime ministry I had seen at our church.

Over the last few years we've had men and women in our church, who were anointed in the area of dance, but many times they ministered to us in *mime*. So as I completed "my version" of the *mime* or *mime ministry,* as I called it; and upon the completion, the Lord told me to research it more before I come to a final conclusion. God told me to search out the **origin** of it; **but pray first!!!**

We must realize that we are absolutely living in the last times. We have to understand that the enemy is not playing games with us. Understand that not to many people would follow the devil if he walked right up to them and said; *follow and worship me.* But the bible explains that he's going to *cause* many to worship him. Remember, the devil is not just a liar, he's a lie. Even if he tells you *truths*, it's only because his underlying motive is a lie. He doesn't tell you the truth; he tells you *truths* in order to set you up with a lie or some type of deception. Isn't that what he did to Eve? He told her some truths, but the ultimate purpose, was to lie and deceive her. He makes something look like **light,** but it's full of *darkness* and *death.*

As I began to pray and ask the Lord for guidance and understanding of what He was about to show me. He spoke to me again and told me to throw out everything that I had already written and He would show me what to do. Of course by now, my study and research mode had kicked in along with the revelation, and my excitement about what He was going to show me concerning the mime.

As I began to pray and ask God to show me what He wanted me to do; the Lord began to tell me that He wants His people to offer up to Him a **pure worship and praise.** Something that is totally *untouched, uncorrupted, uninfluenced or tainted* by the world; but holy and pure unto Him.

To Mime or not to Mime. The Lord told me that even though we're using our gifts and offering up our sacrifices of praise, we're doing it without a level of knowledge and understanding. In the 33rd division of Psalms, verse 3, the Word tells us to use our gifts, **skillfully.** As I began to study the word *skillful* even more, it took me to the word, **understanding.** In other words, God not only wants us to use our gifts skillfully, as in the *mechanics of the gift,* but the skill the bible mentions, also speaks to operating our gifts with *an understanding* as well. So skill speaks to understanding and understanding to knowledge. We are to operate in our gifts with all knowledge. Romans 10: 2, tells us that Israel had zeal for God, but not according to knowledge. What did that mean? Outwardly, they were extremely religious, but their efforts were not according to knowledge. They lacked a total understanding of the kind of worship God wanted and expected of them. Furthermore, they depended on their gifts alone, allowing self righteous ways to keep them from understanding what the will of the Lord was. God wants us to know what He is saying to us concerning our gifts and how He wants us to use them.

As I began to ask the Lord why He was taking me this way, He told me that He wants us to *know* and *understand* what *type* of **sacrifices** we're offering up to Him. **He said to make sure we know where the sacrifice came from.** Remember in the Old Testament, the sacrifices had to be *clean* and of a *pure* and *untainted* nature with no *spots* or *blemishes* in them. In other words, the

origin of the sacrifice had to be perfect. If the animal being sacrificed had a spot or was not of a pure breed without blemish, it could not be used. Even the priests couldn't have blemishes in their skin, and they could not have any missing parts, like fingers or toes.

God wanted the sacrifices and the priests making them, to be pure and untouched by anything **sinful** or of a **strange** sort. Take a look through the Old Testament and see how meticulous God was about the sacrifices that were to be offered up to Him. Do you remember in Leviticus 10:1, when Nadab and Abihu, the sons of Aaron took censers and put fire and incense in them and offered up to God what was considered to be, **strange fire?** Then there came a fire out from the Lord and smote them on the spot. Moses then spoke to Aaron afterwards saying, *This is it that the LORD spake, saying,* <u>*I will be sanctified in them that come nigh me, and before all the people I will be glorified.*</u> *vs. 3*. The sad part about this incident was the fact that those two men *knew* how the correct sacrifice was *supposed* to be offered up to God, but chose to rebel instead.

Some theologians say they may have been intoxicated with alcohol and committed various moral sins. The point being made here is the fact that Gods way is going to be the only way that works. We're bringing all types of *strange* things to God, and in the house of God, and calling it **worship. God calls it strange!** We better be careful people of God! We have to follow God's instructions to the letter, and not be influenced by today's pressure and contemporary way of doing things. Today we're so scared that we may hurt someone's feelings or that it's not politically correct! We better make sure it's God Jehovah correct! God always instructed Israel not to be like any other nation, but He wanted and commanded them to be a separated people. **Doesn't anyone want to be different anymore?** Is anyone still concerned about what God says about it, and not some Preacher, Teacher, Singer or Hollywood movie star? It's yet holiness or hell ya'll!! It's not a very popular message anymore, and it may not draw too many crowds, but it's what God is yet saying. He wants to be worshipped in spirit and truth. We have to get to the place where we want what God wants, and if we do that, we'll have what He has for us. There you go, there's your prosperity sermon. . . . . .Want what God wants!!!!

To Mime or not to Mime. The reason God told me that we need to be careful what we are offering up to Him is because, **there's something else coming on the scene**. He told me that the church was going to embrace this new thing. He said it's coming *in my name* but it's not of me. He also said that some would take this thing into the Houses of God and offer it up to me as worship, but its strange fire *(profane)* to me and I won't accept it. Not only that, but the hidden agenda of Satan would rest in its presentation. This supposedly new move of God would carry spirits of oppression, gloom and even death, both naturally and spiritually.

Finally God started to deal with me for a few weeks, concerning the, *origin* of things.

I remember our Pastors called for the married couples to meet for a marriage enrichment class. It was around the time of Valentines Day. As we all gathered together and began the session, our Pastor came out and began to ask the ladies what Valentines meant to them? Of course many of the ladies began to tell how wonderful their husbands made them feel. They began to talk about how their husbands gave them candy, flowers, dinner and how they were just happy to have a day when they could spend time together. Some said that it was a day that they showed their love and appreciation for each other. Now of course, that's all good stuff, but the fact is we're celebrating a day that had nothing to do with love, candy, flowers or dinner. As the couples completed their mushy words of love, our Pastor began to tell the people, how the Lord had been dealing with **him** concerning guess what? **The *origin of things!*** Where did all this stuff come from? Not only that, but we put so much pressure on one another to perform on all these holy or unholy holidays. If he can't buy it or she didn't receive it, we're depressed? Depression is of the devil. Death and the suicide rates are at their highest during the holidays. People are more depressed during Thanksgiving and Christmas than any other holidays in the year. Do you think Jesus Christ wanted that on the day we celebrate His birthday? *(that's another story)*

The world's system, commercialism, old tales and myths have taken away the original meaning of why we celebrate many holidays. On the other hand, there are things we celebrate that have absolutely nothing to do with the actual event. Remember, anything created, invented or introduced is considered the ***author*** and has the enduring ability to carry the spirit or characteristics of its originator. What should this tell us then? Well, it should tell us that we should be extremely careful and look into the things we allow into our lives, and into our spirits. We need to make sure we understand where it came from before we embrace it, seeing it has the ability to carry the spirit of its originator.

To further substantiate my point, and to the surprise of all the loving couples that were in the meeting that day, our Pastor went on to tell us how Valentines Day was actually about murder and the unpleasant events of a bloody massacre that happened in Chicago, back in 1929, on 2122 N. Clark St. in the time of Al Capone. The event is recognized as the, **St. Valentines Day Massacre**. And before that, you can travel back to the third century in the days of, St. Valentine or Valentinus who served as a Priest in Rome. The Catholic Church recognizes at least three different saints named, Valentine or Valentinus, all of whom were martyred. Read the history and the origin of St. Valentine and figure out why we're actually celebrating this day exactly? If we study the Word of God, it tells us exactly what we should do in the area of love.

To Mime or not to Mime. Ephesians 5:22, 25 tell us; wives, submit unto your own husbands and husbands, love your wives even as Christ also loved the church and gave himself for it. We as people of God should love everyday, for by this all men will know that we are His disciples, because of the love we show one to another. John 13:35 KJV. We should not be waiting for a specific day to show our love to one another, we do it 24/7/365. Let's move on!

One Saturday night while I was conducting an extensive research on the art of mime, God began to unveil revelation knowledge to me as I sat at my desk typing and looking up information on the internet. I remember it was around 12:15am and I was studying the origin of the mime, when all of a sudden my laptop just froze. Now this was a new laptop and I had never had a moments problem with it. As I began to type, it just stopped! When it stopped, I felt a cold presence pass by me and then it seemed to hover just behind me. The Lord allowed me to discern what it was. He told me it was an old demonic spirit that was trying to throw me off track. It didn't want me to look into the origin of what God told me to study.

The Lord immediately spoke to me and said; pray, I told you to pray! As I sat in front of the computer, I began to pray and rebuke the spirit that was in the room. I then got up off my seat and went to the front door, opened it and told that spirit to get out! After sensing that the spirit had departed, I walked back over to my computer and began to type. No restart or rebooting just sat down and began to type. I knew at that point that it had been the presence of a demonic spirit that had caused the laptop to malfunction. I asked God what the name of the spirit was, and he said to me; **fool.** It was an *ancient spirit* God called a *fool*.

As you can imagine, I'm more confused than ever. Here I am conducting a search and in-depth study on the history and origin of the mime, and Gods talking to me about a spirit called a fool. Let me digress by saying that at this point, I had no idea or opinion on the matter of the mime. All I knew is what I stated to you earlier in this chapter. This was all God, believe me folks! My little finite mind could have **never** come up with this here!

Before we dive into this, let me start by saying that I understand that what I'm about to say will most likely be shocking, controversial and even rejected. I can only go by what God showed me. Now what I've found to be true is, many who seek out a spotlight in ministry, usually don't find one. And those who are not looking to be seen are the one's God usually chooses.

The bible says not many noble are chosen, and I feel I'm the least of them, but God is everything in me, and I can do all things *through* him.

Understand that this book or manual God told me to write, deals with, **order.** This is a book to the Levites of today, to remind us that the Levites back in the bible were commanded to be **separated, sanctified** and **set apart.** The same is true today of the people of the Most High God. Just as God spoke to Moses, David, and many of the prophets and kings, that they were not to be like other nations. He's saying it to the Levites of today. They had to listen, learn and understand the commandments of God. They had to know the laws and remember them or they could be struck down right on the spot. They were not to **mimic** any *cultures* from any of the surrounding nations and offer those pagan practices up to God as a holy sacrifice. Therefore I'm sure they had to study, and pay attention to the things they offered up to God. They didn't just grab the closest thing to them and say, this was good enough. They understood God's order. That's all God is asking of us today, is to follow HIS order. . . . . . .Would you agree?

To Mime or not to Mime. I am fully aware of the fact that the mime or pantomime is an age old art form that has been used in the church, and is now on a major up rise in many of our ministries today. Yes, God has the power to use **anything** He wants to use for His glory; **but He doesn't!** If you study the Word of God, you'll find that there were instruments, David could have used in the tabernacle for worship, but God did not want him to. God did allow David to take some of the instruments from Gath, (*Goliath's home)* because it represented victory over their enemies. When King David began to set up music as part of worship in the sanctuary, he could have bought in many of the professional musicians from Assyria and Egypt to play, but God didn't want him to. You may say, what's wrong with ungodly things being used to make a godly point? God will use examples of ungodly things or He may turn a bad or ungodly situation into a good one for His glory. But to say that God will allow or accept anything ***foul*** or ***unholy*** as an object of *true worship* is insane. We might accept it because it's something we're used to doing or something that everyone else is doing, and it seems as if nobody today wants to be different. Who wants to stand up and be contrary to what everybody else is doing anyway?

The church has taken on an; *if you can't beat'em, join'em* attitude. At some point, someone is going to have to stand up and say; *this is what we're doing, but it's not what God wants.*

In the Old Testament, God *(winked)* His eye, or allowed some things to take place because he had not yet *revealed* the total **knowledge** of it until Christ came on the scene. And because your gifts that come from above are so awesome, He allows His anointing to rest on your efforts, because your heart was right towards what you were doing. But **now**, God is beginning to shed a *negative light* on many of the things we're doing or calling ok. He's saying, it's not ok! Even the Apostle Paul before he receive understanding; thought he was correct until the light of the Lord shined and revealed truth to him. Now, God is revealing His will and power to us in a greater way, because of the increased evil day, in which we now live. We are becoming more and more responsible for the things we hear. Once you've come into the revelation knowledge of what God is now requiring, we are commanded to walk therein.

"To be or not to be, that is the question!" *3.1.64-98.* This phrase in its original text came from Shakespeare's "Hamlet." This dialog is the writings of Shakespeare's *Hamlet's Soliloquies. (Part 1)* In general terms, this statement is a question of whether it is better to stay *(live)* in this present life with all its troubles, oppositions, snares and toils and going through the long journey of life with the risk and chance of never being acquainted with any of its happiness and pleasures; or is it better to leave this life *(death)* in search for an eternal happiness, not actually knowing what fate awaits you on the other side of this life? The reason I named this chapter, **To Mime or Not to Mime,** is because like Hamlet's view; we must decide in our walk with God, whether it is better to live this life obeying God, with the chance of not having or achieving some of the things we wish to do in this life, because it's not pleasing to God, or is it better to go on through this life doing things the way we want to do them, and risk the chance of missing out with God because we're not living holy and according to his word? Is it better to continue to do what is right in our own eyes, being assured of eternal death, or is it better to be without what we call *pleasures* for a short season, but gaining eternal life? Why am I saying this? Because we as a people of God, seem to get caught up *so easily* in the ways of the world, and in sins that so easily beset us, without investigating the *spiritual consequences* of what we're doing.

To Mime or not to Mime. The bible teaches us in Luke 16:8 that, *the children of the world of their generations are wiser than the children of light.* Why is that? Well, one reason is they investigate before they jump in head first. Many times as Christians, as soon as something new comes out, we want it, we have to have it, we have to do it, or we must buy it now! We buy the car because it looks ok on the outside but we fail to check out what's under the hood. The Word of God tells us to acknowledge Him in *all* of our ways, and He'll direct our paths.

I know this subject will probably get a lot of feedback, but the fact is, I didn't have any idea what God was about to show me. He told me to let the body of Christ know and understand what He is saying. It's all about what He wants and desires and what pleases Him.

As I mentioned earlier, God had been dealing with me concerning the **origin of things.** I began to study the *mime*, and **exactly** what this art form was. What do you really know about this supposedly theatrical art form that is now considered a ministry in our houses of worship?

Can you tell me where it came from or where it started? Can you really? I must admit that when I saw it performed by some of our young ministers, I always felt a little strange, but couldn't explain why. I didn't want to seem as if I was being narrow minded about the different ways God can use us in the area of worship. I'm as open to *creativity or demonstration* in ministry as the next person, because that's how God uses me in ministry. But no matter how different or creative it is; it must be something that God desires or something that is pleasing in His eye. It must be according to the Word of God.

I began this 3 month journey studying the mime, and what I found out was; there were many different *types* and *stages* of the mime. This art was not the white face non-vocal expression we know it to be in the western world today, no, it was much, much more than that. Basically what I'm going to tell you is actually a brief journey from where it started to where and what it is today.

Prayerfully you've picked it up by now, that all we're trying to accomplish in this book is the fact that we must worship God according to the **order** He instituted and set in place. From the laws He gave to Moses, to the structure of David and his Levites, to the way we are to worship God today. Yes times have changed, but God hasn't, and we have to do things according to the order and pattern God set in place from the beginning.

Once again, here are some of the ***descriptions of mime*** and their ***associations*** that are relative to what I'm about to establish. *1.* **to mimic or copy**. *2. to poke fun with ludicrous actions or gestures. 3. Imagery- to imagine or to make seem as if, but is not. 4. sword swallowers, clowns, jugglers, acrobats, singers, dancers and magicians.* Key Description: *5. jesters, magicians and **fools**.* First of all I was astonished at the descriptions I found. I had to look in many places and research centuries of the evolution of the mime to get the information. Not to mention the revelation knowledge God began to reveal to me as I did my research.

There's a book by Annette Lust called; *"The Origins and Development of the Mime."* It covers the history and the *art* of the mime.

In PRIMIVITE TIMES, mime is considered one of the earliest mediums of *self-expression*. Remember that terminology, self expression because it's going to be a key factor in this subject.

To Mime or not to Mime. Before there was spoken language; mime used to communicate what the primitive people needed or wanted. Instead of fading into obscurity when the spoken language was developed, mime had become a form of entertainment. It then developed into a theatrical form in ancient Greece, where performers enacted everyday scenes with the help of elaborate gestures. I began to find out that there were many types of mime in its evolution.

The principle mimes were known as *ethologues,* and the scenes they would perform would teach goodly moral lessons. *(in it's early years)*

ANCIENT GREEKS AND ROMANS: This is where it is said it all began; in the **Theater of Dionysus** in Athens. *(in honor of the Greek god," Dionysus" the god of intoxication)*

The mime may be tracked back to the sixth century B.C. in Greece, but the earliest record of its appearance in Rome is 212 B.C. *(Br "History" 97)*. Early mimes in Greece were called *phlyakes*. Phlyakes or phallic scenes were short, improvised, and based on mythological burlesque or daily life. *Lovemaking, gluttony, beatings, thievery, trickery or magic* were popular motifs. Masked actors performed outdoors, in daylight, before audiences of 10,000 or more at festivals in honor of Dionysus, also known as, *the god of theater.* If you've studied Greek Mythology, then you will understand that the Greeks had a god for just about everything.

The most elaborate form of mime, known as *hypthesis,* may have approached the level of true drama. This form would be performed by companies of actors, who would often concentrate more on the development of their characters, than the plot itself.

The *comedy* and *tragedy* styles developed in Athens, and flourished in the fifth and fourth centuries B.C. have influenced nearly all subsequent Western drama, starting with that of the Romans. When Rome conquered Greece, they bought the art of mime back home to Italy and set about to make it their own. This is key because, the Romans had a love for *spectacle* and *foolishness*. If you study the time when Christ was crucified, the Roman soldiers spent hours mocking and poking fun at Jesus, while scourging and beating him.

The Romans then took over the Greek theaters and began renovating and rebuilding them for their own spectacles, which included everything from, *pantomime to mocking and jesting*. The remains of the theater Dionysus which can still be seen in Athens today date back to Roman times and not the fifth century BC. The Mime was very successful and experienced growth under Emperor Augustus of Rome. What you have to understand now is that after the fall of the Roman Empire, the **Christian church** showed great opposition to the lewd and often indecent associations of mime, and **excommunicated** all performers, and closed down all the theaters. But despite the fall, the basic form of mime survived as the Catholic Church began to relax its position and attitudes toward it. Mystery and morality plays began to appear with religious themes, many of these plays were performed in mime. Yet many of the Catholic and Christian Churches did not approve of its actors and entertainers with their indecent behaviors and obscene language. When Rome fell, mimes performed at parties and banquets and *courts* all over Europe. The first known mime was a man by the name of Livius Andronicus, who lost his voice during a performance and had to use silent gestures. His original performances did have *voice*.

To Mime or not to Mime. Roman mime and pantomime were performed at the festival, *ludi Florales* that honored fertility goddesses. Naked mime actresses would perform at that festival. Mime was a word used to describe almost any kind of entertainment. Although associated with short dramas, mime could be comical as well. Dirty jokes and sexual subject matter was a *norm* and their actors seem to have been selected either for their physical beauty or comic ugliness, for the plots most typically revolved around sexual desirability or some grotesquerie.

Roman mime was called, *fibula riciniata,* was a mix of silent sketches, dancers and singers.

Roman mime or *fibula riciniatas* included women and commoners but *never nobility.*

They traveled in packs called *troupes* and they wore **tunics** and *ricinium.* (*hoods*)

There were no cultivated audiences; the cruder it was, the more the audience liked it. That was the Romans normal method of operation. Roman performers were called, *mimus or saltator*. Many of them were famous much like the movie stars we have in Hollywood today.

Mimes that mimicked the dead were called the *archimimus or archimima* for females. *Archimimus or Archimimas* would be hired by families who just lost a loved one and the mime would impersonate their dead relative at the funeral rites. The mime would be dressed in the dead person's clothes and he or she would then imitate brief incidents in the deceased person's life. The undertaker's employees would walk in the funeral processions, dressed in black, and mimic the grieving. This happened in Rome and in Greece.

PANTOMIMES: Now Pantomime was more subtle and complex than mime, which was more obvious and exaggerated. Roman pantomime called *fibula saltica,* was a silent interpretive dance performed by only one actor who played many roles. They wore *masks* with closed mouths on them. The Greeks would use two or more dancers, with the chorus narrating the story, which was usually taken from mythology. The orchestra would accompany them performing on flutes, pipes and cymbals. Roman pantomime was similar to modern day ballet. Pantomime was more popular with the *ruling* class of Rome.

There were public performers as well as private troupes. Unlike mimes, it was *pantomimes* who originally wore masks, but their masks had closed mouths. They wore long tunics (*loose garments*) and cloaks that gave them the freedom to move. It wasn't until late Roman times that mime became completely silent like the mime we are familiar with today.

So as you can see in the history of the mime, they were not all silent performers who danced using gestures. They were also comics, dancers, actors and singers.

As I continued to comb through their history, I found that the Roman mime characters were also called **fools.** Then I discovered that the Christians refused mimes, the *communion,* and *holy sacraments* of the Church. I thought the rejection came from the Catholic Church of that day, but it wasn't just the Catholic Church alone, the Christian Churches denounced them as well, excluding them from the Christian community. Mimes were considered *obscene servants of the devil.*

I had to research this history extensively, because I hadn't studied or found much information in the bible, at least I thought I hadn't.

To Mime or not to Mime. I told myself, this couldn't have just been the Catholic's because after the mimes were dis-fellowshipped from the Church, they retaliated by presenting caricatures or cartoons of self-righteous clergy, and Pentecostal emersion style baptisms in their performances. This is where it all started to get a little strange to me. I asked the Lord for more understanding of what was taking place here. It seemed like the Holy Spirit was now taking control of my studies as the information kept coming, and God began to give me divine understanding of what was going on there in Rome. Mimes began to publically *ridicule* the Church's sacraments and beliefs. They would *mimic* and *poke fun* at or make a *mockery* of the Holy rituals of the Church. Again, it had to be the Christian Church as well, because the banished mimes would put on plays that mimicked baptism **in water.** In one illustration they displayed a dying man who was panicked about his salvation, so they baptized him dunking him in water, (*not sprinkling him*) so that he could receive his salvation. But some vulgar humor was added in the fact that they dunked him head first with his naked *buttocks* showing and displaying him having a *phallus*, as if to say you must be some type of *butt* if you receive the Christians way of salvation!

They would make mockery of many of the sacred ceremonies of the Church and thus became vagabonds on the streets, dancing for whoever would watch them. Of course all the mime practices were disapproved by the Church, so they were excommunicated.

Actors were forbidden the sacraments of the church, and between the sixth and tenth centuries, religious authorities issued frequent injunctions both against presenting and attending theatrical performers, thus the relationship between the mimes and the Church became one of hostility.

As I continued my study and search on the history of the Mime, to my amazement, I kept running across the word **jester**. I began to ask the Lord, why was this word showing up while studying the mime? God told me to keep studying and He would make it clear as I go along. As I did so, I remember mentioning before, that when the Romans took over the art form of mime, they changed it in a sense. It became more *lude, rude* and *vulgar* with a lot of *foolish antics*.

I remembered that the Roman mime characters were also called **fools**.

So here I am studying the history of the mime, and I keep running into the words, *jester* and *fool*. As my mind started to race, I began to deny that fact that some of the things I was thinking were actually so. Could it be a relation between the **mime, jester and fool?** There had to be some kind of connection between these three characters, is what I thought in the back of my mind, but I didn't have all the pieces yet. Then I found out that in *medieval times,* the court jesters and the fools were one in the same individuals. Jesting was the *art of clowning* which had existed for thousands of years prior. There were many *pygmy* clowns that performed in front of the **Pharaohs of Egypt.** *(remember that!)*

Now I'm going to skim through this, but you can also study the history of all these characters. You'll find they're not what or who you thought they were. Most court jesters were summoned to lift the monarch out of an angry or melancholic mood. Jesters used laughter as the medicine for many Kings and Noble personalities. Jesters could have more political roles as well. They could speak dangerous truths and disguised it as a joke or even criticized rulers in subtle ways. Many legends and anecdotes portray jesters or fools as informal, cunning advisors.

To Mime or not to Mime. The expression "fools license" is said to come from this medieval custom. All jesters and fools in those days were thought of as special basket cases whom God himself had touched with a childlike madness and mentality—a gift, or perhaps a curse. Mentally handicapped people many times found employment by capering and behaving in an amusing way. Many of the jesters were dwarfs who back in those days were considered cursed human beings by God. So mocking the churches sacraments was their way of getting back at them for not allowing the mimes to take part in their religious ceremonies.

Now after much studying, the Lord began to speak to me these words; *fool hath said in his heart there is no God.* But I still didn't pay it any attention. I had made the connection between the jester and the fool, but I didn't understand how I got there studying the mime. As I went back over the information of my studies, I found that Roman pantomime, *fibula saltica* was a silent interpretive dance performed only by one actor who played many roles on stage. One of the other roles the mime played was, *jester or fool.* Then as I went back over some of the descriptions of mime, one of the descriptions was; *a jester, clown or fool.* So could it be that these characters were *one in the same*, or did they just hang out together, which was it?

As I continued to study, I found that all of these characters were extremely *irreverent and disrespectful* when it came to Christians. In some cases the mimes had to go as far as **hiding their identity** because the church showed such opposition to the point that vigilantes who sided with the church began to take it upon themselves to do them harm. So many of them traveled in groups and *migrated* into other parts of Italy and even France because of the danger.

Now here's where it all began to come together for me. I started putting all the pieces together.

The mime began to reach its height in sixteenth century Italy, in the art form of, **Commedia dell' Art.** Commedia dell' Art originated in the market places of the Italian streets in the early 1500's. Street performers began donning masks with exaggerated *comical features* to draw attention to themselves and to complement their acrobatic skills. The *features* much of the time consisted of oversized breasts or buttocks. This form of Commedia dell' Art became popular because it was a *do whatever you want, however you want to do it* type of self or individual comical expression. Now of course this drew attention to the art of jesting, thus the jesters and the fools joined this art form. By the 1500's, court jesting was already big in Italy and France.

There were traveling groups of *jesters* throughout Italy and mainly France who performed plays featuring stylized characters. These characters were also called, **Commedia dell' Art.**

Another version of this art moved on into *British folk tradition* in the form of a *puppet show* called, Punch and Judy. *(remember them?)*

In France the tradition of the court jester ended with the French Revolution. Divers dignities used the services of the court jesters such as, Elizabeth I and James I of England, from William Shakespeare to King James and Charles I.

By now you've gathered that the *mimes, fools and jesters* are all one in the same or part of the same group of people. *(birds of a feather etc.)* The characters the mime created became known as **Zanni.** But it wasn't until two Zanni performers teamed up with the Commedia dell' Art that it really took root, and by 1550 it had become a firmly established genre. It was a more *freestyle* or *improvisation* type of art form which was geared more toward the serving class of people.

To Mime or not to Mime. To make it clearer to you, Zanni was a *comical style* of antics that the jesters and mimes used back in that time. The joking and jesting Zanni style became so popular, that performers from other countries began to imitate their style.

Now by this time other styles and forms of mime began to rise, and after the Second World War there arose those of the likes of Marcel Marceau who attempted to change the format of mime to what we know as mime today. But there was still an underlying *crude form* of mime and jesting that still existed, and in that vein was where the Lord wanted me to hone in on. One of the problems is there was never a separating distinction between the divers mime art forms.

There was yet something hiding itself in the midst of the mysterious world of mime, and the *theatrical* component of it was not where the Lord was directing me. God insisted that there was more for me to look into and through my diligence and persistence; He would begin to reveal it to me.

As I continued on my journey, I must say, the whole thing began to get more stranger to say the least. My excursion took me all the way back to Africa to a place called, **Egypt.** Once again I heard the Lord say to me; <u>fool hath said in his heart, there is no God</u>. At this point I felt like Peter when Jesus kept asking did he love him? So after the third time of hearing this, I went to the scriptures to look it up.

I found that Psalms 14:1 and 53:1 were two passages of scripture that spoke of man's guilt before God, and how all have sinned and come short of His glory. These verses also explain the fate of one who **does not** believe in God, or live their lives as if there is one.

There are those who live there lives by there own standards and laws and have decided within themselves what is right and wrong, good or evil, not understanding that one who <u>rejects wise counsel lacks wisdom</u>, and is considered a fool according to scripture. (see Prov. 26:12)

So at this point, God instructed me to study the events that took place in the book of Exodus, when He spoke to Moses and Aaron to go before Pharaoh, requesting that the Children of Israel be let go from their bondage. (Ex. 7: 8-13)

God instructed Aaron to cast down his *rod* in the presence of Pharaoh, and when he did this, it became a serpent upon the ground. I guess we could say if the average man would have seen this, he might have been convinced to let the people of Israel go. But Egypt was a nation who *worshipped **its own** gods,* and was fully addicted to **comic folly, magic, dancing, occultism, spiritism** and **sorcery** as part of their religion and culture. Therefore Pharaoh was diminutively impressed at the fact that Aaron's rod turned into a serpent. They actually became amused.

Notice some of the words I used to describe the **Egyptian addictions and traditions;** *comic folly, magic, dancing* and *sorcery,* which by the way are some of the *descriptions that defined the mime* in its original form as I stated at the beginning of this chapter.

All of a sudden. . . . .something clicked, and the Holy Ghost quickened me. It was like I saw it all; I could just see it just the way God wanted me to see it! *(this is what the Lord showed me)*

When Moses and Aaron approached Pharaoh in his courts, Aaron cast down his rod and immediately his rod turned into a serpent. But Pharaoh and his entourage were standing around *jesting and joking, poking fun* at the sight of the serpent squirming around on the ground.

As I stated earlier, this event wasn't some *strange antics* to the Egyptians at all, because they were already into magic, sorcery and witchcraft. They began to mock Moses and Aaron.

To Mime or not to Mime. As if to say that by some *magic,* Moses and Aaron were informed that their god was God!

There were also standing with Pharaoh, **the fools!** *(heard this name before?)* The fools were standing around the courts *with their own rods,* saying in their hearts; <u>there is no other god like our gods.</u> I understand now why God used Psalms chapters 14 and 53, to get my attention.

The magicians and court jesters *(which were fools)* were standing around the courts of Pharaoh saying, there was no God of Israel. How can Israel's god be God, when ours is god? But then the rod of Aaron which turned into a serpent and swallowed up the other serpents, signifying that there was **only one God** and his name is **I AM!**

Now Pharaoh himself was a man proclaiming to be a god, with his men standing in front of Moses and Aaron *chanting* in front of them, *circling around* them and *dancing* saying, *there is no god in Israel like the gods of Egypt, even Pharaoh.* As the magicians and sorcerers began dancing and jesting in the court, they cast their rods upon the ground, and they too became serpents. We know that the rod/serpent of Aaron swallowed up the serpents of the Egyptians, which signified that God's power was greater than any god in Egypt. **But our concentration should be on *whom those characters were* that danced around and accompanied Pharaoh in his court?** Well. . . .they were fools, jesters, magicians, sorcerers and mimes, *(yes I said mimes)* who danced and *mimicked* in the courts of Pharaoh. These are the self same *ancient spirits* which had now made their way to the sixth century in a different form in Greece, worshipping the Greek gods, mocking, poking fun and disrespecting the sacraments of the Christian Church. God told me they were **all the same characters, operating by the same spirit.**

The mimes that were with Pharaoh, were also there in sixth century Greece. . . . . .

Now I understand that many of you at this point may be thinking, this is crazy and can't be true. Yep! I thought the same thing until I did the research in *biblical history*, and referenced the times in *world history* that placed these characters in the same place at the same time. As I began to cross reference times and dates, I found that the mimes, *(which can be tracked back to ancient Greece, with the worship of Greek gods)* started long before that of Greece and Rome. They were also traced back and found in the courts of the Pharaohs of Egypt.

Why am I uncovering this? Because God told me to let you know that we need to pay more attention to the *origins*, before we bring it into His house, calling it worship. Be aware of what we offer up first! But wait! If that's not enough proof; the Lord persuaded me to continue this mime journey. Let's take a quick look again at the names I came across during this search. First; *mime, jester, and fools.* There were some who asked me, where I gathered this information from, since most studies show that the mime originated back in ancient Greece around the 5th and 6th centuries? Well that particular *form* of mime yes, but as I mentioned earlier in this chapter, the mime went through many stages and forms over the ages. But remember, **the origin** is what God wanted revealed, and that's what we're concentrating on now.

I studied the **art of clowning and jesting** and by the time the Romans took over the art form, the *clowns, mime, jester* and *fools* were all understood to be one group of individuals. If you study the <u>art of clowning</u> and <u>jesting</u>, it will take you all the way back to 2500 B.C. in the court of Pharaoh Dadkeri-Assi during Egypt's Fifth Dynasty. There were pygmy performers in his courts that were also *jesters, clowns, mimes and fools.* Performers have been in China since 1818 B.C.

So the art has been around for thousands of years and carries ancient old spirits along with it.

To Mime or not to Mime. I understand fully that laughter is considered good medicine, but it really depends on what we're laughing about. Back in the early days, these groups or *troops* of performers mimicked and made mockery of the sacred and holy things the Lord set up as worship. It's no laughing matter when you make a joke or even use comedy to describe things that are sacred and holy, it's serious. I'm not being too deep, I'm trying to show you how the enemy can take something that seems to be as simple as using jokes to take away the sensitivity of the things the Lord told us to remember as being holy. The awful death on the cross was no joking matter, even though the Roman soldiers thought so.

Taking communion to commemorate His dying isn't funny, casting out devils, and demonic oppression is no laughing matter.

You see, by us allowing jokes, foolish talking and jesting concerning the holy things of the church, we give the devil the opportunity he's been waiting for by **making all things common.**

Pay attention people of God, the enemy is trying to accomplish this in a very subtle way, especially in our music. Comedy was a tool the *rejected mimes* used to poke fun at the Church, making it seem as if the things that are holy, precious and dear, are dung, ignorant or ridiculous.

Don't misunderstand me, I absolutely love to laugh but just like anything else, it has its place. Even the Apostle Paul stated in Ephesians 5:3-7, *³ But fornication, and all uncleanness, or covetousness, let it not be once named among you, as becometh saints; ⁴ Neither filthiness, nor **foolish talking, nor jesting**, which are **not convenient**: but rather giving of thanks. ⁵ For this ye know, that no whoremonger, nor unclean person, nor covetous man, who is an idolater, hath any inheritance in the kingdom of Christ and of God. ⁶ Let no man deceive you with vain words: for because of these things cometh the wrath of God upon the children of disobedience. ⁷ Be not ye therefore partakers with them.* KJV In no way is Paul suggesting that we are not to have fun or be of a joyous nature. We as people of God should be joyous and happy and full of life. But laughter does not mean you have joy. Joy is a spiritual benefit that comes from an obedient lifestyle towards Christ. If it takes entertainment and folly to bring you happiness, then you won't ever experience a real lifestyle of joy that can only come from a true relationship with Jesus Christ.

When Paul speaks of *foolish talking;* it speaks to obscene and lewd discourse, or more generally, such vain discourse as betrays much folly and indiscretion, and is far from *edifying* the hearer. He also speaks of *jesting*, from the Greek word *eutrapelia*, usually described as an abusive **reflection or mocking** that tends to expose others and to make them **appear ridiculous**. *(which by the way is another description of the **mime**)*

The word also carries a hint of mischief in it that is so far from being profitable, it can pollute and poison the listener. It is very unsuitable to our profession and character in Christ. We are to be *cheerful* and *pleasant*; but must be *merry* and *wise* in our choice of jesting. Finally, the apostle adds in verse 4 that we should rather give thanks to God in song and praises to Him which brings us true joy. This is much more profitable to us. For the joy of the Lord is our strength.

NOTE:
I feel the need to digress for moment concerning the *jesting*, as not to leave anyone asking questions or misunderstanding what the Lord instructed me to point out concerning this.

To Mime or not to Mime. Once again, after my review of the words mime, jester and fool; the next word I arrived at in this examination of the mime, was a word called, **Tarot.** It's about to get a little thick from here. Have you heard of this word before? Some of you have if you've ever had your palm read, which by the way is something we as Christians are **not to do!!**

Anyway, once again I began to wonder why I kept running into these strange words while studying the mime. God again says move on! At first sight of this word, it didn't click until I continued. Then it dawned on me that this study of the mime had taken me to the word **Tarot.** Tarot took me to the use of *tarot cards*, which leads you into the areas of *divination, palm reading, horoscopes, chanting, channeling, sorcery, astrology, witchcraft* and other demonic activity. There are **Bold Italicized** words that I'm going to use that you may not know the meaning of, but these words can be **studied and researched**. I wouldn't have time in this book to cover all of this, because there's so much. Therefore I'm going to only point out the issues God intended for me to point out. I will say that if you study some of these words, I advise you to pray first, to see what areas to research and what to *leave alone*. No, we're not afraid of the devil, but if you're not <u>really living</u> a saved, Holy Ghost filled and delivered life, I'd advise you to leave it alone! I've encountered much demonic resistance because of the information I'm releasing and revealing to the body of Christ. When you understand what we're allowing to enter and all it's doing in our spirits, and in our churches today, no wonder God is warning us! We see things as ok or say, *I don't see anything wrong with it.* That's what Satan is depending on, you *not seeing!* He's not forcing men, he's *causing* men to worship him, *cause* we can't see! We are living in the last days and more evil is coming upon the earth. We've got to know without a shadow of a doubt that it's of God before we taste it, handle it, preach it, teach it, sing it, or decide there's nothing wrong with it, and proceed in presenting it to God.

As I began to study this word, I found that there were different types of *tarot cards* that were used for various purposes of life. Each card had a *picture* on the back that represented different situations people went through. But the cards actually had demonic spirits assigned, attached to and controlling them. *(I'll cover that in a moment)*

Here are a few cards in the divers Tarot decks. *"The Fool"* (a card of what is called the **<u>Major Arcana or Ar-ca-num,</u>** also known as the *"fool's journey"*). See dictionary; Arcanum or Alchemist;> *1. a secret; mystery 2. a supposed great secret of nature that alchemists sought to discover 3. a secret and powerful remedy.* This also speaks to; sorcerers, wizards, augurers, charmers, necromancers, occultists, seers, soothsayers, diviners, enchanters, fortune tellers, magicians and mediums. . .etc.

Card 0, in the **<u>Rider-Waite</u>** numbering system, card 22 in Belgian decks, and *(sometimes unnumbered)*, represents; <u>"the Spirit, God,"</u> (notice, not the spirit of God) the <u>Monad</u>, the <u>Lord of the Universe</u>, the <u>Absolute Being</u>. **Other**

permutations (*numberings*) **include:** Eternity, Life Power, Originating Creative Power, the Will of God, the Essence or Essential Self, Tao, Aether, Prana, Akasha, the Void, the White Brilliance, the Radiant Field of God, Omni revelation, the Universal Light, Boundless Space, Super consciousness, the *Inner Ruler*, the Plenitude, the Unman fest, the Ancient of Days (repeated in manifest form within **Key 9 the Hermit**), Mysterium Magnum, the Sun at a 45 degree angle in the Eastern Heaven-always increasing, never decreasing.

Now in initially reading this you would think this is speaking of Jehovah God of heaven, but it's not. It's not speaking of the God of the Bible or His power and authority at all.

To Mime or not to Mime. Two key words that tipped me off in this *"god"* description were the words, **Self** and **Inner Ruler**. It promotes that you are in control of your own destiny and fate. This description of what seems like the God we know to be I AM, actually speaks to the characters on the back of the tarot cards. One of the major spirits on the loose today is the one that's convincing people that they are their own gods or are only dependent on one's inner self. I continued on in disbelief and began to question the Lord again by asking Him was this for real or not? But the Lord assured me that, what He had me studying was exactly as it was appearing and unfolding to be. So in obedience to His word, I continued on in the most stunning study and research I've ever done in all my years.

The tarot description of the ***fool*** includes a man; *(or less often, a woman)* now remember back in the origin of the fools, jesters and mimes, it started mainly with men, and not women.

On the back of the ***fool's tarot card***, it shows a man *juggling* unconcernedly, with a *dog (sometimes a cat)* at his heels. The fool image on the back of the tarot card represents a number of human conditions: innocence, ignorance, **heterodoxy**, freedom, great cheer, freedom from earthly desires, passions, or responsibility but also perversity, audacity, truth, confidence, or cultural power. The root of the word "fool" is from the Latin word *follies,* which means "*bag of wind,*" or that which contains *air* or *breath.* I know you're wondering where all of this is going! It's describing the demonic and blasphemous structure, imagery, history and origin of the tarot decks, which are used for spiritual, esoteric, psychological, occult and/or divinatory purposes. Understand that a fool is someone who despises wise counsel, one who isn't concerned about anything, just running around acting as if he doesn't care about anything. He's in total disregard for feelings or cares of others. He can not keep himself and isn't one who can be trusted. This is a spirit that plagues many people, especially men. Void of understanding and not wanting it either. No cares or feeling of responsibility for himself or others. Doesn't that sound like some of our absentee fathers of today? It is a spirit that is attacking our young men in this society.

For other descriptions of the various cards, study: *Tarot Games and Tarot Disambiguation.* For information about the traditional European card games that were used to control people and situations. See how and what they were used for in those days and even now.

Bear with me in all of these detailed descriptions, because it's going to be important to where we go later. We need to know how some of this stuff operates in order to understand what it is, and the effects it will have if we allow it into our lives. We think its one thing and Satan's coming a whole different way. Just like an army, we want to know the characteristics of the enemy before we attack. Believe me; the devil has checked you out to see what you're about and how he can get to you. So it is with us; we must be ready and equipped with knowledge and understanding in how to combat the enemy. For the weapons of our warfare are not carnal, but mighty through God, to the pulling down of strongholds. For we are fighting against principalities and powers and spiritual wickedness in high places, and demonic forces in the atmosphere.

In the study of the tarot cards, there is usually a deck of 78 cards composed of:

The *major arcana,* consisting of 21 trump cards and the *Fool* card. The *minor arcana,* consisting of 56 cards. Ten cards numbered from Ace to 10 in four different suits; traditionally batons *(wands)*, cups, swords and coins *(pentacles)* (40 cards in total). Four court cards, page, knight, queen and king in the same four suits (4 per suit, thus 16 court cards in total).

To Mime or not to Mime. The earliest extant specimens of Tarot decks are of North Italian origin and date early to mid-15th century. These were called **carte da trionfi** or *cards of the triumphs*. Soon afterwards, the cards were used for the games called, **Tarocchi.** In the 18th and 19th centuries, the cards became popular in *occult* studies, initiated by occultists such as **Etteilla** and **Antoine Court de Gebelin.**

There are many types and variations of tarot cards that would take up too much of time to go through the various names of the tarot card decks. I'll just give you a little surface information to set up where I'm going with all of this.

Using tarot cards was sometimes considered a game, i.e. playing with a deck of playing cards in today's time. There were even different families who had tarot cards made for themselves specifically. One of the oldest surviving tarot card decks are three early to mid-15th century sets, all made for members of the **Visconti family, rulers** of Milan. The oldest of these existing tarot decks were perhaps painted to celebrate a mid 15th century wedding joining the Visconti and Sforza families of Milan. Thus a tarot deck was made and named the **Visconti and Sforza** deck, after the two families. Now it makes me wonder what all this was about. Why were these various decks composed? They were composed based on what people believed or what they were into at that time. So that could mean if someone were into devil worship or witchcraft, then cards would be fashioned in order to represent what that individual believed in. Almost like the use of voo doo dolls.

Now if you were to ask people who use them, of course they're not going to tell you this, but judging by the pattern of how and why these cards were used, my assumption would be correct. Again, the Visconti/Sforza deck, consisted of 78 cards. Of the original cards, 35 are in the **Pierpont Morgan Library**, 26 cards are at the **Accademia Carrara**, 13 are at the **Casa Colleoni** and 4 cards *(the Devil, the Tower of Babel, the Tree of Swords, and the Knight of Coins)* some say were lost, stolen or possibly never made. The earliest known decks known as **Michelino** named after a painter, was produced back in the 1400's and is now lost.

This deck was made to show a Greek god system or ideological idea in that time. So therefore many decks were made in light of special events or occasions. Painters would then be asked to paint the design that would represent the occasion on the back of the tarot card. Back in early tarot history, the tarot cards were known to be used for everything from playing tricks, card games, gambling, and decision making, to *Greek god worship*, which again was a description in the **origination of the mime.**

After going through years and different stages, the cards fell into the interest of the **Egyptians**, which soon inspired occultism.

The tarot cards eventually came to be associated with *mysticism, divination, fortune telling* and *magic*. The tarot was not widely adopted by mystics, occultists and secret societies until the 18th and 19th century. This new tradition and era of the card began when **Antoine Court de Gebelin**, a Swiss *clergyman* and **freemason**, published Le Monde Primitif, a speculative study which included religious symbolism and its survivals in the modern world. De Gebelin first asserted that the symbolism of the **Tarot de Marseille;** *(which was another deck)* represented the mysteries of **Isis** and **Thoth.** *(maybe we'll talk about the freemasons in the next book)*

To Mime or not to Mime. Gebelin's claim was that the name *tarot* came from the Egyptian word *tar*, meaning *royal* and *ro*, meaning *road*, and that the tarot therefore represented a *royal road* to wisdom. As time progressed, all the divers versions of cards became more and more associated with divination, fortune telling, magic and astrology, etc. Now I could go on and on about the history and origin of the tarot cards, but at this point I'm completely torn up, because my question was; *how and why am I running into all of this studying the history of the mime?* All of this stuff was from the origin and study of the mime! The Lord began to show me that we must understand Satan's plan to destroy people, generations, nations, and the world. This is an attack on all people, but the Lord revealed it even more that it's an attack on our seed which is our children. The devil's after that thing that has the ability to produce another righteous harvest which will produce another Godly generation. One thing I found notable was the fact that around the 1500's the tarot was actually recommended for the instruction and guidance of the youth by Catholic Church moralist. Imagine giving your children tarot cards to help them make everyday decisions. You might say; *what's wrong with that?* Well, we finally need to take a look and see what's on the back of these cards to find out exactly what's wrong with it. *(by the way; these cards are now being given to your children in many schools as play toys)* God has been telling me that we are actually bringing these spirits inside or our own houses, and in the House of God. So in review of my search, and going over the history of the mime; it took me to the word ***fool*** and then the word ***jester*** or ***court jester*** and now ***tarot***. I remember being amazed at finding the history on the tarot cards, but what I would discover next is what threw me for a loop. When I looked up the first tarot card in the **Major Arcana deck**, I saw the picture of **The Fool** on the back. I asked God, what did this mean, and who was this character? God said he was a **mime**, a **jester** or as the card depicted;**"a fool."**

MIME/ THE FOOL/ JESTER. The Fool: the unnumbered card in the <u>**Tarot deck, from the Tarot of Marseille.**</u> This character is also known as a mime. ***Can someone please tell me what a mime/fool is doing on the back of the tarot card?***

Well, if that wasn't bad enough, God said keep going, I have something more to show you. Now this next card will take us into the word I'll be showing you later, I'm not going to tell you what the word is, but I am going to show you the next tarot card, with the hopes that I'm not getting ahead of myself. What I want you to understand is the fact that all of the pictures that I will show you have something to do with all that I'm revealing to you in the character of the mime, and the ancient demonic spirits that are attached to it. We as saints of God must not be carnal in our thinking. Satan is a spiritual being and is using spiritual warfare to fight us!

To Mime or not to Mime. The bible lets us know that the wages or payment of sin is death. The last enemy to be destroyed is death. The plan of Satan for your life is to steal, *kill* and destroy. He's all about death, darkness, and destruction. The depiction on this next card shows his character. The Lord revealed to me **where** and **who** the demonic spirit shown on the back of this card was. He also showed me *what* this spirit is *doing now*, and in *what group* of individuals it's currently working in. *(we'll cover that in just a bit)*

Death, the tarot card, from the **<u>Rider-Waite-Smith deck.</u>**

Depending on which depiction is shown of this tarot card, many of the illustrations of it will show this character with a "**white**" *or pale face* **and dark or "black clothing."** Both of which represent death! ***<u>The pale face and black clothing</u> will be very important to recognize as we move forward.***

Le Chariot, from the **Tarot of Marseille.**

The Lovers, ***<u>Rider-Waite-Smith deck</u>***

To Mime or not to Mime. Take note of card VII. It represents Egypt, where much of what I talk about in this whole book originates. You'll also find that in looking into the **origin** of these characters, it will depict a *mockery* and *mimic* of the Holy things of God.

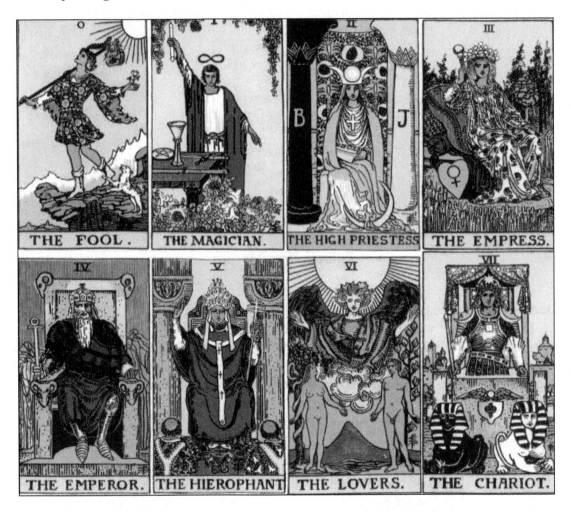

~~~IMPORTANT NOTE~~~

Understand that if you were to research the history and origin of each of these pictures, you would find that they correspond with the theme of this chapter, and the worship of other gods!

To Mime or not to Mime. Other spirits or mockeries are on the back of the tarot cards.

HANGED MAN: In the bible, it teaches us that it was a *curse* to be hanged on a tree. And to be hanged upside down, is a **mockery** of Christ's work on the cross! Many Satanic groups use an upside down cross.

WHEEL OF FORTUNE: I always wondered where they got the name of the television game show from.
To Mime or not to Mime. Not the devil himself but actually a strong demon by the name of; BAPHELMET. (BAFA-METT/ BAPHAL'MAT)

This demon is actually the spirit that resides over one of the leading cults or private organizations in the world. I've actually had an encounter with this particular spirit and he's not who the card is depicting him to be. He has a totally different assignment. But that's how the devil works; he's a deceiver of men. His instructions are directly from Satan and desire to destroy through lust and division.

I'll be honest with you; in my study of this chapter, I still found it hard to accept that I got into all this devilment by studying the art and origin of the mime. It made me begin to understand why so many of our churches are only gifted but possess NO POWER!! We've let the enemy come in and the sad thing about it is, most churches don't even know that he's there because he has disguised himself as an angel of light but is actually a demon of darkness, death and destruction both naturally and spiritually.

To Mime or not to Mime. Look closely, can you see similarities in these pictures that are events in the bible? Babel tower, the worship of the moon and sun, judgment, with the dead raising from their graves and the great hor, which is the world or the world system through lust.

The reason I'm showing you these depictions is the fact that it further substantiates the spirit of *mimic* and *mockery* that is actually stemming from the *origin* and *history* of mime.

To Mime or not to Mime. I could say so much more about the word "tarot", but the Lord told me yet again to move on.

It's been said by some people, *(I'm just going to call them liars)* that the depictions on the back of the tarot cards are reflections of Christian values and morals. No what they are, is mockery of Holy things of God, partnered with blasphemous witchcraft! You can say what you want, but there is no way God is accepting something that has such a foul and demonic beginning.

Now I do want you to understand that this study of mime is in no way a reflection of those of you who God has anointed to portray worship through the art of *dance* by using mime.

One thing God told me was that many people are doing things because they have not been informed or taught. God is now sending a *revelatory word* to let you know what the enemy is planning through many vehicles we use for worship. Even though God allowed you to use the art of mime for a season, He's no longer winking His eye at it and is opening up the understanding of His people in this last day so that we won't be deceived. God still wants to use you in the area of the dance but he does not want to use you in the area of mime. . .**It's not what you thought it was!** Need more proof? You can look up the history for yourselves; don't just take my word on it. Then, earnestly pray and seek God and ask Him to reveal His purpose for you in the area of your dancing gifts. God will answer you and He does not want His will for your life to be a mystery. Read up on the history of the Egyptian Tarot decks with the Egyptians symbols on them. You'll find that in the history of the mimes, they were also back there in the days of the Pharaoh's, right there in their courts along with the court jesters and fools.

Well at this point I thought I couldn't be more shocked than I already was. And I'm sure you've been a little traumatized by such a find. But as shocked and surprised by this information as I was; the Lord told me that he had not yet given me all he wanted me to see. God said there is still more to this than even I had already discovered, and that it was relative to what's going on in our society and churches today.

I began to ask the Lord, what more could there be? Isn't this enough for us to at least seek God before we offer Him just any kind of sacrifice? Well apparently not, because He told me there's more. As I began to ponder what the Lord had already showed me, the last word that I had arrived at was the word "tarot." I continued on from that word and after about two days of intense research, I heard the voice of the Lord saying *"death."* He said all this is bringing death to the world and spiritual death to my house. After he spoke those words, immediately I came across the word, **"Goth."** Actually, the study of the word *tarot* advanced me to this word Goth. At first it didn't dawn on me what this was, I mean I had heard the word *gothic or gothic city* watching Batman, but it hadn't yet hit me. I told the Lord that this was enough and I didn't want to know any more. He said, *I called you to do this and I'll give you the understanding, courage and strength to do it.* Then He showed me that the word **Goth** meant, **"death or darkness."** Now as I had done in the past, once again I asked the Lord why he is showing me this. What does this all mean, and what connection does all this have with your revelation of the mime? After much prayer and fasting concerning this, God caused me to realize that the many things the enemy does are done in *symbols* and *types* just like God himself does. Remember, it is always vital to understand that Satan is a mimicker a deceiver and a copycat! Dictionary says; *to mime or to mimic, is to make something seem as, but actually is not! To imitate, pretend, imagine or to copy something real!*

To Mime or not to Mime. Always remember that Satan is a *mimicker* of holy things.

He always wanted to be God, not just like God but he wanted to be God, so he has his own stuff that gives himself perverted glory.

As I began to look into this word *goth;* many strange things popped up in my search of this word. I found that as many of you probably already know, that there is a culture called, the Goths or the Gothic culture. It is full of a sect of people who are for the most part in rebellion to something or someone, mainly authority. They have their own preachers and teachers, their own hairstyles and clothes, their own jewelry and if you dig deep enough, you'll find they have their own language and music. It's like their own underground world if you will. *(I'll talk about their music later)*

The Goth's also having an infatuation with darkness and gloominess, oppression and death; they normally wear nothing but black and walk around with *"pale faces"* which further represents their obsession with death, darkness, the unseen, and unknown. They thrive on separation and being different from anyone else. They get off on people looking at them strange, it's a spirit of rebellion, and it's a type of high for them. You've seen them; they're the ones with the spiky hair and the black clothes with pale faces with tattoos and piercings, walking through the malls and stores. They are usually depressed about something, doesn't even have to be a big matter, they just want to be indifferent about whatever they can be indifferent about.

What you probably have not seen is some of the things they're in to. That's what I'm going to point out and prayerfully cause you to see and understand what God is saying in this chapter.

All this ties together and you will see the *"underlying"* plan of Satan to bring back *old ancient spirits* causing so much destruction and death.

As I reluctantly entered into the dark study of the Goth culture I began to notice some strange and disturbing similarities between the *spirits* of mimes origin and the dark demonic customs of the Gothic culture.

God wants to let you know and understand that the spirits these cults are dealing with are, the same demonic spirits *the fools, the jesters and the mimes* operated under. Their representation is on the back of the *Tarot Cards* and so are the *Goth's*.

Pay close attention because you must be able to see this in the spirit and not with your carnal mind, because you'll miss it. The Lord told me that we must realize that people who are involved in these divers' cults and religions only understand in part as to what they're involved in. Most of them are very devoted to what they believe. Some have admittedly sold their very souls to the devil and have made agreements in their demonic initiations that hell would be their homes after death. Sound crazy? But this is what many believe in the Goth culture. They think they want to go where their god is. They don't see hell as a place that you will be unhappy or tortured. Actually, torture is a good word to them. They are obsessed with men like Adolph Hitler and others like him.

There are comparisons God caused me to see which caused me understand that there's way more evil involved in this, than we actually want ourselves to believe. Many times when we don't understand something, instead of looking into, or researching it, we tend to put it off to the side, or ignore it.

But God is uncovering it whether we want to believe it or whether we understand it not. No matter how disturbing; God does not want us to be ignorant concerning Satan's deceptive devices. Our knowledge of his plans will teach us how to fight and get the victory over him.

Mime or not to Mime. As I began to seek the Lord and ask Him what were some of the *similarities?* He told me; *Elmus it's all about symbols and types. The symbols and types I'm revealing to you are letting you know, that all of these things are operating by the same* **ancient spirits** *I cast out of heaven centuries ago.*

He asked; *what did the mimes mainly wear in their clothing attire?* I told Him that they mainly wore **black attire** with their **faces painted white**. Then He asked me; *when I showed you the jesters, mimes and fools on the back of the tarot cards; what was the XIIIth card on the back of the Rider tarot deck?* I told Him it was the spirit of death riding on a white horse, wearing black attire with a pale white face. He told me that those same old ancient spirits are roaming the earth today. Finally He asked me; *Elmus, in the Goth culture, what is their main attire?*

All I could do was shake my head because I understood what He was trying to show me. I told Him that in the Goth culture, they mainly wear <u>black clothes</u> and walk around with <u>pale faces!</u>

God told me they only think they know what's going on. They are dealing with a demon of death and destruction! Just as I had mentioned in **chapter 3** in the *goddess Kali* segment; one of the main depictions of the Hindu goddess Kali was a black statue who had lifeless white eyes and in one of her 6 or 8 hands; she had a severed pale white head holding it up. The goddess was called or known as, the goddess of *death and destruction.*

I began to ask God what is going on with all the similarities of all these things. Why am I studying mime and coming up with all of this added stuff? He told me to continue on and He'd bring it all together, and that it would be what He wanted me to show and warn His people of.

So I moved on further into the Gothic movement; its history and religious connections as it pertains to the prior topics in this chapter.

There are many perceptions and misconceptions concerning the gothic movement, but I will hone in on some of the particulars that relate to what I've been talking about. In this rising culture, there are many that are a part of it, who will tell you that being Goth is seeing beauty and its coming destruction. As if to say that there's only destruction in seeing the beauty of something. They say that being Goth is being part of a last dance before the walls of life come tumbling down. The ability to see light in darkness! Now I did say to be able to *see* the light in darkness, but they say that they see *light* in darkness, meaning the *darkness* is the light as far as their concerned.

They love being considered *outcasts* and most of its teenagers are into poetry, music and love wearing dark costumes and are into deeply and inspired by games of chance or fantasy games such as *Dungeons and Dragons.* Their love for horror pictures and mystery movies that are dark, eerie and gloomy is a norm. Some dress up and paint their fingernails black while others immerse themselves in a *pseudo medieval* world of dark images, with tattoo's and strange body piercing in their ears, nose, mouths, bellybuttons, eyebrows and even crotches. Not understanding that it can become a way of making you a slave to the spirit that controls that act.

They're also into the biographies of men such as Hitler and other men that caused great destruction and pain to mankind.

They have their own *unique music* and have fascination with medieval, Victorian and Edwardian history. They will wear a cross, but they don't believe in the cross of Christ or the bloody work that was done thereupon. Which is strange because there are some *Goths* who actually profess to be active *Christians*.

To Mime or not to Mime. Many of them wear an **Egyptian ankh** or the, **Eye of Ra** or **Eye of Horus;** a <u>Wiccan pentacle</u>, a Satanic inverted pentacle. Most either deal or love dealing with oppression and depression, most seem sullen or withdrawn.

Goths often write poetry or listen to music that deals with death or depression and political fault or shortcomings. They are usually most comfortable only around other Goths and say that dark things or dark music reflect their own personal depression, pain or anger. It's said that most Goths come from dysfunctional families. But what I'm finding out is, it's a widely spreading spirit of gloom and hopelessness that is covering the earth and affecting all families.

A lot of our kids are turning to this culture when they're having a hard time in school, feeling alienated, and looking for a way to express themselves that mirrors those feelings. Their music is *thought provoking,* and many times they will *make motions and dance without saying a word.* Humm! *(dance without saying a word?)* Their music also deals with social issues or evils, like racism, war, hatred of groups, etc. . . .*(the same as the mimes did in Italy)*

They have fascinations with death, sex, vampirism and finding a different way of thinking of life, like trying to find beauty in life, through the pain of death. God told me it's a quest for immortality in which only God can cause you to obtain, Satan can't offer you that!

Goth, as a modern movement, started as one component of the *Punk Rock* scene. As the *disco* age began to fade, Goth survived by creating its own subculture. The first use of the term *Goth* in its present meaning is believed to have been on a British Broadcasting TV program.

On this program a man by the name Anthony H. Wilson, a manager of Joy Division described a rock band that was on the program as Gothic compared to some of the pop mainstream bands. The name Goth stuck! That bands use of black clothing was originally something of a backlash to the more colorful disco music of the seventies that was actually associated with homosexuality. Thus the name Goth stuck as a type of rebellion to other styles of music in that era. The Goth movement is said to have started in the *Bat Cave*, a nightclub in London, England back in the early 1980's. Spreading to the U.S., it first became popular in California and then its fame spread too many movies of the 90's.

This dark music began to spread throughout mainstream America, right under the noses of many middle-class Caucasian families.

Many of these young teenagers follow the teachings and associated the music of Marilyn Manson with the Gothic culture, but Manson publicly presents himself as a follower of the *Church of Satan*. He was ordained as a priest in the Church of Satan by the (late) founder, Anton LaVey. Many fans refer to him as the Rev. Marilyn Manson. He says he's not a true follower; he was just ordained and appointed as a Reverend within the Church of Satan by the founder. And from that satanic connection, many Goths have connected themselves with Churches of Satan throughout the world.

Again, I know you're probably wondering why I keep going off into the *history* of these different cults, religions and beliefs? Well, it's because we need to know what's going on around us and how the enemy is planting his seeds, so God can give us wisdom on how to combat and uproot it. We also need to know what we're offering to God in His house and calling it worship. God told me that if His people would just do what John 4: 23-24 says, and worship in spirit and in truth, we won't come up with gimmicks and schemes to get people to worship and praise him. When we operate according to the order of Gods Word, the enemy doesn't have a chance in this world to penetrate the worship. Yes, we expect for this stuff to be out in the world, but God will not stand by and watch these spirits infiltrate the church, contaminating the worship of Himself!

To Mime or not to Mime. Now that we have just a brief origin and history of this dark culture. The Lord told me to put it all together so you could see what the plan of Satan is now, and what it has actually been for thousands of years. Out of all the words you've heard me say; the words *death* and *destruction* are two words we must pay attention to. With all the things that are going on in the world, Satan's plan is to bring it all into the House of God. . . . .Do you see that yet?

Remember, all of this came from God instructing me to study the *origin* of the mime.

To mime or not to mime was the original question here. . . . . .right?

All of this begins to come together and is related folks! From the mimes, to the fools and jesters, from the tarot cards to the Gothic culture. The Lord showed me how much this has ties and connections in one way or another, having its origins in Egypt. God told me that because of it's origins and it's present day hidden demonic forces, He can not in all of his holiness, continue to allow Satan's plan to move forward without giving His people knowledge of what's actually going on out here. There were **no mimes** *worshipping* Almighty God in scripture, but just the opposite. They were *mimickers* of holy things and they went about to poke fun and make mockery of God's holiness!

So who bought the mime into the church? Well as I attempted to show you in going over some of the history of these characters, we found that the jesters, court jesters and mimes were back in the days of the Pharaoh's of Egypt. Many of those characters were sorcerers, practicing in witchcraft and divination, of which Deuteronomy tells us to have no part nor take on the ways of the other pagan nations. Those characters carried the self same spirits and were considered fools; which is one of the descriptions of the mime.

This is not a joke at all! These old spirits are just making their way through time, disguised in a different package. All this is anti-Christ or anti Christian in its origin, and we're trying to give it to God as worship? In scripture, you'll find that God called anointed spirit led *choreographers and dancers,* who danced and gave glory to God in the *order* which He Himself set in place. This is what God created and ordained in scripture.

At first I didn't understand where the Goth culture came into play in all of this. But after studying the culture and God giving revelation. . . .*Revelation!* That's when God gives you unknown or reveals knowledge and understanding not otherwise given by a man or a book.

We still do believe in *revelation knowledge* right, or has the enemy stolen and made that common and unsacred too? See how off base some things have become? We'll believe and run to the palm reader, but won't believe or even hear the Prophets of God! Well too bad; I didn't write this book to get mans approval; I did it because God told me His people are being destroyed because of the lack of knowledge, even revelation knowledge. After God began to enlighten me on how the Goths play a part in all of this, I began to see some of the similar spirits and likeness they had with the mimes and jesters. Remember that these are all anti-Christ in their beliefs. Many see God and His church as nothing more than another social club or just another group of individuals who have a false sense of hope in a god that has no power.

They are fools who have said in their hearts; "There is no God!" It also ties in with the hip hop culture that has their own gods. They give honor to God Almighty, but what they don't know is, the god that rules over that religion is Satan himself. Their actions are anti-God! So how did it get into the church? Through us! Through people who do not have a *lifestyle* of *worship.* Our *cultures* have opened the door to Satan, and ushered him right into the house of God.

To Mime or not to Mime. Many Goths have other gods tattooed on their bodies; the gods of Egypt and other religions, but they continue to give thanks to God Jehovah, making Him as common as all the others. The Goths *mimic* and *poke fun* at holiness in their music and performances. *(just like the mimes did)* You can't say it isn't so! In the Goth culture they have their own music that many times can't be purchased in regular stores. They have an underground network with codes you can't understand. They often discuss religion and for some strange reason many of their artist's music concentrates on Christian themes. Why? It's anti-God that's why. I found a Goth website that has a prophetic but demonic utterance to it. This site was called, **Music from the End of the World.** It is demonic oriented music that blasphemes the name of Christ and all He stood for. It even made fun of the *death, burial and resurrection.* Hear me now as I continue to repeat myself mentioning the words *mimicking* and *poking fun* at holy things! Why are they making fun and blaspheming the work of Jesus on the cross? Satan is working through all types of music. That's why God told us to *sing new, but spiritual songs and hymns.* Gothic music isn't one single style of music at all. It draws from the dark corners of a small family of styles, each of which is loosely related by a sense of tragedy, doom, mystery, or other worldly lusts. Some similarities you will see in this culture that relate to what I've been talking about in this chapter, are the fact that in most of their music, it's wild and has a insane type of vibe that causes many of it's listeners to *jump around foolishly, banging heads* and *slammin'* bodies all over the place. They often make fun of Christian beliefs and make it seem as if the things that they themselves are slaves to, is **the only way** to go and **the only way out**, and the **only way to true life** and happiness. . . . . . . .didn't Jesus say that concerning Himself?

What does some of this music sound like? A lot of this music you can't easily find. I actually had some of this music recorded for an example for one of my Symposiums, but the music was so devilish, God had me pray and anoint all the participants before I allowed them to listen to it. You're going to see in the next year that this music will become common place in our society.

Let's break down and take a look at some of the music they listen to, and musical styles and genres in which they do it; you may be surprised.

Music from the End of the World
[you can use google, bing or other search engines]

Gothic music is not just one *single style* of music. Lets look at the different forms of music they place their musical claim on. What you have to pay attention to, and not get caught up in, is the styles or genres used. The *message* is what's *dangerous* in the music of this and other cultures.

We get caught up on the styles of the music, but you must pay attention to what is being said in the lyrics and what's being released into your spirit.

To Mime or not to Mime. What does this stuff sound like? Lets take a look!

These are some of the genres and styles of music you'll find in gothic vibes. Also a list of some of the bands they listen to and their music titles. **Look these bands up online,** to see what your kids are listening to. Some of these bands and their music are not in mainstream music like what you see on TV. **While you're not paying attention, the devil is stealing their minds.**

Ambient
Delerium
Metamorphosis

Classical
Vivaldi
Pax Hominibus

Dark Wave
Diary of Dreams
Drop Dead

Death Rock
Christian Death
Heresy

EMO, another type of rock.
The EMO culture is much more evil and darker than the Goth.
Celtic Loreena McKennitt
Mummer's Dance , Medieval

EBM, Electric Body Music
Covenant
Go Film
Dark Music

Underground
Ethereal
Lycia

Industrial
Skinny Puppy
Assimilate

New Wave
The Cure
Charlotte Sometimes

Synth Pop
SwitchBlade Symphony
Wallflower

Rock
Nosferatu
Sisters of Mercy
Black Planet

Punk
X-Mal Deutschland
Incubus Succubus

To Mime or not to Mime. NOTE: It if hasn't already started. Hip-Hop will also join this list and you will begin to hear more and more hip-hop/rock and hard rock styles mixed together with blaspheming anti-God lyrics. It has to happen, because it's from Satan! You may think that the hip-hop is a style, but the only reason hip-hop will be invited to this sound it because of it's anti-Christ MESSAGE, not because It's music sounds good with the rock type of musical style. In it's demonic feature, you will begin to hear more *"strings"* being used in the music. It will be a *"whipping, or whoop"* type of *eerie sound*. More strings in the music will also be Satan's way of copying the original sound that came from his body, when he worshipped the true and living God. Also in the secular music, *(mainly hip-hop)* you will begin to hear more and more *organ/ string combinations* in the music. Their style will become more church oriented, although perverted in it's content. **You'll know this is Gods warning to us, because He gave this to me before it actually takes place. He's exposing the devils plan!. . . . .(Prophesied in 2006)**

To Mime or not to Mime. I'll do a brief breakdown of some of this music. It's not very pleasant so we won't dig too deep at this time. You must attend one of my **Levite Symposiums** whenever you get the opportunity. We dig deep into areas that are very uncomfortable, but very real! In this section are the names and *styles* of the music. The names of some of the bands and some of their music tracks they have online. **I would not advise your kids to have free access to this music because of its demonic influence, whether you believe me or not, this stuff does have negative spiritual influences!!** After I'm done showing you this music, I will bring it all together in relation to all of the topics in this chapter. There is an underlying plan to make every music as one music. Its plan to make all music common in order to desensitize people to God. On the previous page in the left hand side, you may have seen the word *Ambient*. Underneath that you will see the word *Metamorphosis*. This is actually a musical track that has an undertone frequency that you can hardly hear. The sound is very gloomy and you can just feel another presence when you listen to it. Understand that spirits have the ability to travel through frequencies, and musical messages can enter your spirit if you're not protected by the spirit of God. Now does that mean that if you have the Holy Spirit you're okay to listen to it? The answer is No! In the upper left corner of the page you saw the

Dark Wave music form. Just under it you will see a song called *Drop Dead*. In the very gloomy and unclear lyrics, they're telling the listener that there's no power in *confessing your sins* to God; so you might as well drop dead. They're making mockery of the fact that Romans 10:9 say's, *that if we confess with our mouths and believe in our hearts, that God has raised Christ from the dead, thou shalt be saved. Verse 10 goes on to say; for with the heart man believeth unto righteousness, and with the mouth confession is made unto salvation.* The devil understands the power of the tongue and what *comes out of your mouth* can *bless* or *curse* you. This music is provoking you to speak against the very Word of God. If he can get you to speak against God; you have given him the keys and the authority to enter in and control you.

On the previous page you will also see in the middle left section the title, *Death Rock*. Yes, I'm afraid this is another form of music the Goths listen to. It's in a category with Rock, Classical, and Punk etc. There's a Death Rock band called **Christian Death** who has a song called, *Heresy*. Look up the word Heresy in a bible dictionary for a better understanding of what it is. However in the song Heresy, by the band Christian Death, speaks of the death of Jesus on the cross with His body covered in blood as nothing but a fictitious story that bares no truth. This sick band often speaks of death to Christians and our beliefs as nothing more than a joke and we as Christians should be stopped at any cost, so that the prince and power of darkness can take his rightful place on his earthly and eternal kingdom.

On the previous page, you will see the word *Rock*. There's a song called *Black Planet* that speaks to *the world living in a wonderful atmosphere of blackness. All dressed in black and living in a dark world.* These types of lyrics are considered good and normal to Goths. They are influenced not to prefer light, because to them it would be a representation of God or godliness. John 3:19, says, *And this is the condemnation, that light is come into the world, and men loved darkness rather than light, because their deeds were evil.* 1 John 1:5b, **God is light**, *and in him is* **no darkness at all.** I could say more on this, but I felt led to stop so I can continue to sum this all up. I felt like I had finished and come to the completion of this subject, but God continued to give me more and more, and I felt like I'd never come to an end of this. *(also look up EMO)*

To Mime or not to Mime. If you look at all the similarities of these subjects, God is revealing that they all have something in common in the fact that they have an origin and history of mimicking and making mockery of godly order. The prince of darkness wants what God is in control of. He wants the credit for all Gods creation. So the devil uses *mockery* to poke fun at holy and sacred things, and by doing this he's slowly trying to make Gods holiness something very common in the eyesight of men. There's a plan from the enemy to make all things as one.

No separation between clean and unclean, holy or unholy. The enemy is calling forth ancient old spirits, calling them back up to do damage today. When you look at the *true history* of the mimes, and who they were in association with the jesters and fools and how all of these characters carry like spirits, not to mention the fact that they can be found on the back of tarot cards. . . .why? What's up with that? Is anyone paying attention to what's going on here?

Are we able to see this in the spirit?

I was shocked and in disbelief myself when the Lord allowed me to come upon these hidden satanic agendas. I found many strange similarities that I thought were just coincidences between them. How the mimes from back in 2500 B.C. wore black tunics with white faces. How the Goths who have taken on a similar image with their infatuation with black and wearing trench coats, walking around with pale faces. They are actually *channeling* into old spirits of darkness and probably don't even realize it. Demons from days of old are just manifesting themselves in today's society. Listen to me, this is very important! One thing the Lord did point out to me was the fact that many of the shocking things He showed me are a *perverted duplication* of how it was done in scripture. What do I mean by that? Well take a look at the music structure in the bible. God anointed musicians, dancers and singers who would minister to Him. There were many writers of songs and psalms who wrote poetry and set it to a beat or tempo. On the hip-hop scene there are now more and more artists who are naming themselves after *holy callings* like, *ministers, prophets, pastors and bishops.* I'm telling you **it's a mockery!** The infatuation and use of wings and angels doing sinful acts and deeds in their concerts. When Snoop Dog gets ready to perform one of his raps, he says, *lets go to church,* and everyone begins to party.

It's a mockery! If you've seen *any* Jay Z or Kanye West video, you know **it's a mockery!!**

We know the word *Golgotha* in scripture is the common name of the spot where Jesus was crucified. It is interpreted as meaning *the place of a skull* (Matthew 27:33; Mark 15:22; John 19:17). This name represents in Greek letters the Aramaic word Gulgaltha, which is the Hebrew Gulgoleth, (Numbers 1:2; 1 Chronicles 23:3, 24; 2Kings 9:35) meaning *a skull*. It is associated with the word *Calvary*. Two explanations of the name are given: (1) that it was a spot where executions ordinarily took place, and therefore abounded in skulls; or (2) it may come from the look or form of the land itself, bald, round and skull-like, and therefore a mound or hillock, in accordance with the common phrase —for which there is no direct authority—*Mount Calvary*. Whichever of these is the correct explanation, Golgotha is known as the spot where our Lord and Savior gave His life for our sins. However, in mockery of this, there have been movies out that use the name Golgotha as a place where you can go to have your future told, and have your destiny set by the use of; that's right. . . .tarot cards! It's suggesting to us that we are not to believe in the death and work of Christ on the cross. His death did not determine or shape our destinies, but if you believe in your future via these cards, that's where your true destiny lies.

I'm sorry, but it was the blood of Jesus that saved, delivered and made me free; not some demon on the back of a card that I allow to run my life. It was the Blood of Jesus, **the Blood of Jesus!!**

To Mime or not to Mime. Satan is continuously throwing out subtle hints of mockery and using tools of destruction while we're standing by watching him. Some still won't admit things are happening, and we just stand by playing *games of chance* with our very lives. Humm! *(games of chance, now there's another subject)*

As mimes did their Acts back in 2500B.C., they used decks of cards to perform what seemed like harmless games and tricks. *(they're just cards; ain't no harm in that. . . .right?)* Okay, if you say so, but the tricks were done with what seemed like a harmless deck of cards. The problem was that many of the tricks were performed with various tarot card decks. Humm! *(makes you wonder how they did some of those tricks!)*

There's an old James Bond movie called, *Live and let Die*, where James confronts a woman by the name of, **Solitaire**, who <u>possesses the power to read tarot cards</u> to predict the future. Did you hear what I said? You have to <u>possess powers</u> to be able to *interpret* tarot cards correctly.

I wonder what type of power that is? And why in the world did they have to name that woman Solitaire? What's the connection there? Humm. . . .could it be the fact that the *very same* mime, fool, joker and jester characters that are on the back of the tarot cards; are on many of the, what we call, *ordinary deck* of *playing cards* which can be purchased right out of the store; the Joker card being one of them? **Sorry, I didn't mean to mess up your poker came tonight!**

Will we continue to say that there's nothing to this? The devil is counting on you saying that. He's trying his best to *cause men and women* to fall down and worship him. If we'll continue to think there's nothing to it and act as if it's okay, then he's doing his job to stop us from operating in the realm of our call as true Levites, unspotted from the world and its devices. Satan's mimic plan is no joke! He's a major **skulk,** who's mastered the art of hiding behind that which *seems so harmless and innocent*. But always has an undercurrent plan to steal, kill and destroy.

The Lord spoke to me again that night I was studying this and told me, He wasn't quite done yet. I felt like Moses when he went to the top of the Mt. Sinai, to receive the Ten Commandments.

He told me to continue on with what seems like *coincidental associations*, but in fact are ancient old undertakings to destroy His righteousness and authority. So as I continued on, He took me to a place in my studies that showed the use of tarot cards as being considered an **_art of storytelling._** Now pay close attention to this, as it's going to begin tying things together even more.

As I've mentioned earlier in this chapter, and also back in chapter 3, the fact of how God set up the Levitcal order, and how He anointed David as King who also set up the order of worship in the tabernacle. David's music department *(if you will)* had *keen musicianship* with *skillful musicians, singers, dancers* and *writers* of *psalms* and *poetry*. I described how they were skilled and anointed to play as they were <u>inspired by the spirit of God</u>. The worship was **spontaneous** in the fact that they moved, sung, danced and even wrote psalms and hymns, as God gave them the ability and inspired them to do so. Just like God has an order; Satan has set up his own way of worship as well. He's been establishing it and putting it all together from that time he was cast out of his own anointed place in heaven. He has his own ministers of music, dancers, singers and writers of songs and poetry. But what you must comprehend is that in his doing so; he is unwilling to established his own *order*. His way can only be a *mimic* of the order that was already established by All mighty God Jehovah Himself.

So as I stated, I found an article on the history of the use of tarot cards, and how the use of them were being described as the **art of storytelling,** which once again is coincidentally or un-coincidentally one of the descriptions of mime.

To Mime or not to Mime. Remember, Satan has set up his own worshippers who have used demonic devises to defend his mimicking worship order.

It's been said that the tarot has inspired *writers* as well as *visual artists. (dancers)*

There's a man by the name of **Italo Calvino** who described the tarot as a **vehicle** for telling stories or even writing novels. They have even been used as a *muse* or a type of *inspiration* for those who would perform mime and dance or the writing of poetry. What I'm getting at is; the devil is using counterfeit replicas of the order of God. God is the creator and doesn't need the help or advice of anyone. Satan has set up his imitations and his whole point is to present his agenda to the *Sons of God*. My brother and my sister, we as Levites and children of the Most High, are the *son*s of which I speak. If he's able to get us to be partakers of his un-holiness and partakers of his unrighteous agenda, then worship as we know it or as it should be as stated in the book of John, will be null and void of its power. We will no longer be true worshippers because we have taken of the accursed thing and have hidden Satan's agenda amongst our own stuff.

We can no longer turn our heads or pretend as if there's nothing to it! There *is* something to it and we should pay attention to the fact that it is what it is. No, the things I'm sharing here are not an easy thing to receive, but I didn't make this up. I didn't put the mimes on the tarot cards.

I didn't put the jesters and the fools together. I'm not the one who caused the hip-hop movement to become a religion and not a form of music. I didn't do that! You explain why there were officers in a Hindu temple who were called Thugs back in the 10th century, who hid *gold* and *diamonds in their mouth* after robbing the worshipers. Now thugs *wear the same* in their mouths today! What or who do you think is behind all of this? Me? I hardly believed it myself. The

Lord and I have had many late night debates on what He was showing and revealing to me. It became so incredible at times that I even asked the Lord not to reveal anymore of these deep events. But God showed me too many comparisons between the demonic activities of the ancient days and what we see going on, not only on the streets, but in our churches as well. We treat these hip-hop and Hollywood stars like gods. We look up to some of them. They walk around with so much pride and act as if they're invincible. We've allowed this same mentality in the church when we lift preachers, teachers and singers higher, and esteem them more than we do God. We're becoming more and more materialistic and have made it seem as if having possession is being godly. This is an attitude that came from Lucifer himself, who was full of pride and arrogance. Now we can see it in today's society, and in our ministries.

God wanted me to point out that we had better pay attention to what the devil is trying to accomplish. If you are paying attention, you will find out that everything the devil is doing is a *mimic* or *copy* of the holy order of God. Now one of the things he's doing is using that same jester spirit of old to poke fun at the church and make its holy things common. I know I keep saying this, but as I tried to let it go, the Lord spoke to me and said the devil is using that same old spirit that the mimes and jesters used when the mimes were rejected by the Christian Church. They began to poke fun at the church because they were not allowed to bring their perverted beliefs into the sanctuary. So the devil attacked it through the mimes in the theaters and tried to make it seem as if the beliefs of the church were nothing more than a weak social establishment. Now through the compromises of leadership, musical artist and weak ministers, we've put out the red carpet to the unholy programs of the world. We've opened up the sanctuary windows to allow a wind of deception to breeze through the house of God. Things that were kept sacred and holy in the church, are now being made fun of, because Gods people won't stand up for holiness!

To Mime or not to Mime. Now this same **comedic spirit** has crept on the scene again. Not just in the secular venues, but in the church too. We are going to see more and more of this spirit trying to make its way into the house of the Lord. God told me it's a *spirit of clowning* that actually originated way back with the origin of the mime and jesters. As I stated before in the book of Ephesians 5:4, Paul speaks of *foolish talking and jesting* which are not convenient.

In other words there's a time for it. But He's also letting us know that the work of Christ and the foundations and order God has set in place are not joking matter. We are in a spiritual warfare and must take it seriously. The devils very serious about what he's trying to accomplish and we need to be more attentive to what the enemy is actually up to. We're not supposed to be ignorant concerning any of his devices and he's well aware that the weapons of our warfare are not carnal, but they're mighty through God to the pulling down of every stronghold.

After taking an overall look at the similar methods from divers events; I began to see even more how related all this was. I began to see an overall picture of the enemy's plan to attack this world, and the church.

When the Lord spoke to me concerning this spirit of comedia or comedy; He told me that it was just another subtle attack. There's a wave of *carelessness* hitting the nation. It's a move of the art of clowning around and making fun. It's showing up everywhere, just pay attention you'll see it. Preachers are cracking jokes instead of preaching the gospel. It's in the music and the dance, it's in the hip hop movement and everywhere you look, it's becoming more visible. It's the same old spirit that started back in Egypt, Greece and Rome with **the art of clowning!**

Even now there's a new wave coming out of just clowning around. There's a dance out called the *clown* or *krumping,* where you throw your body around like you're having a fit. You'll see this dance in many hip-hop and pop videos where they shake and pop their butts. The founder is said to be a man who calls himself *Tommy The Clown* in the hip-hop movement who dresses up like a clown and is getting thousands of young people together and letting them do their thing in dancing and acting crazy. You would have to go to their website to understand what I'm talking about. I don't want to waste too much more paper and ink on them. They will tell you that we're getting kids off the street and this is a good outlet for them. The problem is, we're just taking them from one bad situation to a deeper spiritual evil. Just you watch and see, they'll be trying to get it into the church as well. The founder of this dance says that God allowed him to take this new zombie dancing style to the world.

What they need is the Word of God and someone who will be a godly example not a foolish one. It still takes their mind away from the reality of life and it's many responsibilities. Yes it's hard out there in the streets but what we need is the Lord, not another gimmick.

It's still a part of the hip-hop culture, and it still has the underlying ability to cause even more damage. This is another case where the enemy comes in and hides behind something that seems good on the surface, but it's actually subtly harming. They won't get a firm foundation with solid teaching on how to grow up and be responsible, just get'em out of our hair, put'em in a club and let'em dance around like a bunch of clowns till they feel better. We need to reach out to them; sit them down and teach them how they can get the victory over the devil by living a Godly life. We need to let them know that they can do all things through Christ that strengthens them, not through slam dancing or krumping. . . . . .we need to show them love and compassion!!!

To Mime or not to Mime. I don't like throwing off on anyone or calling out names. That's Not what God told me to do! But he did tell me to cry loud and spare not, because Satan is going to and fro throughout the earth, seeking whom he may devour. He's been up to his bag of tricks for centuries and will not change, especially now because people are now falling for and accepting anything, and he's very pleased at what he's accomplishing in the world and in the church.

The art of clowning has the same vibe as those guys back in the mime theaters whom most of them didn't have regular jobs and didn't want the responsibility of having one. They just traveled around as vagabonds from place to place with no special dwelling place. They did shows for money or would do it for just change in a hat on the street. They didn't want to become subject to any rules or authority. They just wanted to clown!

I wondered and asked God what this is all about? I ask him where is all this taking the church and what are we to do. God told me the reason I wanted you to release this information is because it's hurting His people. He said; *I need men and women who will not bite their tongues when it comes to crying out the truth.* I was very much aware that this would be a touchy subject, because it's something that we're doing. And anytime you come against what people are doing, there's going to be a fight. Well, I didn't come to fight anyone; I had to be obedient to the will of God and what He was saying. It was so hard to say at first because mime was something we did in our own church. But I thank God because there were those who are anointed to dance, and did it in the mime art form, UNITL God sent the revelation that came from His Word. We taught what the Levites did and how God anointed *dancers* to dance before Him. We received the understanding that our vessels must be pure and holy so His spirit can conduit through us.

Just when I thought it was over and I had done what He told me to do. God began to speak to me again and told me to let His people know that none of this is of any coincidence. Just as I mentioned in chapter 3 when He began to show me the *ancient spirits* behind the music and the hip-hop religion. He continued to tell me that we're just being revisited by spirits He cast out of heaven from the beginning. He once again told me that the spirit of clowning is going to rise more and more. Just as it did with the children of Israel when God brought them out of bondage and blessed them, but they rose up to play and had *little* or *no regard* for Gods commandments. It's creeping into the house of God today. We're in His presence putting on performances and shows, and making stars and heroes out of the musicians and preachers. We're *robbing* God's people just like the *thugs* did in the *temple of Kali. (from goddess Kali segment in chapter 3)* We're laughing and joking around and our churches are getting full, but God is not being worshipped in spirit and truth. Now He's being *petitioned* for earthly material gains and prosperity like He's a sugar daddy, but not truly worshipped.

But watch what God is *revealing* to us, and see how He puts it all together. During the 10th-12th century in India a movement arose called *Virasaivism*, which means **heroic worship** or to the Hindus, the heroic worship of the god *Shiva.* (also called Siva) Just like the mimes, jesters and fools mentioned before, the Virasaivites were wandering ascetics who adored the goddess Shiva.

In honor of this Hindu goddess all manner of strange feats and acted **kooky, clowning around** as a way of worshipping their god. Listen to this; they *wrote poetry* and *rhymes* and even wrote what is known as the first *blank verse* in history.

To Mime or not to Mime. Their reason for writing what they called it *blank verses* was because they felt that Shiva, the god of chaos and destruction, wouldn't particularly like **tightly rhymed verses.** These Virasiavite poems were called *Vacanas*, a word which comes from the same root as the English word *vacant*, as in blank verse. Now once again, see the similarities in what we do today. When it speaks of the goddess not liking **tightly rhymed verses**; that's presently a popular *musical sound* and *engineering technique* that's used in today's hip-hop and music industry today. Haven't you heard groups sing or rap and the verse is just 1 or 2 milliseconds off the tempo? The beat almost sounds like its dragging and seems a little off, but the sound and style is very appealing. Well this is what it's talking about, this is what they did. That writing style was a type of *chaotic style* of poetry and music that really didn't have to always *rhyme* or be in *perfect tempo*. I'm prophesying! Because Gods worship music in heaven and with David, were performed in **Major Chords**, with perfect harmonies; Satan can not stand the perfect pitch and timing of the anointing in our music. His music will only be played using predominately *minor progressions*. Watch this in days to come. His music will have a more *chaotic sound* to it. It will be draggy in its tempo. A lazy style with a raggedy edge to it. This will happen with all the genres of secular music in which he's in control of. . . . . .*Let me continue.*

Each of these Virasaivite poets had *signature names*. They would give themselves names that would honor their god. For example; My Lord of *Meeting Rivers* or of *Caves* and another is My Lord *of Cars*, which I mentioned back in chapter 3 where, *Siva* worshippers <u>presently</u> take old beat up cars and restore them to mint condition and offer them as a sacrifice to their god.

So the poets and performers were only known themselves, by the names they used to honor Shiva, their own names being forgotten or not even mentioned, so their *stage* or *performance names* gave *honor to their god*. Wow, what lengths people have gone to in order to give honor to their god. Wouldn't it be a blessing if we as Saints of the Most High God, would give our God that kind of glory and honor? Maybe we wouldn't have so much *self heroic worship*.

I know the things I've been talking about in this chapter, is hard stuff! I felt the same way when I was exposed to this by the Lord. I've lost some friends over many of the things I've shared and revealed. God knows that hurts but I've been obedient to His call on my life in uncovering the plan and agenda of the devil. I know it was Gods will because the devil has fought me tooth and nail, not to reveal some of his tactics. He wouldn't care if I was doing something to build his kingdom, but I know this is tearing away at it. So at this point it really doesn't matter what people think. **I know God's voice,** and I know what He told me to do and I will not make any excuses to make anyone happy. I know there's a lot of information and detail written in this chapter, but all God is saying in a nutshell is He doesn't want to be compromised in any way. He wants to know if you love Him enough to do what His Word says do. His Word alone; with no other added ingredients we use to try and help Him out. He's telling us what it's going to take to give Him a true praise and worship. Are you willing to lay down EVERYTHING for the sake of Christ? If you never ever get to sing or dance or even play music, could you lay down all your gifts at His feet and be willing to forsake all to follow Him? Can you take your thoughts, ideas, and how you feel, out of the equation; to see what God is saying to us as Levites? Understanding that we are a separated people for His use alone? Whatever it is, if He says do it, then do it, and if He says don't, then don't. God just wants to know will you be *willing* and *obedient*. If you can do this, God says you will eat the good of the land and you will prosper in your ministries. . .**To mime or not to mime was the question. Not to mime is the answer!**

CHAPTER 9

SELAH

Se'lah. "*a pause or end of song*" There are actually several descriptions of the word Selah that we would not have time to cover. There are about 138 different variations and derivatives to the word as well. This word, which is found only in the poetical books of the Old Testament, occurs seventy-one times in the Psalms and three times in Habakkuk. It is probably a term which had a meaning in the *musical nomenclature* of the Hebrews, though what that meaning may have been is now a matter of pure conjecture. (Gesenius and Ewald and others think it has much the same meaning as our interlude, —**a pause in the voices singing, while the instruments perform alone.**) A word frequently found in the Book of Psalms, and also in Habakkuk 3:9, 13, about seventy-four times in all in Scripture. Some interpret it as meaning *silence or pause;* others, *end, a louder strain, piano,* etc. Another translation renders the word to mean, *a division.* Here's the area I'd like to cover. . . . . . .

This is a short but sweet chapter about a word or instruction used by the musicians and singers of the Old Testament Tabernacle and Temple.

Do you remember times when you've heard an opening scripture read at the beginning of a worship service, and you heard these various scriptures read like; Psalms 24;6, Psalms 46;7, Psalms 46;11, Psalms 47;4, Psalms 59;13, Psalms 77;15 and Psalms 84;8? What are these scriptures? Well these are songs and psalms written by musicians and singers that have a notation in them with a word called, **Selah** during or at the end of the song or poem.

You may recall someone reading one of those scriptures mentioned above, and when they approached the end of the scripture where it says; *Selah or, oh Jacob, Selah,* and the minister reading the scripture doesn't say anything at the end of the verse. That's because you don't actually say the word Selah, when you read those verses, because it's a musical term that means *pause* or *to be in silence.*

Do you remember times when you've heard a choir sing a song, and when they reached a certain place in that song, the choir director gives a signal for the *choir to stop singing,* and for the *musicians to continue playing?* Now you may think the choir director did it because it simply sounds good to have the music play by itself, but in all actuality, at that moment the *singing stopped*, and the *music continued to play by itself*, that's a **Selah.**

It's a moment when the music and the musicians begin to prophesy on their instruments.

Some scholars have advanced these various improvable theories on **Selah** as; *a pause* either for *silence of singing* or *a musical interlude* or a signal for the congregation to sing, recite or fall prostrate on the ground; a cue for the cymbals to crash; a word to be shouted by the congregation; or a sign to the choir to sing at a *higher pitch* or *louder voice*.

In early Jewish tradition though **Selah** meant *forever*, but the most consistent description of this word is, a *musical notation, instructing a pause in the singing, allowing the music to play*. This is fascinating to me because it shows the creativity of God Himself. Even He likes to hear the sound of worship in a certain manner. Since He created *sound* and *silence,* He uses both elements to bring praise and worship to Himself. There's nothing like anointed music and songs that have the ability to change ones life. God may want to hear vocals at one point and on another occasion He knows that in the midst of a church service or any given situation, the enemy will try to come in and hinder His move. So what God does is He calls musicians to play their instruments *under the anointing to assist in destroying the devils yokes*. One important thing to understand is that a true *Selah* in the *spirit realm* can only be accomplished and is only effective when it is administered by *anointed* music and musicians.

Se'lah. *"a pause or end of song"* You may ask; what's a Selah in the spirit realm? We know what it is and what it sounds like in the natural. . . .it's a silence or pause. But what does it sound like in the spirit realm? Glad you asked. It's a sound that you can only sense when the spirit of the Lord is moving in our midst, and the anointing is operating at a *high level*. You can also sense this level of anointing when it's taking place. If you're listening in the spirit you can actually hear when it's coming. Many of you have heard it, but may not have known what you were hearing. Let me prove my point! If you've ever been in a *hi-spirited* service, now when I say hi-spirited service that doesn't lock it into any one particular style of worship; it does mean that a *yielded* group of spirit filled, holy ghost (Jesus Christ) believers are with one accord, and there is an anointed level that makes you sensitive to the move and voice of God.

As I stated before, if you've been in one of these type of services and anointed singing or music is being ministered, you can actually *hear* when the singing is about to *cease* and the *music* will *continue* to play, or sometimes the overall worship almost comes to a complete silence. So when the singing is taking place, and at the junction where the singing stops, and the music continues to play.. . . . . .AT THAT MOMENT IS A SELAH IN THE SPIRIT REALM.

So this type of Selah can only be heard with a *spiritual ear*, and manifests itself outwardly in the worship that we hear with your *natural ear*.

It all works together for Gods purpose. When you operate under this type of anointing, it has the ability to pave the way for a *prophetic utterance* to come forth. A good example of this is in 2 Kings 3:15 where the prophet Elisha called for a minstrel who the *hand of the Lord* was upon, *(the hand represents the anointing of God was on)* to come in and play, and as he did, Elisha began to prophesy. The prophet Elisha could sense the atmosphere and called for the music to play and break up fallow grounds. Then he could come behind that anointed path that was laid and speak a word to Jehoshaphat. So it's in order to allow the minstrels to play under the anointing of God. Sometimes you may want to *stop or pause,* to allow the music to minister to our spirits,. . . . . .it is a **Selah.**

This is a very fascinating word used in scripture. Other meanings for this word I felt were interesting are; a signal for the congregation to sing, recite, or fall prostrate on the ground to worship; a cue for the cymbals to crash; a word to be shouted by the congregation or a sign to the choir to sing a higher pitched or louder note and tone. Other scholars felt the word simply meant, *forever.* Whatever it's total meaning, it was a word or term consistently used by David and his praise and worship team of singers and musicians.

So let us today, take time out and reflect or pause to think of the goodness of the Lord in the land of the living.

Let us fall down on our knees in reverence of Him and worship the creator of heaven and earth. When we Selah, pause and think of the goodness of Jesus, and all He's done for us; just like the other meaning of this word; let the whole congregation show with a loud voice in praise and adoration to our God.

Finally. . .to me this word **Selah**, is the sum total of a worship experience. It gives us the totality of options in our worship. It calls for us to be *in* **silence**, *to pause* and reflect on His goodness. Selah also allows us to use our expressions of worship through the **playing** of our instruments.

Like Joshua and the children of Israel, it demands that all the people to be with one accord and *shout* unto God with a corporate voice of triumph. . . . .**Shout** for the Lord is giving us the victory!

CHAPTER 10

THE ALTAR

The Altar. The structure on which offerings are made to a deity. The Hebrew word for altar is *mizbeah*, from a verbal root meaning *to slaughter*. Greek renders this word as *thusiasterion*, "a place of sacrifice." In the developed temple ritual, the same word is used for both the altar of holocausts and the altar of incense. Thus, an altar is a place where sacrifice is offered, even if it is not an event involving slaughter. *(the sacrificing of ones self to God)* Altars could be natural objects or man-made constructs. Four materials are recorded as being used in altars: stone, earth, metal, and brick. Archaeology has provided numerous examples of altars from Palestine dating back to approximately 3000 B.C. natural rocks were also used (Judges 6:20). An altar could stand alone, or it was located in the courtyard of a shrine. Their Jerusalem temple had two altars: the altar of incense and the altar of holocausts. The altar of incense was placed inside the sanctuary in front of the curtain screening the Holy of Holies. It was made of gold-covered wood. It stood upright and measured 1 x 1 x 2 cubits. Archaeological data indicate that all four corners of the upper surface were slightly peaked. Twice a day, incense was burned on the altar.

The altar of holocausts stood in the courtyard of the temple. Like the other objects in the courtyard, the altar was made of bronze. It measured 20 x 20 x 10 cubits (2 Chronicles 4).

Ahaz replaced this altar with one modeled on an altar he had seen in Damascus (2 Kings 16).

He moved the old altar, using it for divination. In Ezekiel's vision the courtyard altar also was horned (Ezekiel 43:15).

Altars were places where the divine and human worlds interacted. Altars were places of exchange, communication, and influence. God responded actively to altar activity. The contest between Elijah and the prophets of Baal involving an altar demonstrated interaction between Yahweh and Baal. Noah built an altar and offered a sacrifice to Yahweh. God smelled the aroma and found it pleasing. He responded to Noah's action by declaring that He would never again destroy all living things through a flood. In the patriarchal period, altars were markers of place, commemorating an encounter with God (Genesis 12:7), or physical signs of habitation. Abraham built an altar where he pitched his tent between Bethel and Ai.

Presumably at that altar he *called on the name of the Lord* (Genesis 12:8). Interestingly, we are not told if there was a response. In the next passage, however, Abraham went to Egypt and fell into sin, lying about Sarah out of fear of Pharaoh. Perhaps there was no true communication at the altar between Bethel and Ai. Sacrifices were the primary medium of exchange in altar interactions. The priestly code of Leviticus devotes a great deal of space to proper sacrificial procedure, and to what sacrifices are appropriate in various circumstances. Sacrifice was the essential act of external worship. Unlike the divinities of the nations surrounding ancient Israel, Yahweh did not need sacrifices to survive. The Israelites, however, needed to perform the act of sacrifice in order to survive (Exodus 30; 21). The act of sacrifice moved the offering from the profane to the sacred, from the visible to the invisible world. By this action the worshiper sealed a contract with God. Blood, believed to contain the "life" of an animal *(or a human being)* was particularly important in the sacrificial ritual.

It was sprinkled against the altar (Leviticus 1); once a year, blood was smeared on the horns of the incense altar. The horns of the altar may have functioned as boundary markers, setting apart the sacred space that was the actual place of intersection of the *divine* and *human* spheres. In the stark and moving story of Abraham's encounter with God at Moriah, Abraham built an altar and arranged the wood on it (Genesis 22:9).

The Altar. After Isaac was laid on the altar, but before he was sacrificed, God proclaimed his recognition that Isaac had "not been withheld from Him." By placing Isaac on the altar, Abraham transferred him from the profane to the sacred.

This sacred altar and its horns, where the atoning blood was splashed, provided a place of sanctuary. The altar was a place where an unintentional murderer could gain a haven (Exodus 21:13-14). If the murder was premeditated, however, then the altar was clearly profaned by the murderer's presence and the individual could be taken away and killed. Joab was denied the sanctuary of the horns because he had conspired to kill Amasa and Abner. In an oracle against Israel (Amos 3:14), God declared that "the horns of the altar will be cut off and fall to the ground." The message is clear: There will be no place to intercede with God, and no place to claim His sanctuary.

After the exile, the first thing to be rebuilt was the altar. Then the temple was reconstructed. The *temple* was ultimately *secondary* to the *altar*. In chastising the religious establishment, Jesus underlined the sacredness of the altar, making clear his understanding that the altar "makes the gift sacred" (Matthew 23:19). In Revelation the altar in the heavenly temple shelters martyred souls and even speaks (Revelation 16:7).

The New Testament writer of Hebrews (13:10) implies that the ultimate altar is the cross. Here divine and human interchange is consummated. The cross becomes the sanctuary of the believer, providing protection from the penalties of sin.

Now that you have a description and a little history of the alter, allow me to finalize this.

I've been told by different people, when I've asked them to come to church; that they don't like the *messy stuff* that goes on in church. A co-worker once told me that she believes in God, but she's not comfortable coming to church because of all the *mess* she's seen there. I finally stopped her and admonished her that, *there are no perfect churches. As long as you or I are there, it can't be perfect.* She asked me to explain myself. I told her that the church is a hospital. It's for the sick! Jesus taught that the *well* don't need a physician, the sick do. Jesus came to this earth to save those who were lost. Which means all of us were sick *(sin sick)* at some point. Apostle Paul picks it up and says; we're *striving* for *perfection*. The perfection he speaks of, does not mean perfect. In Genesis 17: 1, God spoke to Abram and said; *walk before Him and be thou perfect.* This *perfection* spoke to the *condition of the heart*. God knew that in our flesh dwelt no good thing. Our *flesh* doesn't have the ability to be perfect. The perfection here deals with the *purpose* and *intent* of the *heart* to do that which is right, and to walk *holy* before God. I explained to the young lady that when you look at it; the altar in the Old Testament was a dirty place. Think about it! The priest had to kill the bulls, slaughter the animals, gut them out and take the fat, flay it and so on. There was a smelly stench at the alter because of the blood. The alter is the place where you come to *clean up* your life. You don't wait until you have yourself all cleaned up to come to the house of God. You come *just as you are*; *dirty, nasty, full of mess, pride* and *condemnation*. Then the blood of Jesus Christ, which was shed on the **ultimate altar of sacrifice**; comes in and *cleanses us* from unrighteousness, *washes us* and *makes us* what we shall be. The church is where all the mess should be. It should be the place where we can come to the altar and get it cleaned up! We can come and get rid of our *pride* and *self-righteousness*, because such were some of you, but now you've been washed. Don't forsake the assembling of yourselves together, because the altar is exactly where all that stuff should be. So just learn to *step over the mess*, and come to Jesus just as **you are**. . . . . . .*messy!*

CHAPTER 11

THE TABERNACLE

The Tabernacle. *A house or dwelling-place* (Job 5:24; 18:6, etc.).

A portable shrine (Compare Acts 19:24) containing the image of Moloch (Amos 5:26).

The human body (2 Corinthians 5:1, 4); a tent, as opposed to a permanent dwelling.

The sacred tent (Heb. *mishkan*, "the dwelling-place"); is the movable tent-temple which Moses erected for the service of God, according to the *pattern* which God Himself showed to him on the mount (Exodus 25:9; Hebrews 8:5). It is called *the tabernacle of the congregation*, rather *of meeting*, i.e., where God promised to meet with Israel (Exodus 29:42); the *tabernacle of the testimony* (Exodus 38:21; Numbers 1:50), which does not, however, designate the whole structure, but only the enclosure which contained the *ark of the testimony* (Exodus 25:16,22; Numbers 9:15); the *tabernacle of witness* (Numbers 17:8); the *house of the Lord* (Deuteronomy 23:18); the *temple of the Lord* (Joshua 6:24); a *sanctuary* (Exodus 25:8).

A particular account of the materials which the people provided for the erection and of the building itself is recorded in Exodus 25: 1-40. The execution of the plan mysteriously given to Moses was entrusted to Bezaleel and Aholiab, who were specially endowed with wisdom and artistic skill, probably gained in Egypt, for this purpose (Exodus 35:30-35).

The people provided materials for the tabernacle so abundantly that Moses was under the necessity of restraining them (Exodus 36:6).

What a blessing it must have been to have more than enough. Pastors today wouldn't have to get up and plead with the congregation to give, we would just give as God has blessed and provided. God wants to do the same today, but can He trust you to give of your substance to the ministry?

These stores, from which the people so liberally contributed for this purpose, must have consisted in a great part of the gifts which the Egyptians so readily bestowed on them on the eve of their exit from Egypt. (Exodus 12:35, 36)

The Tabernacle

The tabernacle was a rectangular enclosure, in length about 45 feet (i.e., reckoning a cubit at 18 inches) and in breadth and height about 15 feet. Its two sides and its western end were made of boards of *acacia wood*, placed on end, resting in sockets of *brass*, the eastern end being left open (Exodus 26:22).

This framework was covered with four coverings, the first of *linen*, in which figures of the symbolic *cherubim* were wrought with needlework in *blue* and *purple* and *scarlet* threads, and probably also with threads of *gold* (Exodus 26:1-6; 36:8-13). Above this was a second covering of twelve curtains of *black goats'-hair cloth*, reaching down on the outside almost to the ground (Exodus 26:7-11). The third covering was of *rams' skins* dyed red, and the fourth was of *badgers' skins* (Heb. *Tahash*, i.e., the dugong, a species of seal), Exodus 25:5; 26:14; 35:7, 23; 36:19; 39:34. Internally it was divided by a veil into two chambers, the exterior of which was called the *holy place*, also *the sanctuary* (Hebrews 9:2) and the *first tabernacle* (6); and the interior, the holy of holies, *the holy place, the Holiest,* the *second tabernacle* (Exodus 28:29; Heb. 9:3, 7).

The veil separating these two chambers was a double curtain of the finest workmanship, which was never passed except by the high priest once a year, *the great Day of Atonement.*

The holy place was separated from the outer court which enclosed the tabernacle by a curtain, which hung over the six pillars which stood at the east end of the tabernacle, and by which it was entered.

The Tabernacle. The *order* as well as the typical character of the services of the tabernacle are recorded in Hebrews 9; 10:19-22.

The holy of holies, a cube of 10 cubits, contained the *ark of the testimony*, i.e., the oblong chest containing the two *tables of stone*, the *pot of manna*, and *Aaron's rod* that budded.

The holy place was the western and larger chamber of the tabernacle. Here were placed the table for the *shewbread*, the *golden candlestick,* and the golden *altar of incense.*

Round about the tabernacle was a court, enclosed by curtains hung upon sixty pillars (Exodus 27:9-18). This court was 150 feet long and 75 feet broad. Within it were placed the *altar of burnt offering*, which measured 7 1/2 feet in length and breadth and 4 1/2 feet high, with horns at the four corners, and the *laver of brass* (Exodus 30:18), which stood between the altar and the tabernacle.

The whole tabernacle was completed in seven months. On the first day of the first month of the second year after the Exodus, it was formally set up, and the cloud of the divine presence descended on it (Exodus 39:22-43; 40:1-38). It cost 29 talents, 730 shekels of gold, 100 talents 1,775 shekels of silver, 70 talents, 2,400 shekels of brass (Exodus 38:24-31).

The tabernacle was so constructed that it could easily be taken down and conveyed from place to place during the wanderings in the wilderness. The first encampment of the Israelites after crossing the Jordan was at Gilgal, and there the tabernacle remained for seven years (Joshua 4:19).

It was afterwards removed to Shiloh (Joshua 18:1), where it remained during the time of the Judges, till the days of Eli, when the ark, having been carried out into the camp when the Israelites were at war with the Philistines, was taken by the enemy (1 Samuel 4), and was never afterwards restored to its place in the tabernacle. The old tabernacle erected by Moses in the wilderness was transferred to Nob (1 Samuel 21:1), and after the destruction of that city by Saul (22:9; 1 Chronicles 16:39, 40), to Gibeon. It is mentioned for the last time in 1 Chronicles 21:29. A new tabernacle was erected by David at Jerusalem (2 Samuel 6:17; 1 Chronicles 16:1), and the ark was brought from Perez-uzzah and deposited in it (2 Samuel 6:8-17; 2Chr 1:4).

The word thus rendered ('ohel) in Exodus 33:7 denotes simply a tent, probably Moses' own tent, for the tabernacle was not yet erected.

The tabernacle instituted by Moses was called:

Sanctuary Exodus 25:8
Tabernacle (KJV), *Tent of Meeting* (RSV) (Exodus 27:21) Exodus 33:7; 2 Chronicles 5:5
Tent of Testimony (KJV) Exodus 38:21; Numbers 1:50
Tent of Testimony (RSV) Numbers 17:7, 8; 2 Chronicles 24:6
Temple of the Lord 1 Samuel 1:9; 3:3 *House of the Lord* Joshua 6:24
Pattern of, revealed to Moses,
Exodus 25:9; 26:30; 39:32,42,43; Acts 7:44; Hebrews 8:5
Materials for, voluntarily offered,
Exodus 25:1-8; 35:4-29; 36:3-7
Value of the substance contributed for,
Exodus 38:24-31
Workmen who constructed it were inspired,
Exodus 31:1-11; 35:30-35
Description of the frame,
Exodus 26:15-37; 36:20-38
The outer covering,
Exodus 25:5; 26:7-14; 36:14-19
The second covering,
Exodus 25:5; 26:14; 35:7, 23; 36:19; 39:34
The curtains of,
Exodus 26:1-14, 31-37; 27:9-16; 35:15, 17; 36:8-19, 35, 37
The courtyard of,
Exodus 27:9-17; 38:9-16, 18; 40:8, 33
The Holy Place of,
Exodus 26:31-37; 40:22-26; Hebrews 9:2-6, 8
The Most Holy Place,
Exodus 26:33-35; 40:20, 21; Hebrews 9:3-5, 7, 8

The Tabernacle

The furniture of,
Exodus 25:10-40; 27:1-8, 19; 37; 38:1-8
Study the *Altar*
Study the *Ark*
Study the *Candlestick* (lampstand)
Study the *Cherubim* (cherubs)
Study the *Laver*
Study the *Mercy-Seat*
Study the *Shewbread*
The Completion,
Exodus 39:32
Dedication of,
Numbers 7
Sanctified,
Exodus 29:43; 40:9-16; Numbers 7:1
Anointed with holy oil,
Exodus 30:25, 26; Leviticus 8:10; Numbers 7:1
Sprinkled with blood,
Leviticus 16:15-20; Hebrews 9:21, 23
Filled with the cloud of glory,
Exodus 40:34-38
How they prepared for removal during the travels of the Israelites,
Numbers 1:51; 4:5-15
How and by whom carried,
Numbers 4:5-33; 7:6-9
Strangers (foreigners) forbidden to enter,
Numbers 1:51
Duties of the Levites concerning,
Study the *Levites*
Defilement of, punished,
Leviticus 15:31; Numbers 19:13, 20; Ezekiel 5:11; 23:38
Duties of the priests in relation to,
Study the *Priest*
Israelites worship at,
Numbers 10:3; 16:19, 42, 43; 20:6; 25:6; 1 Samuel 2:22; Psalms 27:4
Offerings brought to,
Leviticus 17:4; Numbers 31:54; Deuteronomy 12:5, 6, 11-14
Causes tried at,
Deuteronomy 12:5, 6, 11-14
Tribes encamped around, while in the wilderness,
Numbers 2
All males required to appear before, three times each year,
Exodus 23:17

Tabernacle tax,
Exodus 30:11-16
Carried in front of the people of Israel in the line of march,
Numbers 10:33-36; Joshua 3:3-6
The Lord reveals himself at,
Leviticus 1:1; Numbers 1:1; 7:89; 12:4-10; Deuteronomy 31:14, 15
Pitched at Gilgal,
Joshua 4:18, 19
At Shiloh,
Joshua 18:1; 19:51; Judges 18:31; 20:18, 26, 27; 21:19; 1 Samuel 2:14; 4:3, 4; Jeremiah 7:12, 14
At Nob,
1 Samuel 21:1-6
At Gibeon,
1 Chronicles 21:29
Renewed by David, and pitched upon Mount Zion,
1 Chronicles 15:1; 16:1, 2; 2 Chronicles 1:4
Solomon offers sacrifice at,
2 Chronicles 1:3-6
Brought to the temple by Solomon,
2 Chronicles 5:5; 1 Kings 8:1, 4, 5
Symbol of spiritual things,
Psalms 15:1; Hebrews 8:2, 5; 9:1-12, 24

The structure referred to in Scripture as the tabernacle was the center of the worship of Yahweh by the people of Israel from shortly after the exodus until it was replaced by Solomon's temple around 960 b.c. The term *tabernacle* is sometimes used to refer to one part of a larger complex: the *tent-like* structure that stood within a court enclosed by linen curtains. At other times the term describes the entire complex. The inner structure was comprised of gold-plated planks linked together and standing on edge. They formed three sides of a rectangle, with the fourth closed by a heavy curtain. The whole structure was draped with several layers of cloth and leather. Here God was understood to be especially present for his people. Even more important, the tabernacle and the sacrificial system connected with it are understood by the Bible to be richly symbolic of truths concerning God and the possibility of human fellowship with him.

The first references to the tabernacle appear in Exodus 5, where Moses begins to receive the instructions for making this structure. These instructions continue through chapter 31. Then, after a three-chapter interlude dealing with the *golden calf* episode and its aftermath, chapter 35 resumes the story of the tabernacle, reporting how the complex was built. This report repeats the previous instructions almost word for word. The report carries on through chapter

40, where the book reaches its climactic conclusion with God's glory filling the tabernacle.

Part of the significance of the tabernacle is seen through the placement of this block of material in the Book of Exodus. The book contains three segments: chapters 1-15, *the account of the deliverance from Egypt, culminating in the Red Sea crossing;* chapters 16-24, *the account of the journey to Sinai, culminating in the sealing of the covenant;* and chapters 25-40, *the account of the building of the tabernacle, culminating in its being filled with the glory of God.*

This literary structure shows that the ultimate need of the people was not for deliverance from physical oppression or from theological darkness, but from alienation from God. Deliverance from bondage and from spiritual darkness are not ends, but means to the end of fellowship with God. This is the significance of the title *tabernacle* (or *tent,* Heb. *Ohel* [l,hoa]) *of meeting.* Apparently first applied to the interim tent where Moses met God before the tabernacle was complete (Exodus 33:7), the phrase aptly sums up the function of the tabernacle. Not only does the structure symbolize the presence of God with his people; it also shows how it is that sinful people can come into, and live in, the presence of a holy God.

The incident of the golden calf, which is reported between the instructions for the tabernacle and its building, highlights both the significance and function of the tabernacle.

The Tabernacle. The people recognized they needed divine protection and guidance, especially in the light of Moses' inexplicable failure to return from the mountain (Exodus 32:1). And they were sure they could not have these unless God was tangibly present with them. The tragedy of the story is that at the very moment they were demanding that Aaron meet their needs, God was giving Moses the instructions that would meet those needs in a much more complete way than Aaron's feeble efforts ever could.

When human needs are met in God's way the results far surpass anything we could conceive on our own. The golden calf could hardly compare to the tabernacle. In the tabernacle there was beauty of design, color, texture, and shape. There was a satisfying diversity in objects and spaces. There was a sense of motion through separate stages from the profane to the sacred. There was a profound, yet evident, symbolism capable of conveying multiple truths to different persons.

Moreover, the impact upon people is profoundly different when our needs are met in God's way. Here, instead of limited gifts and no participation (Ex. 32:3-4), everyone has something to contribute, whether in talent or material (Ex. 35:4-10). Here persons give freely, without coercion (Ex. 35:21, contra Ex. 32:2). Here work is done according to *Spirit-imparted gifts,* not according to rank appearance (Ex. 35:30-36:2). And here, instead of further alienation from God (Ex. 32:9), the glory of God's presence is revealed in the midst of human life (Ex. 40:35).

Thus, Exodus 32-34 is an integral part of the whole final segment of the book, illustrating by contrast the same truths that chapters 25-31 and 35-40 teach in a positive way.

Beyond a tangible representation of the presence of God, the tabernacle also is intended to teach by visual means the theological principles whereby that presence is possible. It is necessary to exercise care at this point because the Bible does not explain all the visual symbolism, and it is possible to expend too much energy in speculation. However, the main lines are clear enough. The color **white**, which was especially prominent in the linen curtains of the court, calls attention to the purity of God and the necessary purity of those who would live in His presence. **Blue** speaks of God's transcendence; **purple**, of his royalty; and **red**, of the blood that must be shed if a Holy God is ever to live with a sinful human. The accents of **gold** and **silver** that occurred throughout the structure speak of the riches of the divine kingdom and its blessings.

Possibly the multiple coverings over the Holy Place and the Holy of Holies speak of the security that attends those who live with God.

The most significant symbolism is surely that found in the arrangement of spaces and objects. The court itself speaks of the separation between God and the sinner. It is impossible for us to come into the presence of God in our normal state. This gulf is further reinforced by the veil at the door of the Holy Place, and by the one that closed off the Holy of Holies.

It is impossible that good intentions and honest effort can ever bring us to God.

We come in the ways He has dictated, or not at all.

Then, how is it possible for us to come into that Presence which is life itself?

The tabernacle shows the way. The first object encountered is the altar. Here, in the starkest visual terms, is the representation of the truth that *without the shedding of blood there is no forgiveness* (Hebrews 9:22). But the altar raises its own questions; how can a bull or a sheep or a goat die in the place of a person who has been made just a little lower than God Himself? (Micah 6:6-8)

The Tabernacle. For the Old Testament believer, the solution to this enigma was, in many ways, a mystery. Nevertheless, there is no other way to the Holy of Holies than past the altar. Behind the altar is the *laver*. Here we are reminded that God is clean. *Clean* describes the essential character of God, who is faithful, upright, merciful, and true. To be unclean is to fail to share that character, and that which does not share God's character cannot exist in His white-hot presence (Isaiah 6:5). Thus, it is necessary for those who would come into His presence to be washed and made clean (Psalms 51:7), and the laver represents both that necessity and that possibility.

Inside the Holy Place three objects demand attention. On the right is a *table with twelve loaves of bread* on it. In pagan temples this is where the gods were believed to sit and eat. But in Israel's tabernacle, this is where God was understood to feed His people (Psalms 23:5).

He had no need of food (Psalms 50:12-13), but Israel was famished for Him (Psalms 107:9; Isaiah 65:13).

On the left was the *lampstand* where the light was never permitted to go out. This represented the light that God was to His people in the darkened world of sin (Psalms 27:1). Directly in front of the worshiper at the far end of the space was the *altar of incense.*

Here incense burned day and night, symbolizing both the sacred presence and the prayer of worshipers that can rise to God like sweet perfume at any moment of the day (Psalms 141:2; Revelation 8:3-4). Thus, the objects in the Holy Place were the evidence of the blessings that are for those who live in the presence of God: light, sustenance, and communion. In all the pagan temples the innermost space was reserved for the idol, the visual expression of the pagan insistence that the divine is clothed with this world, and that this world is the body of the divine. Alone of all the ancient peoples, the Hebrews insisted this is not true. God is not part of this world, and may not be represented by any natural object. So what was in the innermost space of the tabernacle? A box! We usually refer to the object with the a.d. 1611 term *ark*, but that is just an archaic word for *box*. A box to represent the presence of God? To be sure it was a beautifully ornamented box, with winged figures of some sort molded into its golden top.

But for all that, it was still just a box.

Why would the Hebrew's use something as mundane as a box to convey the presence of the almighty God? Negatively, a box simply cannot be worshiped as somehow being God. It is neither a human figure nor a natural object. To be sure, some translations have God sitting *upon* the cherubim, but the Hebrew does not use the preposition *upon*. Rather, it uses no preposition, or *with respect to*—a clear attempt to avoid even that potential confusion of object and reality. If it is desired to have an object that will remind us of God's real presence while underscoring the prohibition of images, a box is an excellent choice. But the ark has positive significance as well.

It represents the true basis of divine-human relations. Those relations do not rest upon ritualistic manipulation—magic—as idol-worship assumes. Rather, the basis is covenant, a relationship of mutual commitment whereby grace is responded to in obedience, especially on an ethical plane. Surrender, trust, and obedience are the operative principles, not magical identification.

How appropriate that all these truths should be represented in the box in the Holy of Holies. Aaron's rod represents the delivering grace of God, both in the exodus events and in God's selection of the Levitical priests as mediators; the *manna* represents God's sustaining grace; and the tablets of the *Ten Commandments* summarize the terms of the relationship.

The Tabernacle. The ark tells us that we cannot manipulate the essence of God; we can only remember what He has done for us and relate to Him and one another accordingly. The sad truth is that the human spirit is not able to fulfill the terms of the covenant, no matter how pure the initial intentions may have been. As the Hebrews first broke their covenant with God in less than six weeks, so every human who has ever lived has learned that living for God is not a matter of good intentions. Every one who has ever sought to live for God has discovered that when all has been done, we have fallen far short of God's moral perfection, and His glory.

What then is to be done? The covenant was sworn to with the most solemn oaths. Now it lies broken in the presence of God, calling out for justice. How can God be *Justice* and *Love* at the same time? The answer is the *cover* (mercy-seat). The Hebrew word for the nullification of the effects of sin is *kapar*, "to cover." It is surely not a coincidence that the lid of the box is called *the cover*.

For this lid not only covers what it is in the box; it is also the place where covering for sin, particularly unconscious sin, is made once a year through sprinkling the blood of a sacrificial animal upon that cover (Leviticus 16:11-17). The broken covenant, calling out for the death of those who swore in the name of God that they would be obedient or die, was satisfied by a representive sacrificial death.

But this brings to the forefront the question raised by the great altar in the court outside. If the fundamental tenet of the Hebrew faith, God's transcendence, is true, if God cannot be magically manipulated through the creation, then of what ultimate good is the sacrifice of one bull, or, for that matter, tens of thousands of bulls? What's the use? This seems a hopeless dilemma.

God's justice cannot be satisfied magically, but it must be satisfied. God cannot simply ignore it.

To do so would be to destroy the whole basis of a world of cause and effect.

This is the dilemma that came to such a dramatic resolution for the persons of the first century a.d., who suddenly realized what the coupling of Jesus Christ's divinity and His unjust death, and His glorious resurrection meant. Here was the perfect sacrifice! Here was the one to whom the sacrificial system and the tabernacle pointed.

That system and that structure had no magical efficacy in themselves. They were only efficacious in removing sin insofar as they pointed to the One who could indeed die for all.

If God could die and then return to life, that death could indeed be in the place of all who would ever live and sin. This is the vision that captured the writer of the Book of Hebrews and is recorded in chapter 9 of that book.

He realized that the tabernacle and the sacrificial system were simply symbolic of an eternal reality. The language used there might suggest that the author thought the earthly tabernacle was a copy of an eternal heavenly one. But to take that position is to miss the point of the passage. The author is saying that the earthly tabernacle and the sacrifices offered there are representative of eternal, spiritual truth: the all-sufficiency of the sacrifice of Christ for all eternity. The tabernacle represents truth, not some other material entity. The author is possibly using the language of Platonic philosophy, but the biblical philosophy of transcendence is diametrically at odds with Plato's insistence that this world is unreal. The writer of Hebrews knows this is evident in 9:25-26, where he shows that Christ is not being continually sacrificed in some heavenly reality, but that he died once for all here on earth, and so *here* fulfilled what the **tabernacle** was all about.

Today, we are to be like Him. We are now that tabernacle for Christ to dwell and abide in.

CHAPTER 12

THE TEMPLE

The Temple. There is perhaps no building of the ancient world, which has attracted so much attention since the time of its destruction as the temple, which Solomon built by Herod.

Its spoils were considered worthy of forming the principal illustration of one of the most beautiful of Roman triumphal arches, and Justinian's highest architectural ambition was that he might surpass it. Throughout the middle ages it influenced to a considerable degree the forms of Christian churches, and its peculiarities were the watchwords and rallying-points of all associations of builders. When the French expedition to Egypt, in the first years of this century, had made the world familiar with the wonderful architectural remains of that country, every one jumped to the conclusion that Solomon's temple must have been designed after an Egyptian model. The discoveries in Assyria by Botta and Layard have within the last thirty years given an entirely new direction to the researches of the restorers. Unfortunately, however, no Assyrian temple has yet been exhumed of a nature to throw much light on this subject, and we are still forced to have recourse to the later buildings at Persepolis, or to general deductions from the style of the nearly contemporary secular buildings at Nineveh and elsewhere, for such illustrations as are available. THE TEMPLE OF **SOLOMON**: It was David who first proposed to replace the tabernacle by a more permanent building, but was forbidden for the reasons assigned by the prophet Nathan, (2 Samuel 7:5) etc.; and though he collected materials and made arrangements, the execution of the task was left for his son Solomon. The gold and silver alone accumulated by David are at the lowest reckoned to have amounted to between two and three billion dollars, a sum which can be paralleled from secular history.

Solomon, with the assistance of Hiram king of Tyre, commenced this great undertaking in the fourth year of his reign, B.C. 1012, and completed it in seven years, B.C. 1005. There were 183,000 Jews and strangers employed on it, of Jews 30,000, by rotation 10,000 a month; of Canaanites 153,600, of whom 70,000 were bearers of burdens, 80,000 hewers of wood and stone, and

3600 overseers. The parts were all prepared at a distance from the site of the building, and when they were brought together the whole immense structure was erected without the sound of hammer, axe or any tool of iron. (1 Kings 6:7) The building occupied the site prepared for it by David, which had formerly been the threshing-floor of the *Jebusite Ornan or Araunah, on Mount Moriah. (study this)* The whole area enclosed by the outer walls formed a square of about 600 feet; but the sanctuary itself was comparatively small, inasmuch as it was intended only for the ministrations of the priests, the congregation of the people assembling in the courts. In this and all other essential points the temple followed the model of the tabernacle, from which it differed chiefly by having chambers built about the sanctuary for the abode of the priests and attendants and the keeping of treasures and stores. In all its dimensions, length, breadth and height, the sanctuary itself was exactly double the size of the tabernacle, the ground plan measuring 80 cubits by 40, while that of the tabernacle was 40 by 20, and the height of the temple being 30 cubits, while that of the tabernacle was 15. *(Compare the following account with the chapter,* **TABERNACLE**) As in the tabernacle, the temple consisted of three parts, the porch, the holy place, and the holy of holies.

The Temple. The front of the porch was supported, after the manner of some Egyptian temples, by the two great brazen pillars, Jachin and Boaz, 18 cubits high, with capitals of 5 cubits more, adorned with lily-work and pomegranates (1 Kings 7:15-22). The places of the two *veils* of the tabernacle were occupied by partitions, in which were folding-doors. The whole interior was lined with woodwork richly carved and overlaid with gold. Indeed, both within and without the building were conspicuously chiefly by the lavish use of the gold of Ophir and Parvaim.

It glittered in the morning sun *(it has been well said)* like the sanctuary of an El Dorado.

Above the sacred ark, which was placed, as of old, in the most holy place, were made two new cherubim, one pair of whose wings met above the ark, and another pair reached to the walls behind them. In the holy place, besides the altar of incense, which was made of cedar overlaid with gold there were seven golden candlesticks instead of one, and the table of shew-bread was replaced by ten golden tables, bearing, besides the shew-bread, the innumerable golden vessels for the service of the sanctuary. *(can't you feel the presence of the Lord right about now?)*

The *outer court* was no doubt double the size of that of the tabernacle; and we may therefore safely assume that it was 10 cubits in height, 100 cubits north and south, and 200 east and west. It contained an inner court, called the *court of the priests*; but the arrangement of the courts and of the porticos and gateways of the enclosure, though described by Josephus, belongs apparently to the temple of Herod. The outer court there was a new altar of burnt offering, much larger than the old one. Instead of the brazen laver there was *a molten sea* of brass, a masterpiece of Hiram's skill for the ablution of the priests. It was called a *sea* from its great size.

Sea, Molten *(study this also)* the chambers for the priests were arranged in successive stories against the sides of the sanctuary; not, however, reaching to the top, so as to leave space for the windows to light the holy and the most holy place. We are told by Josephus and the Talmud that there was a superstructure on the temple equal in height to the lower part; and this is confirmed by the statement in the books of Chronicles that Solomon overlaid the *upper chambers* with *gold*. (2 Chronicles 3:9) Moreover, *the altars on the top of the upper chamber*, mentioned in the books of the Kings, (2 Kings 23:12) were apparently upon the temple. *(The dedication of the temple was the grandest ceremony ever performed under the Mosaic dispensation)*.

The temple was destroyed on the capture of Jerusalem by Nebuchadnezzar, B.C. 586.

TEMPLE OF **ZERUBBABEL**. We have very few particulars regarding the temple, which the Jews erected after their return from the captivity (about B.C. 520), and no description that would enable us to realize its appearance. But there are some dimensions given in the Bible and elsewhere which are extremely interesting, as affording points of comparison between it and the temple which preceded it and the one erected after it. The first and most authentic are those given in the book of Ezra, (Ezra 6:3) when quoting the decree of Cyrus, wherein it is said, *"Let the house be builded, the place where they offered sacrifices and let the foundations thereof be strongly laid; the height thereof three-score cubits, and the breadth thereof three-score cubits, with three rows of great stones, and a row of new timber."* Josephus quotes this passage almost literally, but in doing so enables us to translate the word **rows** as meaning *stories*.

The Temple. We see by the description in Ezra, that this temple was about one third larger than the temple built by King Solomon.

Ezra 3:12-13, gives us interesting commentary of how the Jews felt after the construction of the new temple. There was a remarkable mixture of affections upon laying the foundation of the temple. Those that only knew the misery of having no temple at all, praised the Lord with shouts of joy. To them, even this foundation seemed great. We ought to be thankful for the *beginnings of mercy*, though it wasn't yet perfect. But those who remembered the glory of the first temple, and considered how far inferior this new temple was likely to be, wept with a loud voice.

There was reason for it, and if they bewailed the sin that was the cause of this melancholy change, they did well. Yet it was wrong to cast a damper on the dedication of the new temple, knowing they despised the day of small things, and were unthankful for the good they enjoyed. But let not the remembrance of former afflictions drown the sense of present mercies. It was the lavish display of the precious metals, the elaboration of carved ornament, and the beauty of the textile fabrics, which made up their splendor and rendered them so precious in the eyes of the people, thus having mixed emotions in the streams of their tears during its construction.

TEMPLE OF **EZEKIEL**. The vision of a temple which the prophet Ezekiel saw while residing on the banks of the Chebar in Babylonia, in the twenty-fifth year of the captivity, does not add much to our knowledge of the subject. It is not a description of a temple that ever was built or ever could be erected at Jerusalem, and can consequently only be considered as the *beau ideal* of what a Shemitic temple ought to be.

TEMPLE OF **HEROD**. Herod the Great announced to the people assembled at the Passover, B.C. 20 or 19, his intention of restoring the temple; *(probably a stroke of policy on the part of Herod to gain the favor of the Jews and to make his name great.)* if we may believe Josephus, he pulled down the whole edifice to its foundations, and laid them anew on an enlarged scale; but the ruins still exhibit, in some parts, what seem to be the foundations laid by Zerubbable, and beneath them the more massive substructions of Solomon. The new edifice was a stately pile of Graeco-Roman architecture, built in white marble gilded *acroteria*. It is minutely described by Josephus, and the New Testament has made us familiar with the pride of the Jews in its magnificence. A different feeling, however, marked the commencement of the work, which met with some opposition from the fear that what Herod had begun he would not be able to finish. He overcame all jealousy by engaging not to pull down any part of the existing building till all the materials for the new edifice were collected on its site. Two years appear to have been occupied in preparations among which Josephus mentions the teaching of some of the priests and Levites to work as masons and carpenters and then the work began.

The holy *house*, including the *porch, sanctuary* and *holy of holies*, was finished in a year and a half, B.C. 16. Its completion, on the anniversary of Herod's inauguration, was celebrated by lavish sacrifices and a great feast. About B.C. 9, eight years from the commencement, the court and cloisters of the temple were finished, and the bridge between the south cloister and the upper city *(demolished by Pompey)* was doubtless now rebuilt with that massive masonry of which some remains still survive.

The Temple. *(The work, however, was not entirely ended till A.D. 64, under Herod Agrippa II. So the statement in* John 2:20 *is correct)* The temple or holy *house* itself was in dimensions and arrangement very similar to that of Solomon, or rather that of Zerubbabel, more like the latter; but this was surrounded by an inner enclosure of great strength and magnificence, measuring as nearly as can be made out 180 cubits by 240, and adorned by porches and ten gateways of great magnificence; and beyond this again was an outer enclosure measuring externally 400 cubits each way, which was adorned with porticos of greater splendor than any we know of as attached to any temple of the ancient world. The temple was certainly situated in the southwest angle of the area now known as the Haram area at Jerusalem, and its dimensions were what Josephus states them to be, 400 cubits, or one stadium, each way. At the time when Herod rebuilt it, he enclosed a space *twice as large* as that before occupied by the temple and its courts, an expression that probably must not be taken too literally at least, if we are to depend on the measurements of *Hecataeus*. According to them, the whole area of Herod's temple was between four and five times greater than that which preceded it. What Herod did apparently, was to take in the whole space between the temple and the city wall on its east side, and to add a considerable space on the north and south to support the porticos which he added there.

As the temple terrace thus became the principal defense of the city on the east side, there were no gates or openings in that direction, and being situated on a sort of rocky brow, as evidenced from its appearance in the vaults that bounded it on this side, it was at all later times considered unattackable from the eastward.

The north side, too, where not covered by the fortress Antonia, became part of the defenses of the city, and was likewise without external gates. On the south side, which was enclosed by the wall of Ophel, there were notable gates nearly in the centre. These gates still exist at a distance of about 365 feet from the southwestern angle, and are perhaps the only architectural features of the temple of Herod which remain *in situ*. This entrance consists of a double archway of Cyclopean architecture on the level of the ground, opening into a square vestibule measuring 40 feet each way. From this a double funnel nearly 200 feet in length, leads to a flight of steps which rise to the surface in the court of the temple, exactly at that gateway of the inner temple which led to the altar, and is one of the four gateways on this side by which any one arriving from Ophel would naturally wish to enter the inner enclosure. We learn from the Talmud that the gate of the inner temple to which this passage led was called the "water gate;" and it is interesting to be able to identify a spot so prominent in the description of Nehemiah (Nehemiah 12:37). Toward the west there were four gateways to the external enclosure of the temple. The most magnificent part of the temple, in an architectural point of view, seems certainly to have been the cloisters which were added to the outer court when it was enlarged by Herod. The cloisters in the west, north and east sides were composed of double rows of Corinthian columns, 25 cubits or 37 feet 6 inches in height, with flat roof, and resting against the outer wall of the temple. These, however, were immeasurably surpassed in magnificence by the royal porch or **Stoa Basilica**, which overhung the southern wall. It consisted of a **nave** and two aisles, facing toward the temple being open, and toward the country, being closed by a wall.

The Temple. The breadth of the centre aisle was 95 feet of the side aisles, 30 from centre to centre of the pillars; their height 50 feet, and that of the centre aisle 100 feet. Its section was thus something in excess of that of York Cathedral, while its total length was one stadium or 600 Greek feet, or 100 feet in excess of York or our largest Gothic cathedrals. This magnificent structure was supported by 162 Corinthian columns. The porch on the east was called

The Temple

Solomon's Porch. The court of the temple was very nearly a square. It may have been exactly so, we don't have all the details to enable us to feel quite certain about it. To the eastward of this was the court of the women. The great ornament of these inner courts seems to have been their gateways, the three especially on the north and south leading to the temple court.

These according to Josephus, were of great height, strongly fortified and ornamented with great elaboration. But the wonder of all was the great eastern gate leading from the court of the women to the upper court. It was in all probability the one called the *beautiful gate* in the New Testament. Immediately within this gateway stood the altar of burnt offerings. Both the altar and the temple were enclosed by a low parapet, one cubit in height, placed so as to keep the people separate from the priests while the latter were performing their functions.

Within this last enclosure, toward the westward, stood the temple itself. As before mentioned, its internal dimensions were the same as those of the temple of Solomon. Although these remained the same, however, there seems no reason to doubt that. The whole plan was augmented by the *pteromata*, or surrounding parts being increased from 10 to 20 cubits, so that the third temple, like the second, measured 60 cubits across and 100 cubits east and west.

The width of the facade was also augmented by wings or shoulders projecting 20 cubits each way, making the whole breadth 100 cubits, or equal to the length.

There is no reason for doubting that the sanctuary always stood on *identically the same spot* in which it had been placed by Solomon a thousand years before it was rebuilt by Herod.

The temple of Herod was destroyed by the Romans under Titus, Friday, August 9, A.D. 70.

A Mohammedan mosque now stands on its site.

I know you may be asking yourself, why I'm covering all this information concerning the temple. There's a saying that states; *it's hard to know where you're going, if you don't know where you've been or where you come from.*

If you paid attention to the chapters covering the Altar and the Tabernacle, you can see how they paid attention to every *antiquated* detail. **They followed God's plan to the letter. Understand that when you follow *order* or *structure* as they did, you to will come away with the same results they did in scripture. Every piece of furniture was in its rightful place. From the length of the curtains, to the weight of the gold that overlaid the wood, to the measurements of the building structure itself.**

When we as Levites and people of God come together and abide in the place where God has ordained us to be, and operate in the area where God instructed you to, *then* we'll see the manifestation of God's presence in *our temples* and places of worship.

Just like the furniture was *set in order* in their tabernacles; whether it was **two or three holy items gathered together in His name**, there God was *in the midst of them,* behind the veil.

So now you understand that yes, it can be a tedious job, following the plan of God to the letter.

But when we *get in our places* and follow Gods *order*, we'll also find Him *in our midst* today.

The Temple. His anointing will rest rule and abide in our ministries if we will yield to the spirit of God and allow Him to move in our midst.

Therefore it was important that we covered the building and the structure of the tabernacles and temples.

It's like being on a job; you want to know as much about the job as possible, in order to be the best you can at that job.

God expects us to invest in our gifts and ministries and produce a profit. By following His instructions, that profit will be the **salvation and saving of our souls, and the souls of men.**

And just like the splendid Temples of old, **that's worth its weight in gold.**

SOLOMONS TEMPLE STRUCTURE

CHAPTER 13

SATAN'S PLAN IN HOMOSEXUALITY

Satan's Plan in Homosexuality. I'm not going to spend a tremendous amount of time on this, but to say; the **bible teaches** that those who do such things shall not inherit the Kingdom of God. Yes, this is a touchy subject, only because it seems to be the spirit of our day, which is actually a sign that we are living in the last days.

Now as the Lord leads me to talk about this, I must give you the reason why. We are not speaking on this to belittle anyone, or to run anyone down. The Lord wants only truth and reality to be spoken on this subject. You have to know what the enemy is doing, and what his plans are to move people further away from the truth of God's Word, into a deeper state of deception!

In this life naturally speaking, there are things that can disqualify you from obtaining certain positions. For example; if you were a child molester; you would probably have a hard time finding a job as a pre-school or a kindergarten teacher. Or if you were a convicted felon or one who's robbed banks; you may find it a little difficult to get employment as a teller. So what am I saying? There are ministries that God has for us, that if we're not in right standing with Him, can disqualify ourselves from ministry, and run the risk of missing heavens gates altogether.

The Lord wanted me to put a different spin on this subject. Not to pacify or dance around the truth, but to give you something else to look at other than being CONDEMNED!!! God wants you to understand the truth of His word, that all of us can be removed from areas of ministry, if our *moral lifestyles* don't line up with the Word of God. Don't just take my word for it, STUDY the BOOK!! Don't let any preacher come and tell you otherwise. If we don't line up to the Word, we CAN NOT be His ministers! Don't allow *anyone* who is *gifted* and *skillful* in *twisting* and *perverting* scriptures, tell you it isn't so! The devil will go as far as using Gods Word to confuse and deceive you. Remember what Paul said in Galatians 1:8-9; *but though we, or an angel from heaven, preach any* ***other gospel*** *unto you than that which we have preached unto you, let him be* *accursed. Verse 9; as we said before, so say I now again, if any man preach any **other gospel** unto you than that ye have received, let him be accursed.*

There are Bishops, Evangelists and Pastors out here teaching people that the Bible doesn't really mean what it says. They say that we're all misinterpreting the Word. The men and women teaching this are cunning and crafty in their speech. The average Christian *(or those of you who don't bother studying the Word for yourselves)* will fall for this *false teaching,* because it sounds good, and they are convincing in their dialog and delivery! Most have strong personalities, along with a perverted *gift of persuasion,* thereby deceiving those who don't know Gods Word, or have already involved and compromised themselves with those in that lifestyle. **Gifts of persuasion** can also be manifested in the form of prophecy! Therefore guiding many into the realm of being *controlled;* which is **witchcraft!**

Notice in verse 8, Paul admonished the people that if any come preaching *another gospel,* let them be accursed. Seems like Paul could have said, if any one comes preaching *a lie,* let them be accursed. But he used the term, *another gospel.* This signifies that there are many voices out there today. If you don't know the truth, these voices can deceive you because they sound good and have *partial truths* to them. That's how Satan deceives so many because he tells you just enough truth, in order to establish his lie! Paul let the Galatians know that there are other words and voices out there that sound good, but if it's not matching up with the words you've already heard from Christ and of the Apostles, let every man be a lie, and Gods Word be true. A lie can only be a lie, when it's based off of something that is true! So if it's not Bible, it's another gospel, and it's not true! *(John 17:17, Sanctify them through thy truth: thy word is truth.)*

Satan's Plan in Homosexuality. We must eat the whole roll, and not just the part of the roll that we like! Now I'm one who doesn't necessarily like the crust on the bread, and there are certain parts of the chicken I don't prefer. But if I get hungry enough, I will eat all of the bread, and all pieces of the chicken in order to be full. That's how we have to treat Gods Word. We have to eat the whole thing, not just the parts we agree with, but the parts that speak against the way we're actually living as well. I'd rather have the truth, than to have my own way. The truth will make me free, but my way has usually ended up wrong and has gotten me off course, every time!!

This is said in much love, and not with a voice of condemnation!

God takes this very seriously because it's something He warns against. It's all in the scriptures, but somehow we have by-passed or ignored it, because we refuse to separate and be holy.

I know many of you will say, *we have all come short, even you!* You're Right! So the Word goes out to **all of us**, who know to do right but don't! If we intend on God using us, and anointing us; we have to have a mentality, that if God says it, then it's so! Even if we don't agree, or want to believe that it's true!

If we have purposed to be holy before God, we must come in line with His Word. Need more proof; let's take a look shall we?

1 Corinthians 6:9: "*Know ye not that the unrighteous shall not inherit the kingdom of God? Be not deceived: neither **fornicators**, nor **idolaters**, nor **adulterers**, nor **effeminate**, nor **abusers of themselves with mankind**.*" (KJV)

What do you think "effeminate" means? Go a head; take the time to look it up!!! That word speaks to our men, but the passage speaks to the lifestyle. (see the other bible versions)

1 Corinthians 6:9: *9"Do you not know that the unrighteous and the wrongdoers will not inherit or have any share in the kingdom of God? Do not be deceived (misled): neither the impure and **immoral**, nor idolaters, nor adulterers, nor **those who participate in homosexuality**.*" (AMP)

1 Corinthians 6:9: *9"Or do you not know that the unrighteous[a] will not inherit the kingdom of God? Do not be deceived :[A] neither the sexually immoral, nor idolaters, nor adulterers, **nor men who practice homosexuality**,[b]* (ESV)

Footnotes:
- *1 Corinthians 6:9 Or wrongdoers*
- *1 Corinthians 6:9 The two Greek terms translated by this phrase refer to the passive and active **partners in consensual homosexual acts**."* (ESV)

1 Corinthians 6:9: *9 "Or know ye not that the unrighteous shall not inherit the kingdom of God? Be not deceived: neither fornicators, nor idolaters, nor adulterers, nor effeminate, nor **abusers of themselves with men**.*" (ASV)

1 Corinthians 6:9:
9"Do ye not know that unrighteous [persons] shall not inherit [the] kingdom of God? Do not err: neither fornicators, nor idolaters, nor adulterers, nor those who make women of themselves, nor who abuse themselves with men." (Darby Translation)

1 Corinthians 6:9:
9 "Don't you realize that those who do wrong will not inherit the Kingdom of God? Don't fool yourselves. Those who indulge in sexual sin, or who worship idols, or commit adultery, or are male prostitutes, or practice homosexuality." (NLT)

This should make it a little clearer of what God is saying to each of us. We cannot make excuses, or compromise with the Word of God. You cannot use the same old lame excuses that all have sinned and come short, or that WE ALL are Gods Children, and God wouldn't destroy His own children. Really? Again, you better eat the whole roll of His Word! It is true that He is the Creator of all souls, but you need to study what God says in His Word.

He did say in; **Ezekiel 18:4**:

*Behold, all **soul**s are mine; as the **soul** of the father, so also the **soul** of the son is mine: the **soul** that **sinneth**, it shall die.* (KJV)

God also says in; Luke 6:46; "*and **why call ye me, Lord, Lord**, and do not the **things** which **I say**?*" (KJV)

Now the scriptures that prove we were all *created* by God, but *God is not a Father to all*, are these......

John 8:44: "*Ye are of **your father** the **devil**, and the lusts of **your father** ye will do. He was a murderer from the beginning, and abode not in the truth, because there is no truth in him. When he speaketh a lie, he speaketh of his own: for he is a liar, and the **father** of it.*" (KJV)

Romans 8:9: "*But **ye** are not in the flesh, but in the Spirit, if so be that the Spirit of God dwell in you. Now if any man have not the Spirit of Christ, he is **none** of **his**.*"

You see, a natural child is *born* of its father and mother. But you must be *born again* of the spirit, to be a **child of God**.

Notice when you read the story of Nicodemus in John 3:1-15, Jesus essentially tells him that he must be *born again*, **before** he can be considered a *child* or citizen of the kingdom. It's not until after verses 1-15 take place, that verse 16 tells us that God so loved the world that he gave His only begotten son. This signifies that we are all *NOT* His children, if we don't meet the *conditions* of being a *child of the king*. To be clear; the condition is, a lifestyle of **holiness.**

Satan's Plan in Homosexuality. The reason I'm using the Word of God is because all of our personal opinions really don't matter. I'm not telling you what I think about the situation, so if anyone is mad, I'm not the one to be mad at. It's God you have to answer to, Not Me!

But I'm willing to be a sacrificial lamb for the sake of the gospel.

As I was about to mention earlier, there's something you can pick up by those who will defend this lifestyle. Pay attention and you'll see it, because there's no way they can hid it. No matter how nice the personality of a person is. What's on the inside must come out. When you begin to speak on this subject and what God's Word says about homosexuality, most will immediately become defensive and then very aggressive. What's on the inside will cause them to be in the attack mode. You'll see the *personality* of that spirit actually cause them to change. I guess it's like anything else when it comes to someone speaking in contrast to what we think or believe. There are things I know I could be better or change in my life, and when the Word of God comes to challenge it, if I'm not careful, *the spirit* which causes me to do what I do, can make me rise up in *defense* of the *wrong* that I know is there within me.

Romans 1:18-32, not only picks it up and talks about it, but also shows another side of God. Again, many times when this subject is challenged, one of the first things you'll hear is; *we're all God's children and God loves everyone.* It's a partially true statement, but shallow in its attempt to compromise the

Holiness of God. Yes God loves you, but He hates the sin. He called it an abomination! Something He detests or hates! You won't make it into His heaven, doing something He hates! We always want to pull the, "*He loves everyone card,*" but no one wants to talk about the fact that God has *another side* to Him that is *full of His fury and wrath*. He cannot, and will not compromise HOLINESS, because that's what He is. But even in His wrath, He's still a God of love! He loves us so much that He'll allow us to make your own decisions on where our souls spend eternity.

We are made in His *image* and *likeness*. We feel happiness, and we get angry! God is the same way. And if we are made in His image and likeness, you need to understand that, Gods nature is not of a *homosexual nature*, neither does He possess any perverted tendencies. His attributes are holy and we must carry the same attributes within us.

We've come up with so *many excuses*, and try and justify them by the Word of God. Yes, God is love, but He has another side to Him, and before you so quickly justify your ways, you might want to read the good book a little closer to see if you *indeed* have *eternal life* with Him, carrying this type of spirit.

The Word of God in **Romans 1: 18-32** speaks of the *wrath of God* in unrighteousness. . . . . . .

[18] ***for the wrath of God is revealed from heaven against all ungodliness and unrighteousness*** *of men, who suppress the truth in unrighteousness, [19] because what may be known of God is manifest in them, for God has shown it to them. [20] For since the creation of the world His invisible attributes are clearly seen, being understood by the things that are made, even His eternal power and Godhead, so that they are without excuse, [21] because, although they knew God, they did not glorify Him as God, nor were thankful, but became futile in their thoughts, and their foolish hearts were darkened. [22] Professing to be wise, they became fools, [23] and changed the glory of the incorruptible God into an image made like corruptible man—and birds and four-footed animals and creeping things.*

Satan's Plan in Homosexuality. *[24] Therefore God also gave them up to uncleanness,* **in the lusts of their hearts, to dishonor their bodies among themselves,** *[25] who exchanged the truth of God for the lie, and worshiped and served the creature rather than the Creator, who is blessed forever. Amen.*

[26] For this reason God gave them up to **vile passions***. For even their* **women exchanged the natural use** *for what is against nature.*

[27] Likewise also the **men, leaving the natural use of the woman***, burned in their lust for one another,* **men with men** *committing what is shameful, and receiving in themselves the penalty of their error which was due. [28] And even as they did not like to retain God in their knowledge, God gave them over to a debased (reprobate)mind, to do those things which are not fitting; [29] being filled with all unrighteousness,* **sexual immorality***, wickedness, covetousness, maliciousness; full of envy, murder, strife, deceit, evil-mindedness; they*

*are whisperers, ³⁰ backbiters, haters of God, violent, proud, boasters, inventors of evil things, disobedient to parents, ³¹ undiscerning, untrustworthy, unloving, unforgiving, unmerciful; ³² who, knowing the **righteous judgment of God**, that those who practice such things are deserving of death, not only do the same but also approve of those who practice them.* (NKJV, New King James Version)

Now notice all the other sins mentioned in this passage. Don't feel picked on, this is talking to all that fit these categories. . .(*sexual immorality, wickedness, covetousness, maliciousness; full of envy, murder, strife, deceit, evil-mindedness; they are whisperers, ³⁰ backbiters, haters of God, violent, proud, boasters, inventors of evil things, disobedient to parents, ³¹ undiscerning, untrustworthy, unloving, unforgiving, unmerciful*). We all have some work to do, because Satan is using all of these things to work his plan of attacking the church, and the world.

So it wasn't a natural thing, no matter how people try to justify it. It's not meant to become a common thing in life, and certainly not to be a common thing in the house of God. The church can't afford to accept it as being ok. We cannot sit back and allow people to be deceived, thinking everything is ok and have them believing *that's just the way they are*. God wants to heal and deliver you from this bondage, and all others for that matter.

The Lord revealed this to me many years ago, and I've said this so many times. You have to understand how *lust* operates. The **spirit of lust** doesn't care how it's gratified; **it just wants to be gratified!** No one could ever say; *I wouldn't do what those people do.* Okay! But if you allow that spirit inside, and don't seek or receive deliverance from that type of lust, you could fall into the same conditions. That *spirit* is *never* satisfied. . . . .**NEVER!** It's like a drug. Once you've tried one thing, you're compelled to move on to stronger stuff. You can't help it!

When speaking of sexual lusts, the Bible says in Proverbs 6:27; *can a man take fire in his bosom, and his clothes not be burned?* The answer is, no! You're not able to defeat that spirit alone.

It takes the delivering power of God to loose your **heart, mind and soul** from that spirit!

Lucifer lost his place in the worship of God, and now wants his place back! He knows he can never be God, so he mimics or copy's God. But his plan is to get into the worship and *defile it*, thus starting an epidemic of *false worship*. So how is he going about it? Remember, he not only wanted to be *like* God, he wanted to *be* God, or take the place of God. You know what happened to him when he decided that. He was kicked out of his place in heaven and the worship, of which he was the leader. Ever since then, his plan has been to get revenge on God.

Satan's Plan in Homosexuality. He's trying several ways to get back at God, and one of the ways is his undercurrent plan to creep into the church. Yes, the church, where the true worship of God is *supposed* to be taking place.

Lucifer was used to being the head of stuff, as the head of the heavenly choir and worship. He played the instruments, and was the *anointed cherub* that *covered*. In other words, he was over the *atmosphere* of heaven, the *first sound* of the morning.

Now that he's lost his place, he's mad and wants to get back at God. So he's trying to rule, and get his place back by slipping into the church. He was accustomed to being **the head**, and now the **leadership in the church** is where you'll find him trying to re-surface. When the devil wants to make his way into a church, he tries to enter in **two places** first. The **pulpit** or the **music department!** That's right, the **Priesthood** and the **Musicians**. These were two areas he occupied before his dismissal from the presence of God. He understands that if he can get to *the head*, he can destroy *the body*. That's why we can't afford to let just anything and anyone in our pulpits or on our instruments. They are holy! THEY ARE HOLY people of God! Stand up and stop compromising in the house of God. Satan is doing all he can to make *worldly things* and *holy things,* **common** or the same. How can someone **unclean**, clean us up? How can someone in homosexuality, teach us about holiness, or how can a homosexual praise and worship leader, usher us into the presence of God? It stinks in His nostrils! Have we *no fear* of God? *(respect)* What needs to happen is; we DO need to allow them to come into the church; get somewhere and take a seat, so they can hear the Word of God and receive deliverance. We're not to look down on anyone, but show godly love and compassion; for such were some of you, but now you are washed and cleansed, aren't you?

This is not a chapter to down trod or bash anyone. But we must preach the Word of God in reality and truth. In season and out, whether people like it or not. They didn't like Jesus, and they're probably not going to like us as well. The Bible tells us to arm ourselves likewise with the same mind to suffer. Suffer being talked about, suffer being lied on, and hated of men.

It's not an accident that the church is in a fight, allowing homosexuals to enter into the pulpit. No matter how intelligent or reasonable their excuses may sound, this should not be so. They will preach to their own, passing the word on that it's ok to remain the way they are. God made you this way. That's Satan's deception and there's no truth to it! Watch in the coming days and years, they will push their agenda through the *laws* of the land, not understanding that they are actually *paving the way* for the spirit and deception of the anti-Christ. The devils plot is to make it a *law,* and you'll make it the truth in the *minds* of people. Excuses are being made for the unclean way they have decided to live, but God didn't make you that way my brother and sister. There's nothing unclean about the Lord! Don't make excuses for the **lust of your own flesh.**

Let's look at the scripture in James 1: 1-25. *[13"]Let no man say when he is tempted,* **I am tempted of God:** *for* **God cannot be tempted with evil**, *neither tempteth he any man:*

^{14}*But every man is tempted, when he is **drawn away of his "own lust," and enticed.** ^{15}Then when lust hath conceived, it bringeth forth sin: and sin, when it is finished, bringeth forth death. ^{16}Do not err, my beloved brethren. ^{17}Every good gift and every perfect gift is from above, and cometh down from the Father of lights, with whom is no variableness, neither shadow of turning. ^{18}Of his own will begat he us with the word of truth, that we should be a kind of firstfruits of his creatures. ^{19}Wherefore, my beloved brethren, let every man be swift to hear, slow to speak, slow to wrath: ^{20}For the wrath of man worketh not the righteousness of God.*

Satan's Plan in Homosexuality. ^{21}*Wherefore lay apart all filthiness and superfluity of naughtiness, and receive with meekness the engrafted word, which is able to save your souls. ^{22}But be ye doers of the word, and not hearers only, deceiving your own selves. ^{23}For if any be a hearer of the word, and not a doer, he is like unto a man beholding his natural face in a glass: ^{24}For he beholdeth himself, and goeth his way, and straightway forgetteth what manner of man he was. ^{25}But whoso looketh into the perfect law of liberty, and continueth therein, he being not a forgetful hearer, but a doer of the work, this man shall be blessed in his deed."* (KJV)

We must not embrace the homosexual agenda, and make it seem like a *natural* or *common* thing.

God is already dealing with many other pastors, elders and prophets along these lines, who will be obedient to Him. They will not compromise with this sin, as other leaders and ministers have already done. There are areas that I will speak on that other ministers may not be appointed to. And at the same time, there will be other areas concerning this subject which I will not touch on, that God has anointed other's to minister the Word of God concerning this. Some are planting, some are watering, but God will give the increase.

The whole purpose of this chapter is to *expose* the plan of the enemy in the use of this weapon!

*"It is going to be a fight to the very end; the devil does not want this type of knowledge and information to get out about the things he's doing against the body of Christ. But God is going to raise up saved, sanctified, Holy Ghost filled and anointed young ministers of God who **will not** compromise the holy things of God to make a mockery of them." "God is going to speak loud and clear in the coming months and years to let the devil and all who follow, understand that there will be a **separation** between clean and unclean, holy and unholy. It will come out of the mouths of many of our **sold out** young people who will operate with no fear of the devil, no fear of peer pressure, for God is already grooming them to withstand all of the fiery darts of the wicked."*

Pray for those who God will draft into this army, to stand on the front lines and fight this war. We already have the victory on our side, but we want to take as many prisoners for Christ as we possibly can. We don't want to see anyone lost through the deception of Satan. We are exposing these things so we can ultimately win some to Christ. John 8:32 says; *ye shall know the truth, and the truth shall make you free!* That's what it's all about, the ministry of reconciliation, reconciling the world back to God, *(Jehovah)* the Only True and Living God!! Thank God! *"I can feel the presence of the Lord right now as I'm writing this."*

Understand that the power of the almighty God is with us, because greater is He that is in us, than he who is in this world. If God be for us, **who** can be against us? If we would just give the world the *Word of God* in our preaching and in our songs, and *live the life* that we preach and sing about, the *Word* alone has the power to draw men. God just needs a few *sold out* people who will stand on the *truth* and *power* of His Word. Stand against the things that are wrong, and the corruption we see slithering into our houses of worship. If we would do this, we will see a move of God that we've never experienced before. It is the end time, and God is calling you Priests and Levites to come forth and stand against the *false prophets* that are in the world and in the church as well. The spirit of **apostasy** is running rampant in the church right now, and for years we've allowed sin to come in, take a seat and become comfortable in our churches.

Satan isn't intimidated by our preachers because they've watered down the gospel with faith and prosperity messages, and have utterly stopped telling people that they must come out of their sins in order to make it to heaven.

Satan's Plan in Homosexuality. We are now petting and pacifying them in their sins, and not feeding them the whole loaf of bread. Just the slices of the Word that *taste good and tickle the ear.* God told me that the reason many leaders and pastors won't preach against immoral sins, is because they're not willing or able to preach on subjects, they themselves are involved in! Therefore, they will not preach or teach people in areas where they are not living up to the Word themselves. Therefore, health, wealth and prosperity are the only areas they will preach on, as if that's the only words God has to say to His people. God is not only judging the world concerning this, but judgment WILL and IS beginning at His house, among His people.

We are commanded to declare the whole council of God.

So to all the sincere pastors and true preachers of the gospel, don't be alarmed if your churches aren't always filled with people, as long as you are preaching the truth of the gospel. God is going to bless you! For *success in ministry* is not gauged by the quantity of your congregation but the quality of the Word of Truth that is being preached. By that I mean, when the gospel is being preached and souls are being added to the church such as will be *saved,* that's success! When *healing* and *deliverance* is taking place, people are being *restored, set free* and the spirit of reconciliation is in the house; my brothers and sisters, you have successful ministry!

As I said earlier, Satan isn't intimidated by our big churches and or fancy cars, and how well we can dress, preach, or sing. Evil spirits are scarcely being chased away by the music in our churches much anymore, mainly because our musicians are now more concerned about making a dollar and gaining fame. Many of our **Minstrels** are living *sexually perverted* live-styles, and are not concerned with playing or singing under an anointing that destroys yokes off of those who are in bondage. Some of our **Prophets** aren't even hearing what God is saying for their own lives, let alone speaking into the lives of someone else who need to hear a Word from the Lord. Our choirs are now promoting themselves and singing songs to receive awards for their efforts instead of singing to the glory and honor of God. Not understanding that the greater reward is in heaven. We need your voices to sing the praises of God and create an atmosphere of worship.

We better get it together and stop this cycle of compromise. The Lord told me not long ago that, many ministers are ministering with a *lack of knowledge*, and some have a direct assignment from Satan to destroy the *holy fabric* of the church of God. If you're ministering with a lack of knowledge, this book will help you to understand that the devil isn't trying to use *sinners* to destroy the church; no, he's trying to deceive the *weak* Christian to do his *dirty work* within the house of God. He's lying to you when he tells you it's ok to be homosexual and minister to God also. **Not so!** You have to read the rest of the Bible concerning God's judgment on those who commit such acts. You can't just read John 3:16 and close the book! You should search the entire book, for in it, you think you have eternal life. John 5:37-44 says; $_{37}$ *and the Father who sent me has himself borne witness about me. His voice you have never heard, his form you have never seen,*

$_{38}$*and you do not have his word abiding in you, for you do not believe the one whom he has sent.*

$_{39}$**you search the Scriptures because you think that in them you have eternal life**; *and it is they that bear witness about me,* $_{40}$*yet you refuse to come to me that you may have life.* $_{41}$*I do not receive glory from people.* $_{42}$*but I know that you do not have the love of God within you.*

$_{43}$ *I have come in my Father's name, and you do not receive me. If another comes in his own name, you will receive him.* $_{44}$*how can you believe, when you receive glory from one another and do not seek the glory that comes from the only God?* ESV.

Satan's Plan in Homosexuality. God cannot tolerate it, and according to His Word, will judge it very soon. As a matter of fact, He's already judged this and other sins, and the manifestation of the judgment is just a matter of time. You don't have to stay the way you are. God can and will free you if you want to be free! This is why it's so important, that preachers and leaders stand up and preach THE TRUTH, because like any other sin or bondage, there are some people who actually don't want to be in this particular bondage. They just need to hear a Word from us letting them know that it's ok to be free. You can reverse the curse and step out! Come out of the closet and **declare** that you **don't** have to be this way. For whom the Son has set free can be free indeed. It's up to you! There are preachers and Bishops that have told their congregations that they themselves have sought God to take this away, but nothing happened. Yep, you're right, nothing happened, because you have to *want* God to do it, you have to separate from people who influence you in that lifestyle, and you have to be in a church, or a place of **deliverance and power!** You can't be in a place where the Word of God isn't operating with power. Many ministries have preachers and pastors, who can break down the scriptures, and write flawless dissertations about the Word, and use the correct homiletics or hermeneutics, speaking with smooth cunning words. But the thing many lack is the anointing and power to back all that wonderful presentation up. Allow God to lead you to a place of deliverance. He's is not intimidated by you coming. He will deliver you from it, and you can finally experience what *freedom* and the *real Power of God* feels like in your life!

Don't misunderstand me; we're coming against the SIN, not people who are involved in it.

We love every man because God is love. We don't want anyone to be deceived by telling you that it's alright, God *understands* it's just the way you are.

Yes, He understands, but in the words of my co-pastor; *He'll understand, but he won't say* ***well done****!*

As I come to a conclusion of this topic. I'm reminded of something the Lord shared with me that really made me think. He pointed out that Lucifer actually understood that he could never be God, because God was *creator*. Therefore Satan could only be a **perverted opposite** of God. God is *pro-creation*. And in creation, after Adam and Eve sinned in the garden, God set the man to over-see the woman because of their disobedience.

Genesis 3:1-19 says; *14So the LORD God said to the serpent: "Because you have done this, You are cursed more than all cattle, And more than every beast of the field; On your belly you shall go, And you shall eat dust All the days of your life. 15 And I will put enmity between you and the woman, And between your seed and her Seed; He shall bruise your head, And you shall bruise His heel." 16 To the woman He said: "I will greatly multiply your sorrow and your conception; In pain you shall bring forth children;* **Your desire shall be for your husband, And he shall rule over you."** *17 Then to Adam He said, "Because you have heeded the voice of your wife, and have eaten from the tree of which I commanded you, saying, 'You shall not eat of it: "Cursed is the ground for your sake; In toil you shall eat of it All the days of your life. 18 Both thorns and thistles it shall bring forth for you, And you shall eat the herb of the field. 19 In the sweat of your face you shall eat bread Till you return to the ground, For out of it you were taken.* NKJ Genesis 5:1-3 says; *1 This is the book of the genealogy of Adam. In the day that God created man,* **He made him in the likeness of God.** *2* **He created them male and female,** *and blessed them and called them Mankind in the day they were created.* NKJV

Satan's Plan in Homosexuality. By setting the man over the woman, God was setting things in order. That's the key word; *order*. God created a *man* and a *woman*, and if you read the beginning chapters of Genesis, you'll find that God had an *established order* from the very outset. Adam received the commandment from God and instructed Eve in the particulars of it. Notice that nothing happened when *Eve ate* of the tree. The voice of God didn't come inquiring through the garden until *Adam ate*. Why? Because there was an *order* that God had set up when He created Adam in His own image. It was *man and woman* He set together, not *man and man or woman and woman*. There could be no **help meet** for Adam without his *rib*. He took the woman *out from* the man and commanded them to live together in harmony and multiply. God didn't make any mistakes in creation. As a matter of fact, when you look in the beginning chapters of Genesis, you'll find that when God was in the creating mode, the bible says that when God spoke everything into existence; He looked at His creations and called them *good*. When things are out of order, and the plan of God is altered, death sets in and destroys. Satan is trying to destroy the original order God set in place from the beginning. Satan understands that when *headship* is out of its place, it causes a trickling effect. When headship is out of place, it weakens the home, weakens the church and ultimately the nations. Death then has a *rite of passage* to come in and destroy the fabric of society. Remember, nothing happened until Adam ate of the forbidden tree. That was because **Adam represented the glory of God or "headship."** Satan wants to remove *headship* in order to destroy the order God originally intended.

Here's what I'm getting at and what the Lord showed me. Satan deceived Eve, but that's not who he was after. His desire was to destroy the **head** or the one with the direct command from God. **He wants the man!** If he can get us men out of our place of **authority** that God gave us, he will succeed in taking away the *blessings* that would be in our homes, churches and society. We would forfeit the power and authority in the earth that was given to us by God Himself. Satan's plan is to destroy God's order by destroying the man. He has commanded his demons around the world to, *get the man out of the homes*. Don't give 'em jobs so they feel worthless. Make the man feel like a nothing or a nobody! Put 'em in jail, send them to war or cause them to act in such a feminine way that it *strips them* of their God given, appointed **authority.** This authority has the anointed power to destroy the very works of hell! This authority can destroy Satan's kingdom in the earth! Satan is trying to place a *spirit* on our men that will cause them not to have the God given *desires for a woman*. You know that's not the way God set it up, because in Genesis, God saw that <u>it wasn't good for man to be alone,</u> so God gave Adam, Mrs. Eve, not Mr. Steve.

Also, two women together are totally *out of God's order*, because they can't *naturally reproduce* between themselves. Remember this, it's so simple. **God is pro-creation, pro-reproduction!**

This is the spirit of the anti-Christ which will be *anti-creation,* and *anti-God.* He will be totally opposite of anything God set in order. Satan's plan is to get into the houses of God with a *spirit of homosexuality.* This can cause spiritual death in the church, and is already causing a deadly decay in the morals of our society. By replacing the position of the man in his rightful place, he's setting up his **homosexual agenda.**

This is actually a sign of the spirit of the anti-christ, causing mankind to worship him through this gross disobedience of Gods commandment. The Lord showed me how cunning the devil really is. By believing that the devil is **only** trying to enter and destroy the house of God by sending in a homosexual spirit, would be incorrect.

Satan's Plan in Homosexuality. His plan is to corrupt the church through an influx of homosexuality. But the thing to pay attention to, is the different avenues by which he's using to accomplish this. Remember, his plan is to discredit and do away with *headship.* His cunning plan is presently working in the secular arenas. He's *reconditioning* our *mindset* and *conscience.* Just watch some of the sit-coms and reality shows on television today. You'll find that the *woman* is the strong one, the educated one with the great job, and is usually depicted as the dominant of the two. While the *male figure* is some weak minded, unintelligent couch potato that is incapable of effectively or efficiently making decisions, or leading his family. By seeing this over and over, it begins to enter our **sub- conscience**, and we begin to act upon what we continually see through our *eye gates.* We have to be careful not to allow this **role reversal** type of spirit to creep into the church.

Example; you've probably noticed that in many of our churches across the country, that our sisters out number us men. In many cases the difference is 2 to 1. *"Well praise the Lord Brothers;"* there's absolutely nothing wrong with that, it's just a fact! But have you ever wondered where many of these brothers are? Sisters, I believe you can answer this question without my help. It's *not a coincidence* that our men are *out of position.* We've lost many to war, drugs, violence, jail, and yes, homosexuality. Look at the attack of the enemy on our men.

The music is telling them *to hit it and run, crush as much as you can, be some baby's daddy, but not a father figure, and the list goes on and on.* And because our sisters have had to step in and carry the load and responsibility of our men in so many cases, it's become the norm in our society today. Don't get it twisted; it's been Satan's plan from the very start. Now because of the **absence** of men and fathers in the home, church and society, some of our women have taken on **another spirit**. Now, women don't need a man, or they've been hurt by a man. He's slowly being replaced in the minds and hearts of our women. Now because the man many times is not found in his rightful place, both *naturally and spiritually,* the women have taken on the leadership roles which God intended for the man to occupy. Can't blame the women though; they're just doing what a good woman was created to do. She was placed in the garden as a *help meet* to the man, and since the man cannot be found, the woman is still there to meet the need, but now there's no man to help. So therefore, her help meet gifts *yet* have to operate, and the devil knows this. So now her gifts that **are** intended for the desire of a man, have now *shifted* to an *abnormal appetite* for a woman. Because of the way God made them; when women see a need, they attend to it and get it taken care of. And if we men would be honest; we oft times will procrastinate and allow the woman to do it, even if it's our job or *responsibility* to take care of. So what happens now is; you'll visit a church and many times, it's the women who are on fire, anointed and working in the church, *(not in all cases)* but many times our men are just standing idly by watching our sisters go forth. When they put on programs in church you'll hear the sisters say; *the brothers need to come up, the sisters are doing this and accomplishing that, get with it brothers, don't let the women out shine you!*

Now don't get mad at me brothers and sisters, but here's what the Lord showed me. If we're not careful, that same **roll reversal spirit** that I told you about in the sit-coms and media, can carry over into the church. What am I saying? Satan's plan is to plant a spirit *(sub consciously)* in the women, to feel like they don't have any need for a man! They can do *everything* that a man can do and more. But there's a danger in this way of thinking that will begin to breed a spirit of lesbianism. Once again the man is being *replaced* and **order** has been thrown out the window.

Satan's Plan in Homosexuality. Those of you who can *hear me in the spirit!* I'm not talking about the *gifts* and *abilities* of our women in *natural* or *spiritual* things. I'm talking about the *order* God set in place. He told us to give *honor* to the woman as unto the *weaker vessel*. The weaker vessel means the weaker physical vessel, not the weaker spiritual one. A woman *(no matter how she tries to walk, talk, act or look like a man)* is not naturally built to take on the physical stress of a man, because God didn't make her that way.

But in the Kingdom of God, we are neither male nor female, and God is using whoever will be obedient to Him in the body of Christ.

What I'm trying to get across to you is that Satan understands what God did in setting up order between a man and a woman. He understands the blessing that comes within the *marital union*. God told us in, Proverbs 18:22 that the man who finds a *wife*, finds a *good thing* and *obtains favor* of the Lord. The Bible also says in, Hebrews 13:4 that marriage in all is *honorable*, and the **bed is undefiled.** You DO NOT obtain Gods favor nor is the bed undefiled between persons of the same sex. . . . . .If you don't believe that then read *(part b)* of verse 4.

By following and obeying Gods commandments and His order in the earth, we allow the blessings of God to be upon our families and lives. It gives us the ability to possess the power and authority from God to defeat the enemy's devices in our lives and in our churches.

But when we find ourselves *out of order*, we allow Satan to confuse and rearrange nature, and the order God set up for us, which was originally provided for us in the garden. When the head is cut off from the body, the body can no longer live. We can no longer afford to stand by and watch Satan use homosexuality to discredit and replace our men in or out of the church. Satan's plan in homosexuality is to get into the church, even if he has to start on the outside of it. Don't be deceived, his plan is to corrupt, defeat and render powerless, the house of God through this spirit. He's dishonoring the holiness, the awesome creation and order of God.

Let's stand up men and women of God, let's be in the place that God has ordained for us to be in. Let's find ourselves in our rightful places, both in natural and spiritual things. Then God will grant us His power so that we may defeat the plan of the enemy. Remember, no matter what's going on in the world and in the church, God is going to have a holy people! A church within the church, who are going to stand up and call right, right and wrong, wrong! Not compromising or settling, but walking in holiness and sanctification. As God's people we must set our own agenda against Satan and his plan to corrupt God's house. I know this is a strong word but, the only time we should allow that spirit in our churches is if those who carry the spirit, are coming in to hear the Word of the Lord, which will ultimately lead to them to their salvation and deliverance. We should welcome all persons with love, but come against that spirit with *power and authority,* and hate then things God hates.

The church does need you. We need your gifts to assist in fighting this warfare in the spirit. But let us be perfectly clear; God will not use you with this spirit hanging on you. You may be the gifted of the gifted, you may have been able to fool or deceive many who DON'T have a gift of discernment, but God is requiring that you come before Him correct. You can't keep offering Him a tainted sacrifice, and expect to continue on as usual. God is sending His Word to you now!! Choose ye this day whom you will serve, because God is getting ready to UNCOVER MANY IN THE HOUSE OF GOD, who have been hiding. God is going to start with HIS LEADERS who have done this in HIS FACE, and have not seen it necessary to REPENT!!!

No matter what Satan's plans are. . . . . .God Will Have Order in His Courts!!!

CHAPTER 14

LEVITES

Levite. Levite, a descendant of the tribe of Levi (Exodus 6:25; Leviticus 25:32; Numbers 35:2; Joshua 21:3, 41). This name is, however, generally used as the title of that portion of the tribe which was set apart for the subordinate offices of the sanctuary service as assistants to the priests (1 Kings 8:4; Ezra 2:70).

When the Israelites left Egypt, the ancient manner of worship was still observed by them, the eldest son of each house inheriting the priest's office. At Sinai the first change in this ancient practice was made. A hereditary priesthood in the family of Aaron was then instituted (Exodus 28:1). But it was not till that terrible scene in connection with the sin of the golden calf that the tribe of Levi stood apart and began to occupy a distinct position (Exodus 32).

The religious primogeniture was then conferred on this tribe, which henceforth was devoted to the service of the sanctuary (Numbers 3:11-13). They were selected for this purpose because of their zeal for the glory of God (Exodus 32:26), and because, as the tribe to which Moses and Aaron belonged, they would naturally stand by the lawgiver in his work.

The Levitical order consisted of all the descendants of Levi's three sons, Gershon, Kohath, and Merari; whilst Aaron, Amram's son (Amram, son of Kohat), and his issue constituted the priestly order.

The age and qualification for Levitical service are specified in Numbers 4:3, 23, and 30, 39, 43, 47. They were not included among the armies of Israel (Numbers 1:47; 2:33; 26:62), but were reckoned by themselves. They were the special guardians of the tabernacle (Numbers 1:51; 18:22-24).

The Gershonites pitched their tents on the west of the tabernacle (Numbers 3:23), the Kohathites on the south (Numbers 3:29), the Merarites on the north (Numbers 3:35), and the priests on the east (Numbers 3:38). It was their duty to move the tent and carry the parts of the sacred structure from place to place. They were given to Aaron and his sons the priests to wait upon them and do work for them at the sanctuary services (Numbers 8:19; 18:2-6).

As being wholly consecrated to the service of the Lord, they had no territorial possessions. Jehovah was their inheritance (Numbers 18:20; 26:62; Deuteronomy 10:9; 18:1, 2), and for their support it was ordained that they should receive from the other tribes the tithes of the produce of the land. Forty-eight cities also were assigned to them, thirteen of which were for the priests *to dwell in*, i.e., along with their other inhabitants. Along with their dwellings they had *suburbs*, i.e., *commons*, for their herds and flocks, and also fields and vineyards (Numbers 35:2-5).

Nine of these cities were in Judah, three in Naphtali, and four in each of the other tribes (Joshua 21). Six of the Levitical cities were set apart as *cities of refuge*. Thus the Levites were scattered among the tribes to keep alive among them the knowledge and service of God. Pentateuch, the Hebrew word for Levite *(lew)* indicates a descendant of Levi, the son of Jacob and Leah (Genesis 29:34).

There were three family clans within the tribe of Levi—Gershon, Kohath, and Merari—but it was only Kohath who supplied the Aaronic priests. Subsequent to the induction of Aaron and his sons into the priesthood, the entire tribe of Levi was *set apart* following the golden calf incident (Exodus 32:26-29). They were blessed and chosen because their actions signified their loyalty to the covenant.

Levite. Thus, the prophecy of Jacob that Levi's descendants would be scattered throughout Israel (Genesis 49:5-7) was fulfilled, not as a curse but as a blessing (Exodus 32:29; Deuteronomy 33:8-9). Their zeal for the Lord caused the male Levites *(except for Aaron's family, who were already designated as priests)* to be set apart as caretakers of the tabernacle and as aides to the priests (Numbers 1:47-53). Each clan in the tribe now had specific duties related to the tabernacle (Numbers 3:14-18). Because this appointment came about due to their actions and was not based on their relationship with Aaron or his family, it was *providentially coincidental* that it was the tribe that contained the priests. Because of this a progression can be demonstrated in terms of separation and responsibilities from nation to tribe *(Levi)* to priesthood. The Levites *set apart* status is demonstrated by their taking the place of the firstborn, who by right belonged to God (Numbers 3:41). Another indication of Levi's distinction is found in Numbers 1:47-54, where God instructs Moses not to number the Levites with the other tribes. The Levites were set apart but their status must still be seen as significantly different from that of the priests. *(even though all priests were Levites too)* As aides, not officiating priests, theirs is an intermediate status between the people in general and that of the priesthood. *(i.e., the priests were made holy, the Levites were made clean; the priests were anointed and washed, the Levites were sprinkled; the priests were given new garments, the Levites washed theirs; blood was applied to the priests, but was waved over the Levites)* The Levites were explicitly permitted to go near the *Tent of Meeting* and this special privilege more than any other duty distinguished them from ordinary Israelites (Num 8:19; 16:9-10).

Part of the support of the Levites was to come from the tithe they were to be allotted of the income of the other tribes (Numbers 18:20-25). Since the reception of this tithe was dependent on the faithfulness of all the people, the financial position of the Levite was unpredictable. The Levites are therefore included in the legislation, along with the aliens, fatherless, and widows, as those whom the people must remember to care for (Deuteronomy 12:19; 14:27-29).

In Deuteronomy, with a view to entering the land, the Levites were given an additional duty since their tabernacle transport obligations would be diminished. It was now the important duty of the Levites and the Levitical priests, who would live throughout the land, to instruct the people in the law (Deuteronomy 33:10).

At the conquest the Levites received no tribal inheritance but were given forty-eight cities with their pastures (Joshua 21:1-42). This along with the tithe was to be their means of support as they pursued their work as aides to the priests and helpers at the sanctuary. This lack of land inheritance is to be understood by the statement that *the priestly service of the Lord is their inheritance* (Joshua 18:7).

During the temple period, with the ark permanently in Jerusalem and in view of their numbers, the Levites were given additional responsibilities as officials, judges, gatekeepers, and musicians, all of which assisted the priests (1 Chronicles 23:4-5). They also continued to serve as teachers and administrators of the law. That function was not always carried out well; hence the need for specific times of teaching (2 Chronicles 17:7-9; 35:3).

Levite. Postexilic Historical Books. While 4,289 priests *(approximately one-tenth of the entire returning number of exiles)* returned from captivity with Zerubbabel, only 341 Levites, singers, and gatekeepers are recorded as returning (Ezra 2:36-58). Ezra succeeded in persuading only thirty-eight Levites to return with him (Ezra 8:15-19). The fact that many of the menial tasks of temple service were the responsibility of the Levites and that the temple first had to be rebuilt and when it was, it was not as glorious as Solomon's temple (Ezra 3:12). This may have affected the willingness of the Levites to return. Some of the Levites became involved in the interpretation and teaching of the law (Nehemiah 8:7-8) and in the leading of the people in worship (Nehemiah 9:4-5; 12:8-9, 27-47).

Prophets, though rarely referred to, and even then usually in the context of priests who are Levites, the Levites as distinct from the Zadokite priests are mentioned in Ezekiel 44:11. The future acquisition and redistribution of the land would include a specific area in which the Levites could live (Ezekiel 45:5).

The term *Levite(s)* is only used three times in the New Testament. They were still a distinct class connected to the temple in Jerusalem along with the priests (John 1:19). As teachers of the law, the Levites, together with the priests, were probably sent with this role in mind, to question John the Baptist. It is possible that many scribes were Levites. In the parable of *the good Samaritan*, both a priest and Levite are mentioned, though not in a commendable manner (Luke 10:31-32). Barnabas is referred to as a Levite (Acts 4:36).

In summary, though the conclusions of the majority of modern critical scholars concerning the identity and purpose of the Levites *(and priests)* are in sharp contrast to the view presented here, the Scriptures clearly indicate that the Levites should be seen as a tribe that was below the priestly group of Aaronic priests but still distinct from other Israelites. They were set apart, handled the sacred articles of the tabernacle, served as substitutes for the firstborn who belonged to God, taught the law of God, served as judges, enhanced the worship at the temple in music, and guarded the treasures and moneys associated with the temple, but did not serve as mediators of the covenant. Their significant contribution was that they made it possible for the people to worship and fulfill their obligations to God. Along with the honor that the Levites had in their unique appointment, there was the need for their total dedication to the work of the Lord, *not that of pursuing material gain,* and the necessity to look to Him to supply some of their needs through the people. It was a life of sacrifice and service with their service to the Lord being their valuable inheritance that they could pass on to the next generation. They did not always value their function and inheritance, as evidenced after the exile.

Levite.

Levi

- Son of Jacob
  Genesis 29:34; 35:23; 1 Chronicles 2:1
- Avenges the seduction of Dinah
  Genesis 34; 49:5-7
- Jacob's prophecy regarding
  Genesis 49:5-7
- His age at death
  Exodus 6:16
- (Descendants of, made the ministers of religion)

The third son of Jacob by Leah. The origin of the name is found in Leah's words, "This time will my husband be joined [Heb. yillaveh] unto me." (Genesis 29:34)

He is mentioned as taking a prominent part in avenging his sister Dinah (Genesis 34:25-31).

He and his three sons went down with Jacob (Genesis 46:11) into Egypt, where he died at the age of one hundred and thirty-seven years (Exodus 6:16). The father of Matthat, and son of Simeon, of the ancestors of Christ (Luke 3:29).

Levi, one of the apostles, the son of Alphaeus (Mark 2:14; Luke 5:27, 29), also called, **Matthew** (Matthew 9:9).

1. The name of the third son of Jacob by his wife Leah. (B.C. about 1753.) The name, derived from lavah, "to adhere," gave utterance to the hope of the mother that the affections of her husband, which had hitherto rested on the favored Rachel, would at last be drawn to her: "This time will my husband be joined unto me, because I have borne him three sons." (Genesis 29:34) Levi, with his brother Simeon, avenged with a cruel slaughter the outrage of their sister Dinah. [**DINAH**] Levi, with his three sons, Gershon, Kohath and Merari, went down to Egypt with his father Jacob (Genesis 47:11). When Jacob's death draws near, and the sons are gathered round him, Levi and Simeon hear the old crime brought up again to receive its sentence. They no less than Reuben, the incestuous firstborn, had forfeited the privileges of their birthright. (Genesis 49:5-7) **LEVITES**
2. Two of the ancestors of Jesus. (Luke 3:24, 29)
3. Son of Alphaeus or Matthew; one of the apostles. (Mark 2:14; Luke 5:27, 29)

CHAPTER 15

HISTORY OF THE PRIEST, PRIESTHOOD

Priest, Priesthood. *Old Testament Priesthood*: The primary word for *priest* in the Old Testament is the Hebrew masculine noun **kohen**, for which I have no certain etymology. *(origin)* It occurs approximately 740 to 750 times and can refer to priests of the one true God or of other supposed gods that other nations and sometimes also the ancient Israelites themselves worshiped *(for the latter, see, Gen 41:45, 50; 2 Kings 10:11, 19)*. Related terms are the verb **kahan**, *to act as (or become) a priest (23 occurrences)*, the feminine abstract noun **kehunna**, *priesthood (14 occurrences see* Exod 29:9; 40:15; Num 3:10; 18:1, 7; 1 Sam 2:36; Ezra 2:62; Neh 7:64; 13:29, referring to the exclusivity and eternal responsibility of the Aaronic office of *priesthood* cf. Num 16:10; for Korah's rebellion against the Aaronic exclusivity, and Joshua 18:7; for the *priesthood* of the tribe of Levi as a whole*)*, and the Aramaic masculine noun **kahen** *priest (8 occurrences, all in* Ezra 6-7). Another Hebrew word, **komer**, *(idolatrous) priest*, occurs only three times in the Old Testament (2 Kings 23:5; Hosea 10:5; Zeph 1:4) referring exclusively to priests of foreign gods.

The first occurrence of *priest* in the Old Testament is the reference to the pre-Israelite *Melchizedek king of Salem. . . .priest of the Most High God* (Gen 14:18). Jethro, Moses' father-in-law and the priest of Midian, was also recognized as non-Israelite priest of the true and living God of Sinai by Moses, Aaron, and the elders of Israel (Exod 2:16; 3:1; 18:1, 10-12). Priests of foreign gods in foreign lands referred to in the Old Testament are Potiphera, Joseph's father-in-law, who was a *priest of On* in Egypt (Gen 41:45, 50; 46:20), the whole priestly organization in Egypt (Gen 47:22, 26), the *priests of Dagon* in Philistia (1 Sam 5:5; 6:2), the *priests of Chemosh* in Moab (Jer 48:7), and the *priests of Malcam* in Ammon (Jer 49:3).

Unfortunately, there were also priests of foreign gods who practiced their priesthood within the boundaries of Israel, sometimes even under the auspices of certain unfaithful Israelite rulers (see, 2 Kings 10:11, 19, 23; 23:5). 2 Kings

23:4-20 lists *five categories of priests* that existed in ancient Israel before Josiah's reformation, and arranges them according to their proximity to the Jerusalem temple: (1) **the high priest** (v. 4), (2) **the second-order priests** (v. 4), (3) **the idolatrous priests** in the cities of Judah and in the area surrounding Jerusalem (v. 5); (4) **the priests of the high places in the cities of Judah** from Geba to Beersheba (vv. 8-9); and (5) **the priests of the high places in Samaria** (i.e., the remnants of the priests of the former northern kingdom, v. 20).

According to this passage, a significant feature of Josiah's religious reformation was his eradication of all priests *(and their cultic accouterments)* except those who functioned legitimately within Jerusalem temple. Therefore, only the first two categories of priests in 2 Kings 23 retained their office: the *high priest* (v. 4, here Hilkiah) and *the priests of the second order (v. 4; i.e., other descendants of Aaron).*

NOTE: The books of the bible used in this chapter are abbreviated, i.e., Gen= Genesis, Num=Numbers, Exod= Exodus, Zeph= Zephaniah, 1 Sam= 1 Samuel, Duet= Deuteronomy, Chron= Chronicles, Jer=Jeremiah, Isa= Isaiah, Matt= Matthew, Rom= Romans. . . . .

Priest, Priesthood. A Kingdom of Priests: One of the foundational principles of the Israelite covenant with God at Sinai was that the nation as a whole would become *a kingdom of priests* (Exod 19:6a). There have been many proposed interpretations of this expression. Some say that it refers to Israel as a kingdom ruled by priests or a nation whose kings are also priests.

In the immediate context as well as in the theology of the Old Testament overall, however, this expression seems to support two main ideas corresponding to the surrounding statements that covenant Israel would become the Lord's *special treasure* and *holy nation* (Exod 19:5b, 6b). First, the closest Old Testament parallel is Isaiah 61:6 (cf. 66:21), which designates the nation of Israel as the priestly mediators for all the nations of the world when they come to worship the Lord on Mount Zion in the eschatological future. This seems to be part of the intended meaning in Exodus 19:5b-6a as well, since Israel was to become the Lord's special treasure among all the people.

Although the whole earth is mine, you will be for me a kingdom of priests.

In Hebrew, the *you* is emphatic, contrasting Israel with any other nation.

Second, the covenant ratification ritual in Exodus 24:3-8 actually inaugurated Israel as a *kingdom of priests*, that is, a nation that had direct access to God through his *presence in the tabernacle* and to which they would come and worship. The ritual procedure itself involved splashing the blood of the burnt and peace offerings (v. 5) *both on the altar* (v. 6) *and on the people* (v. 8).

There is a striking similarity between this ritual in Exodus 24 and the consecration of the Aaronic priests by putting some of the blood of the ordination peace offering on the right ear, thumb, and big toe of Aaron and his sons, and afterwards splashing some of it around on the altar (Exod 29:20; Lev 8:23-24).

That differences between Exodus 24:5-8 and Exodus 29:20 are due primarily to one or both of the following factors: (1) the consecration in Exodus 24 was for the priesthood of the whole nation so that the corporate general splashing of blood was appropriate to the meaning of the ritual; and (2) in the instance of Exodus 24 specific touching of each person's body by Moses was precluded by the large number of people involved. Moreover, the connection between Exodus 24 and 29 is confirmed by the blood manipulation *(or usage)* for the guilt offering used to cleanse the leper in Leviticus 14 *(presumably the same for all lepers whether or not they were priests)*. The procedure there is virtually identical to the one performed for the consecration of the priests. The rationale seems to have been that since the leper had been expelled *(i.e., desecrated)* from the *holy* community (Lev 13:46), therefore, it was necessary to re-sanctify him *(i.e., make him holy once again)* and thereby readmit him to the community that had originally been established as a consecrated community by the ritual in Exodus 24.

The manipulation or usage of oil in the case of the leper (Lev 14:15-18) also corresponds to priestly consecration procedures (cf. Exod 29:21; and Lev 8:30) and further substantiates this suggestion that, from the start *(i.e., from Exod. 24 forward)*, the whole nation was a *kingdom of priests*, they were *a holy people* (Exod 19:6, immediately following *a kingdom of priests*).

Priest, Priesthood. Finally, the sect granted the entire nation the privilege of eating at the Lord's table on regular occasions in accordance with the peace offering regulations in Leviticus 3 and 7:11-34. Therefore, Israel was to be a *kingdom of priests* in terms of its corporate participation in the service of worship to the Lord in the sanctuary (Exod 24:3-8) as well as in its position and ministry toward the nations roundabout them (Isa 61:6).

The Aaronic Priesthood: Moses functioned as the original priest of Israel by initially consecrating (1) *the whole kingdom of priests* (Exod 24:3-8), (2) *the perpetual priesthood of Aaron and his descendants*, who would in turn mediate for that kingdom of priests (Exod 29; Lev 8), and (3) *the tabernacle* (Num 7:1). However, there are several passages that seem to indicate that Aaron and his sons functioned as priests in Israel even before the official consecration of the Aaronic priesthood (Exod 19:24; 24:1; 32:3-6). Of course, as brothers and sons of Amram and Jochebed (Exod 6:20) Moses and Aaron were both from the tribe of Levi through Kohath. Therefore, it was natural that the Lord should then choose the whole tribe of Levi to assist the group of Aaron with all their priestly duties in place of the firstborn of all Israel (Num 8:14-19). So, although the entire nation constituted *a kingdom of priests*, the Lord established Aaron's descendants as the perpetual priestly group in Israel.

Together they were responsible for maintaining a proper relationship of the people toward the Lord in regard to the two major focuses of the Mosaic covenant: (1) *the administration and ministry of the sanctuary* and (2) *the custody and administration of the law of Moses.*

The Administration and Ministry of the Sanctuary: The ministry of priesthood focused especially on administering and ministering at the place of the Lord's *Presence (see esp. Exod 33:14-15; Lev 10:2)* according to the basic principles of holy versus profane (Lev 10:10a), clean versus unclean (v. 10b), and atonement (v. 17). Following these rules and procedures was a matter of survival for the nation in general *(Lev 15:31b, so they will not die in their uncleanness for defiling my dwelling place, which is among them cf. Exod 32:35; 33:2-3, 14-15)* as well as for the priests in particular *(see the death of Nadab and Abihu in Lev. 10).* It was not just the sons of Aaron but the whole tribe of Levi who were responsible for maintaining proper levels of sanctity and purity in regard to the sanctuary presence of the Lord as a whole *(Num 18:1a; You [Aaron], your sons and your father's family [i.e., the Levites] are to bear the responsibility for offenses against the sanctuary, note the clarification regarding the Levites in Num 18:2-6; and cf. Deut 18:5-8).*

Initially, the duties of the Levites in assisting the priests focused on such tasks as the transportation of the tabernacle *(see, e.g., Num. 3-4; 1 Chron 15:2)* and guarding the doorway to the tabernacle *(see, e.g., 1 Chron 9:19, 22-27).* David assigned them other tasks in assisting the priests within the sanctuary *(e.g., purification procedures, preparing the showbread and other grain offerings, leading in the praising of the Lord through song, special responsibilities for festival burnt offerings, etc., 1 Chron 23:27-32; 1 Chron 25:1-8).* The importance of the Levites in the priestly functions of the sanctuary are well illustrated by their involvement in the reforms of Hezekiah *(2 Chron. 29-31)* and Josiah *(2 Chron 34:9; 35:10-15).*

Priest, Priesthood. On the other hand, although the Levites assisted the priests, it was the priests alone, Aaron and his descendants (*no other Levites*), who were responsible for dealing directly with the burnt offering altar or anything inside the Holy Place or Holy of Holies (Num 18:1b).

First, they had the oversight of the various offerings and sacrifices in the tabernacle, certain specific responsibilities regarding the actual handling of the blood, fat, flesh, and special portions, and the benefit of certain parts of the offerings as their payment for performing the requisite rituals. The priestly responsibilities and prerogatives for each of the major ritual procedures is prescribed in detail in Leviticus 6:8-7:36. There were also daily, weekly, monthly, and periodic festival offerings that the priests were responsible to offer as part of the regular pattern of tabernacle worship (Num. 28-29). Regular daily responsibilities included keeping the lamps burning continually in the tent of meeting by attending to them each evening and morning (Lev 24:3-4; cf. Exod 27:20-21), and keeping the fire continually burning on the burnt offering altar as part of the regular morning and evening burnt offering rituals (Lev 6:12-13; cf. Num 28:3-8).

Weekly responsibilities included replacing the twelve cakes of the *bread of presence* on the table in the tent of meeting each sabbath (Lev 24:5-9; cf. Exod 25:30), and the regular additional Sabbath burnt offerings (Num 28:9-10). At the special festival times the priests had specific responsibilities in handling the offerings brought by the people (Lev 23:9-21, 25, 36-38).

In addition to the normal regulations for offering sacrifices and offerings the priests were in charge of the valuation for the redemption of vows and things consecrated to the Lord (Lev 27), the oversight of the sin offering for jealousy (Num 5:11-31), and the regulations for the *Nazirite vow* (Num 6:1-21). They also blew the trumpets in Israel for summoning and directing the congregation and its leaders in their travels (Num 10:2-6), convening the congregation (Num 10:7-8), blowing the alarm in battle (10:9), or on worship and festival occasions (10:10).

Second, the Aaronic priests were responsible to maintain the sanctity and purity of the sanctuary (Lev 10:10). Since the Lord was physically present within the physical tabernacle structure in their midst, therefore, the physical purity of Israel was essential to the habitation of the Lord among them. *(note the contrast between cleansing the "flesh" by the Old Testament sacrifices as opposed to the cleansing of the "conscience" by the sacrifice of Christ in Heb 9:8-10, 13-14)*. They were to accomplish this by teaching the people the laws of purity (Lev 11:46; 12:7; 13:59; 14:57; 15:32) and by functioning as the regulators of certain aspects of the society based on those rules. Sometimes this involved presiding over certain specified sacrificial cleansing procedures on irregular occasions, for example, the burnt and sin offering rituals for the woman after childbirth (Lev 12:6-8), the combination of two bird, guilt, sin, and burnt offering rituals for the cleansing of the leper (Lev 14:4-20), the sin and burnt offering rituals for the man or woman with an irregular discharge (Lev 15:13-15, 25-30), and the preparation of the ashes of the red heifer for purification for touching a dead corpse (Num 19:1-10).

Priest, Priesthood. In addition, they diagnosed and regulated the expulsion and readmission of people with infectious skin diseases (Lev 13); cf. the cleansing procedures in Lev 14 referred to above), and were responsible to preside over the removal of bloodguiltiness for an unsolved homicide in the land (Deut 21:1-9, esp. v. 5).

The Custody and Administration of the Mosaic Law: Leviticus 10:10 relates primarily to issues of *the holy and the common* and *the unclean and the clean*. The next verse introduces the matter of administration of the Mosaic Law: *"you must teach the Israelites all the decrees the Lord has given them through Moses" (10:11)*. Deuteronomy 21:5 is particularly instructive regarding these responsibilities of the priests: *The priests, the sons of Levi* were charged to *pronounce blessings in the name of the Lord and to decide all cases of dispute and assault.*

The standard priestly blessing formula found in Numbers 6:24-26 was given as a means of invoking the name of the Lord upon the nation so that he might bless them in their various endeavors (Num 6:27). This may have been particularly important in situations where there was a need to clear the nation of guilt, in this case bloodguiltiness for an unsolved homicide (Deut 21:1-9). The last clause of Deuteronomy 21:5 especially highlights the judicial side of the priestly office. The resolution of disputes was not always achieveable in the local courts.

Since the levitical priests were the custodians and teachers of the Mosaic Law (Deut 17:18; 24:8; 31:9-13, 24-26; cf. 2 Chron 15:3; 31:4; 35:3; Ezra 7:24-26), those who staffed the central sanctuary were naturally the final court of appeal in Israel (Deut 18:8-13; 19:17).

The Levites shared not only in the sanctuary duties of the Aaronic priests but also in their judicial duties *(see 2 Chron 17:8-9; 35:3; Ezra 7:5-10; Neh 8:1-2, 9-11, etc.)*. Samuel is a good example of a Levite who legitimately did both *(cf. 1 Sam 1:1; 8:2, with 1 Chron 6:28, 33-38)*. In his early days he was levitical assistant to Eli the Aaronic high priest in the service of the tabernacle (1 Sam. 2-3). Later he became a judge of Israel (1 Sam 7:15-17). **The High Priesthood**, *Special Obligations*: There were special obligations for which the high priest alone was responsible. On any normal day any priest might perform atoning sacrificial procedures, but not on the **Day of Atonement** (Lev 16). On this day, and only this day, the high priest would enter alone into the Most Holy Place to purge it from the impurities of the priests (vv. 11-14) and the people (v. 15) by sprinkling sin offering blood on the mercy seat. After this he also purged the other parts of the sanctuary with blood (vv. 16-19), performed the scapegoat ritual (vv. 20-22), and offered his burnt offering, the burnt offering of the people, and the fat of the sin offerings on the burnt offering altar (vv. 23-27). Thus, the high priest would yearly cleanse *(i.e., purify)* himself, the other priests, and all the people of the assembly (vv. 30, 33b) by purging *(i.e., atoning)* the Most Holy Place, everything in the tent of meeting, and the burnt offering altar (v. 33a) on their behalf (vv. 30, 33b). Furthermore, all the priests were under strict restrictions to avoid defilement by contact with a corpse *(except for their immediate family)*, or by marriage to a divorced woman or former harlot (Lev 21:1-4, 7). The high priest, however, could not defile himself even by attending to his dead father or mother, and marriage was restricted to a virgin.

Priest, Priesthood. He could not marry a widow, much less a divorced woman or former harlot Lev 21:10-14). Moreover, he was responsible to function as the head of the priestly system at the festivals and was in charge of everything that happened in the tabernacle *(see, e.g., Eli's supervision in 1 Sam 1:9, 12-17)*, including the actions of the other priests *(see, e.g., the problem of Eli's rebellious priestly sons in 1 Sam 2:29)*. Finally, another well-known and exclusive function of the high priest was to possess and manipulate the *Urim* and *Thummim* housed in the breast piece of judgment, which was attached to the high priest's ephod (Exod 28:28-30).

He used them to obtain oracular answers from the Lord regarding specific situations in Israel. **History:** The history of the Old Testament high priesthood is complex. After the death of Nadab and Abihu, Eleazar seems to have been the oldest remaining son and it is he who became the next high priest (Num 20:22-29; 26:1-4; 27:21; Joshua 19:51), his brother Ithamar being second to him. Certain passages suggest that Phinehas followed Eleazar his father (Num 31:6; Joshua 22:13, 30-32; Judges 20:28). The high priestly line evidently shifted from the descendants of Eleazar to Ithamar during the period of the judges. Eli, the high priest and Judge of Israel at Shiloh (1 Sam 1:9), was from the line of Ithamar. The line of Eli continued in the high priesthood for a time *(see 1 Sam 14:3, 18; 21:1; 22:19-20)*. However, the judgment of the Lord against Eli in 1 Samuel 2:22-36 would eventually bring the office back to the line of Eleazar when Solomon dismissed Abiathar (1 Kings 2:27) and appointed Zadok to be the high priest (1 Kings 2:35). Thus, the Lord's *covenant of a perpetual priesthood* with Phinehas was fulfilled (Num 25:13).

New Testament Priesthood: The primary New Testament Greek word for *priest* is *hiereus* [iJereuv"] (32 occurrences). Six other terms derive from it: the verb *hierateuo* [iJerateuvw] for Zacharias *serving as priest* (Luke 1:8), the verb *hierourgeo* [iJerourgevw] referring to Paul *serving as a priest* by offering the Gentiles up as a holy offering to God (Rom 15:16), and the nouns *hierateia* [iJerateiva] for the *priestly office* of Zacharias (Luke 1:9) and the sons of Levi (Heb 7:5), *hierateuma* [iJeravteuma] in reference to the *priesthood* of the church (1 Peter 2:5,9), *archieratikos* [ajrcieratikov"] referring to those of *high priestly* descent (Acts 4:6), and especially *archiereus* ["] *(high or chief priest(s), 123 occurrences)*. With only one exception (Acts 14:13, the priest of Zeus), all the New Testament references to priests or priesthood are in some kind of continuity with the Old Testament.

High Priests, Chief Priests and Priests: The Old Testament Aaronic and specifically Zadokite line of high priests continued down into the intertestamental period until about 172 b.c., when the Syrian *(i.e., Seleucid)* ruler of Palestine, Antiochus IV (Epiphanes), began to assign the office to whomever was in political and financial favor with him at any particular time (2 Macc. 4). Although they were not Zadokites, the Maccabeans *(i.e., Hasmoneans)* were a priestly family that successfully led a revolt against the Syrian rulers and eventually became not only the political leaders of the Jews but also assumed the role of high priest *(i.e., beginning with Jonathan, ca. 152 b.c., 1 Matt. 10:18-21)*. During this time the Qumran community prided itself on being the enclave of the legitimate Zadokite high priesthood over against the Hasmonean high priesthood in Jerusalem.

Priest, Priesthood. In 37 b.c. the rule of the Hasmoneans came to an end and the family of Herod the Great began the practice of appointing high priests from various priestly families again, not necessarily Zadokites, from time to time, sometimes year by year *(note: John 18:13, Caiaphas, the high priest that year)*. This led to an oligarchy of a few privileged high priestly families who obtained their position through bribery. The New Testament refers often to the *chief priests*, apparently referring to a group of priests who had the oversight of the cultus, many of whom belonged to these privileged families. This group seems to have included the current high priest (John 18:13), all those still alive who had previously held the position (Luke 3:2; John 18:19, 24), and those of high priestly descent *(see esp. Acts 4:6, 23)*. Three New Testament high priests are specifically named; Annas (Luke 3:2; John 18:19, 24), Caiaphas (Luke 3:2; John 18:13b, 24), and Ananias (Acts 23:2; 24:1).

Of course, the priests *(i.e., the high priests, chief priests, and regular priests)* were the source of much opposition to Jesus and the apostolic spread of the gospel. Nevertheless, Paul confirmed his respect for the office of Ananias after unintentionally insulting him (Acts 23:2-5).

Jesus refused the same to Annas (John 18:19-24), but during his ministry he sometimes affirmed the priests (see, e.g., Matt 8:4; *the cleansing of the leper*). Zecharias, the father of John the Baptist, was a priest (Luke 1:8). Interestingly, the high priest Caiaphas unwittingly prophesied the substitutionary death of Jesus for Israel and for all believers even among the gentiles (John 11:47-53; 18:14). Moreover, it was not long before "a large number of priests became obedient to the faith" (Acts 6:7).

Jesus as Priest and High Priest: Although the high priesthood of Jesus is often described solely in terms of his status according to the order of Melchizedek, Hebrews 2-4 devotes a great deal of attention to the matter of the high priesthood of Jesus before introducing Melchizedek in 5:6. In 2:17 the writer of Hebrews describes Jesus as the one who has come to our aid as our high priest by making *atonement for the sins of the people*. The emphasis is on the fact that, because He Himself suffered the same sorts of temptations that we face, He is a *merciful and faithful* high priest (Heb. 2:17-18) and, as such, He is *the apostle and high priest whom we confess* (Heb. 3:1). After a lengthy digression about the faithfulness of Jesus and the importance of a corresponding faithful commitment to Him on our part (Heb. 3:7-4:13), the writer returns to the same issue and exhorts us to *hold firmly* to our sympathetic high priest (Heb. 4:14-16) because it is in Him that *we may receive mercy and find grace to help us in our time of need*. This argument regarding the gentle and sympathetic nature of our high priest and mediator continue in Hebrews 5:1-10. Old Testament high priests could sympathize with the people for whom they mediated because they had to offer sacrifices for their own sins before they could offer for the people (Lev 5:2-3; 7:27; and cf. Lev 16:11-14 with Lev 16:15-19). Jesus as our

New Testament high priest is sympathetic because, even though He was the son of God, He suffered agony in the face of death (Heb 5:7-8). This is where Melchizedek comes into the picture. The first occurrence of the term *priest* in the Old Testament is in reference to the pre-Israelite Melchizedek king of Salem, priest of God *Most High* (Gen 14:18), to whom Abram paid a tithe.

Priest, Priesthood. Melchizedek reappears in Psalm 110:4, referring to the royal Davidic *priest forever, in the order of Melchizedek* (v. 4). This, in turn, became the pattern for the thematic development of the Melchizedekian priesthood of Jesus Christ in Hebrews 5-7 since, not being a descendant of Aaron, he could not be a priest according to the order of Aaron (Heb 7:11-14). Nevertheless, just as Aaron was divinely appointed to this office so was Jesus (vv. 4-5), but the high priesthood of Jesus was *in the order of Melchizedek* (vv. 6, 9-10). This makes the high priesthood of Jesus distinct and superior from that of Aaron and his successors on several counts. First, Jesus *has become a high priest forever* (6:20). Aaronic priests died and therefore had only a *temporary* priesthood (7:23). But Jesus abides forever as a priest according to the order of Melchizedek and therefore has a permanent priesthood through which he can save us completely and *eternally* (7:24-25). Second, since the Old Testament Levitical priests paid a tithe to Melchizedek while they were still in the loins of Abraham, their order of priesthood is inferior to the order of Melchizedek (7:4-10). Third, if the Aaronic priesthood had brought perfection there would have been no need for another priest to arise according to another order *(i.e., the order of Melchizedek, 7:11)*. Moreover, in this connection, there was a necessary and corresponding shift from the old and obsolete covenant mediated by the old priesthood *(i.e., the Mosaic covenant with its relatively weak and useless law, 7:11, 18-19; 8:13)* to a new and better covenant mediated by the better priesthood *(i.e., the New Covenant with its better promises, 7:22; 8:1-13)*. Direct references to Melchizedek and to Jesus as a priest according to the order of Melchizedek as opposed to the order of Aaron are limited to Hebrews 5-7.

Therefore, just as the discussion of the high priesthood of Jesus in the Book of Hebrews begins without direct reference to Melchizedek *(see page 363)*, so it ends without it.

In fact, the references to the *(high)* priesthood of Christ in Hebrews 9:7-11 and 9:24-10:25 focus more on the offering of his own blood as a sacrifice than on his priestly office, which is forever. However, in Hebrews 10:13 the writer once again alludes to Psalm 110:1 when he refers to Jesus as the priest who has offered himself up as our sacrifice and since that time, waits for his enemies to be made his footstool. This is, of course, a royal motif. This suggests that Jesus, like Melchizedek, is a king who is also a priest. In fact, in some sense David, who is likely to have been the initial referent in Psalm 110, also legitimately exercized priestly prerogatives on some occasions *(see esp. 2 Sam. 6)*. According to some scholars, even if David wrote Psalm 110 *(as the title of the psalm seems to suggest*), still *my lord* in verse 1 may be a formulaic way of saying *me* (thus yielding the translation, *The Lord says to me* but see Matt 22:41-46).

The Priesthood of Believers: This *(royal)* high priesthood of Jesus Christ connects to the *royal priesthood* of believers: *"you are a royal priesthood, a holy nation"* (1 Peter 2:9a).

The obvious reference to Exodus 19:6 suggests that the church functions in this present age as God's New Testament kingdom of priests much like the nation of Israel did in the Old Testament. As such we are responsible to carry out the ministry of proclaiming to the world *the praises of him who called you out of darkness into his wonderful light* (1 Peter 2:9b). A closely related idea (but without the *royal* connections) is Peter's earlier description of the church as a group of believers who are being, or should allow themselves to be, built into a spiritual house.

Priest, Priesthood. Jesus Himself being the living and choice cornerstone, (1 Peter 2:4, 6-8) to be a holy priesthood, offering spiritual sacrifices acceptable unto God through Jesus Christ (1 Peter 2:5). Thus, as fellow priests with Jesus we offer up to God our sacrifices of praise (Heb 13:15), our good deeds and sharing (Heb 13:16), and ultimately our present physical bodies in the interest of conforming to his standards (Rom 12:1-2). It is important to observe that here the corporate priesthood of the church shades into the priesthood of the individual believer. Moreover, our ministry in the gospel can be described as an offering of our very life in priestly service to the church (Phil. 2:17), by which we can produce a harvest of sanctified people whom we present to God, a holy and acceptable offering.

Finally, corporate Israel in the Old Testament functioned as a kingdom of priests in both its mediation between God and the other nations and in its service of worship to the Lord in the sanctuary (Exod 19:5-6). Similarly, the priesthood of the church has mediatorial features as well as aspects that correspond to the sanctuary worship of the Old Testament, sometimes expressed separately and sometimes jointly in the various New Testament passages related to the priesthood of believers.

The Priesthood Today: We as spiritual Israelites are a called out group of people who are to give our own bodies now as living sacrifices. 1 Peter 2: 1-9 says; *¹ Wherefore laying aside all malice, and all guile, and hypocrisies, and envies, all evil speakings, ² As newborn babes, desire the sincere milk of the word, that ye may grow thereby: ³ If so be ye have tasted that the Lord is gracious. ⁴ To whom coming, as unto a living stone, disallowed indeed of men, but chosen of God, and precious, ⁵ Ye also, as lively stones, are built up a spiritual house,* **an holy priesthood***, to offer up spiritual sacrifices, acceptable to God by Jesus Christ. ⁶ Wherefore also it is contained in the scripture, Behold, I lay in Sion a chief corner stone, elect, precious: and he that believeth on him shall not be confounded. ⁷ Unto you therefore which believe he is precious: but unto them which be disobedient, the stone which the builders disallowed, the same is made* *the head of the corner, ⁸ And a stone of stumbling, and a rock of offence, even to them which stumble at the word, being disobedient: whereunto also they were appointed. ⁹* **But ye are a chosen generation, a"royal priesthood," an holy nation, a peculiar people; that ye should shew forth the praises of him who hath called you out of darkness into his marvellous light.** KJV.

We are now a kingdom of priests, here to show forth the praises of our God. We are to tell all nations of His goodness and let them see His glory through our daily lives. We are the priests of our homes, leading our families and our children in the way they should go. We are to tell our sons and daughters about Him and teach them the Word of God so that they can perpetuate righteousness and godliness in the earth. We are to be a separated nation of people showing this present world that there is a risen savior that is able to keep us from falling and to present us faultless. We are the ones to make the living sacrifices today and present ourselves to God so He can use us in whatever capacity He chooses. When we are dead in Him, then God can become alive in manifesting Himself in our lives.

Priest, Priesthood. We as a kingdom of priests to the world today are as Paul says in scripture; always bearing about in our bodies, the dying of the Lord Jesus, so that the life of Him might be made manifest in our bodies. In other words we become the sacrifice for the people, always being made weak that others may become strong.

We have now become in a sense, the high priests as witnesses and a go-between from the world to God. We now stand in the middle, bidding men to come to God, we are the ones who will guide them to the throne of grace and become intercessors for the world to come to Christ.

And God, who is faithful and just to forgive, will forgive all of unrighteousness.

What an awesome responsibility we have as priests in the world today. We can bring the world to God by living that sacrificed life and being who we say we are. For we are living epistles, read of men! Let us as people of God become that **Kingdom of Priests** in the earth that people can pick from us and see God. The Word of God tells us that if any among you be great, let him become a servant. We are dealing with real people with real problems and situations. We must be as the priests to the world and go to God on the behalf of the people. We must lay ourselves on the alter and become the sacrifice in order to obtain the grace and mercy of God toward the people. "**God our lives are on the altar of your will; do with us as you see fit.**" Can you say that? Are you willing to lay down your life and die to your own desires for the good of the people? Just like Jesus Christ our example in who God was well pleased to bruise and batter so that from his death came the life in many. So it should be with you, priest of the Most High. Gods taking you and breaking you into pieces so the body of Christ can eat from your ministry.

CHAPTER 16

THE WORSHIP

---

*T*he **Worship.** This is a *short* chapter on worship only because the whole book is based on *true worship*. Much has been written concerning worship. Some good, and some not so good. People have so many concepts and philosophies on what worship actually is. Worship is not just the raising of the hands, or the lifting of the voices. Worship is not showing up early for church service just to get your favorite seat. It's not in listening to the Pastor teach a bible story or hearing the choir sing your favorite song; no, that's not worship at all. Worship isn't even the clapping of your hands, or in tears flowing down your face. There's more to it than all of that.

It's time we understand what worship is all about. We have to know what God wants when He says He's *seeking* for those who will do so.

In John 4:25, the women who met Jesus at the well was actually looking and waiting on the Messiah to come and tell them how and where to worship. Not understanding that the one she should have been worshipping was staring her in the face. She was like many of us today. We're waiting on some super manifestation of worship to take place in the church. We're waiting on the Pastor to preach the perfect sermon, or on the choir to sing just the right song. But like the woman at the well, we don't actually know what we're waiting on, and even if we did; many times there's too many objects in our lives we actually worship other than God.

In John 4: 22, Jesus told the women; *ye worship ye know not what: we know what we worship: for salvation is of the Jews*. Now that sounds a little harsh, but in essence what Jesus pointed out to her was the fact that they worshiped, and didn't know what they were worshipping.

He showed her that; the Samaritans were ignorant, not only of the place to worship, but of the very **object of worship.** Indeed, they feared the Lord after a fashion; but at the same time served their own gods, 2 Kings 17:33. Salvation is from the Jews. So spake all the prophets that the Saviour should arise out of the Jewish nation; and that from thence the knowledge of Him should spread to all nations under heaven.

Jesus wanted her to see, that worship was not just the reverence of a certain day, time, or a physical place to gather.

He told her; *but the hour cometh, and now is, when the true worshippers shall worship the Father in spirit and in truth: for the Father seeketh such to worship him.*

God is a Spirit; and they that worship him must worship him in spirit and in truth.

God is searching and seeking for this thing called worship. He's looking in the church to find it. He's looking in your homes to find it. He's searching your places of employment to see if He can spot it there. He's even watching when you're all alone, thinking no one can see you.

Jesus let the woman know that, the **true worshippers** shall worship the Father, *not here* or *there only, (meaning in the mountain or in Jerusalem)* but *at all times* and in *all places.*

God is a Spirit, not only remote from the body, and all the properties of it, but likewise full of all spiritual perfections, power, wisdom, love, holiness. And our worship should be suitable to His nature. We should worship Him with the truly spiritual worship of *faith, love,* and ***holiness***, animating all our *tempers, thoughts, words,* and *actions.*

What God is seeking for is a holy lifestyle. That's true worship! It's your everyday life, prostrate before a holy God. It's your faith, it's your love and patience, it's your total obedience to Him on a daily and consistent bases. It's your willingness to say yes to His perfect will. If the world could only see this true worship in us, then they would do like the woman did when Jesus had finish speaking to her. They will drop everything and tell others to come and see how a true worshiper lives their life. Let's do it yall. . . . . . . .The Father is waiting!

The Worship.

1. **Perpetual Service.** In an important sense the worship of the Hebrews was incessant. At the inauguration of the tabernacle service by the consecration of Aaron and his sons (Exodus 40:1-38; Leviticus 8:1-36), fire fell from heaven upon the altar of burnt sacrifices (Leviticus 9:1-24), and they were commanded to keep it burning continually (Leviticus 6:12, 13). They were also required to keep the golden lamps in the holy place burning continually (Leviticus 24:1-3) and the showbread was *set in order before the Lord continually* (Leviticus 24:5-9).
2. **Elements of the Service.** The continual service was characterized by,
    a. sacrifice
    b. bread
    c. life

3. **Daily Sacrifices.** They were commanded to offer upon the brazen altar two lambs, one in the morning, and the other in the evening, continually. With each lamb, they offered flour, oil and wine (Exodus 29:38-43; Numbers 28:1-8). The offerings were doubled on the Sabbath Day (Numbers 28:9, 10).
4. **Irregular Offerings.** The class of offerings embraced all individual sacrifices, chiefly comprehended under *five classifications,* and the people were at liberty to present them whenever necessity demanded it.
   a. **The burnt offering** was an animal sacrifice and was wholly consumed upon the brazen altar (Leviticus 1:1-17);
   b. **The meat offering** was bloodless and part of it was burnt, and the remainder was consumed by Aaron and his sons (Leviticus 2:1-16);
   c. **The peace offering** consisted of an animal, part of which was burnt on the altar, the remainder being eaten by the priests and the worshipper (Leviticus 3:1-17; Leviticus 7:11-38);
   d. **The sin offering** consisted of an animal, part of which was consumed upon the altar of burnt offerings and the remainder burnt without the camp (Leviticus 4:1-35);
   e. **The trespass offering** consisted of an animal and the presentation was similar to that of the sin offering (Leviticus 7:1-7). It was distinguished from all other offerings by the restitution that the worshipper was required to make (Leviticus 5:1-19; Leviticus 6:1-7; Leviticus 7:1-7).
5. **Requirements of Sacrifices.**
   a. The irregular sacrifices were characterized by offerings for sin, consumption by fire, reformation of life, peace, voluntary gifts to the Lord.
   b. They were required to offer animals without blemish (Leviticus 1:1-3; Leviticus 22:17-25).

The Worship.

   c. They were required to offer salt with all their sacrifices (Leviticus 2:13).
   d. The blood of the sin offerings for the priests and for the whole congregation was sprinkled seven times before the Lord, before the vail of the sanctuary, and some of it was put upon the altar of incense (Leviticus 4:1-21).
   e. They were prohibited from eating any part of an animal whose blood was carried into the tabernacle (Leviticus 6:24-30).

6. **Periodical Offerings.** All the males of the Hebrews were required to appear before the Lord three times a year: at the Passover, feast of weeks and feast of tabernacles (Exodus 23:14-19; Leviticus 23:1-44), at which

time numerous sacrifices were offered (Numbers 28:16-31; Numbers 29:1-40).

7. **Day of Atonement.** This was by far the most important day in the Hebrew calendar. It was the day on which reconciliation was made for the entire nation. After the ordinary morning sacrifice was presented (Exodus 28:38-42), a special offering was made, consisting of one young bullock, seven lambs, one ram, one kid of the goats, accompanied by meat offerings of flour mingled with oil (Numbers 29:7-11). Very probably it was before the presentation of this special offering that the high priest laid aside his garments of glory and beauty and arrayed himself in spotless linen.

He then brought a bullock for a sin offering and a ram for a burnt offering to the north side of the altar, after which he bathed his hands and feet at the laver, took a censer full of fire from the brazen altar and a handful of incense which he immediately burnt within the second vail. He then returned to the altar of burnt offerings and slew the bullock of the sin offering. Taking of its blood he returned within the vail and sprinkled it upon the mercy seat and seven times upon the ground before it: this was the sin offering for himself and his family. After making atonement for himself and house, he returned and slew the goat for a sin offering for the people, which had been previously provided. Taking of its blood he returned the third time within the vail and sprinkled it upon the mercy seat eastward, and seven times upon the ground before it. Coming out of the most holy place he stained the horns of the altar of incense with the blood; returning to the brazen altar, he stained the horns thereof with the blood of both sin offerings, and sprinkled it with his finger upon the altar seven times. When the atonement for the priests, tabernacle and people had been completed, the second goat of the sin offering for the people, the one for the scapegoat, had the sins of the people confessed over it by the high priest who laid his hands upon its head, after which it was led into the wilderness by a man selected for the purpose. The high priest then went into the tabernacle where he removed the plain linen garments, and after bathing his person again, resumed his official dress. Returning to the altar he offered his burnt offering and that of the people, and burnt the fat of the sin offerings upon the altar.

During this service no one was allowed in the tabernacle. The bodies of the sin offerings were burnt without the camp. The man who burned the bodies of the sin offerings, and the one who led away the scapegoat, were required to wash their clothes and bathe their flesh before returning to the camp. On this day the people were required to refrain from work and afflict their souls (Leviticus 16:1-34).

CHAPTER 17

CHERUB, ANGELS, SERAPHIM

Cherub, Angels, Seraphim. Cherub plural cherubim, the name of certain symbolical figures frequently mentioned in Scripture. They are first mentioned in connection with the expulsion of our first parents from Eden (Genesis 3:24). There is no information given of their shape or form. They are next mentioned when Moses was commanded to provide furniture for the tabernacle (Exodus 25:17-20; 26:1, 31). God promised to commune with Moses "from between the cherubim" (25:22). This expression was afterwards used to denote the Divine abode and presence (Numbers 7:89; 1 Samuel 4:4; Isaiah 37:16; Psalms 80:1; 99:1). In Ezekiel's vision (10:1-20) they appear as living creatures supporting the throne of God. From Ezekiel's description of them (1; 10; 41:18, 19), they appear to have been compound figures, unlike any real object in nature; artificial images possessing the features and properties of several animals. Two cherubim were placed on the mercy-seat of the ark; two of colossal size overshadowed it in Solomon's temple. Ezekiel 1:4-14 speaks of four; and this number of "living creatures" is mentioned in Revelation 4:6. Those on the ark are called the "cherubim of glory" (Hebrews 9:5), i.e., of the Shechinah, or cloud of glory, for on them the visible glory of God rested. They were placed one at each end of the mercy-seat, with wings stretched upward, and their faces "toward each other and toward the mercy-seat." They were anointed with holy oil, like the ark itself and the other sacred furniture. The cherubim were symbolical. They were intended to represent spiritual existences in immediate contact with Jehovah. Some have regarded them as symbolical of the chief ruling power by which God carries on His operations in providence (Psalms 18:10).

Others interpret them as having reference to the redemption of men, and as symbolizing the great rulers or ministers of the church. Many other opinions have been held regarding them which need not be referred to here. On the whole, it seems to be most satisfactory to regard the interpretation of the symbol to be variable, as is the symbol itself. Their office was, (1) on the expulsion of our first parents from Eden, to prevent all access to the tree of life; and (2) to form the throne and chariot of Jehovah in His manifestation of Himself on earth. He dwelleth between and sitteth on the cherubim (1 Samuel 4:4; Psalms 80:1; Ezekiel 1:26, 28).

Cherub, Cherubim.

The symbolical figure so called was a composite creature-form which finds a parallel in the religious insignia of Assyria, Egypt and Persia, e.g. the sphinx, the winged bulls and lions of Nineveh, etc. In a cherub guarded paradise, (Genesis 3:24) figures of Cherubim were placed on the mercy-seat of the ark. (Exodus 25:18) A pair of colossal size overshadowed it in Solomon's temple with the canopy of their contiguously extended wings. (1 Kings 6:27) Those on the ark were to be placed with wings stretched forth, one at each end of the mercy-seat. *Their wings were to be stretched upwards, and their faces towards each other and towards the mercy-seat.*

It is remarkable that with such precise directions as to their position, attitude and material, nothing, save that they were winged, is said concerning their shape. On the whole it seems likely that the word *cherub* meant not only the composite creature-form, of which the man, lion, ox and eagle were the elements, but, further, some peculiar and mystical form.

Cherub, Angels, Seraphim. Some suppose that the cherubim represented *God's providence* among men, the four faces expressing the characters of that providence: its wisdom and intelligence (man), its strength (ox), its kingly authority (lion), its swiftness, far-sighted (eagle). Others, combining all the other references with the description of the living creatures in Revelation, make the cherubim to represent *God's redeemed people*. The qualities of the four faces are those which belong to God's people. They are facing four ways, towards all quarters of the globe, represents their duty of extending the truth. The wings show swiftness of obedience; and only the redeemed can sing the song put in their mouths in (Revelation 5:8-14).

Angels

A superhuman or heavenly being who serves as God's messenger. Both the Hebrew *malak* [J; 'm] and the Greek *angelos* [a [ggelo"] indicate that these beings also act decisively in fulfilling God's will in the world. But these two terms also apply to human beings as messengers (1 Kings 19:2; Hag 1:13; Luke 7:24). *Angels* are mentioned almost three hundred times in Scripture, and are only noticeably absent from books such as Ruth, Nehemiah, Esther, the letters of John, and James.

The Old Testament From the beginning, angels were part of the divine hierarchy.

They were created beings (Psalm 148:2, 5), and were exuberant witnesses when God brought the world into being (Job 38:7). By nature they were spiritual entities, and thus not subject to the limitations of human flesh.

Although holy, angels could sometimes behave foolishly (Job 4:18), and even prove to be untrustworthy (Job 15:15). Probably these qualities led to the *fall* of some angels, including Satan, but the Bible contains no description of that event.

When angels appeared in human society they resembled normal males (Gen 18:2, 16; Ezek 9:2), and never came dressed as women. In whatever form they occurred, however, their general purpose was to declare and promote God's will. On infrequent occasions they acted as agents of destruction (Gen 19:13; 2 Sam 24:16; 2 Kings 19:35, etc.). Sometimes angels addressed people in dreams, as with Jacob (Gen 28:12; 31:11), and could be recognized by animals before human beings became aware of them, as with Balaam (Num 22:22). Collectively the divine messengers were described as the *angelic host* that surrounded God (1 King 22:19) and praised His majesty constantly (Psalm 103:21). The Lord, their commander, was known to the Hebrews as the *Lord of Hosts*. There appears to have been some sort of spiritual hierarchy among them. Thus the messenger who instructed Joshua was a self-described *Commander of the Lord's Army* (Josh. 5:14-15), although this designation probably meant that it was God Himself who was speaking to Joshua. In Daniel, two angels who interpreted visions were unnamed (Dan. 7:16; 10:5), but other visions were explained to Daniel by the angel Gabriel, who was instructed by a *man's voice* to undertake this task (Dan. 8:15-16). When a heavenly messenger appeared to Daniel beside the river Hiddekel (Tigris), he spoke of Michael as *one of the chief princes* (Dan. 10:13, 21). This mighty angel would preside over the fortunes of God's people in the latter time (Dan. 12:1). Thereafter he was regarded by the Hebrews as their patron angel.

Cherub, Angels, Seraphim. In the postexilic period the term *messenger* described the teaching functions of the priest (Malachi 2:7), but most particularly the individual who was to prepare the way for the Lord's Messiah (Malachi 3:1). Two other terms relating to spiritual beings were prominent at various times in Israel's history. The first was *cherubim*, a plural form, conceived of as winged creatures (Exodus 25:20), and mentioned first in connection with the expulsion of Adam and Eve from Eden (Genesis 3:24). Apart from their functions as guardians, however, nothing is said about their character. When the wilderness tabernacle was being fashioned, God ordered two gold cherubim to be placed on top of the *mercy seat* or lid of the covenant ark to screen it. These came to be known as the *cherubim of the Glory* (Hebrews 9:5). Cherubim designs were also incorporated into the fabric of the inner curtain (Ezekiel 26:1) and the veil of the tabernacle (Exodus 26:31).

Solomon placed two wooden cherubim plated with gold leaf in the Most Holy Place of the temple, looking toward the Holy Place. They stood ten cubits (about fourteen feet) high and their wings were five cubits (about seven feet) long. Near Eastern archeological excavations have shown how popular the concept of winged creatures was in antiquity. The throne of Hiram at Byblos (ca. 1200 b.c.) was supported by a pair of creatures with human faces, lion's bodies, and large protective wings. It was above the cherubim that the Lord of hosts sat enthroned (1 Samuel 4:4).

The seraphim were also thought of as winged, and in Isaiah's vision they were stationed above the Lord's throne (Isaiah 6:1-2). They seemed to possess a human figure, and had voices, faces, and feet. According to the vision their task was to participate in singing God's praises *antiphonally*. They also acted in some unspecified manner as mediums of communication between heaven and earth (Isaiah 6:6). The living creatures of Ezekiel 1:5-14 were composites of human and animal parts, which were typically Mesopotamian in character, and they seem to have depicted the omnipotence and omniscience of God.

The Apocrypha: In the late postexilic period angelology became a prominent feature of Jewish religion. The angel Michael was deemed to be Judaism's patron, and the apocryphal writings named three other archangels as leaders of the angelic hierarchy. Chief of these was Raphael, who was supposed to present the prayers of pious Jews to God (1 Tobit 2:15). Uriel explained to Enoch many of his visions (1 Enoch 21:5-10; 27:2-4), interpreted Ezra's vision of the celestial Jerusalem (2 Esdras 10:28-57), and explained the fate of the fallen angels who supposedly married human women (1 Enoch 19:1-9; cf. Gen 6:2). Gabriel, Michael, Raphael, and Uriel (1 Enoch 40:3, 6) reported to God about the depraved state of humanity, and received appropriate instructions. According to contemporary thought, Gabriel sat on God's left, while Michael sat on the right side (2 Enoch 24:1). The primary concern of these two angels, however, was supposedly with missions on earth and affairs in heaven, respectively. In rabbinic Judaism they assumed a character which, while sometimes dramatic, had no factual basis in divine revelation.

The New Testament Against this background of belief in angels who were involved in human affairs, it was not surprising that the angel Gabriel should be chosen to visit Zechariah, the officiating priest in the temple, to inform him that he was to become a father, and that he had to name his son John (Luke 1:11-20). Gabriel was not referred to here as an archangel, the Greek term *archangelos* [ajrcavggelo"], appearing only in 1 Thessalonians 4:16 to describe an otherwise unnamed executive angel, and also in Jude 9, which refers to *Michael the archangel.*

Cherub, Angels, Seraphim. Six months after his announcement to Zechariah, Gabriel appeared to Mary to inform her that God had selected her to become the mother of Jesus, the promised Messiah (Luke 1:26-33).

Nothing in Gabriel's behavior is inconsistent with Old Testament teachings about angels. It has been pointed out frequently that, just as they were active when the world began, so angels were correspondingly prominent when the new era of divine grace dawned with the birth of Jesus.

On three occasions an angel visited Joseph in a vision concerning Jesus (Matt 1:20; 2:13, 19).

On the first two occasions the celestial visitor is described as *the angel of the Lord*, which could possibly be a way of describing God Himself. On the last visit the heavenly messenger was described simply as *an angel of the Lord*. In the end, however, the celestial beings were most probably of the same order, and were fulfilling among humans those duties normally assigned to such angels as Gabriel (Luke 1:19).

There is nothing recorded about the actual form of the latter, but Zechariah appears to have recognized the angel immediately as a celestial being, and was terrified (Luke 1:12). His penalty for not having learned anything from his ancestor Abraham's experience (Luke 1:18; cf. Gen 17:17) would only be removed when his son John was born (Luke 1:20). When Gabriel announced to Mary that she would bear Jesus (Luke 31), she seems to have been more disturbed by his message than his appearance. The birth of Jesus was announced to Bethlehem shepherds by the angel of the Lord, and since he was accompanied by the divine glory he may well have been the Lord Himself. The message of joy having been proclaimed, the heavenly host of angels praised and glorified God (Luke 2:13-14) for a short period, as they had done at the creation of the world (Job 38:7), after which they departed. During His ministry, angels came and ministered to Jesus after He had resisted the devil's temptations (Matthew 4:11). Again, when Jesus was submitting Himself to God's will in the garden of Gethsemane (Luke 22:40-44), an angel came from heaven to strengthen Him. At the resurrection, the angel of the Lord rolled back the stone from Jesus' burial place (Matt 28:2), and He was described as having a countenance like lightning and garments as white as snow (Matt 28:3). Again, this celestial being performed a service of reassurance and love for Mary and Mary of Magdala, who subsequently reported seeing *a vision of angels* (Luke 24:23).

In John's Gospel Mary Magdalene saw two angels in white clothing, sitting in the empty tomb, just before she met the risen Lord (John 20:12-16).

In Acts, the imprisoned apostles were released by an angel (Acts 5:19). Philip was ordered by an angel to meet an Ethiopian official (Acts 8:26-28), while another celestial being appeared to Cornelius (Acts 10:3).

The angel of the Lord released Peter from prison (12:7-11), and subsequently afflicted Herod with a fatal illness (12:23). When Paul and his companions were about to be shipwrecked the apostle assured them of the presence of a guardian angel (27:23-24).

Paul referred subsequently to angelic hierarchies *thrones, powers, rulers, or authorities* when proclaiming the cosmic supremacy of Jesus (Colossians 1:15-16; cf. 1 Peter 3:22), and prohibited the worship of angels in the Colossian church (Col 2:18) in an attempt to avoid unorthodox practices.

Cherub, Angels, Seraphim. His reference to *angels* in 1 Corinthians 11:10 may have been a warning that such things observe humans at the time of worship, and thus the Corinthians should avoid improper conduct or breaches of decency. Wow, the angels can watch us worship?

The angelology of 2 Peter and Jude reflects some of the intertestamental Jewish traditions concerning *wicked angels*. In Revelation there are numerous symbolic allusions to angels, the worship of which is forbidden (Revelations 22:8-9). The *angels of the seven churches* (Rev. 1:20) are the specific spiritual representations or personifications of these Christian groups.

A particularly sinister figure was Abaddon *(Apollyon in Greek)*, the *angel of the bottomless pit* (Rev. 9:11), who with his minions was involved in a fierce battle with Michael and his angels (Rev. 12:7-9). Jesus accepted as valid the Old Testament references to angels and their functions (Matt. 22:30), but spoke specifically of the *devil and his angels* (Matt. 25:41) as destined for destruction. He fostered the idea of angels ministering to believers (cf. Heb 1:14), and as being concerned for the welfare of children (Matt. 18:10). He described angels as holy creatures (Mark 8:38) who could rejoice when a sinner repented (Luke 15:10). Angels were devoid of sexual characteristics (Matt 22:30), and although they were highly intelligent ministers of God's will they were not omniscient (Matt 24:36). Christ claimed at His arrest in Gethsemane that more than twelve legions of angels (numbering about 72,000) were available to deliver Him, had He wanted to call upon them for assistance (Matt 26:53). He taught that angels would be with Him when He returned to earth at the second coming (Matt 25:31), and that they would be involved significantly in the last judgment (Matt 13:41, 49). Finally, angels set a model of obedience to God's will in heaven to which the Christian church should aspire (cf. Matt 6:10).

Some writers contrast the celestial beings with *fallen angels*, of which there are two varieties. The first consists of unimprisoned, evil beings working under Satan's leadership, and generally regarded as demons (Luke 4:35; 11:15; John 10:21). The second were imprisoned (2 Peter 2:4; Jude 6) spirits because they forsook their original positions in heaven. For New Testament writers they were particularly dangerous. The precise difference in function and character is not explained in Scripture. Presumably the imprisoned angels are the ones who will be judged by the saints (1 Corinthians 6:3).

In a material world that is also populated by good and evil spirits, the Bible teaches that the heavenly angels set an example of enthusiastic and resolute fulfillment of God's will.

They acknowledge Jesus as their superior, and worship Him accordingly. Angels continue to perform ministering duties among humans, and this function has led to the concept of *guardian angels*, perhaps prompted by Christ's words in Matthew 18:10.

It is not entirely clear whether each individual has a specific angelic guardian, but there is certainly no reason for doubting that an angel might well be assigned to care for the destinies of groups of individuals such as families. These celestial ministries will be most effective when the intended recipients are receptive to the Lord's will for their lives. It's through Gods love for us that He dispatches His heavenly creatures to watch over His earthly creation. They desire to look into the fact they we have an ability to boast in something they themselves cannot. We have been redeemed by the blood of the lamb!

The Cherubim and Seraphim
[CHEER oo beam] [SER uh fim]
(Meaning uncertain) (Fiery, burning ones)

These angelic creatures had special assignments in scripture and have special tasks in heaven before the presence of the Lord.

Winged angelic beings often associated with worship and praise of God. The cherubim are first mentioned in the Bible in Genesis 3:24. When God drove Adam and Eve from the Garden of Eden, He placed cherubim at the east of the garden, and a flaming sword, which turned every way, to guard the way to the tree of life.

According to the prophets, cherubim belong to the category of fallen angels; at one time, however, Satan or Lucifer was a cherub (Ezekiel 28:14; Ezekiel 28:12-19).

Symbolic representations of Cherubim were used in the Tabernacle in the Wilderness. Two Cherubim made of gold were stationed at the two ends of the Mercy Seat, above the Ark of the Covenant in the Holy of Holies, (Ex. 25:17-22; 1 Chronicles 28:18; Hebrews 9:5).

A careful comparison of the first and tenth chapters of the book of Ezekiel shows clearly that the *four living creatures* (Ezek. 1:5) were the same beings as the Cherubim in Ezekiel 10. Each had four faces-that of a man, a lion, an ox, and an eagle and each had four wings. In their appearance the Cherub had the likeness of a man (Ezek. 1:5). These Cherubim used two of their wings for flying and the other two for covering their bodies (Ezek. 1:6; 11, 23). Under their wings the Cherubim appeared to have the form, or likeness of a man's hand (Ezek. 1:8; 10:7-8, 21).

The imagery of Revelation 4: 6-9; seems to be inspired, at least in part, by the prophecies of Ezekiel. The *four living creatures* described here, as well as the *Cherubim* of Ezekiel, served the purpose of magnifying the holiness and great power of God. This is one of the main responsibilities throughout the Bible. In addition to singing God's praises, they also served as a visible reminder of the majesty and glory of God and His abiding presence with His people.

In some ways, the *Cherubim* were similar to the *Seraphim*, another form of angelic being mentioned in the Bible. Both were winged beings, and both surrounded God on His throne (Isaiah 6: 2-3). But the Seraphim of the prophet

Isaiah's vision were *very vocal* in their praise of God, singing, *Holy, holy is the Lord of hosts* (Isaiah 6:3).

Nowhere else in the Bible do the Cherubim break forth in such exuberant praise. They apparently played a *quieter*, more *restrained* role in worship, but the Seraphim were more *vibrant* and *vocal* in nature. Isn't it interesting though that Lucifer who was the *anointed cherub that covered*, was over the worship in heaven, yet the Cherubim's were very quiet in their nature? He was also a musical instrument who must have had the ability to *speak* or *communicate* with his music!! Huummm! *(read more about him in chapter 5)*

It's a lot of information but I think it's neat to hear and learn more about the creatures we'll be in fellowship with when the saints of God get to heaven. I can't wait to see them!

CHAPTER 18

THE AMEN!

The Amen. Transliteration of the Hebrew word signifying something as certain, sure and valid, truthful and faithful. It is sometimes translated **so be it.** In the Old Testament it is used to show the acceptance or the validity of a curse or an oath *(Num. 5:22; Deut. 27:15-26; Jer. 11:5)*, to *indicate acceptance of a good message (Jer. 28:6)*, and to join in a doxology in a worship setting to *affirm what has been said or prayed (1 Chron. 16:36; Neh.8:6; Ps. 106:48).*

Amen may confirm what *already is*, or it may indicate a hope for *something desired.*

In Jewish prayer *amen* comes at the end as an affirmative response to a statement made by others, and is so used in the New Testament epistles *(Rom. 1:25; 11:36; 15:33; 1Cor. 16:24; Gal. 1:5; Eph. 3:21; Phil. 4:20).* Paul ended some of his letters with *amen (Romans. 6:27; Gal.: 18).*

Ancient authorities add *amen* in other letters, but translations reflect this only in their notes. In the Gospels Jesus used *amen* to affirm the truth of His own statements. English translation often uses *verily, truly, I tell you the truth* to translate Jesus' *amen.* He never said it at the end of a statement but always at the beginning: *Amen, I say to you (Matt. 5:18; 16:28; Mark 8:12; 11:23; Luke 4:24; 21:32; John 1:51; 5:19).* In John's Gospel Jesus said Amen, *"amen."* That Jesus prefaced His own words with *amen* is especially important, for He affirmed that the kingdom of God is bound up with His own person and emphasized the authority of what He said.

Jesus is called *the Amen in Revelation. 3:14* meaning that *He Himself is the reliable and true witness of God.* Perhaps the writer had in mind *Isaiah 65:16* where the Hebrew says *God of Amen.*

"The Lord spoke to me and gave me a vision to write this Levites Manual. It has taken a total of about 9 and a half years to complete, with the Lord's help.

It is my prayer that this book be a blessing to as many who will read it. It was our endeavor to inform, enhance and give understanding to the called out of God. *(the levites)* We are a powerful force in this world if we would stand up and be who God has called us to be.

I know this manual covered a variety of subjects, but as the Lord kept speaking, I had to keep writing, and He told me to touch on all of the subjects written here. God is concerned about His people, and He desires that true worship John mentions. He's searching the earth wondering where His Levites are. He's calling us NOW, and wants to do a greater work in the earth.

I thank God for my best friend, my help meet, my confidant, my love and my original editor; my wonderful wife who constantly tells me I can do anything I put my mind to. God truly gave her to me, and I often say that I've been blessed over the years with many things, but God gave me the best thing first. My wife Valerie! I love you *"Punkin."*
She was a major part of the writing of this book because she helped me spell all the BIG words.

I would also like to thank God for one of my main influences, my Pastor, **Apostle Dr. Thomas H. Vinson.** *He's the studier's study and a teacher of teachers.* He lives in the Word of God and God gives him so **many nuggets** to share with the body of Christ. Many things I know and understand about the Word of God are because of him. He's my hero, Thanks Father! You are absolutely one of Gods chosen men for this end time, and God has truly blessed me through you. Thanks for your encouragement and wisdom, I love you Gods man!"

The Amen. Thanks also to my First Lady, **Evangelist Dr. Carolyn Vinson.** God put us together years ago and there's **no one** who can separate us but God! She's been my friend, my mother, my guide and an excellent example in the house of God. She is soooo gifted, and God is doing great things in her life. You haven't seen it all yet! She's before her time. She's a *song writer, musician and singer, arranger, producer, author, gospel dj, radio and TV personality, mother of six daughters, evangelist and Co Pastor.* Need I say more? Mom I love you with all my heart, you've helped me in many areas of my life, and my life WOULD NOT be the same if God hadn't seen fit to place you and Pastor in it. Thank you! I love you to **My Six**, you are my sisters!

I give thanks for my brother Eric High, who you'll be hearing more from real soon. He's a true Levite, psalmist, prophetic-minstrel and our *Chief Musician.* Thanks for always encouraging me in the things I set out to do. Thanks to my blood sisters Sheila and Sharon, for making me feel smarter than I actually am. I love you all so much. To Sylvia Graham and Brenda Taylor who I know without a shadow of a doubt, have my back and are in my corner. You are my true sisters in Christ fo sho! Love you! To my *"middle sized"* bro, Elder Jerome Mack. . .a great example!

To my parents, Elder Elmus L. *(preacha man!)* and First Lady *(songbird)* Roberta High Sr.

You put all of this in me! Thanks for praying for my brothers and sisters and prophesying that we would become anointed Levites from the womb. For telling us we were different and special and that God had an anointed call on our lives. **We miss you very much, but we'll see you soon!**

Also, a shout out to my youngest son Aaron. Thanks for your help man. He always corrects me, saying; "Dad, rephrase this, put it like that, don't say it like that," he's such a **smart guy!!!** *(The College Man Prophet!)*

To my two elder sons, Anthony *(the rhyming prophet)* and Andrew *(my preachin armor bearer)* I thank God for lending you to me to father. I want Gods best for you men! The mantle is yours to have if you want it.

Thanks to all who influenced my life, way too many to count or name. To all the Pastors and evangelists, musicians, singers, dancers and friends I've met over the years. Let's get this thing done for God. We as Levites are going to tear down and destroy the devils kingdom!

The "<u>Amen</u>," "the end." "<u>So be it</u>," "affirmation," or an "<u>acceptance of what has been said</u>." We pray that this is accepted as a Word from the Lord, for I wouldn't have said a word without Him.

(Use this book/manual as a reference and study guide to aid you in your own studies!).

"THE AMEN SOUND" A "<u>CRESCENDO OF PRAISE</u>"......Psalms 150: 6.
"Let everything that hath breath, praise the Lord".
Elder Elmus L. High, Jr. Author

Now let all the people say; AMEN!

Final Note

There have been a lot of issues covered in this book. I pray this book has been a blessing to all who have read it. I pray that it has opened your eyes to the ministry and separated life of a Levite.

God has gifted us in so many areas, and He wants to make sure that His anointing is attached to our gifts in order to affect the world and destroy the yokes that need to be expelled from people's lives. It doesn't matter if you're a preacher, usher, musician, or a greeter. We need to have God's anointing on everything we do.

I also want to make something perfectly clear! When the Lord began to reveal the information concerning the different groups or cults; you must understand that God is just uncovering the plan of the enemy in his plot to destroy man. We are not the judge, God is. But He does allow us to inspect the fruit. If it's an apple tree then it should bear apples.

But understand this; regardless of who you are, God is calling all of us to come together to worship Him in spirit and in truth. God is calling you even with your baggy pants, colored hair, black lips and toe nails, nose rings, pale faces or anything of the sort. Doesn't matter if you're on drugs, have *the can't help it's*; just off the streets or sitting right in the House of God.

He's reconciling all men and women back to Himself.

His Word says; *whosoever will let them come and drink of the waters of life freely, come without money or price.* He also said, *other sheep I have which are not of this fold; them also He will bring in and there will be one fold and one Shepard.*

So if you have a problem with any of these people that I've mentioned; you might as well get it together and get used to it, because God is pouring out of His spirit upon *ALL FLESH,* and all the flesh He's calling may not look like yours!

The reason God commissioned me to cover the diver's cultures and touch on so many sensitive issues is because He's calling for us to reach out and go into the highways and hedges and *compel men and women to come* to Christ, who IS the ONLY WAY!

But in order to go and get them effectively, you must understand something about them or be *discerningly aware* of the spirit that's driving or oppressing them. You never want to go out and witness to anyone without an understanding of what spirit (s) you're dealing with.

So in this book, the Lord first instructs us on what's required of us as *true* ministers of Christ. He's making sure we're well equipped with the necessary tools and anointing it will take to win these multiple souls to Him. He's counting on us to know what our calling and election is. Our call is the call to salvation. Therefore He's teaching us who we are, and where we come from, so we can walk in the skill and anointing that is to accompany our gifts. We have to know God's election of us is sure! You must have POWER with God! You can't minister in your own strength and expect to defeat the oppositions you will face. We wrestling not against flesh and blood, but it's an *invisible* spiritual war, that is making itself more *visible* in the lifestyles of mankind.

So go ahead in the strength of the Lord, go ahead and minister to the world in the skills and anointing God has placed on your lives. Many are coming, and the fishing net of ministry is being cast out. There will be many types of fish in the net, and you must understand how to minister to them all. You must know how to catch them before you scale them. You can't throw any of these fish back. *You're dealing with real people with real issues*, and they need an answer to the reason why you believe the way you do. The answer is Jesus Christ!!! God Bless You!

IF YOU READ THIS BOOK; MUCH HAS BEEN GIVEN, MUCH IS REQUIRED!

Questions & Answers

QUESTIONS AND ANSWERS

WORKBOOK & DISCUSSION GUIDE

COMPILED BY

Elmus L. High Jr.

Message to the Levites Workbook
& Discussion Guide

Copyright 2013 by Elmus L. High Jr. All Rights Reserved. Printed in the

United States of America

I put together this Q&A section to help you further learn and understand the information in this book. The questions and answers will go over selected parts of each chapter.

This can assist Pastors, Teachers, Worship Leaders and Musicians with information that can be used as a learning tool to help sharpen our skills as Levites!

This workbook can be used for the following

- *Pastors and Leaders*
- *Teachers of the Word & Classrooms*
- *Bible Study Groups/ Seminars & Workshops*
- *Bible Colleges/ Christian Schools & Academies*
- *Youth Groups or Explosions!*
- *Worship Leaders & Psalmists*
- *Musicians/ Singers*
- *Ministers, Elders and Lay Members*
- *Ushers & Porters*
- *Helpful tool for Everyday Individual Studies. . . .etc*
- *Use this workbook to compare notes with others*
- *Educating, inspiring, training, discussions*
- *Use twitter & face-book to go over questions & answers with others readers*

INTRODUCTION:

1. *Review the chapter of the book.*
2. *Once you've review the chapter, answer the questions for that chapter.*
3. *If you have difficulty with a question, you can review the chapter or flip to the answers at the end of the workbook.*
4. *If the workbook is completed by a group or class, the facilitator can prepare questions and or discuss issues in any particular chapter.*
5. *This workbook section is intended to inform the reader and to make you aware of Gods purpose while understanding the devils plans to prevent Gods will.*
6. *Share this workbook or the book with unbelievers as well.*
7. *If you have any questions for me, (the author) you can email me directly at: leviteminister@aim.com. You can also contact me through the information on the front of the book.*
8. *I'm also available to teach in my <u>Levites Symposiums</u> where we teach, and go through a spiritual activation session which helps you identify what your God given gifts are, and how to skillfully use them. This session usually ends with an anointed concert where all will use their giftings to usher in the presence of the Lord. . . . .its great!!!*

Chapter 1 - It's been my experience

1. When God spoke to Elder High about writing this book, what did God tell him to use that would qualify him to write? _____.

2. How old was Elder High when he started play the saxophone? _____ _____.

3. Name 4 pastors that influenced Elder High's life in the early years? _____. _____, _____, _____.

4. Who were the 2 people the prophet told Elder High he would meet? _____ and _____.

5. What passage of scripture is this book based on? _____ _____.

6. Finish and explain this statement. "You don't have "authority," unless you're _____
_____
_____.

7. Discuss in your class or groups how your life experiences help you in ministry. And what advantages you have? Notes: _____
_____
_____
_____
_____.

8. Why is it important for you to have leadership covering? Discuss and Answer _____
_____.

Questions and Answers

Chapter 2 - **What you don't know can hurt others**

1. Chapter 2 explains that Gods people are destroyed for _____ of knowledge.

2. In the last days, what will be prevalent in Christianity? _____.

3. According to this chapter, as ministers of Christ, what are some of the things we as Levites should be? (give at least 5 answers of your own and compare notes) _____
_____
_____.

4. Since the lack of bible knowledge is no longer an excuse for the Christian. What did Paul admonish us to do in 2 Timothy? _____ to show _____ unto God _____ be ashamed, rightly dividing _____.

5. Is it necessary for one to have seminary training to be an affective minister? If yes, tell why? If no, give your reasoning for that as well. (you may want to discuss this in your group or have your pastor speak on this. Notes: _____
_____
_____.

6. Give your explanation of this passage of scripture? 2Cor 3:6 Who also hath made us able ministers of the new testament; not of the letter, but of the spirit: for the letter killeth, but the spirit giveth life. KJV (discuss this) _____
_____
_____.

7. The bible warns that in latter times, some shall depart from the faith. Why?
   a. because of their lack of faith in God
   b. because pastors will be preaching too much truth
   c. some will give ear to seducing spirits & demonic doctrine
   d. there will be fewer and fewer churches to attend in the last days
   e. sports and television shows will take over peoples interest, more than church

(circle the one that applies)

8. According to 1 Timothy 4, what will make you a good minister?
a. being able to speak well
b. putting the brethren in remembrance of truths already taught
c. remembering as many scriptures as you can
d. nourished up with many words
e. being sound in faith & doctrine

(circle all that apply)

9. Other than the gifs you are born with. What's another way you can receive gifts?
a. by a prophetic word
b. by naming it, and claiming it
c. by the Holy Ghost
d. the laying on of hands by the elders

(circle all that apply)

Chapter 3 - About the Levites

1. What is a Levite? _____
   _____
   _____.

2. Where did they come from? _____
   _____
   _____.

3. What were some of their responsibilities? _____
   _____
   _____.

4. Who started the "paying" of the musicians in worship? _____
   _____
   _____.

5. Name 3 of David's "Chief Musicians?" _____
   _____
   _____.

6. Name at least 3 feasts before Israel's exile into Babylon? _____
   _____, _____, _____.

List the purpose of each feasts?
   _____
   _____
   _____

7. Levi was the _____ song of Jacob.

Chapter 4 - The Levites shall set it up, take it down and camp

1. Name some of the furniture the Levites were responsible for moving, when the presence of the Lord changed locations? (answer and compare notes) _____
   _____.

2. Name Elder High's Pastors _____
   _____.

3. According to chapter 4, your Pastors represent who?
   The _____ of God.

4. Explain the Levites pitching around the tabernacle and discuss _____
   _____.

5. When the spirit of the Lord moved locations. What was the job of the Levites? _____
   _____.

6. Numbers chapter 1 speaks of a, "inner circle" of Levites. What was this for? _____
   _____.

7. Explain Psalms 133:1-3. Why is it so important in ministry? _____
   _____
   _____
   _____.

Chapter 5 - Vision of the anointed cherub Lucifer

1. What type of Angel was Lucifer? _____
   _____.

2. Based on the text in this chapter, what differentiated the Cherubim from the Seraphim? _____
   _____.

3. What is a twofold meaning in Ezekiel 28 _____
   _____
   _____

4. In the vision of Lucifer, what did Elder High see under his wings?
   _____.

5. When he saw these under his wings; what were their purpose?
   _____ _____
   _____.

6. Lucifer was an Angel and he was what musical instrument? _____
   _____.

7. _____ carries the spirit of the original author. (complete this statement)

8. What is one of the descriptions of "Iniquity?" _____
   _____ .

9. Discuss with your Minister of Music or Worship Leaders how we can "avoid" taking on the same prideful spirit Lucifer had?

Notes: _____
_____

10. Review this chapter and complete the following sentences. . . . . . .

Thou wast perfect in all they ways, from the day that thou wast _____, till _____ was found in thee.

Lucifer was the _____ Cherub that covereth.

Pride goes before _____, and a haughty spirit _____.

Lucifer was an anointed Cherub and a _____
_____.

This chapter establishes that Lucifer didn't want to be like God, he _____.

11. When Lucifer was cast out of heaven, he lost all of his gifts. True? False?

12. It is possible to know that you're anointed without having pride? True? False?

13. Because of the way God honors spiritual authority. Lucifer yet has rank amongst the Angels, even in heaven? True? False? If true, please explain! _____ _____ _____ .

14. David allowed secular oriented music into the worship? True? False?

15. God should just accept the music we offer Him in worship, as long as our hearts are right?   True?   False?

16. Since God is full of love and mercy; if Satan and the fallen angels repent, they can get their places back in heaven? True?   False?

Questions and Answers

Chapter 6 - Asaph, Ethan and Heman

1. Who was considered David's Chief CEO over his music ministry?
_____.

2. Jeduthan was also known as, _____.

3. Whose name meant, "who gathers together?" _____
_____.

4. If two individuals had the same gift, what was King David's rule as far as jealousy? _____
_____.

5. Ministers of Music or Chief Musicians, when you get the opportunity, gather your music department together and have a forum where you can talk about the order and positioning of your department.

When you look in chapter 6, you'll see that David's music department was set up like a corporation, with everyone in their own proper and assigned places. In order for your music ministry to truly be affective, everyone must know and understand their gifting and how to operate in them. This is important because it blocks out envy and jealousy when everyone in the house understands their roll and understand that they're all important in the overall construction of the department.

Here are some questions you can ask your members to get a feel of whom you have and who you're ministering with. The bible does teach us to know them that labor among us. Get to know them naturally and spiritually. . . . . . .

- *Ask each member what they believe their gifting is, and why?*
- *Ask each member their views on worship and what it is*
- *How important is the anointing to you, and do you know the difference between a gifted person, and an anointed one?*
- *If you're a great singer, but you're continuously asked to sing background, what is your attitude?*
- *What's more important, skill, or anointing and why?*

You can create your own questions as well, based on this subject. It's so important to understand that if we expect a great move of God, we need to be with one accord, with one mind, and one purpose. Everyone understanding what's expected of them.

Message to the Levites

Chapter 7 - Psalms and the dance

1. Who were the leaders of the Kohathite Singers? _____.

2. Psalms 7 & Habakkuk 3 use the word; Shiggaion, what does it mean? _____.

3. According to true worship, what is a good reason we should not mix secular music with worship? (give your own answers a discuss in your group or compare notes)

   _____
   _____
   _____
   _____
   _____

4. Do you believe songs have the ability to get into your spirit? If so; why? _____.

   If you don't believe songs can get into your spirit, explain why not?
   _____
   _____.

5. Name at least 3 "characteristics" an anointed dancer has?
   _____, _____, _____ .

6. Give your understanding on Prophetic Dancing? _____.

   (you can compare notes or discuss in a group if you wish)

7. Who sung the first recorded song in scripture? _____
   _____.

8. What was the first recorded songs theme? _____
   _____
   _____.

9. Who sung the second recorded song in biblical history? _____
   _____.

10. Sit down for a minute and think of the last situation or trial you just came out of.

When you get that situation in your mind, I want you to write a short song about how you came out victorious. . . . .Ready?

_____
_____
_____
_____
_____
_____
_____
_____
_____. *Amen! If you have something to record the song with, give a copy to one of the "anointed dancers" in your ministry, and allow them to come up with choreography for the song. Also give a copy to your Chief Musicians so they can structure it for worship. You've now ministered the way they did under King David. Songs were also given "spontaneously" based on their victories!*

Chapter 8 - To mime or not to mime

1. Where does history tell us this art form began? _____
   _____
   _____.

2. After reading this chapter, where was the origin discovered? _____
   _____
   _____

3. Why is origin so important? (give your opinion) _____
   _____
   _____.

4. Give five descriptions of the word; Mime? _____
   ___, _____, _____, _____,
   _____.

5. How does mime differ from dance in your opinion? _____
   _____
   _____
   _____.

6. Name some of the characters, mentioned in this chapter, that were in the courts of the Pharaoh's of Egypt? _____
   _____
   _____.

7. Mimes in the Theaters of Greece & Rome worshipped what god in Athens? _____.

8. What similarities were pointed out in the garments of the mimes, fools (on the tarot cards) and the Goths? _____ clothing and _____ faces.

9. In the Hindu culture, what was the description of, Blank Verse? ___
   _____
   _____.

10. To mime or not to mime was the question. What's your answer? ___
    _____.

11. **Many people don't believe in what they don't understand. True? False?**

    If your answer was false, why don't you believe this statement? ____
    _____
    _____.

    If your answer was true, please explain. _____
    _____
    _____.

12. **After reading the mime history, do you feel we should yet use it in ministry? Yes / No.**

    Explain your answer. _____
    _____
    _____.

Chapter 9 - Selah

1. Give 3 meanings of the word Selah? _____, _____, _____ _____.

2. Around how many times was this word used in the Bible? _____ times.

3. Explain how a Selah can be used today in the spirit realm? (review chapter for answer)
_____
_____
_____
_____.

4. Discussion notes here. _____
_____.
_____
_____
_____.

5. Selah also means to be in "reflection" and to "lift up." This is interesting that the word is actually a sum total of our worship expression. It can mean to be quiet and reflect, or to lift up your voice in adoration & praise. This is a symbol that worshipping God covers every space in our lives. He's near to answer every situation we have. In worship, we cause Him to be nigh us, filling the room with His presence, being omni-present!

   What are your thoughts?
   _____
   _____
   _____

Chapter 10, 11, 12 - The Altar, the Tabernacle and the Temple

Write your own thesis or dissertation on these three subjects. Tell what happened at the Altar and what it was for.

Talk about the Tabernacle (tent) of Moses and David. Tell us the comparisons and the differences between the two. Come up with your own view on this and teach it to your class, or compare it in your groups or seminars. Base it on the scriptures given in the book and of course any references to other scriptures in the bible.

Take a look into the Temple of Solomon and the rebuilt Temple during the time of Hezekiah.

Put together a short synopsis dealing with all 3 and how they coincide with each other based on the times in biblical history. I believe we'll all learn more about this if we have different views and inputs on this subject. Submit your work to a facilitator of your class or group.

NOTES:

Chapter 13 - Satan's plan in Homosexuality

1. What is the main focus of this chapter?
a. condemnation?
b. sexual preference?
c. homosexuality?
d. Satan's plans?
e. All of the Above?

2. According to the Bible, is this a sin? YES / NO (circle one)

    If it's a sin, find scripture on it. _____
    _____.

    If it's not, find scripture on this also. _____
    _____

3. According to the scriptures, are we ALL God's children? If yes, give backing scriptures. _____, _____, _____, _____.

    If we are not ALL His children, find that as well. _____, _____. _____, _____.

4. According to the bible, when is a man tempted? (give the scripture(s) _____.

5. Name two areas of ministry you'll find homosexuality the most prevalent? _____ _____ and _____. (there is a reason for that!)

6. Where is this passage of scripture found? "you search the scriptures because you think in them, you have eternal life?" (English standard version) _____

7. According to the "revelation" in this chapter, what is Satan's plan in homosexuality? _____
_____.

8. God is love only. True? False?

9. God never gets upset. True? False?

10. Finish this verse. "For the wrath of God is revealed from heaven against, _____
_____."

Questions and Answers

11. Satan wants his place back. True? False?

12. Satan is pro-creation. True? False?

13. God tempts mankind with evil. True? False?

14. God will overlook our sins, because we live in the grace dispensation? True? False?

15. God would not punish us, and allow us to be lost if He loves us. True? False?

Chapter 14 - Levites

1. Who were the Levites, and where did they come from? _____
   _____
   _____
   _____.

2. Since they were not given a portion of land with the other tribes, how did they make their money or get paid? _____
   _____.

3. Where in scripture does it show God's choice of this tribe? _____
   _____

   What happened that God made choice of them? _____
   _____
   _____.

4. Explain how we are all Levites today? _____
   _____
   _____
   _____.

5. Levite is derivative of the word? _____
   _____.

6. The term Levite(s) is only used how many times in the New Testament? _____ times.

7. Levi was also one of the Apostles. True? False?

8. Name 3 of Levi's sons that went with their grandfather Jacob down to Egypt? _____, _____, _____
   _____.

9. Who was Jacobs's son Levi's mother? _____
   _____.

Chapter 15 - History of the Priest, Priesthood

1. Before we can become priest in the church, we should be priest, _____.

2. Who was the first High Priest of Israel? _____
   _____.

3. What was the main reason God destroyed Nadab and Abihu? _____
   _____
   _____.

4. Who is the High Priest after the order of Melchizedek? _____
   _____

5. What event took place in the bible, which signified that we no longer have to go to a priest to have our sins forgiven? (also find the scriptures)
   _____
   _____
   _____.

6. Why was "Yom Kippur" one of the most important days on the Jewish calendar? _____
   _____
   _____.

7. What was the commemorative reason for the Passover Feast? _____
   _____
   _____
   _____.

8. What was the use of the "Urim & Thumim?" _____
   _____
   _____
   _____.

9. Name five categories of priest? (review the chapter for the answer)
   1._____. 2. _____.
   3. _____. 4. _____. 5._____.

10. What did the priests of Israel wear on the bottom of their priestly robes? _____.

11. Have a discussion on the subject of being a priest of your home.

- *What are the duties and responsibilities of being a priest of your own home?*
- *How does the church and the body of Christ benefit from you successfully overseeing your home?*
- *How does it affect the worship in the church?*
- *Does it matter if the priest of the home is a woman or a man?*

Notes from this subject

_____
_____
_____
_____
_____
_____ .

Chapter 16 - The Worship

Discuss this in your class or group:

In your own words, explain John 4:23-24, "True Worshippers" _____
_____
_____
_____.

*In the Old Testament, there were animal sacrifices unto God. What is our sacrifice today?*_____
_____
_____
_____

In your own words, show how worship is different from praise? ____
_____
_____
_____.

Do this exercise on your own or in a group:

Go down in prayer and speak something nice to the Lord while you're on your knees. Tell Him how great He is! Don't ask Him for anything! As you feel His presence come into the room, I want you to listen for a sound or a melody. . . . .

As you begin to hear the melody in the midst of your worship of God; I want you to begin to "say what you hear" right at that moment! You're going to hear a melody, or an "Expression of Worship" in the form of a musical sound. Start to speak out what you hear. It's an expression of worship and what God wants to hear spoken in the spirit realm.

You may be asking what this or what is for. . . . .

If you're serious about this when you go down in prayer, and begin to speak well of Him, you will begin to hear a "sound of worship." You will hear a melody in the atmosphere. Once you hear the melody, "say what you hear." You may sing it, or you may just hear the words in the midst of the melody. THIS IS WHAT IT IS. . . . .!!!

YOU'RE NOW HEARING WHAT GOD WANTS TO SAY IN YOUR WORSHIP OF HIM.

YOU'LL HEAR WHAT HE WANTS YOU TO SAY BACK TO HIM OUT OF YOUR MOUTH.

THIS WILL BE A TRUE WORSHIP EXPERIENCE FOR YOU, BECAUSE YOU WILL KNOW AND UNDERSTAND WHAT GOD IS SAYING AT THAT MOMENT!!!!

In this chapter, what else is considered worship based? Is worship singing or lifting our hands or speaking well of God only? (explain)

_____
_____
_____
_____
_____.

Questions and Answers

Chapter 17 - Cherub, Angels, Seraphim

1. *Search out and find scriptures concerning these creatures for your own research.*

   _____
   _____
   _____
   _____
   _____.

2. *Share what differences you find in the Cherubim and the Seraphim?*

   _____
   _____
   _____
   _____.

3. *What type of Angel was Michael?* _____
   _____.

4. *When Angles came down as messengers, there were times they came dressed as women? True? False?*

5. *When an Angel came down to earth carrying a message from God. The person they came to give the message to, always had to bow down before them to receive the Word from God. True? False?*

6. *Angeles have sexual emotions just like humans. True? False?*

Message to the Levites

Chapter 18 - The Amen

1. **What does the word Amen mean?** _____
   _____
   _____
   _____.

2. **What is Elder High's wife's name?** _____
   _____.

3. **What are the names of his 3 sons?** _____, _____,
   _____.

4. **What instrument does Elder High play?** _____
   _____.

5. **How many years did it take Elder High to compile and write this book?** _____ yrs.

Benediction: [ben-i-dik-shuh n]
   an utterance of good wishes. the form of blessing pronounced by an officiating minister, as at the close of a service. a ceremony by which things are set aside for sacred uses, as a church vestments, or bells. cap. a service consisting of prayers, at least one prescribed hymn, censing of the congregation and the Host, and a blessing of the congregation. the advantage conferred by blessing; a mercy or benefit. conclusion of a matter or subject!

ANSWERS TO THE WORKBOOK

WORKBOOK AND DISCUSSION GUIDE

Here are the answers in the workbook to review with your class or study group. Have discussions and activation sessions to get a total understanding of the essence of this book.

Chapter 1 It's been my experience

1. his own experiences
2. 11 years old
3. Pastor Justus Morgan, Pastor Elmus L. High Sr., Apostle Ruben Beechum and Apostle Thomas H. Vinson
4. Thomas Vinson and Carolyn Vinson
5. John 4: 23-24
6. You don't have authority unless you're under authority. Don't be a spiritual vagabond ministering on your own. Always have the blessing of your leaders.
7. Class or Group discussion and Notes. . . .
8. Class or Group discussion and Notes. . . . *(spiritual protection & authority given to minister)*

Chapter 2 What you don't know can hurt others

1. lack of knowledge
2. Apostasy, False Teaching or Doctrine
3. Examples, Good Ministers, Nourished up in the Word, Prepared, Well Equipped, *(there are other correct answers you can add)*
4. Study—thyself approved—a workman that needeth not—the word of truth.
5. Review your answers with others to get different views.
6. Discuss your answer with others in a group or class setting.
7. c. possibly a.
8. b., e.
9. a., c., & d.

Chapter 3 About the Levites

1. Give your answer and review the history.
2. We know the derivative is from Levi.
3. They were responsible for the care of the Tabernacle & Temple. Priestly duties and sacrifices. The Music. Moving of the furniture. . . . . . .etc.
4. King David started it by bringing in "professional" musicians.
5. Asaph, Heman and Jeduthan (who is also Ethan)
6. Passover Feast, Feast of Weeks or Pentecost, Feast of Tabernacles or Sukot. Feast of Trumpets (4th feast is a bonus)
7. 3rd son of Jacob, born to Leah

Chapter 4 The Levites shall set it up, take it down and camp

1. The tent – the ark of the covenant – candlestick – musical instruments utensils – tapestry - compare notes, and go to the scriptures. 2 Chronicles 5 will give you a lot of the information needed.
2. Apostle Dr. Thomas H. Vinson and Evangelist Dr. Carolyn Vinson
3. The spirit or presence of God as those who lead God's people, the same way the presence of the Lord lead the children of Israel through the wilderness. It's the same shadow and type of God's leading his people.
4. Discuss this answer with others to find the understanding. It does point to the Levites and us in ministry being one.
5. This should be easy since answer 1 gives you a hint. Add more.
6. Give your answer and also understand it also speaks to a type of undergirding of leadership or armor bearing.
7. Give your answers and share with others. A hint for discussion is Unity amongst the ministers. . . . . .

Chapter 5 Vision of the anointed cherub Lucifer

1. Cherub
2. Based on the text in this chapter, the difference that was pointed out was the fact that the Seraphim were more "vocal in nature" than the Cherubim.
3. The passage in chapter 28 speaks to the King of Tyre or (Tyrus) who had become lifted up in pride, but was soon going to be bought down. It also speaks of the same spirit Lucifer had before his down cast from heaven. All who would lift themselves up as a deity would and will be made low!
4. Bellow(s)
5. The bellows produced a thrush that traveled through his body that would provide air to sound off the viles or organ pipes that were embedded in Lucifer's back.
6. Something similar to a piped like organ or accordion. (no keys)
7. Music.
8. The spirit of lawlessness.
9. Discuss with your group. One way is to understand your place and who you are in comparison to Almighty God. Without Him we are nothing. Seek humility, even if you're extremely gifted, as Lucifer was.
10. Created – iniquity / Anointed / Destruction – before a fall / musical instrument / wanted to be God.

11. False
12. True.
13. True. *(see the example in scripture with Michael the archangel when contending with Satan)* Michael gives perfect example of authority; that even though Satan no longer in his heavenly appointment, was yet respected because of the authority once given him in heaven as Lucifer. . . . .

Commentary on Authority:

<u>**greater**</u> — than these blasphemers. Jude instances *Michael* (Jud_1:9).

<u>**Railing accusation**</u> — *Greek,* "blaspheming judgment" (Jud_1:9).

<u>**Against them**</u> — against "dignities," as for instance, the fallen angels: once exalted, and still retaining traces of their former power and glory.

<u>**Before the Lord**</u> — In the presence of the Lord, *the Judge,* in reverence, they abstain from judgment. Judgment belongs to God, not the angels.

2 Peter 2:11
*Whereas angels, which are greater in power and might, bring not railing **accusation** against them before the Lord.*

Jude1:4-9 – verse 9, *Yet Michael the archangel, when contending with the devil he disputed about the body of Moses, durst not bring against him a railing **accusation**, but said, The Lord rebuke thee.*

14. False
15. False
16. False

Chapter 6 Asaph, Ethan and Heman

1. Chenaniah was Chief CEO, considered the "Master of the Song." Director of the Music and President of the Music Ministry.
2. Ethan
3. Asaph
4. If two showed jealousy between them in ministry, King David would have the removed from ministry and or replaced.
5. Leaders make sure that in this exercise, you receive a clear answer from each of our members on their purpose in ministry. Make sure you have a clear understanding of the gifts that lie in each of your

musicians, singers, dancers and choir members. This will assist you in properly placing people where they can shine and grow, which in return will help boost the worship experience.

Chapter 7 Psalms and the dance

1. **The sons of Korah.** (they were also entrusted with song arrangements in Psalms 44, 49, 84, 85, 87 and 88).
2. **To sing with a frenzied or emotional style.**
3. **Explain your answer. One of my answers is. . . .worship to God must be of a pure origin and nature. You can't mix the message, it confuses the unbeliever. Also how can you justify it when God always wanted worship that was spotless! Didn't you read the book?**
4. **After reviewing this chapter, give a reason why you wouldn't think music can have this affect after it's been proven in the Word of God, and companies like Wal-Mart conducting advertising studies to this fact. If you can' t believe God, at least believe Wal-Mart!**
5. **The ability to "see" the music – The ability to "see" the motions of music and sound - The inability to hide facial expressions. (bonus) The inability to sit still when they hear music of any kind, it takes all that's in them not to do so.**

6. **One thing to understand is that prophetic dancing can reveal Gods Word through a visual expression. We can actually "see" a manifestation of the verbal word.**
7. **Miriam** (Moses and Aaron's sister).
8. **How God delivered them from the hand of Pharaoh and Egypt.**
9. **Moses.**
10. **Please pay attention to this exercise. Once you've written this spontaneous song, and given a copy to an anointed dancer. If you've already put your song into the hands of an anointed chief musician. I want you to pay close attention to why God doesn't need our help structuring a song.**

    Once the musician has put music to the song you heard during your worship. IF the musician is anointed, take a closer look at the song. It's probably ALREADY STRUCTURED into a song that can be sung without much additional arrangement. This should tell you that the way they got their songs in scripture many times came spontaneously with no outside help from secular oriented music. God doesn't need help!!!!!!!

HAVE A DISCUSSION HERE:

NOTES:

Chapter 8 To mime or not to mime

1. Ancient Greece and Rome.
2. 2500 B.C. in the court of Pharaoh Dadkeri-Assi during Egypt's Fifth Dynasty and probably before.
3. It's important to know where things come from before implementing them in as a major part of your life. . . . .like worship.
4. To mimic or copy – to appear as something else – to poke fun or emulate – to appear as is, but is not.
5. Dance originated from the pure worship of God in heaven. Mime originated from a not so pure imagination of man.
6. Fools, Jesters – Court Jester – Magician – Joker – Sorcerer – Diviners. . . . .etc.
7. **Dionysus.** (the god of intoxication)
8. Black clothing and White faces.
9. Blank Verse was a style of writing poetry or poetry with the music. Instead of tightly rhyming verses, the poets would skip out verses, or write in a was to make sure the poem didn't always rhyme. (a secular technique you'll hear more and more as time goes along. As the world gets more and more corrupt, the sounds, lyric and music will become more and more off tempo and make little sense.) **You'll see!!!**
10. Not to mime.
11. Many studies have shown this to be true.
12. According to the revelation God revealed in this book. The answer would be No!

NOTES:

Chapter 9 Selah

1. To pause. To be in silence. Musical notation for the singers to stop, allowing the music to continue playing under the anointing.
2. Seventy four times.
3. When songs are being sung under the anointing, and as the spirit leads, the singers will stop singing, and the musicians will continue to play, "whether directed to or not." It's done by the direction of the holy spirit, not by the direction of the choir director. Understand that if the Minister of Music or Choir director are anointed and operating in the spirit, they can sense a Selah coming, and direct the singers and musicians accordingly.
4. Have a discussion about this with your friends, music group or music ministry teams. It's so important in the worship experience to be able to sense this musical motion. It has the ability to change the whole atmosphere of worship. . . .how fascinating!!!!!!
5. A time to be quiet and reflect His goodness. A time to lift up our voices and make known His deeds among the people.

NOTES ON SELAH

Chapters 10, 11 and 12 The altar, the tabernacle and the temple

Write down any additional information or interesting facts you came across by studying the Altar, the Tabernacle and the Temple. It's a lot of reading but will give you a great foundation of the structure and order of the God we serve.

Answers to the Workbook

Chapters 13 Satan's plan in homosexuality

1. d. Satan's plans.
2. Yes.
3. No, Luke 6:46 – John 8:44 – Romans 8:9
4. When he is drawn away of his own lust and enticed. James 1:14.
5. **The pulpit and the music ministry.** (Satan wants his place back in the worship)
6. John 5:39.
7. His plan in using homosexuality is to infiltrate this spirit inside the church and body of Christ. This is a direct opposite of the nature of God!
8. True.
9. False.
10. all ungodliness and unrighteousness of men, who hold the truth in unrighteousness. Romans 1:18
11. True.
12. False.
13. False.
14. False.
15. False.

Explain your answer on number 15:

Chapters 14 Levites

1. They originated from the tribe of Levi, who was one of Jacob's sons born to Leah.
2. The Lord commanded that they receive of the tithes given from the other 11 tribes.
3. Any part of this answer will be correct: (a.) When the Israelites left Egypt, the ancient manner of worship was still observed by them, the eldest son of each house inheriting the priest's office. At Sinai the first change in this ancient practice was made. A hereditary priesthood in the family of Aaron was then instituted (Exodus 28:1). But it was not till that terrible scene in connection with the sin of the golden calf that the tribe of Levi stood apart and began to occupy a distinct position (Exodus 32). (b.) It happened back in Exodus 32:26, when Moses came down from the Mt. and the children of Israel had sinned with the golden calf. When Moses cried out and asked, "*who is on the Lord's side? Let him come to me*," it was the sons of Levi who gathered themselves together "*first*" to come before Moses and repented. Therefore when the time came for God to make choice of who would operate in the tabernacle and the priesthood, He made choice of the Levite tribe because of their *swift and humble heart* to repent.
4. A short explanation is the fact that back in the Old Testament, they were the natural Israelites. *(sons of God)* Today we are the spiritual Israelite sons of God. God's worship order is yet instituted and in place today for our benefit.
5. Levi.
6. Only 3 times.
7. True. **Levi,** one of the apostles, the son of Alphaeus (Mark 2:14; Luke 5:27, 29), also called, **Matthew** (Matthew 9:9).
8. Gershon, Kohath, and Merari.
9. Leah.

Chapter 15 History of the priest, priesthood

1. of our homes.
2. Aaron.
3. They attempted to operate in a place that was not theirs. They were out of order.
4. Jesus Christ, who is the everlasting to everlasting.
5. When the Vail of the temple rent (tore) and Jesus gave up the ghost on the cross.
6. The Feast of Trumpets: Was a feast and ritual of *blowing* the *trumpets* to call the people to a *fast* at the end of the summer, before the beginning of the New Year, Rosh Hashanah. This feast ended on the seventh day with the, *Day of Atonement, or Yom Kippur* as it was so called. This date was considered one of the most important days on the Jewish Calendar. It was held on the final day of the feast, when *Repentance and Forgiveness* took place throughout the nation.
7. This was to commemorate the night the death angel passed through the land of Egypt, killing every firstborn child, but "passed over" the firstborn of the children of Israel, in preparation for their exit out of Egypt.
8. In most of its instances, it was used for decision making. It was a part of the high priest's garment. This was housed in the breast piece of judgment, which was attached to the high priest's ephod (Exod 28:28-30). He used them to obtain oracular answers from the Lord regarding specific situations in Israel
9. 2 Kings 23:4-20 lists *five categories of priests* that existed in ancient Israel before Josiah's reformation, and arranges them according to their proximity to the Jerusalem temple: (1) **the high priest** (v. 4), (2) **the second-order priests** (v. 4), (3) **the idolatrous priests** in the cities of Judah and in the area surrounding Jerusalem (v. 5); (4) **the priests of the high places in the cities of Judah** from Geba to Beersheba (vv. 8-9); and (5) **the priests of the high places in Samaria** (i.e., the remnants of the priests of the former northern kingdom, v. 20).
10. **Bells & Pomegranates**
11.
    - The priest of the home should pray for the home, and cover the household.
    - The church benefits by having members whose homes are in order.
    - The affect is unneeded strain off of the leaders and help assist in the worship experience. A strong home means a strong church.
    - Whoever is head of the household is to be considered the priest of their home.

Message to the Levites

Chapters 16 The worship

Group Discussion Answers:

- Give your answer of true worship: Mine based on John 4:23-24 is simply my everyday lifestyle before God. My life prostrate before Him. Therefore when I enter into His gates with thanksgiving and into His courts with praise, it's just an overflow of my everyday communication with Him.
- According to Romans 12:1, we are now a *"living sacrifice"* unto the Lord. To be holy and acceptable to Him, which is our reasonable service.
- In my opinion, worship is different than praise in the fact that anyone saint or sinner can give God praise. Psalms 150 invites all who have breath to praise the Lord. You can praise Him for what He's done and who He is to you.

  But a worshipper is one who has a personal relationship with Him, based on His requirements and conditions, not our own. Many people today will tell you they have a relationship with Him, but their actions show much different. To be a true worshipper of God calls to intimacy with Him. Once you've become intimate with God, you won't want to do anything to jeopardize that relationship.

The Worship Exercise results:
- If you followed the recipe to the "t". You should have experienced a visitation from God. When you study the Word of God, you'll find that in order to truly benefit from worship, you MUST follow the total order of God!

Chapters 17 Cherub, Angels, Seraphim

1. Genesis 3:24 – Exodus 25: 17-26 – Numbers 7:89 – 1 Samuel 4:4 – Isaiah 37:16 – Psalms 80: 1;99:1 – Ezekiel 10: 1-20, 41:18,19 – Ezekiel 1:4-14 – Hebrews 9:5 – Revelations 4:6 – Psalms 18: 10 and much more. Study these for a start.
2. One thing to look at was their different purposes and assignments.
3. Archangel. *(study the theory that this angel was a shadow or type of the everlasting God)* See 1Thes. 4:16, Jude1:9 and Revelation 12:7. . . . .
4. False.
5. False.
6. False.

Chapters 18 The Amen

1. So be it – It is so – to be in agreement with what has been spoken. Something valid, sure, truthful or faithful. To indicate the acceptance of a message..etc.
2. Valerie.
3. Anthony, Andrew & Aaron.
4. His main instrument is the saxophone.
5. 9 years.

ACTIVATION TIME

WORKBOOK AND DISCUSSION GUIDE

In this section I want you to have a session where you begin to activate the gifts you have. After gaining understanding in this book, you should have learned what it means to be skilled and anointed. The skill you have speaks to having understanding of how to properly operate your gifts and gifts of the spirit.

In this Activation Session we want you to gather together whether you're a group of prophets, singers, musicians or ministers. This section is geared toward you not only recognizing and identifying your gifts, but activating them.

Hebrews 5:14 lets us know that by *reason of use having our senses exercised*, we learn how to operate and be efficient in our gifting. We learn to discern good and evil, right and wrong.

This will be so helpful to our several ministries, when we learn how to be in touch with the spirit of God and discern His presence, and what He's doing in the spirit realm. We have to be sensitive enough to follow His leading and hear what He wants done in the midst of our worshipping Him.

These Activation Sessions will help us learn and respect each other's gifting, which will in return, weed out envy and jealousy.

Before you begin, make sure everyone takes this seriously. We're dealing in the spiritual realm where there's also principalities that are not in agreement with what we're doing and learning, because as we continue this activation, we're understanding more and more that the weapons of our warfare are not carnal, but mighty through God to the pulling down of demonic strongholds!

So before you start this session with your groups anoint everyone and pray God's blessings.

~ACTIVATION TEN COMMANDMENTS~
Instructions

i. This consists of 5 Activation Sessions. Thou shalt follow the instructions and allow God to move in your midst. Some of you have more than one gift, so you can participate in one or all 5 Activation Sessions.

ii. These sessions should be facilitated by a *"delegated authority"* of each department.

iii. Thou shalt hold these sessions separately, or combine them all in a setting.

iv. Always pray before each session to bind up any principalities that may want to hinder. Even if the hindrance is coming from one of the participants!

v. Before starting the sessions, and after you've prayed; anoint each person!

vi. Thou shalt conduct these sessions with the utmost respect for one another, and in love. We're here to learn and receive from the Lord.

vii. Understand that no matter how gifted you are, you are always subject to a higher authority, whether that authority was delegated or the authority of your leaders.

viii. Be open and honest in these sessions as God begins to reveal Himself in, and through us. We want to come out with the substance and understanding He wants for us to have, in order to be effective ministers of Christ.

ix. If at all possible before each session, always have a minstrel play and worship under the anointing at least 15 minutes before you begin. This sets the atmosphere for the prophetic to come forth.

x. **IMPORTANT NOTE: THOU SHALT NOT**, conduct any session without the knowledge, authority and blessing of your pastors! We must always be in order. God honors His "appointed authority", and will honor us if we honor them!

~THE PROPHETS~

The point of this exercise is to make sure that we're hearing *properly* from the Lord.

Understand that when you have a verbal prophetic gift, you're a perfect candidate to hear all types of voices. But as you're learning to be sensitive to the voice of God, you must also understand when God is revealing things to you for the purpose of speaking those things, and when it's your gift actually picking it up in the spirit. You see, not all time when something is revealed to you, are you to actually speak on it. You're gift just allows you to know and perceive it.

Now there are many who have the gift to prophecy, but this exercise is mainly geared towards those who walk in the "office" of a Prophet.

Start this session with the Lead or Master Prophet calling the group to order.

Begin Here:

- Remember to have an anointed musician set the atmosphere with music. *(pref. strings)*
- Start by praying for God to speak a "specific word" to your school of prophets.
- Remember this is all done by the spirit, so make every attempt to weed out carnality.
- While in worship, God will begin giving the *specific word* to the Lead Prophet.
- It is important that the Lead be in the spirit and hears correctly from the Lord. This will cut down on errors. Please don't be afraid if the *word* is misrepresented. Just go back and hear again. We are here to learn, not here to point fingers!
- When the Lead Prophet is confident they have the word, then as the other prophets are standing prayerfully by, hand a piece of paper to each prophet so they can write down what they hear in the spirit. Now understand there are different exercises you can do to ask God to speak a *continual word* or a *series of words* in order to come up with a *sum total* of what God may be saying. But in this particular exercise, we're asking God to give a ***precise word!***
- Once each prophet is confident that they've have sought the heart and mind of God to the point of hearing, have someone gather the words together and discuss what each one heard.

- ❖ In the discussion, try and dissect any words that may have come forth that differ from the *specific word* we're seeking. Remember this is not to point fingers, but to get understanding.
- ❖ One thing you may discover and teach is how to block out voices and imaginations when trying to hear from God. You'll also discover how "separated" a prophet must be in order to hear from God. Encourage each participant to seek the Lord and stay in consecration in order to avoid error. Your gift is vital to the ministry and to the headship of the church.

~PSALMIST & SINGER~

The point of this exercise is to become skillful in your understanding toward these gifts.

As was taught in the book; these two gifts have two separate anointing and purposes in the order of worship.

Remember a Psalmist's gift is an anointing by inquiry. Their gift inquires of God to know what God wants to hear or say in the midst of worship. A Psalmist's concern or first priority in ministering, is actually to minister to people, but unto the Lord. They can sense the very heartbeat of God and are to inquire of Him to know what should be ministered.

A singers anointing is quite different in its application. Once they receive the order of what is to be sung, they have an anointing to minister the song(s) to the audience. Their gift should carry an anointing that can destroy yokes off of the individuals listening.

Therefore the *skill and understanding* is in recognizing the characteristics of another person's gift, and how it operates in the body of Christ. What this does is cuts out confusion, envy and jealousy in ministry. This is the skill the bible references to as well, not just the mechanical skills of how well you can sing. Start this session with your delegated Worship or Praise Leader.

Begin Here:

- Remember to have an anointed musician set the atmosphere with music. *(pref. strings)*
- Have the delegated Leader pray and ask God to give you a song in the midst of worshipping.
- As the musician begins to play under the anointing, everyone begin to move into worship.
- Understand that the Worship Leader is the facilitator of this exercise.
- As the spirit begins to move, the Psalmists in your midst should begin to sense what God wants to hear in worship. Don't get this confused, because the Worship Leader, the Psalmist and the Chief Musician could be one in the same person, so it's up to the facilitator to guide this exercise.
- As the spirit is moving, chose one Psalmist that you sense may be hearing Gods voice. Notice, this psalmist's give is also prophetic, so have any other psalmists in the group be in silence but listen in the spirit. Now this is not like the Prophet exercise; we're not looking for one specific word, but a series words.
- As the delegated Psalmist begins to hear God's heart, they will begin to flow in songs of worship to the Lord. Allow time for them to minister unto the Lord to hear ALL God is saying in the song!

- As they're ministering the song to the Lord, have the facilitator get the attention of the singers to use their skill to pick up the song being ministered by the Psalmist.
- As each anointed singer begins to sing the song have someone in your group who can scribe or write out the song being "spontaneously sung."
- Once the move of God has tapered off, give the "written song" to your musician, *(who should also be skillful to play)* to begin playing music for the newly acquired words.
- Pay **close attention,** and all who are there witnessing this spontaneous worship should notice that the song the Psalmist received from God's heart, and the anointed singers who picked it up and began to sing, and the musician who put music to the song; notice that it should be a perfectly structured song! The song will make sense and will have prophetic purpose to it. This song will be the words to what God wanted to hear in worship at that point and time.
- How wonderful! This is actually they way they did in David's time during worship and with all the anointed gifts of music he had in the tabernacle. They sang their own songs of worship!!!!
- You can do this for each of your Psalmists if you wish to, or have the time. You will experience a beautiful experience of worship. You'll understand and be satisfied that TRUE WORSHIP has taken place, because we've now completed what God wants in worship and not what flesh and blood wanted!!!!

Comments:

~PROPHETIC DANCERS~

The point of this exercise is to show you the importance of this powerful anointing that stems from the visual worship ministry.

Dancing is not only in order when it comes to worship; it's prophetic, and has the anointing to proclaim God's voice without uttering a word. Lucifer well understands this gift because he himself operated in *motions*, while worshipping God before His throne.

This is a wonderful ministry of worship that most people misunderstand. It is our purpose in this exercise for you to not only *hear* the voice of God, but to *SEE* what God is saying! This should be facilitated by your dance ministry leader, or another who's been delegated to do so. In King David's time, this would have been a man by the name of, Mahalath! Mahalath is mentioned 3 times in scripture, and 1 of them was an anointed choreographer who had the anointed ability to "see the music" in worship. He would write down what he saw in worship to God, and would give the motions names. He then would teach these motions to the dancers of the tabernacle.

I've done this exercise in some of my Levite Symposiums; it's absolutely awesome!!!

Begin Here:

- ❖ Again, if possible. Have one of the anointed musicians in your ministry play music at least 15 minutes before starting this exercise. *(preferably strings or synth strings on keyboard)*
- ❖ Start with prayer by your facilitator. Pray for God to manifest Himself by anointing and giving the dancers an "expression of worship" through the visual ministry of dance. Pray for a prophetic utterance in motion.
- ❖ Get across to your dancers that this is not just a dance class. This is to be a prophetic display of God's presence in the room. The non spoken voice of God can declare victory. It can declare warfare and as it's been done in scripture; can also prophesy the destruction of our enemies!!
- ❖ Next, have your musician begin to play. Now if the musician is just playing the instrument in a carnal mindset, this will not work!!! Instruct them to worship and play on the instrument under the anointing.
- ❖ As you sense the presence of God, get 2 or 3 of your dancers and set them out in front of everyone in your pulpit or stage. Blindfold them and have them stand still in one place side by side. Instruct them that as they begin to worship, their gift will cause them to be in tune with the "anointed music." As I've said before, an anointed dancer has the ability to see the music.

- ❖ Instruct the dancers, NOT TO MOVE UNTIL, they can see the music or sense its motion in body. As the spirit begins to move on you, THEN MOVE.
- ❖ Note: Each dancer may or may not begin moving at the same time, and that's ok! Each one may have their own expression of worship.
- ❖ Those of you sitting by watching this ministry are to write down what you see in the motions of the dancers. Scribe out what you feel God is saying to us through the visual.
- ❖ When the move of God releases; take the notes and compare them with the whole group to see if you notice a similarity and pattern in what each person saw. Don't be offended by this, but there are some who have trained or learned to dance. And there are some who are anointed to dance, and probably had this gift from birth. This is also ok for now!
- ❖ As you compare notes, you may find that those who may have had the gift of dance from birth, have a more consistence view or of what they saw in the other dancers. So, since this is the case, it is up to the dance leaders to be skilled and spiritual enough to teach the others how to flow in the spirit. . . . . . .this is so good!!!
- ❖ Have a discussion about this exercise. Understand that if you need new choreography for your dance ministry; use exercises like this to write down what you saw and teach the spontaneous moves to the other dancers in your group. People of God, this is what I've been trying to tell you throughout this whole book. This is how it was done many times in the bible. This is how they worshipped the Lord in spirit! They would worship God, in the dance, and there were anointed scribes who would write down what took place in the midst of spontaneous worship. Then they would use it in their daily and weekly worship sevices.
- ❖ Instruct your dancers NOT to bring in any worldly or secular dances into the house of God. That is not worship and God will not accept it!!!

Comments:

_____
_____
_____
_____
_____
_____

~MUSICIANS~

The purpose of this exercise is to teach our Musical Levites how to flow in the spirit and operate in worship. To instruct how to lead us into the presence of the Lord through anointed music; which will set the tone and atmosphere for a prophetic utterance of God's word.

Musicians *(by that I mean those who play musical instruments)* are a different breed of human being. No one really understands the struggles an anointed musician has; like another musician!

Lucifer understands this! He knows the power and authority you posses, if you understand how to use it. Musicians have the ability to play their instruments and tear down the very kingdom of darkness! This is why he try's so hard to get you off track by using your gifts for other purposes than worshipping God. He's mad at you because he used to be who you are!

Begin Here:

- Open this exercise by having your "Chief Musician" play their instrument before the Lord.
- Once the atmosphere is settled by the anointed prelude; have someone anointed pray for this activation exercise. Pray that the anointed music sets the atmosphere for a prophetic word to come forth. Ask God to cause each musician to be on one accord with the same mind.
- In this exercise, it would be good to have a minister or a prophet, even your pastor present.
- No singing is necessary at this time. We want to feel the anointing of God through the performed music.
- If you have a organist or keyboard player present, ask them to begin worshipping on their instrument. As they move into the spirit, continue to add more musicians to the worship.
- Make sure there's no talking. The Chief Musician should be leading the worship on their instrument. As each musician begins to play, I want those of you standing by, to listen in the spirit. There is a "sound within the sound" that you can hear!
- I can not tell you whether to play a fast tempo song, or a slow one. All I can tell you is be lead by the spirit of God.
- While you listen; if you can sense a spiritual climax in the music, each musician should be given a chance to minister on their instrument and become the lead of the worship on their instrument.
- As those of you standing by feel the presence of the Lord, begin to shout out in a praise to the Lord. Let the praise be only about the goodness of

the Lord; not asking for anything. This will be a shout of victory in the presence of the Lord.

- ❖ As the instruments are playing and the shout is going up to the Lord in victory; you will all feel a "shifting" in the spirit! When all of you sense this shifting, the atmosphere is going to change and a spirit of prophecy should come forth.
- ❖ While the prophetic word is being spoken, everyone be in silence! No music, no other sound but the word of God.
- ❖ Once the prophetic word has come to an end, the Chief Musician can direct someone to sing a soft song in worship.
- ❖ Allow the singing to continue for a moment, and then instruct the singers to cease their singing and allow the musicians to finish the worship on their instruments.
- ❖ The moment the instrument begin to play here, is called a Selah!
- ❖ Since God is God and He moves the way He wants. I will not instruct you how to end this worship session. All I ask is that you allow God to have His way, and stay in order, not allowing the enemy to take away what was just imparted in the worship, that was induced by the anointed music!!!!
- ❖ At the end of this session, speak a short word to all the musicians if you feel lead. Point out to them how important it is to stay before the Lord and seek humility! I say this, because Satan constantly buffs at the musician to cause them to be lifted in pride because of their gifts. Stay humble before the Lord and pray before and after ministering on your instrument!

God Bless You!

Comments:

_____
_____
_____
_____
_____
_____
_____
_____
_____

Activation Time

~PRIESTHOOD~

The purpose of this exercise is to bring "oneness" among the priesthood. It is vital to a church and ministry that the priesthood under gird leadership. God gives the set person a vision, and it's up to the priesthood to assist in carrying out that vision. There nothing more that a pastor could ask for than his/her ministers, be on one accord with one mind and spirit.

Even when Jesus was about to leave off the scene and go back to His place of authority in heaven. He prayed a heart felt prayer for all people, but mainly for the disciples who walked so close to Him in ministry. Pastors can identify with this passage of scripture in John 17, because it speak their own sentiments of how they feel concerning those ministers God has given them to help in the burden of ministry!

As we begin this exercise, we want to concentrate on the words of Christ in verses, 16 thru 23.

Begin Here:

- ❖ Have your Pastor call the session to order. The Pastor may also delegate one of the Elders to call the session to order. They can open up with a prayer.
- ❖ Pray for the "unity of the priesthood", and that all who are called to ministry would come in line with the vision of the Pastor. Rebuke envy and jealousy in the body, and pray that God will give each minister a mind to do what a minister is called to do. . . . . .serve!!!!!
- ❖ Whoever the Pastor uses to facilitate this session, start out by reading John 17:16-23 aloud.

John 17:16 They are not of the world, even as I am not of the world.
John 17:17 Sanctify them through thy truth: thy word is truth.
John 17:18 As thou hast sent me into the world, even so have I also sent them into the world.
John 17:19 And for their sakes I sanctify myself, that they also might be sanctified through the truth.
John 17:20 Neither pray I for these alone, but for them also which shall believe on me through their word;
John 17:21 <u>That they all may be one</u>; as thou, Father, art in me, and I in thee, <u>that they also may be one in us</u>: that the world may believe that thou hast sent me.
John 17:22 And the glory which thou gavest me I have given them; <u>that they may be one</u>, even as we are one:

John 17:23 I in them, and thou in me, <u>that they may be made perfect in one</u>; and that the world may know that thou hast sent me, and hast loved them, as thou hast loved me.

Note: Jesus repeated that they be one. He prayed that they be one so that the world could take notice. He prayed that they would be made perfect in their love toward one another.

- ❖ **Read this passage:** *John 13:35 By this shall all men know that ye are my disciples, if ye have love one to another. (expound on this scripture and allow others to comment)* 10 mins.
- ❖ As we start this exercise, it is important that every minister understand that they should have an attitude to "be for one another." What that means, it back one another, boost or push one another to be the best minister of Christ they can be. It's up to the facilitator to get this point across.
- ❖ Point out that as the days grow worse, it will be vital that the ministers of Christ be rooted and grounded in "sound doctrine."

Expound on this scripture: 1 Timothy 4:1-6. *¹Now the Spirit speaketh expressly, that in the latter times some shall depart from the faith, giving heed to seducing spirits, and doctrines of devils; ²Speaking lies in hypocrisy; having their conscience seared with a hot iron; ³Forbidding to marry, and commanding to abstain from meats, which God hath created to be received with thanksgiving of them which believe and know the truth. ⁴For every creature of God is good, and nothing to be refused, if it be received with thanksgiving: ⁵For it is sanctified by the word of God and prayer. ⁶If thou put the brethren in remembrance of these things, thou shalt be a good minister of Jesus Christ, nourished up in the words of faith and of good doctrine, whereunto thou hast attained. KJV.*

- ❖ Discuss this passage with your ministers, and allow them to respond. (3 mins. or less)
- ❖ **Expound on this scripture: 2 Timothy 2:15.** *¹⁵Study to shew thyself approved unto God, a workman that needeth not to be ashamed, rightly dividing the word of truth.*
- ❖ Discuss this passage with your ministers, and allow them to respond. (3 mins. or less)
- ❖ The facilitator is establishing the fact the as Minster's of Jesus Christ, ignorance in the Word of God can no longer be an excuse. Point out that people in other religions who are in error, but they know almost every there is to know about what they believe. Now we have THE TRUTH and won't deliver it correctly or in the correct contents.

Activation Time

- Here's an exercise for your ministers. The facilitator can pick out a passage of scripture of their choice. Choose 3 ministers to come up and expound on that scripture. Instruct each minister that they only have **5 mins.** I'll say that again! Instruct each minister that they only have 5 minutes! ☺
- Here's a few things the facilitator can look for in each sermonette. *(now if you're a pastor, you may already know what you're looking for in your ministers.*

    - As the minister gets up. Pay attention to their intro.
    - Did they greet the audience properly?
    - Did the recognize the Pastors and or the conductor of the service?
    - Did they engage or interact well with the audience?
    - Was the message based on the scripture given, clear and presice?
    - From 1 to 10, what would be their overall grade base on the total delivery and effectiveness of the message? (grade on a separate sheet)

- Call as many ministers as you feel necessary. Then go over the points with the ministers over all. Try not to pick out just one ministers issue, but discuss the issues in a general term. This will allow all who may not have ministered in this particular session, a chance to learn so that when their time comes, they know what and what not to do.

Note: Your grading techniques can be totally up to you. You can even get a panel of more seasoned Elders to grade each speaker. But to be thorough; you should even have the seasoned Ministers go through this exercise, to make sure they're saying the same and correct things as well.

- It wouldn't be a bad idea to record these session sermons for reference purposes!
- One thing the facilitator can note. While the ministers are speaking, take note of the reaction of the other ministers listening.

    - Are they getting with the speaker in support?
    - Are they paying attention?
    - Observe facial reactions of the ministers listening.
    - Did the ministers act like they have a favorite, or were they supportive of all?
    - How was their reaction once the minister completed their sermonette?

Note: This is very important in the relationship growth & development of the priesthood. We all need to be of one mind, with the same goals and purpose. No one having their own agenda but understanding that the way you become blessed in your ministry, is by being faithful in another's ministry. God will honor you!

Take the time to reflect on the different sermons and discuss any situation openly that may have arisen during this session. Don't miss out on the nuggets of learning more about your gift and how to use it with excellence!

Conclusion

If you're using the workbook for your class or study group:

You can set up your own scoring system or test scores to see how much your students have learned. Encourage others who have this book to pass it on to others in their church or job.

We recommend you request this book and workbook for your ministry's bookstores. It will be a blessing to all who read.

Prayerfully you have gained a better understanding of your gifts and call on your life. We pray that you understand the importance of who you are in the earth and in the church. You are a powerful anointed gift from God.

It is imperative that we represent Christ in all purity, honesty and sanctification. We must be separate from the worldly system. We operate in a Kingdom system, not a democracy. God wants His Levites to show His glory in the earth! He wants us to show forth His praises, without compromising the Word of God and its principles.

God wants to bless each of you!

No matter where you operate in ministry, give God your all; give Him all the glory, praise and honor. Be holy! He's seeking for such to worship Him in spirit and truth. God is sending you this message. He's sending a **Message to the Levites!**

God Bless You
Elder Elmus L. High Jr.

FINAL NOTES FROM THE SESSIONS:

Message to the Levites

FINAL NOTES FROM THE SESSIONS:

Message to the Levites

FINAL NOTES FROM THE SESSIONS:

FINAL NOTES FROM THE SESSIONS:

Message to the Levites

FINAL NOTES FROM THE SESSIONS:

Message to the Levites

FINAL NOTES FROM THE SESSIONS:

Message to the Levites

FINAL NOTES FROM THE SESSIONS:

Message to the Levites

FINAL NOTES FROM THE SESSIONS:

Message to the Levites

FINAL NOTES FROM THE SESSIONS:

Message to the Levites

FINAL NOTES FROM THE SESSIONS:

Message to the Levites

FINAL NOTES FROM THE SESSIONS:

Message to the Levites

FINAL NOTES FROM THE SESSIONS:

Message to the Levites

FINAL NOTES FROM THE SESSIONS:

Message to the Levites

FINAL NOTES FROM THE SESSIONS:

Message to the Levites

FINAL NOTES FROM THE SESSIONS:

Message to the Levites

FINAL NOTES FROM THE SESSIONS:

Message to the Levites

FINAL NOTES FROM THE SESSIONS:

Message to the Levites

FINAL NOTES FROM THE SESSIONS:

Message to the Levites

FINAL NOTES FROM THE SESSIONS:

Message to the Levites

FINAL NOTES FROM THE SESSIONS:

Message to the Levites

FINAL NOTES FROM THE SESSIONS:

Message to the Levites

FINAL NOTES FROM THE SESSIONS:

Message to the Levites

FINAL NOTES FROM THE SESSIONS:

Message to the Levites

FINAL NOTES FROM THE SESSIONS:

Message to the Levites

FINAL NOTES FROM THE SESSIONS:

Message to the Levites

FINAL NOTES FROM THE SESSIONS:

Message to the Levites

FINAL NOTES FROM THE SESSIONS:

Message to the Levites

FINAL NOTES FROM THE SESSIONS:

Message to the Levites

FINAL NOTES FROM THE SESSIONS:

Message to the Levites

FINAL NOTES FROM THE SESSIONS:

Message to the Levites

FINAL NOTES FROM THE SESSIONS:

Message to the Levites

FINAL NOTES FROM THE SESSIONS:

Message to the Levites

FINAL NOTES FROM THE SESSIONS:

Message to the Levites

FINAL NOTES FROM THE SESSIONS:

Message to the Levites

MESSAGE TO THE LEVITES

COMMENTARY

COMMENTARY, ON THE "MUSICAL MEN" WITH KING DAVID

"Based on 1 Chronicles 25"

"**I**nstruments" *David, having settled the courses of these Levites that were to attend the priests in their ministrations, proceeds, in this chapter, to put those into a method that were appointed to be singers and musicians in the temple. Here is, I. The persons that were to be employed, Asaph, Heman and Jeduthun (v. 1), their sons (v. 2-6), and other skilful persons (v. 7). II. The order in which they were to attend was determined by the casting of lots (v. 8–31).*

VERSES 1-7 Observe, I. Singing the praises of God here is called *prophesying* (v. 1-3), not that all those who were employed in this service were honored with the visions of God, or could foretell things to come. Heman indeed is said to be the *king's seer in the words of God* (v. 5); but the psalms they sang were composed by the prophets; "prophet-minstrels" and many of them were prophetical; and the edification of the church was intended in it, as well as the glory of God. In Samuel's time singing the praises of God went by the name of *prophesying* (1 Sa. 10:5; 19:20), and perhaps that is intended in what Paul calls *prophesying* in, 1 Cor. 11:4; 14:24. II. Here it is called a *service,* and the persons "employed" in it are *workmen,* v. 1. It is considered the greatest liberty and pleasure to be *employed* in praising God. This speaks to the fact that it is our duty to make the praises of God *our business.* Our praises should continually be stirred up within us, even in the midst of our trials and infirmities. We must understand that the praise of God will not be done as it should be done, without *labor* and *struggle.*

So when the word, "*employed*" is used here, it's actually saying, praising God is a continual sacrifice. The writer said; "I will bless the Lord at all times, His praises shall continually be in my mouth." And in order for that to happen, you'll find it to be a sacrifice many times. We must take pains with our hearts to bring them, and keep them, to this work, and to engage all that is within us. III. Here were, in compliance with the temper of that dispensation, a great variety of musical **instruments** used, *harps, psalteries, cymbals* (v. 1, 6), and here was one that *lifted up the horn* (v. 5), that is, used wind-music. The bringing of such concerts of music into the worship of God now is what none pretend to. But those who use such concerts for their own entertainment should feel themselves obliged to preserve them always free from anything that savors of immorality or profaneness, by this consideration, that time was when they were sacred; and then *those* were justly condemned who brought them into *common use,* Amos 6:5. *They invented to themselves **instruments** of music like David.* IV. The glory and honor of God were principally intended in all this temple-music, whether vocal or instrumental. It was *to give thanks, and praise the Lord,* that the singers were employed, v. 3. It was *in the songs of the Lord that they were instructed* (v. 7), that is, *for songs in the house of the Lord,* v. 6. This agrees with the intention of the perpetuating of psalmody in the gospel-church, which is *to make melody with the heart,* in conjunction with the voice, *unto the Lord,* Eph. 5:19. V. The order of the king is likewise taken notice of, v. 2 and again v. 6.

In those matters indeed David acted as a prophet; but his taking care for the due and regular observance of divine institutions, both ancient and modern, is an example to all in authority to use their power for the promoting of holiness, and the enforcing of the laws of Christ. Let them thus be *ministers of God for good.* VI. The fathers presided in this service, Asaph, Heman, and Jeduthun (v. 1), and the children were *under the hands of their father,* v. 2, 3, 6. This gives a good example to parents to train up their children, and indeed to all seniors to instruct their juniors in the service of God, and particularly in praising him, than which there is no part of our work more necessary or more worthy to be transmitted to the succeeding generations.

It gives also an example to the younger to *submit themselves to the elder* (whose experience and observation fit them for direction), and, as far as may be, to do what they do *under their hand.* It is probable that Heman, Asaph, and Jeduthun, were bred up under Samuel, and had their education in the "*schools of the prophets*" which he was the founder and president of; then they were pupils, now they came to be masters. Those that would be eminent must begin early, and take time to prepare themselves. This good work of singing God's praises Samuel revived, and set on foot, but lived not to see it brought to the perfection. Solomon perfects what David began, so David perfects what Samuel began. Let all, in their day, do what they can for God and His church, though they cannot carry it so far as they would; when they are gone God can out of stones raise up others who shall build upon their foundation and bring forth the top-stone.

VII. There were others also, besides the sons of these three great men, who are called their brethren *(probably because they had been wont to join with them in their "**private concerts**")*. "I'll explain that in the post commentary section." They were *instructed in the songs of the Lord,* and were cunning or well skilled therein, v. 7. They were all Levites and were in number 288 strong. Now, these were a good number, and a competent number to keep up the service in the house of God; for they were all skilful in the work to which they were called.

When David the king was so much addicted to divine poesy and music many others and all that had a genius for it, applied their studies and endeavors that way. Those do worship a great deal of good service that bring the exercises of devotion into reputation. Yet these were but a small number in comparison with the 4000 whom David appointed thus to *praise the Lord; (choir members)* ch. 23:5. Where were all the rest, when only 288, and those but by twelve in a course, were separated to this service? It is probable that all the rest were divided into as many courses, and were to follow as these led. Or, perhaps, these were *for songs in the house of the Lord* (v. 6), with whom any that worshipped in the courts of that house might join; and the rest were disposed of, all the kingdom over, to preside in the country congregations, in this good work: for, though the sacrifices instituted by the hand of Moses might be offered but at one place, the psalms penned by David might be sung every where, 1 Timothy 2:8.

<u>VERSES 8-31</u> Twenty-four persons are named in the beginning of this chapter as sons of those three great men, Asaph, Heman, and Jeduthun. Ethan was the third (ch. 6:44), but probably was dead before the establishment was perfected and Jeduthun came in his room. Ethan and Jeduthun were two names for the same person. Of these three Providence so ordered it that Asaph had four sons, Jeduthun six [only five are mentioned v. 3; Shimei, mentioned v. 17, is supposed to have been the sixth], and Heman fourteen, in all twenty-four (who were named, v. 2-4), who were all qualified for the service and called to it. But the question was, in what order must they serve? This was determined by lot, to prevent strife for precedency, a sin which most easily besets many that otherwise are good people. xI. The lot was thrown impartially. They were placed in twenty-four companies, twelve in a company, in two rows, twelve companies in a row, and so they cast lots, *ward against ward,* putting them all upon a level, small and great, teacher and scholar. They did not go according to their age, or according to their standing, or the degrees they had taken in the music-schools; but it was referred to God, v. 8. small and great, teachers and scholars, stand alike before God, who goes not according to our rules of distinction and precedency. See Mt. 20:23. II. God determined it as he pleased, taking account, it is probable, of the respective merits of the persons, which are of much more importance than seniority of age or priority of birth. Let us compare them with the preceding catalogue and we shall find that, 1. Josephus was the second son of Asaph. 2. Gedaliah the eldest son of Jeduthun. 3. Zaccur the eldest of Asaph. 4. Izri the second of Jeduthun. 5. Nethaniah the third of Asaph.

6. Bukkiah the eldest of Heman. 7. Jesharelah the youngest of Asaph. 8. Jeshaiah the third of Jeduthun. 9. Mattaniah the second of Heman. 10. Shimei the youngest of Jeduthun. 11. Azareel the third of Heman. 12. Hashabiah the fourth of Jeduthun. 13. Shubael the fourth of Heman. 14. Mattithiah the fifth of Jeduthun. 15. Jeremoth the fifth of Heman. 16. Hananiah the sixth of Heman. 17. Joshbekashah the eleventh of Heman. 18. Hanani the seventh of Heman. 19. Mallothi the twelfth of Heman. 20. Eliathah the eighth of Heman. 21. Hothir the thirteenth of Heman. 22. Giddalti the ninth of Heman. 23. Mehazioth the fourteenth of Heman. And, *lastly,* Romamti-ezer, the tenth of Heman.

See how God increased some and preferred the younger before the elder. III. Each of these had in his chorus the number of twelve, called *their sons and their brethren,* because they observed them as sons, and concurred with them as brethren. Probably twelve, some for the voice and others for the instrument, made up the concert. Let us learn with one mind and one mouth to glorify God, and that will be the best concert.

COMMENTARY ON SONGS OF PURPOSE AND THE MERCIES OF GOD
"Based on Psalms 78"

"Sing of His mercies"

This psalm is historical; it is a narrative of the great mercies God had bestowed upon Israel, the great sins wherewith they had provoked him, and the many tokens of his displeasure they had been under for their sins. The psalmist began, in the foregoing psalm, to relate God's wonders of old, for his own encouragement in a difficult time; there he broke off abruptly, but here resumes the subject, for the edification of the church, and enlarges much upon it, showing not only how good God had been to them, which was an earnest of further finishing mercy, but how basely they had conducted themselves towards God, which justified him in correcting them as he did at this time, and forbade all complaints.

"Here is, I. The preface to this church history, commanding the attention of the present age to it and recommending it to the study of the generations to come (v. 1-8). II. The history itself from Moses to David"; it is put into a psalm or song that it might be the better remembered and transmitted to posterity, and that the singing of it might affect them with the things here related, more than they would be with a bare narrative of them. The general scope of this psalm we have (v. 9–11) where notice is taken of the present rebukes they were under (v. 9), the sin which brought them under those rebukes (v. 10), and the mercies of God to them formerly, which aggravated that sin (v. 11).

As to the particulars, we are here told, 1. What wonderful works God had wrought for them in bringing them out of Egypt (v. 12–16), providing for them in the wilderness (v. 23–29), plaguing and ruining their enemies (v. 43–53), and at length putting them in possession of the land of promise (v. 54, 55). 2. How ungrateful they were to God for his favors to them and how many and great provocations they were guilty of. How they murmured against God and distrusted him (v. 17–20), and did but counterfeit repentance and submission when he punished them (v. 34–37), thus grieving and tempting him (v. 40–42). How they affronted God with their idolatries after they came to Canaan (v. 56–58). 3. How God had justly punished them for their sins (v. 21, 22) in the wilderness, making their sin their punishment (v. 29–33), and now, of late, when the ark was taken by the Philistines (v. 59–64). 4. How graciously God had spared them and returned in mercy to them, notwithstanding their provocations. He had forgiven them formerly (v. 38, 39), and now, of late, had removed the judgments they had brought upon themselves, and brought them under a happy establishment both in church and state (v. 65–72). As the general scope of this psalm may be of use to us in the singing of it, to put us upon recollecting what God has done for us and for his church formerly, and what we have done against him, so the particulars also may be of use to us, for warning against those sins of unbelief and ingratitude which Israel of old was notoriously guilty of, and the record of which was preserved for our learning. *"These things happened unto them for ensamples,"* 1 Corinthians 10:11; Hebrews 4:11. **Maschil of Asaph.**

VERSES 1-8 these verses, which contain the preface to this history, show that the psalm answers the title; it is indeed *Maschil—a psalm to give instruction;* if we receive not the instruction it gives, it is our own fault. Here, I. The psalmist demands attention to what he wrote (v. 1): *Give ear, O my people! to my law.* Some make these the psalmist's words. David, as a king, or Asaph, in his name, as his secretary of state, or scribe to the sweet singer of Israel, here calls upon the people, as his people committed to his charge, to give ear to his law. He calls his instructions his *law* or *edict;* such was their commanding force in themselves. Every good truth, received in the light and love of it, will have the power of a law upon the conscience; yet that was not all: David was a king, and he would interpose his royal power for the edification of his people. If God, by His grace, made great men good men, they will be capable of doing more good than others, because their word will be a law to all about them, who must therefore give ear and hearken; for to what purpose is divine revelation brought our ears if we will not incline our ears to it, both humble ourselves and engage ourselves to hear it and heed it? Or the psalmist, being a prophet, speaks as God's mouth, and so calls them *His People,* and demands subjection to what was said as to a law. Let him that has an ear thus *hear what the Spirit saith unto the churches,* Revelation 2:7. Remember as I stated in other parts of the book, that God is calling his Musical Levites to come forth and seek His face and **birth spiritual songs into the atmosphere.** He will give you events and circumstances to write about, and one of the best tools you have to minister to the masses is your own *experiences* in life, and your personal walk with God.

Don't be afraid to be transparent in your ministry and God can trust you and use you for His glory. We need songs from the Lord; can you see how important it is?" That's why I'm sharing comments and information from these excellent sources, to give you a full picture of how it was intended for us to operate in the body of Christ as His special called out ones. Your gift from the Lord is far too precious to be taken lightly or with little concern on how or where it is used. Don't cast your pearls before swine and don't sing songs in a strange land. Don't just tell me about your success and how well you're doing. Don't just show me your best side and how wonderful things are for you now. Tell me about the time you failed, and the time when you were discouraged and wanted to quit. Tell me about how you had to wait on God even when you didn't understand what He was doing in your life. Tell us how you almost lost your mind in the midst of trials and temptation. Tell us how you overcame the evil one and how you bounced back from a horrible pit even *since you've been saved.*

That's the type of message or song we need to hear. We need to hear how you came from literally nothing to the place where you sit now and how God brought you all the way into a wealthy place, wealthy both naturally and spiritually. You will be much more effective if you can allow yourself to be made a spectacle or even risk being talked about and criticized for speaking truth. That doesn't mean throw all of your business in the street for some to step on and point fingers at you, but to the point where you don't mind sharing with someone how God can take you through any situation if you turn to Him with all your heart, mind and soul.

Give it all to Jesus and He'll make it all right. When you are able to do this your ministry can help more people who are in need. One thing my father always told me, he said, "always take it seriously, ministering to Gods people, you're dealing with real people with real issues and they don't need to hear your thoughts or opinions about it, they need to hear what thus said the Lord. The reason I'm using the title, *Songs of purpose and the Mercies of God,* is because the Word of God in song or in melody is so powerful. Musicians have figured it out, they have tapped into the fact that music and a song can control or change a life. It has the ability to cause a person to alter the way they think, move, walk or even act. The problem is, as musicians, (*Godly Musicians*) we are guilty of taking away the *sacredness* and the *original purpose* of the song.

I don't care how you slice it up, re arrange and misinterpret God's word, if you search in the bible you will understand that God only meant for the song and the music to worship him. The mercy of God is that he hasn't struck us down because we have taken that which is holy and made it common. We have taken the worship of God to another level, but that level isn't up, it isn't anointed, it sounds good to the ear, it's popular, it's right now, it has a tight beat but it's not what's called for at all when tainted by worldly and unclean beginnings. Give the songs back to God or He's getting ready to take what's His and He won't need your help to get it.

There are yet sold out ministers of God, true Levites that are going to keep God's commandment when he said for us to sing praises to Him. But we're finding our music mixed with the worlds stuff, mixed with the accursed things of this world and calling it okay. God have mercy on us!

COMMENTARY ON FALLEN LUCIFER AND THOSE WHO CARRY LIKE SPIRITS
"Based on Ezekiel 28"

"Pride comes before a fall"

In this segment we have, I. A prediction of the fall and ruin of the king of Tyre, who, in the destruction of that city, is particularly set up as a mark for God's arrows (v. 1-10). II. A lamentation for the king of Tyre, when he has thus fallen, though he falls by his own iniquity (v. 11-19). III. A prophecy of the destruction of Zidon, which as in the neighborhood of Tyre and had a dependence upon it (v. 20-23). IV. A promise of the restoration of the Israel of God, though in the day of their calamity they were insulted over by their neighbors (v. 24-26).

VERSES 1-10 Now dealing with Tyrus in this chapter, now the prince of Tyrus is to be singled out. Here is something to be said to him by himself, a *message to him from God,* which the prophet must send him, whether he will hear or whether he will forbear. I. He must tell him of his pride. His people are proud (ch. 27:3) and so is he; and they shall both be made to know that *God resists the proud.* Let us see, 1. What were the expressions of his pride: *His heart was lifted up,* v. 2. He had a great conceit of himself, was puffed up with an opinion of his own sufficiency, and looked with disdain upon all about him. Out of the abundance of the pride of his heart he said, *I am a god;* he did not only say it in his heart, but had the impudence to speak it out. God has said of princes, *"They are gods"* (Psalms. 82:6); but it does not become them to say so of themselves; it is a high affront to Him who is *God alone,* and will not give His glory to another.

He thought that the city of Tyre had as necessary a dependence upon him as the world has upon the God that made it, and that he was himself independent as God and unaccountable to any.

He thought himself to have as much wisdom and strength as God Himself, and as incontestable an authority, and that his prerogatives were as absolute and his word as much a law as the word of God. He challenged divine honors, and expected to be praised and admired as a god, and doubted not to be defied, among other *heroes,* after his death as a great benefactor to the world. Thus the king of Babylon said, *I will be like the Most High* (Isa. 14:14), not like the *Most Holy.* "I am the strong God, and therefore will not be contradicted, because I cannot be controlled. *I sit in the seat of God;* I sit *as high* as God, my throne is equal with his." *Divisum imperium cum Jove Caesar habet—Caesar divides dominion with Jove.* I sit as safely as God, as safely *in the heart of the seas,* and as far out of the reach of danger, as he in the *height of heaven.* He thinks his guards of men of war about his throne as pompous and potent as the hosts of angels that are about the throne of God. He is put in mind of his meanness and mortality, and, since he needs to be told, he shall be told, that self-evident truth, *Thou art a man, and not God,* a depending creature; thou art *flesh, and not spirit,* Isa. 31:3. Note, men must be made to know that they are *but men,* Ps. 9:20. The greatest wits, the greatest potentates, the greatest saints, are *men, and not gods.* Jesus Christ was both God and man. The king of Tyre, though he has such a mighty influence upon all about him, and with the help of his riches bears a mighty sway, though he has tribute and presents brought to his court with as much devotion as if they were sacrifices to him.

Though he is flattered by his courtiers and made a god of by his poets, yet, after all, he is *but a man;* he knows it; he fears it. But *he sets his heart as the heart of God;* "Thou hast conceited thyself to be a god, hast compared thyself with God, thinking thyself as wise and strong, and as fit to govern the world, as he." It was the ruin of our first parents, and ours in them that they would be *as gods,* Gen. 3:5. And still that corrupt nature which inclines men to set up themselves as their own masters, to do what they will, and their own carvers, to have what they will, their own end, to live to themselves, and their own felicity, to enjoy themselves, *sets their hearts as the heart of God,* invades His prerogatives, and catches at the flowers of His crown a presumption that cannot go unpunished. 2. We are here told what it was that he was proud of. (1.) His wisdom. It is probable that this prince of Tyre was a man of very good natural parts, a philosopher, and well read in all the parts of learning that were then in vogue, at least a politician, and one that had great dexterity in managing the affairs of state. And then he thought himself to be *wiser than Daniel,* v. 3. We found, before, that Daniel, though now but a young man, was celebrated for his prevalency in prayer, ch. 14:14. Here we find he was famous for his prudence in the management of the affairs of this world, a great scholar and statesman, and withal a great saint, and yet not a prince, but a poor captive. It was strange that under such external disadvantages his lustre should shine forth, so that he had become *wise to a proverb.* When the king of Tyre dreams himself to be a god he says, I am *wiser than Daniel. There is no secret that they can hide from thee.*

Probably he challenged all about him to *prove him with questions,* as Solomon was proved, and he had unriddled all their enigmas, had solved all their problems, and none of them all could puzzle him. He had perhaps been successful in discovering plots, and diving into the counsels of the neighboring princes, and therefore thought himself omniscient, and that no thought could be withholden from him; therefore he said, *I am a god.* Note, *Knowledge puffeth up;* it is hard to know much and not to know it too well and to be elevated with it. He that was *wiser than Daniel* was prouder than Lucifer. Those therefore that are knowing must study to be humble and to evidence that they are so. (2.) His wealth. That way his wisdom led him; it is not said that by his wisdom he searched into the arcana either of nature or government, modeled the state better than it was, or made better laws, or advanced the interests of the commonwealth of learning; but his *wisdom and understanding* were of use to him in *traffic.* As some of the kings of Judah *loved husbandry* (2 Chr. 26:10), so the king of Tyre loved merchandise, and by it he *got riches, increased his riches, and filled his treasures with gold and silver,* v. 4, 5. See what the wisdom of this world is; those are cried up as the wisest men that know how to get money and by right or wrong to raise estates; and yet really *this their way is their folly,* Ps. 49:13. It was the folly of the king of Tyre, [1.] That he attributed the increase of his wealth to himself and not to the providence of God, forgetting him who *gave him power to get wealth,* Deu. 8:17, 18. [2.] That he thought himself a wise man because he was a rich man; whereas a fool may have an estate (Eccl. 2:19), yea, and a fool may get an estate, for the world has been often observed to favor such.

When bread is not to the wise, Eccl. 9:11. [3.] That *his heart was lifted up because of his riches,* because of the increase of his wealth, which made him so haughty and secure, so insolent and imperious, and which *set his heart as the heart of God.* The *man of sin,* when he had a great deal of worldly pomp and power, *showed himself as a god,* 2 Th. 2:4. Those who are rich in this world have therefore need to charge that upon themselves which the word of God charges upon them, *that they be not high-minded,* 1 Tim. 6:17. II. Since *pride goes before destruction, and a haughty spirit before a fall,* he must bell him of that destruction, of that fall, which was now hastening on as the just punishment of his presumption in setting up himself a rival with God. "Because thou hast pretended to be a god (v. 6), therefore thou shalt not be long a man," v. 7. Observe here, 1. The instruments of his destruction: *I will bring strangers upon thee* —the Chaldeans, whom we do not find mentioned among the many nations and countries that traded with Tyre, ch. 27. If any of those nations had been brought against it, they would have had some compassion upon it, for old acquaintance-sake; but these strangers will have none. They are people of a *strange language,* which the king of Tyre himself, wise as he is, perhaps understands not. They are the *terrible of the nations;* it was an army made up of many nations, and it was at this time the most formidable both for strength and fury. These God has at command, and these he will bring upon the king of Tyre. 2. The extremity of the destruction: *They shall draw their swords against the beauty of thy wisdom* (v. 7), against all those things which thou gloriest in as thy beauty and the production of thy wisdom.

Note, it is just with God that our enemies should make that their prey which we have made our pride. The king of Tyre's palace, his treasury, his city, his navy, his army, these he glories in as his brightness, these he thinks, made him illustrious and glorious as a god on earth. But all these victorious enemy shall defile, shall deface, shall deform. He thought them sacred, things that none durst touch; but the conquerors shall seize them as common things, and spoil the brightness of them. But, whatever becomes of what he has, surely his person is sacred. No (v. 8): *They shall bring thee down to the pit,* to the grave; thou shalt *die the death.* And, (1.) It shall not be an honorable death, but an ignominious one. He shall be so vilified in his death that he may despair of being deified after his death. He shall die *the deaths of those that are slain in the midst of the seas,* that have no honor done them at their death, but their dead bodies are immediately thrown overboard, without any ceremony or mark of distinction, to be a feast for the fish. Tyre is *likely to be destroyed in the midst of the sea* (ch. 27:32) and the prince of Tyre shall fare no better than the people. (2.) It shall not be a happy death, but a miserable one. He shall *die the deaths of the uncircumcised* (v. 10), of those that are strangers to God and not in covenant with him, and therefore die under his wrath and curse. It is *deaths,* a double death, temporal and eternal, the death both of body and soul. He shall die the *second death;* that is dying miserably indeed.

The sentence of death here passed upon the king of Tyre is ratified by a divine authority: *I have spoken it, saith the Lord God.* And what He has said He will do. None can gainsay it, nor will He unsay it.

(3.) The effectual disproof that this will be of all his pretensions to deity (v. 9): "When the conqueror sets his sword to thy breast, and thou seest no way of escape, *wilt thou then say, I am God?* Wilt thou then have such a conceit of thyself as thou now hast? No; thy being overpowered by death, and by the fear of it, will force thee to own that thou art not a god, but a weak, timorous, trembling, dying man. *In the hand of him that slays thee* (in the hand of God, and of the instruments that He employed) *thou shalt be a man, and not God,* utterly unable to resist, and help thyself." *I have said, You are gods; but you shall die like men,* Ps. 82:6, 7. Note, those who pretend to be rivals with God shall be forced one way or other to let fall their claims. Death at furthest, when we come into his hand, will make us know that we are men.

<u>VERSES 11-19</u> As after the prediction of the ruin of Tyre (ch. 26) followed a pathetic lamentation for it (ch. 27), so after the ruin of the king of Tyre is foretold it is bewailed. I. This is commonly understood of the prince who then reigned over Tyre, spoken to, v. 2. His name was *Ethbaal,* or *Ithobalus,* as Diodorus Siculus calls him that was king of Tyre when Nebuchadnezzar destroyed it. He was, it seems, upon all external accounts an accomplished man, very great and famous; but his iniquity was his ruin. Many expositors have suggested that besides the literal sense of this lamentation there is an *allegory* in it, and that it is an *allusion to the fall of the angels that sinned,* who undid themselves by their pride. And (as is usual in texts that have a mystical meaning) some passages here refer primarily to the king of Tyre, as that of his merchandises, others to the angels, as that of being *in the holy mountain of God.*

But, if there be any thing mystical in it (as perhaps there may), I shall rather refer it to the fall of Adam, which seems to be glanced at, v. 13. *Thou hast been in Eden the garden of God, and that in the day thou wast created.* II. Some think that by *the king of Tyre* is meant the whole royal family, this including also the foregoing kings, and looking as far back as Hiram, king of Tyre. The then governor is called *prince* (v. 2); but he that is here lamented is called *king.* The

Commentary

court of Tyre with its kings had for many ages been famous; but sin ruins it. Now we may observe two things here:—1. What was the renown of the king of Tyre. He is here spoken of as having lived in great splendor, v. 12–15. He as a man, but it is here owned that he was a very considerable man and one that made a mighty figure in his day. (1.) He far exceeded other men. Hiram and other kings of Tyre had done so in their time; and the reigning king perhaps had not come short of any of them: *Thou sealest up the sum full of wisdom and perfect in beauty.* But the powers of human nature and the prosperity of human life seemed in him to be at the highest pitch. He was looked upon to be as wise as the reason of men could make him, and as happy as the wealth of this world and the enjoyment of it could make him; in him you might see the utmost that both could do; and therefore *seal up the sum,* for nothing can be added; he is a complete man, perfect *in suo genere—in his kind.* (2.) He seemed to be as wise and happy as Adam in innocency (v. 13): "*Thou hast been in Eden,* even *in the garden of God;* thou hast lived as it were in paradise all thy days, hast had a full enjoyment of every thing that is *good for food* or *pleasant to the eyes,* and an uncontroverted dominion over all about thee, as Adam had."

One instance of the magnificence of the king of Tyre is, that he outdid all others princes in jewels, which those have the greatest plenty of that trade most abroad, as he did: *Every precious stone* was *his covering.* There is a great variety of precious stones; but he had of every sort and in such plenty that besides what were treasured up in his cabinet, and were the ornaments of his crown, he had his clothes trimmed with them; they were his *covering.* Nay (v. 14), he *walked up and down in the midst of the stones of fire,* that is, these precious stones, which glittered and sparkled like fire. His rooms were in a manner set round with jewels, so that he walked in the midst of them, and then fancied himself as glorious as if, like God, he had been surrounded by so many angels, who are compared to a *flame of fire.* And, if he be such an admirer of precious stones as to think them as bright as angels, no wonder that he is such an admirer of himself as to think himself as great as God. Nine several sorts of previous stones are here named, which were all in the high priest's ephod. Perhaps they are particularly named because he, in his pride, used to speak particularly of them, and tell those about him, with a great deal of foolish pleasure, "This is such a precious stone, of such a value, and so and so are its virtues." Thus is he upbraided with his vanity. *Gold* is mentioned last, as far inferior in value to those precious stones; and he used to speak of it accordingly. Another thing that made him think his palace a paradise was the curious music he had, the *tabrets and pipes,* hand-instruments and wind-instruments.

The *workmanship* of these was extraordinary, and they were prepared for him on purpose; prepared *in thee,* the pronoun is **feminine**— in thee, O Tyre! or it denotes that the king was **effeminate** in doting on such things. They were prepared *in the day he was created,* that is, either born, or created king; they were made on purpose to celebrate the joys either of his birth-day or of his coronation-day. These he prided himself much in, and would have all that came to see his palace take notice of them. (3.) He looked like an incarnate angel (v. 14): *Thou art the anointed cherub that covers* or *protects;* that is, he looked upon himself as a guardian angel to his people, so bright, so strong, so faithful, appointed to this office and qualified for it. Anointed kings should be to their subjects as anointed cherubim, that cover them with the wings of their power; and, when they are such, God will own them. Their advancement was from him: *I have set thee so.* Some think, because mention was made of Eden, that it refers to the cherub set on the east of Eden to cover it, Gen. 3:24. He thought himself as able to guard his city from all invaders as that angel was for his charge. Or it may refer to the cherubim in the most holy place, whose wings covered the ark; he thought himself as bright as one of them. (4.) He appeared in as much splendor as the high priest when he was clothed with his garments for glory and beauty: *"Thou wast upon the holy mountain of God,"* as president of the temple built on that holy mountain; thou didst look as great, and with as much majesty and authority, as ever the high priest did when he walked in the temple, which was *"garnished with precious stones"* (2 Chr. 3:6).

Had his habit on, which had precious stones both in the breast and on the shoulders; in that he seemed to *walk in the midst of the stones of fire."* Thus glorious is the king of Tyre; at least he thinks himself so. 2. Let us now see what was the ruin of the king of Tyre, what it was that stained his glory and laid all this honor in the dust (v. 15): *"Thou wast perfect in thy ways;* thou didst prosper in all thy affairs and every thing went well with thee; thou hadst not only a clear, but a bright reputation, *from the day thou wast created,* the day of thy accession to the throne, *till iniquity was found in thee;* and that spoiled all." This may perhaps allude to the deplorable case of the angels that fell, and of our first parents, both of whom *were perfect in their ways till iniquity was found in them.* And when iniquity was once *found in him* it increased; he grew worse and worse, as appears (v. 18): *"Thou hast defiled thy sanctuaries;* thou hast lost the benefit of all that which thou thoughtest sacred, and in which, as in a sanctuary, thou thoughtest to take refuge; these thou hast *defiled,* and so exposed thyself *by the multitude of thy iniquities."* Now observe, (1.) What the iniquity was that was the ruin of the king of Tyre. [1.] The *iniquity of his traffic* (so it is called, v. 18), both his and his people's, for their sin is charged upon him, because he connived at it and set them a bad example (v. 16): *By the multitude of thy merchandise they have filled the midst of thee with violence,* and thus *thou hast sinned.* The king had so much to do with his merchandise, and was so wholly intent upon the gains of that, that he took no care to do justice, to give redress to those that suffered wrong and to protect them from violence; nay, in the multiplicity of business, wrong was done to many by oversight.

In his dealings he made use of his power to invade the rights of those he dealt with. Note, those that have much to do in the world are in great danger of doing much amiss; and it is hard to deal with many without violence to some.

Trades are called mysteries; but too many make them mysteries of iniquity. [2.] His pride and vain-glory (v. 17): *"Thy heart was lifted up because of thy beauty;"* thou wast in love with thyself, and thy own shadow. And thus *thou hast corrupted thy wisdom by reason of the brightness,* the pomp and splendor, wherein thou livedst." He gazed so much upon this that it dazzled his eyes and prevented him from seeing his way. He appeared so puffed up with his greatness that it bereaved him both of his wisdom and of the reputation of it. He really became a *fool in glorying*. Those make a bad bargain for themselves that part with their wisdom for the gratifying of their gaiety, and to please a vain humor, lose a real excellency. (2.) What the ruin was that this iniquity brought him to. [1.] He was thrown out of his dignity and dislodged from his palace, which he took to be his paradise and temple (v. 16): *I will cast thee as profane out of the mountain of God.* His kingly power was high as a *mountain,* setting him above others; it was a *mountain of God,* for the powers that be are ordained of God, and have something in them that is sacred; but, having abused his power, he is reckoned profane, and is therefore deposed and expelled. He disgraces the crown he wears, and so has forfeited it, and shall be destroyed *from the midst of the stones of fire,* the precious stones with which his palace was garnished, as the temple was; and they shall be no protection to him.

[2.] He was exposed to contempt and disgrace, and trampled upon by his neighbors: *"I will cast thee to the ground* (v. 17), will cast thee among the *pavement-stones,* from the midst of the *precious stones,* and will *lay thee* a rueful spectacle *before kings, that they may behold thee* and take warning by thee not to be proud and oppressive." [3.] He was quite consumed, his city and he in it: *I will bring forth a fire from the midst of thee.* The conquerors, when they have plundered the city, will kindle a fire in the heart of it, which shall lay it, and the palace particularly, in ashes. Or it may be taken more generally for the fire of God's judgments, which shall devour both prince and people, and bring all the glory of both *to ashes upon the earth;* and this fire shall be *brought forth from the midst of thee.* All God's judgments upon sinners take rise from themselves; they are devoured by a fire of their own kindling. [4.] He was hereby made a terrible example of divine vengeance. Thus he is reduced *in the sight of all those that behold him* (v. 18): *Those that know him shall be astonished at him,* and shall wonder how one that stood so high could be brought so low. The king of Tyre's palace, like the temple at Jerusalem, when it is destroyed shall be *an astonishment and a hissing,* 2 Chr. 7:20, 21.

So fell the king of Tyre.

<u>VERSES 20-26</u> God's glory is his great end, both in all the good and in all the evil which *proceed out of the mouth of the Most High;* so we find in these verses. 1. God will be glorified in the destruction of Zidon, a city that lay near to Tyre, was more ancient, but not so considerable, had a dependence upon it and stood and fell with it.

God says here, *I am against thee, O Zidon! I will be glorified in the midst of thee*, v. 22.

And again, "those who do not know be shall be made to know *that I am the Lord,* and I alone, and that I am a just and jealous God, *when I shall have executed judgments in her,* destroying judgments, when I shall have done execution according to justice and according to the sentence passed, and so shall be *sanctified in her."* The Zidonians, it should seem, were more addicted to idolatry than the Tyrians were, who, being men of business and large conversation, were less under the power of bigotry and superstition. The Zidonians were noted for the worship of Ashtaroth; Solomon introduced it, 1 Kings 11:5. Jezebel was daughter to the king of Zidon, who brought the worship of Baal into Israel 1 Kings 16:31; so that God had been much dishonored by the Zidonians. Now, says he, *I will be glorified, I will be sanctified.* The Zidonians were borderers upon the land of Israel, where God was known, and where they might have got the knowledge of him and have learned to glorify him; but, instead of that, they seduced Israel to the worship of their idols. Note, when God is sanctified He is glorified, for His holiness is His glory; and those whom He is not sanctified and glorified by He will be sanctified and glorified upon, by executing His holy and righteous judgments upon them, which declare Him a just avenger of His own and His people's injured honor. The judgments that shall be executed upon Zidon are war and pestilence, two wasting depopulating judgments, v. 23. They are God's messengers, which he sends on His errands, and they shall accomplish that for which He sends them.

Pestilence and *blood* shall be sent *into her streets;* there the dead bodies of those shall lie who perished, some by the plague, occasioned perhaps through ill diet when the city was besieged, and some by the sword of the enemy, most likely the Chaldean armies, when the city was taken, and all were put to the sword. Thus the wounded shall be judged; when they are dying of their wounds they shall judge themselves, and others shall say they justly fall or, as some read it, *they shall be punished by the sword,* that sword which has commission to destroy *on every side.*

It is God that judges, and He will overcome. Nor is it Tyre and Zidon only on which God would execute judgments, but on all those that despised His people Israel, and triumphed in their calamities; for this was now God's controversy with the nations that were *round about them,* v. 26. Note, when God's people are under His correcting hand for their faults He takes care, as He did concerning malefactors that were scourged, *that they shall not seem vile* to those that are about them, and therefore takes it ill of those who despise them and so *help forward the affliction* when He is but *a little displeased,* Zechariah 1:15. God regards them even in their low estate; and therefore let not men despise them. 2. God will be glorified in the restoration of His people to their former safety and prosperity. God had been dishonored by the sins of His people, and their sufferings too had given occasion to the enemy to blaspheme Isaiah 52:5; but

God will now both cure them of their sins and ease them of their troubles, and so *will be sanctified in them in the sight of the heathen,* will recover the honor of His holiness, to the satisfaction of all the world, v. 25.

For, (1.) They shall return to the possession of their own land again: *I will gather the house of Israel* out of their dispersions, in answer to that prayer Psalms 106:27, "*save us, O Lord our God!*" "*Gather us from among the heathen;*" and in pursuance of that promise Deut. 30:4, thence will *the Lord thy God gather thee.* Being gathered, they shall be brought in a body, to *dwell in the land that I have given to my servant Jacob.* God had an eye to the ancient grant, in bringing them back, for that remained in force, and the discontinuance of the possession was not a defeasance of the right. He that gave it will again give it. (2.) They shall enjoy great tranquility there. When those that have been vexatious to them are taken off they shall live in quietness; there shall be no more *a pricking brier nor a grieving thorn,* v. 24. They shall have a happy settlement, for they shall *build houses,* and *plant vineyards;* and they shall enjoy a happy security and serenity there; they shall *dwell safely,* shall *dwell with confidence,* and there shall be none to disquiet them or make them afraid, v. 26. This never had full accomplishment in the body of that people, for after their return out of captivity they were ever and anon molested by some bad neighbor or other. Nor has the gospel church been ever quite free from pricking briers and grieving thorns; yet sometimes *the church has rest,* and believers always dwell safely under the divine protection and may be *quiet from the fear of evil.* But the full accomplishment of this promise is reserved for the heavenly Canaan, when all the saints shall be gathered together, and every thing that offends shall be removed, and all grief's and fears for ever banished. I can't wait for that day to come, even *come Lord Jesus!*

THE PRIESTHOOD IN BIBLE HISTORY

"The Priesthood"

1. **Ancient History**. The idea of a priest and his intercessory work underlies all religion. From the time that the smoke of Abel's sacrifice ascended to God to the death of Jesus Christ on the cross, the history of the human race is inseparably associated with altars, priests and sacrifices. It may be safely asserted that in the early ages every man was his own priest. Cain and Abel "brought" their sacrifices and presented them to Jehovah (Genesis 4:1-5). The fact that the distinctions "clean" and "unclean" (Genesis 7:1-3) were recognized in the antediluvian ages, goes to prove that offering sacrifice was a general custom among men. After the flood, Noah, in acknowledgment of God's goodness, erected an altar upon the purified earth and offered sacrifices to his great Deliverer (Genesis 8:20). Further on, the head of the family officiated at the altar and led the family worship. Numerous examples are offered;

a. Abram built altars at Sichem, between Bethel and Hai (Genesis 12:6-8; Genesis 13:1-3) and on Mount Moriah (Genesis 22:1-9);
   b. Isaac built an altar at Beersheba (Genesis 26:18, 23-25);
   c. Jacob offered sacrifices at Beersheba on his way to Egypt (Genesis 46:1). During the ages before the exodus there was not established priesthood, and no special law regulating the offering of sacrifices; but the sacrifices were undoubtedly offered in obedience to Divine command (Genesis 4:1-5; Genesis 22:1-9; Genesis 35:1-3; Romans 10:17; Hebrews 11:4). God was gradually preparing the people of his choice for a more perfect revelation of Himself and a more explicit code of laws for their government.
   d. He was gradually cutting them off from other nations in order to preserve the blood of Abraham. During the sojourn in Egypt the chosen people largely fell into the corruptions of their surroundings. Tribal relations and conditions had to some extent been developed and preserved, even during the enslavement; but there is no proof that there was any general bond of union or any public worship.

2. *The Lords Choice.* During the last night in Egypt the angel of the Lord passed through the land of Egypt, smiting all the firstborn of man and beast among the Egyptians (Exodus 12:1-29). In memory of the preservation of the firstborn of the children of Israel, he subsequently took unto Himself the firstborn of man and beast (Exodus 13:2, 11-16). After this, He chose the entire tribe of Levi in place of the firstborn of the children of Israel, and the cattle of the Levites in the place of their cattle (Numbers 3:40-43).

3. *Divisions of the Levites.* The first intimation of the selection of the Levites was in the choice of Moses and Aaron (Exodus 3:1-10, Exodus 4:14-16). The Levites first showed their devotion to God when Moses returned from the mountain and found all Israel engaged in idol worship. In obedience to the invitation of Moses they gathered around him, and, at his command, slew many of the idolaters (Exodus 32:1-28). The tribe was divided as follows:
   a. Aaron and his sons were to be priests (Exodus 28:1; Numbers 18:1-7);
   b. The Kohathites were charged with the responsibility of transporting the holy vessels of the tabernacle and court (Numbers 4:1-15).
   c. The Gershonites had charge of the coverings, curtains, hanging and cords, or fabrics of the tabernacle (Numbers 4:21-28);
   d. The Merarites had charge of the boards, bars, pillars, sockets, pins and cords of the tabernacle and court, and the tools needed in setting them up (Numbers 4:29-33).

4. *Period of Service.* The Kohathites, Gershonites, and Merarites entered partially upon their service at the age of twenty-five (Numbers 8:24), fully upon their duties at the age of thirty (Numbers 4:2-49), and were relieved at the age

of fifty (Numbers 8:23-26); the age at which the sons of Aaron became priests were not specified by the law. In the time of David they entered upon their duties at age of twenty (2 Chronicles 31:17). *Consecration of the Levites.* The rites by which the Levites were consecrated to the service of the Lord were, first, they had water of purifying sprinkled upon them; they then shaved themselves and washed their clothes; afterward they offered a young bullock with its meat offering for a burnt offering, and a second bullock for a sin offering; the Israelites approached and laid their hands on the heads of the Levites to the Lord as an offering from the Israelites; the Levites then placed their hands on their burnt offering and sin offering which were slain, and atonement was made for them (Numbers 8:5-15). *Consecration of Aaron and His Sons.* The Lord commanded Moses to bring Aaron and his sons before the door of the tabernacle and call all the congregation of Israel together.

A young bullock for a sin offering, a ram for a burnt offering, and a ram of consecration were then brought, with a basket containing loaves of unleavened bread, oiled cakes of unleavened bread and wafers anointed with oil. Aaron and his sons were then washed, and their official raiment, which was made for "glory and for beauty" (Exodus 28:2), and was put on them, and the holy anointing oil was poured upon Aaron's head. The bullock was then brought to the north side of the altar, and was killed after Aaron and his sons put their hands upon its head; Moses then took its blood upon his finger and put it upon the horns of the altar and poured the remainder at the side of the altar. The fat of the bullock he burned upon the altar, but the skin, flesh and dung he burned without the camp. Aaron and his sons then placed their hands on the head of the ram for a burnt offering; it was then killed, and Moses took of its blood and sprinkled it upon and round about the altar; he then cleansed and washed it and burned its fat and flesh upon the altar. The ram of consecration was next brought, and after Aaron and his sons had put their hands on its head, it was slain, and Moses took its blood upon his finger and put it upon the tip of the right ears of Aaron and his sons, and on the thumbs of their right hands, and on the great toes of their right feet. Moses then took the fat and rump, and placed them upon the right shoulder of the ram, and also took a loaf of the unleavened bread and a cake of the oiled unleavened bread, and an oil-anointed wafer, and placed them all on the hands of Aaron and his sons to be waved before the Lord; after which he burned them on the altar. And Moses took the breast of the ram of consecration and waved it before the Lord.

Moses then took the anointing oil and the blood which was upon the altar, and sprinkled it upon Aaron and his sons. He also took the flesh of the ram of consecration and boiled it, and commanded Aaron and his sons to eat it with the unleavened bread in the basket, requiring them to remain at the door of the tabernacle for seven days. On each of the seven days of consecration a bullock was sacrificed at the altar to consecrate it. On the eighth day Aaron and his sons offered sin, burnt, and peace offerings on the altar; and Aaron lifted up his hands toward the people and blessed them, and came down from the altar. Then Moses and Aaron went into the holy place, and when they came out Aaron blessed the people, and fire came out from the presence of the Lord and consumed the offerings on the altar, and when the congregation saw it, they fell on their faces and shouted (Exodus 29:1-37; Leviticus 8:1-36; Leviticus 9:1-24).

5. *Dress of the Priests.* The dress of the ordinary priest was made of fine linen and consisted of a coat, girdle, bonnet, and breeches (Exodus 28:40-42; Exodus 39:27-29).

6. *Dress of the High Priest.* The dress of the high priest consisted of breeches, broidered coat, girdle, robe of the ephod, ephod, curious girdle, breastplate, mitre, and in all eight parts (Exodus 28:4, 40-42; Leviticus 8:7).
    a. The breeches were made of fine twined linen, and reached from the loins to the thighs (Exodus 28:42).
    b. The broidered coat was a long robe of fine twined linen, with sleeves, and reached from the neck to the ankles (Exodus 28:39; Exodus 39:27).
    c. The girdle was made of fine twined linen embroidered with blue, purple and scarlet (Exodus 28:40; Exodus 39:29).
    d. The robe of the ephod was made entirely of blue material, and was woven (Exodus 39:22). It was worn under the ephod, but was much longer than the ephod. It had a hole for the head to pass through. It had a strong band around the hole to prevent it from rending. The bottom of it was ornamented with bells alternating with pomegranates (Exodus 28:31-35; Exodus 39:22-26).
    e. The ephod was made of gold wire, blue, purple, scarlet, and fine twined linen. It consisted of two parts; one part covered the back and the other the front of the upper portion of the body. The two parts were fastened together on the shoulders with two large onyx stones on which were engraved the names of the children of Israel according to their birth. It was further united by the curious girdle (Exodus 28:6-14; Exodus 39:2-4).
    f. The curious girdle was made of blue, the same material as the ephod (Exodus 28:8; Exodus 39:5).
    g. The breastplate was the high priest's outermost article of dress, and was worn above the ephod to which it was closely bound. It was made of gold wire, blue, purple, scarlet, and fine twined linen, and was two spans long and one span wide; but it was doubled and was therefore square.

    It was fastened at the top by rings and chains of gold to the two onyx stones on the shoulders, and at the bottom to the ephod by a lace of blue, fastened in its rings and the rings of the ephod (Exodus 28:15-29; Exodus 39:8-21). Three rows, of four each, of precious stones in gold settings, were inserted in the breastplate, having engraven on them the names of the twelve sons of Jacob, one on each stone (Exodus 28:16-21; Exodus 39:8-14). The great mystery of the high priest's dress was the Urim and Thummim. In some way not explained in Scripture the Lord communicated to the high priest through the stones of the breastplate (Exodus 28:30; Judges 20:28; 1 Samuel 14:3, 18, 19; 1 Samuel 23:2, 3, 11, 12).

  h. The mitre was the high priest's head dress and was made of fine linen. A plate of gold with the words "Holiness to the Lord" inscribed on it, was fastened with a blue ribbon to the forefront of the mitre (Exodus 28:36-38; Exodus 39:30, 31).

7. **Stones of the Breastplate**.

8. *Representative of the twelve "Sons of Jacob"*

9. Twelve "Tribes of Israel"

10. | Carbuncle | Topaz | Sardius

11. | Zebulon | Issachar | Judah

12. | Fire-red | Golden tinge | Blood-red

13. | Diamond | Sapphire | Emerald

14. | Gad | Simeon | Reuben

15. | Sky-blue | Shining-green |

16. | Amethyst | Agate | Ligure

17. | Benjamin | Manasseh | Ephraim

18. | Violet-blue| Diverse colors

19. | Jasper | Onyx | Beryl

20. | Naphtali | Dan | Asher

21. | Dark-red | Sea-green | Deep golden

22. *Terms of Office.* All the priests continued in office from the time of their consecration until their death (Hebrews 7:23, 28). The firstborn of Aaron's

family in regular succession was the high priest, and to him the holy garments descended by Divine requirement (Exodus 29:29 Numbers 20:20-29).

23. *Appellation of the High Priest.* The high priest was known as the anointed priest (Leviticus 4:3-16; Psalms 133:1-3). At the consecration of Aaron and his sons the anointing oil was poured profusely upon Aaron's head (Leviticus 8:12). He was also anointed with blood and oil combined, while the other priests were only anointed with the blood and oil (Leviticus 8:30).

24. *Personal Duties of the High Priest.* The high priest was required to lead a life of sobriety, marry and live according to the requirements of the laws of God (Leviticus 10:8-11; Leviticus 21:1-12).

25. *Qualifications Necessary to the Priestly Office.* Every priest was required to prove his descent from Aaron, but only those who were without physical imperfections were eligible to the office (Leviticus 21:16-24).

26. *Representative Character of the High Priest.* The high priest represented the entire nation, hence he bore upon his shoulders and his breast the names of all the tribes of Israel (Exodus 28:9-21).

27. *Duties of the Priests, Aaron's Sons.* The priests, Aaron's sons, officiated at the brazen altar and in the holy place from day to day (Leviticus 1:1-17; Hebrews 9:6).

28. *Public Duties of the High Priest.* The high priest was required to attend to the golden candlestick, burn incense morning and evening (Exodus 30:1-10), and stand before the ark of the covenant and make atonement for the children of Israel once every year (Leviticus 16:1-34 Hebrews 10:9). He was also required to teach the people the law of God (Leviticus 10:8-11; Deuteronomy 17:8-13).

29. *Blessing the People.* It was the high priest's duty to bless the people. The occasions on which he was to do this are not specified, but we may reasonably suppose that it was at the national festivities (Leviticus 9:22-24). The form of the blessing is given and is superlatively grand. He called upon the Lord to bless and keep them, to make his face shine upon them, and be gracious unto them; to lift His countenance upon them, and give them peace (Numbers 6:22-27).

4. *Priests as Types;*

   a. The priests were types of Christians (Exodus 29:38-42; Romans 12:1; Hebrews 10:5-7).

b. The high priest was a type of Jesus Christ (Leviticus 16:1-34; Hebrews 10:7-14).

30. *Support of the Priesthood.* The priests derived their living from:

a. One-tenth of the tithes which the people paid to the Levites (Numbers 18:26-28);
b. a special tithe every third year (Deuteronomy 14:28;; Deuteronomy 26:12);
c. redemption money (Numbers 18:14-19);
d. redemption money of things specially devoted to the Lord (Leviticus 27:1-34);
e. spoils of war (Numbers 31:25-47);
f. showbread and parts of certain offerings (Leviticus 6:25-30; Leviticus 7:6-10; Numbers 18:8-14);
g. an undefined amount of the first fruits of corn, wine and oil (Exodus 23:19; Leviticus 2:14; Deuteronomy 26:1-10);
h. on their settlement in Canaan they were given thirteen cities, with pasture grounds of their flocks (Joshua 21:13-19).

THE SPIRIT OF CARNAL PRIDE AND SELF-SUFFICIENCY
"Based on Ezekiel 28"
"Critical and Explanatory Information of Ezekiel 28"

1. Ezekiel 28:1-26. PROPHETICAL DIRGE ON THE KING OF TYRE, AS THE CULMINATION AND EMBODIMENT OF THE SPIRIT OF CARNAL PRIDE AND SELF-SUFFICIENCY OF THE WHOLE STATE. THE FALL OF ZIDON, THE MOTHER CITY. THE RESTORATION OF ISRAEL IN CONTRAST WITH TYRE AND ZIDON. **2. Because,** and repeated in Ezekiel 28:6. The apodosis begins at Ezekiel 28:7. "The prince of Tyrus" at the time was Ithobal, or Ithbaal II; the name implying his close connection with Baal, the Phoenician supreme god, whose representative he was.

I am a god, I sit in the. . . seat of God . . . the seas—as God sits enthroned in His heavenly citadel exempt from all injury, so I sit secure in my impregnable stronghold amidst the stormiest elements, able to control them at will, and make them subserve my interests. The language, though primarily here applied to the king of Tyre, as similar language is to the king of Babylon (Isaiah 14:13,14), yet has an ulterior and fuller accomplishment in Satan and his embodiment in Antichrist (Daniel 7:25, 11:36, 37, 2 Thessalonians 2:4, Revelation 13:6). This feeling of superhuman elevation in the king of Tyre was fostered by the fact that the island on which Tyre stood was called "the holy island" [SANCONIATHON], being sacred to Hercules, so much so that the colonies looked up to Tyre as the mother city of their religion, as well as of their political existence. The Hebrew for "God" is El, that is, "the Mighty One."

Thou thinkest of thyself as if thou wert God.

3. Ezekiel ironically eludes to Ithbaal's overweening opinion of the wisdom of himself and the Tyrians, as though superior to that of Daniel, whose fame had reached even Tyre as eclipsing the Chaldean ages. "Thou art wiser," namely, in thine own opinion (Zechariah 9:2).

4. **No secret**—namely, forgetting riches (Ezekiel 28:4), **that they can hide**—that is, that can be hidden.

5. (Psalms 62:10).

6. **Because,** and resumptive of Ezekiel 28:2.

7. **Therefore terrible of the nations**—the Chaldean foreigners noted for their ferocity (Ezekiel 30:11, 31:12), **against the beauty of thy wisdom**—that is, against thy beautiful possessions acquired by thy wisdom on which thou pridest thyself (Ezekiel 28:3-5), **defile thy brightness**—obscure the brightness of thy kingdom.

8. **The pit**—that is, the bottom of the sea; the image being that of one conquered in a sea-fight,

the deaths—plural, as various kinds of deaths are meant (Jeremiah 16:4),

of them . . . slain—literally, "pierced through." Such deaths as those pierced with many wounds die.

9. **Yet say**—that is, still say; referring to Ezekiel 28:2.

But thy blasphemous boastings shall be falsified, and thou shalt be shown to be but man, and not God, in the hand (at the mercy) of Him.

10. **Deaths of . . . uncircumcised**—that is, such a death as the uncircumcised or godless heathen deserve; and perhaps, also, such as the uncircumcised inflict, a great ignominy in the eyes of a Jew (1 Samuel 31:4); a fit retribution on him who had scoffed at the circumcised Jews.

11. **Sealest up the sum**—literally, "Thou art the one sealing the sum of perfection." A thing is sealed when completed (Daniel 9:24). "The sum" implies the full measure of beauty, from a Hebrew root, "to measure." The normal man—one formed after accurate rule.

12. **In Eden**—The king of Tyre is represented in his former high state (contrasted with his subsequent downfall), under images drawn from the primeval man in Eden, the type of humanity in its most Godlike form.

13. **Garden of God**—the model of ideal loveliness (Ezekiel 31:8, 9, 36:35). In the person of the king of Tyre a new trial was made of humanity with the greatest earthly advantages. But as in the case of Adam, the good gifts of God were only turned into ministers to pride and self.

14. **Every precious stone**—so in Eden (Genesis 2:12), "gold, bdellium, and the onyx stone." So the king of Tyre was arrayed in jewel-bespangled robes after the fashion of Oriental monarchs. The nine precious stones here mentioned

answer to nine of the twelve (representing the twelve tribes) in the high priest's breastplate (Exodus 39:10-13, Revelation 21:14, 19-21).

There is an ulterior reference to Antichrist, who is blasphemously to arrogate the office of our divine High Priest (Zechariah 6:13). Here are relative instruments and key descriptions for this subject matter:

Tabrets—tambourines.

Pipes—literally, "holes" in musical pipes or flutes.

Created—that is, in the day of thine accession to the throne. Tambourines and all the marks of joy were ready prepared for thee ("in thee," that is, "with and for thee"). Thou hadst not, like others, to work thy way to the throne through arduous struggles. No sooner created than, like Adam, thou wast surrounded with the gratifications of Eden. Fairburn, for "pipes," translates, "females" (having reference to Genesis 1:27), that is, musician-women. Maurer, explains the Hebrew not as to music, but as to the setting and mounting of the gems previously mentioned.

15. Anointed cherub—Gensenius, translates from an Aramaic root, "extended cherub." English Version, from a Hebrew root, is better. "The cherub consecrated to the Lord by the anointing oil."

Covereth—The imagery employed by Ezekiel as a priest is from the Jewish temple, wherein the cherubim overshadowed the mercy seat, as the king of Tyre, a demi-god in his own esteem, extended his protection over the interests of Tyre.

The cherub—an ideal compound of the highest kinds of animal existence and the type of redeemed man in his ultimate state of perfection—is made the image of the king of Tyre, as if the beau ideal of humanity. The pretensions of Antichrist are the ulterior reference, of whom the king of Tyre is a type. Compare "As God . . . in the temple of God" (2 Thessalonians 2:4).

I have set thee—not thou set thyself (Proverbs 8:16, Romans 13:1), **upon the holy mountain of God**—Zion, following up the image.

In midst of . . . the stones of fire—In ambitious imagination he stood in the place of God, "under whose feet was, as it were, a pavement of sapphire," while His glory was like "devouring fire" (Exodus 24:10, 17).

16. Perfect—prosperous; "Grotius," and having no defect. So Hiram was a sample of the Tyrian monarch in his early days of wisdom and prosperity (1 Kings 5:7), **till iniquity . . . found in thee**—Like the primeval man thou hast fallen by abusing God's gifts, and so hast provoked God's wrath.

17. Filled the midst of thee—that is, they have filled the midst of the city; he as the head of the state being involved in the guilt of the state, which he did not check, but fostered.

Cast thee as profane—no longer treated as sacred, but driven out of the place of sanctity (see Ezekiel 28:14) which thou hast occupied (compare Psalms 89:39).

18. Brightness—thy splendor. **Lay thee before kings**—as an example of God's wrath against presumptuous pride.

19. Thy sanctuaries—that is, the holy places, attributed to the king of Tyre in Ezekiel 28:14, as his ideal position. As he "profaned" it, so God will "profane" him (Ezekiel 28:16).

Fire . . . devour—As he abused his supposed elevation amidst "the stones of fire" (Ezekiel 28:16), so God will make His "fire" to "devour" him.

20. Zidon—famous for its fishery (from a root, *Zud,* "to fish"); and afterwards for its wide extended commerce; its artistic elegance was proverbial. Founded by Canaan's first-born (Genesis 10:15). Tyre was an offshoot from it, so that it was involved in the same overthrow by the Chaldeans as Tyre. It is mentioned separately, because its idolatry (Ashtaroth, Tammuz, or Adonis) infected Israel more than that of Tyre did (Ezekiel 8:14, Judges 10:6, 1 Kings 11:33). The notorious Jezebel was a daughter of the Zidonian king.

21. Shall be sanctified in her—when all nations shall see that I am the Holy Judge in the vengeance that I will inflict on her for sin.

22. No more . . . brier . . . unto . . . Israel—as the idolatrous nations left in Canaan (among which Zidon is expressly specified in the limits of Asher, Judges 1:31) had been (Numbers 33:55, Joshua 23:13). "A brier," first ensnaring the Israelites in sin, and then being made the instrument of punishing them.

Pricking—literally, "causing *bitterness.*" The same *Hebrew* is translated "fretting" (Leviticus 13:51, 52). The wicked are often called "thorns" (2 Samuel 23:6).

23. Fulfilled in part at the restoration from Babylon, when Judaism, so far from being merged in heathenism, made inroads by conversions on the idolatry of surrounding nations. The full accomplishment is yet future, when Israel, under Christ, shall be the center of Christendom; of which an earnest was given in the woman from the coasts of Tyre and Sidon who sought the Saviour (Matthew 15:21, 24, 26-28; compare Isaiah 11:12).

24. Dwell safely—(Jeremiah 23:6). *I know you're wondering why so much emphasis on King Tyre or this spirit? It's because my brothers and sisters, it is a **spirit that's flowing** through the land with our **priests** and **musicians**. We must be so very careful how we carry the **"beauty"** of God's **gifts** and **anointing**. Somehow we have begun to act as if the gifts are ours. People flock to us like **stars** and are running to hear a **word** or a **beat** while looking to us more than they're looking to the one who gave the gifts and anointing. Another problem is, we're allowing people to **give us glory!** Be very careful! These gifts and talents do not belong to us, and we must watch how we handle what actually **belongs to God**, he just made us stewards of these things. Even the **angelic messengers** sent by God in scripture made very sure that when men tried to bow down to them, they swiftly spoke out and said, **"see thou do it not."** Even the angels with all their power and authority to do God's will, understood that the glory belongs to God! Do you?*

COMENTARY ON CHRISTS' SUPERIOR PRIESTHOOD
"Based on Hebrews 5: 1-16"
"Knowledge of God and the Perpetual Priesthood of Christ"

Paul speaks to the Hebrews about their lack of knowledge and digging into scripture to understand the priesthood of Christ.

In this chapter the apostle begins his discourse upon the priesthood of Christ, a sweet subject, which he would not too soon dismiss. And here, I. *He explains the nature of the priestly office in general (v. 1-3). II. The proper and regular call there must be to this office (v. 4-6). III. The requisite qualifications for the work (v. 7-9). IV. The peculiar order of the priesthood of Christ; it was not after the order of Aaron, but of Melchisedec (v. 6, 7, 10). V. He reproves the Hebrews, that they* **had not made those improvements in knowledge** *which might have made them capable of looking into the more abstruse and mysterious parts of scripture (v. 11–14).*

Verses 1-9, we have here an account of the nature of the priestly office in general, though with an accommodation to the Lord Jesus Christ. We are told, I. Of what kind of beings the high priest must be. He must be taken from among men; he must be a man, one of ourselves, bone of our bones, flesh of our flesh, and spirit of our spirits, a partaker of our nature, and a standard-bearer among ten thousand.

This implies, 1. That man had sinned. 2. That God would not admit sinful man to come to Him alone without a high priest, who must be taken from among men. 3. That God was pleased to take one from among men, by whom they might approach God in hope, and He might receive them with honour. 4. That every one shall be welcome to God that comes to Him by the priest.

II. For whom every high priest is ordained: *For men in things pertaining to God,* for the glory of God and the good of men, that he come between God and man. So Christ did; and therefore let us never attempt to go to God but through Christ, nor expect any favour from God but through Christ. III. For what purpose every high priest was ordained: *That he might offer both gifts and sacrifices for sin.* 1. That he might offer gifts or free-will offerings, brought to the high priest, so offered for the glory of God, and as an acknowledgment that our all is of Him and from Him; we have nothing but what He is pleased to give us, and of His own we offer to Him an oblation of acknowledgment. This intimates, (1.) That all we bring to God must be free and not forced; it must be a gift; it must be given and not taken away again. (2.) That all we bring to God must go through the high priest's hands, as the great agent between God and man. 2. That he might offer sacrifices for sin; that is, the offerings that were appointed to make atonement, that sin might be pardoned and sinners accepted. Thus Christ is constituted a high priest for both these ends. Our good deeds must be presented by Christ, to render ourselves and them acceptable; and our evil deeds must be expiated by the sacrifice of Himself, that they may not condemn and destroy us.

And now, as we value acceptance with God and pardon, we must apply ourselves by faith to this our great high priest. IV. How this high priest must be qualified, v. 2. 1. He must be one that can have compassion on two sorts of persons:—(1.) *On the ignorant,* or those that are guilty of sins of ignorance. He must be one who can find in his heart to pity them, and intercede with God for them, one that is willing to instruct those that are dull of understanding. (2.) *On those that are out of the way,* out of the way of truth, duty, and happiness; and he must be one who has tenderness enough to lead them back from the by-paths of error, sin, and misery, into the right way: this will require great patience and compassion, even the compassion of God. 2. He must also be compassed with infirmity; and so be able from himself feelingly to consider our frame, and to sympathize with us. Thus Christ was qualified. He took upon Him our sinful infirmities; and this gives us great encouragement to apply ourselves to Him under every affliction; for in all the afflictions of His people He is afflicted. V. How the high priest was to be called of God.

He must have both an internal and external call to his office: *For no man taketh this honour to himself* (v. 4), that is, no man ought to do it, no man can do it legally; if any does it, he must be reckoned a usurper, and treated accordingly. Here observe, 1. The office of the priesthood was a very great honour. To be employed to stand between God and man, one while representing God and His will to men, at another time representing man and his case to God, and dealing between them about matters of the highest importance.

Entrusted on both sides with the honour of God and the happiness of man must render the office very honourable. 2. The priesthood is an office and honour that no man ought to take to himself; if he does, he can expect no success in it, nor any reward for it, only from himself. He is an intruder who is not called of God, as was Aaron. Observe, (1.) God is the fountain of all honour, especially true spiritual honor. He is the fountain of true authority, whether he calls any to the priesthood in an extraordinary way, as he did Aaron, or in an ordinary way, with successors. (2.) Those only can expect assistance from God, and acceptance with Him, and His presence and blessing on them and their administrations, that are called of God; others may expect a blast instead of a blessing. VI. How this is brought home and applied to Christ: *So Christ glorified not himself,* v. 5. Observe here, Though Christ reckoned it His glory to be made a high priest, yet He would not assume that glory to Himself. He could truly say, *I seek not my own glory,* John 8:50. Considered as God, He was not capable of any additional glory, but as man and Mediator He did not run without being sent; and, if He did not, surely others should be afraid to do it. VII. The apostle prefers Christ before Aaron, both in the manner of his call and in the holiness of his person. 1. In the manner of his call, in which God said unto him, *Thou art my Son, this day have I begotten thee* (quoted from Psalm 2:7), referring to His eternal generation as God, his wonderful conception as man, and His perfect qualification as Mediator. Thus God solemnly declared His dear affection to Christ, His authoritative appointment of Him to office of Mediator.

His installment and approbation of Him in that office, His acceptance of Him, and of all He had done or should do in the discharge of it. God never said thus to Aaron. Another expression that God used in the call of Christ we have in Psalms 110:4, *Thou art a priest for ever, after the order of Melchisedec*, v. 6. God the Father appointed Him a priest of a higher order than that of Aaron. The priesthood of Aaron was to be but temporary; the priesthood of Christ was to be perpetual: the priesthood of Aaron was to be successive, descending from the fathers to the children; the priesthood of Christ, after the order of Melchisedec, was to be personal, and the high priest immortal as to His office, without descent, having neither beginning of days nor end of life, as it is more largely described in the 7th chapter, and will be opened there. 2. Christ is here preferred to Aaron in the holiness of his person. Other priests were to offer up sacrifices, as for the *sins of others, so for themselves*, v. 3. But Christ needed not to offer for sins for Himself, *for He had done no violence*, neither was there *any deceit in His mouth*, Isaiah 53:9. And such a high priest became us. VIII. We have an account of Christ's discharge of this His office, and of the consequences of that discharge, v. 7-9. 1. The discharge of His office of the priesthood (v. 7): *Who in the days of his flesh, when he had offered up prayers and supplications, etc.* Here observe, (1.) He took to Him flesh, and for some days tabernacled therein; He became a mortal man, and reckoned His life by days, herein setting us an example how we should reckon ours.

Were we to reckon our lives by days, it would be a means to quicken us to do the work of every day in its day. (2.) Christ, in the days of His flesh, subjected Himself to death; He hungered, He was a tempted, bleeding, dying Jesus! His body is now in heaven, but it is a spiritual glorious body. (3.) God the Father was able to save Him from death. He could have prevented His dying, but He would not; for then the great design of His wisdom and grace must have been defeated. What would have become of us if God had saved Christ from dying? The Jews reproachfully said, *Let him deliver him now, if he will have him,* Matthew 27:43. But it was in kindness to us that the Father would not suffer that bitter cup to pass away from Him; for then we must have drunk the dregs of it, and been miserable for ever. (4.) Christ, in the days of His flesh, offered up prayers and supplications to His Father, as an earnest of His intercession in heaven. A great many instances we have of Christ's praying. This refers to His prayer in His agony (Matthew 26:39, and ch. 27:46), and to that before His agony (John 17) which He put up for His disciples, and all who should believe on His name. (5.) The prayers and supplications that Christ offered up were joined with strong cries and tears, herein setting us an example not only to pray, but to be fervent and importunate in prayer. How many dry prayers, how few wet ones, do we offer up to God! (6.) Christ was heard in that He feared. How? He was answered by present supports in and under His agonies, and in being carried well through death, and delivered from it by a glorious resurrection: He *was heard in that he feared.*

He had an awful sense of the wrath of God, of the weight of sin. His human nature was ready to sink under the heavy load, and would have sunk, had He been quite forsaken in point of help and comfort from God; but He was heard in this, He was supported under the agonies of death. He was carried through death; and there is no real deliverance from death but to be carried well through it. We may have many recoveries from sickness, but we are never saved from death till we are carried well through it. And those that are thus saved from death will be fully delivered at last by a glorious resurrection, of which the resurrection of Christ was the earnest and first-fruits. 2. The consequences of this discharge of His office, v. 8, 9, etc. (1.) By these His sufferings *he learned obedience, though he was a Son,* v. 8. Here observe, [1.] The privilege of Christ: *He was a Son;* the only-begotten of the Father. One would have thought this might have exempted him from suffering, but it did not. Let none then who are the children of God by adoption expect an absolute freedom from suffering. *What Son is he whom the Father chasteneth not?* [2.] Christ made improvement by His sufferings. By His passive obedience, He learned active obedience; that is, He practiced that great lesson, and made it appear that He was well and perfectly learned in it; though He never was disobedient, yet He never performed such an act of obedience as when He became obedient to death, even to the death of the cross. Here He has left us an example, that we should learn by all our afflictions a humble obedience to the will of God.

We need affliction, to teach us submission. (2.) By these His sufferings He was made perfect, and became the author of eternal salvation to all who obey Him, v. 9. [1.] Christ by His sufferings was consecrated to His office, consecrated by His own blood. [2.] By His sufferings He consummated that part of His office which was to be performed on earth, making reconciliation for iniquity; and in this sense He is said to be *made perfect,* a perfect propitiation. [3.] Hereby He has become the author of eternal salvation to men; He has by His sufferings purchased a full deliverance from sin and misery, and a full fruition of holiness and happiness for His people. Of this salvation He has given notice in the gospel; He has made a tender of it in the new covenant, and has sent the Spirit to enable men to accept this salvation. [4.] This salvation is actually bestowed on none but those who obey Christ. It is not sufficient that we have some doctrinal knowledge of Christ, or that we make a profession of faith in Him, but we must hearken to His word, and obey Him. He is exalted to be a prince to rule us, as well as a Saviour to deliver us; and He will be a Saviour to none but to those whom He is a prince, and who are willing that He should reign over them; the rest He will account His enemies, and treat them accordingly. But to those who obey Him, devoting themselves to Him, denying themselves, and taking up their cross, and following Him, He will be the author, *aitios* —the grand cause of their salvation, and they shall own Him as such for ever.

Verses 10-14 Here the apostle returns to what He had in v. 6 cited out of Psalms 110, concerning the peculiar order of the priesthood of Christ, that is, the order of Melchisedec. And here, I. He declares He had many things which He could say to them concerning this mysterious person called Melchisedec, whose priesthood was eternal, and therefore the salvation procured thereby should be eternal also. We have a more particular account of this Melchisedec in ch. 7.

Some think the things which the apostle means, that were hard to be uttered, were not so much concerning Melchisedec himself as concerning Christ, of whom Melchisedec was the type.

And doubtless this apostle had many things to say concerning Christ that were very mysterious, hard to be uttered; there are great mysteries in the person and offices of the Redeemer; Christianity is the great mystery of godliness. II. He assigns the reason why he did not say all those things concerning Christ, our Melchisedec, that he had to say, and what it was that made it so difficult for him to utter them, namely, the dullness of the Hebrews to whom he wrote: *You are dull of hearing.* There is a difficulty in the things themselves, and there may be a weakness in the ministers of the gospel to speak clearly about these things; but generally the fault is in the hearers. Dull hearers make the preaching of the gospel a difficult thing, and even many who have some faith are but dull hearers, dull of understanding and slow to believe; the understanding is weak, and does not apprehend these spiritual things; the memory is weak, and does not retain them. III. He insists upon the faultiness of this infirmity of theirs.

It was not a mere natural infirmity, but it was a sinful infirmity, and more in them than others, by reason of the singular advantages they had enjoyed for improving in the knowledge of Christ: *For when, for the time, you ought to be teachers, you have need that one teach you again which are the first principles of the oracles of God,* v. 12. Here observe, 1. What proficiency might have been reasonably expected from these Hebrews—that they might have been so well instructed in the doctrine of the gospel as to have been teachers of others. Hence learn, (1.) God takes notice of the time and helps we have for gaining scripture-knowledge. (2.) From those to whom much is given much is expected. (3.) Those who have a good understanding in the gospel should be teachers of others, if not in a public, yet in a private station. (4.) None should take upon them to be teachers of others, but those who have made a good improvement in spiritual knowledge themselves. 2. Observe the sad disappointment of those just expectations: *You have need that one should teach you again,* etc. Here note, (1.) In the oracles of God there are some first principles, plain to be understood and necessary to be learned. (2.) There are also deep and sublime mysteries, which those should search into who have learned the first principles, that so they may be complete in the will of God. (3.) Some persons, instead of going forward in

Christian knowledge, forget the first principles they had learned long ago; and indeed those that are not improving under the means of grace will be losing. (4.) It is a sin and shame for persons that are men for their age and standing in the church to be children and babes in understanding.

IV. The apostle shows how the various doctrines of the gospel must be dispensed to different persons. There are in the church babes and persons of full age (v. 12–14), and there are in the gospel milk and strong meat. Observe, 1. Those that are babes, unskillful in the word of righteousness, must be fed with milk; they must be nourished with the plainest truths, and these delivered in the plainest manner; *there must be line upon line, precept upon precept, here a little, and there a little,* Isaiah 28:10. Christ despises not His babes; He has provided suitable food for them. It is good to be babes in Christ, but not always to continue in that childish state; we should endeavor to pass the infant state; we should always remain in malice children, but in understanding, grow to a manly maturity. 2. The deeper mysteries of religion belong to those that are of a higher class in the school of Christ, who have learned the first principles and well improved them; *so that by reason of use they have their senses exercised to discern both good and evil, duty and sin, truth and error.* Observe, (1.) There have been always in the Christian state children, young men, and fathers. (2.) Every true Christian, having received a principle of spiritual life from God, stands in need of nourishment to preserve that life. (3.) The Word of God is food and nourishment to the life of grace: *As new-born babes desire the sincere milk of the word that you may grow thereby.* (4.) It is the wisdom of ministers rightly to divide the word of truth, and to give to every one his portion-milk to babes, and strong meat to those of full age. (5.) There are spiritual senses as well as those that are natural.

There is a spiritual eye, a spiritual appetite, a spiritual taste; the soul has its sensations as well as the body; these are much depraved and lost by sin, but they are recovered by grace. (6.) It is by use and exercise that these senses are improved, made more quick and strong to taste the sweetness of what is good and true, and the bitterness of what is false and evil. Not only reason and faith, but spiritual sense, will teach men to distinguish between what is pleasing and what is provoking to God, between what is helpful and what is hurtful to our own souls.

STUDY GUIDE TO KNOW YOUR GOD

"*In this guide there are areas of study that will help sharpen your skills as a minister of Christ and Levite that is called of God to reach the lost. Now we can't assume that when we minister in whatever capacity, that our audience is ignorant or unlearned. When the Jehovah's Witness or other groups go out, even though they are in error, they usually know about the things they are about to tell you. Now they get hung up when they run into one of us who "KNOW" Gods Word. So study and know about the faith you're in. There are many study helps available to learn from. God will lead you in what to read and what to avoid. Know your gifts or callings, wait on your ministry. Know about the instrument you play, practice on it and become skillful, understand Hermeneutic and Homiletics and be aware how to go in and out among God's people, know about the God you serve and how you can be the most effective minister possible. The world is waiting on you; they're waiting on the manifestation of your ministry so "Minister the them!"*

Here are a few subjects to study:

Ministry, Minister

It is reasonably clear in Scripture that (1) ministry means the service of God and his creatures; (2) the one essential ministry is that of Jesus Christ; (3) the whole membership of the old and the new Israel is called to share in ministerial service, of which there are many forms; and (4) certain persons in both the old and the new Israel are set apart for special ministry, within the total ministry.

The Old Testament. There are three distinct ministries in the Old Testament: the prophetic, the priestly, and the kingly.

All three are essential within the covenantal relation between Yahweh and Israel. However, more basic than these three is that the whole people, Israel are the ministers of God. The election and call of Israel is the foundation of the service of Israel to God. Nowhere is this made clearer than in Isaiah 40-66, where the missionary calling of the people of God is made explicitly clear. Much earlier the people had been told that they were "a kingdom of priests and a holy nation" (Exodus 19:6). Thus, in a basic sense every person, male and female, insofar as he or she is a member of Israel is a minister/servant of Yahweh; so the whole of life has a God-ward dimension (as the Law makes very clear).

The service rendered by prophet, priest, and king was that of maintaining the personal relation between Israel (the bride) and Yahweh (the Bridegroom) required by the covenant. Within this relation of grace there was need of a minister of God who would speak for him to the people (thus the prophet Isaiah 6:8; 50:4); of a minister to stand before God to teach the people, lead in worship, and offer sacrifice on their behalf (on many occasions priests and Levites are called,

Ministers — e.g., Exod 30:20; and of a king to express the sovereignty and kingship of Yahweh unto and within Israel and to show that the sacred and secular realms belong together. *The New Testament.* Each of these ministries comes to fulfillment in Jesus Christ, who is himself the Prophet, Priest, and King. At the same time, the corporate ministry of Israel as a people finds fulfillment first in Jesus Christ as the new Israel and then in his body, the church. *Christ in His Church.* Jesus Christ came not to be ministered to but to minister (Matt 20:28). In his life and particularly in his death, Jesus fulfilled the prophecy of the Messiah as the Suffering Servant of Yahweh (Isa 52:13-53:12).

By washing the feet of his disciples he gave an example (John 13:15) of true service; and in the Upper Room he declared, "I am among you as one who serves" (Luke 22:27).

The unique, ministerial servant example of Jesus is beautifully commended by Paul (Philippians 2:5-8) and Peter (1 Peter 2:21-25). The Word Incarnate ministered to people in their deepest need. He entered fully into the pitiful and perverse condition of the human race as it exists before God, sharing its pain and estrangement. He did this in order, by meek and gracious service in doing good and bringing healing and liberation, to bring peace and reconciliation between man and God. The climax of his diaconal, servant ministry was to offer himself as a atonement for sin on the cross of Calvary.

This diaconal ministry of Jesus Christ continued after his exaltation into heaven. As the Head of the church, which is his body, he continually ministers to and through his members as their King, Priest, and Prophet. He rules and guides, prays and intercedes, proclaims and teaches, loves and rejoices for, in, and through them. The whole church is a holy priesthood and a chosen race, a royal priesthood, God's own people (1 Peter 2:5, 9). In union with Christ, his body shares in his priestly, kingly, and prophetic work. The whole point of Paul's argument in both Romans 12 and 1 Corinthians 12 is that each and every member of the church has a part to play in the service of God. By three basic words—*doulos* [dou'lo], *leitourgos* [leitourgov], *diakonos* [diavkono]—the call to serve God in Christ is made clear. Christians are to be slaves and servants of Jesus Christ.

They were bought from slavery to Satan, sin, and death by a great price (1 Cor 6:19-20; 1 Peter 1:18-19) and now they are slaves of Jesus Christ (Rev 1:1; 1 Peter 2:16) who are to serve righteousness in Christ (Rom 6:15-16). These Christian ministers were made bondservants (*doulos* [dou'lo] of Jesus Christ.

There exists within the church, by God's will, a universal duty and right of service; however, with this there also exists the greatest possible differentiation of forms and functions of service. *Ministries in the Church.* The ways of serving the Lord in his church are many and varied. These types overlap and members of the body will partake of more than one type.

There is ministry of the Word in evangelism, founding and guiding churches *(apostles, prophets, evangelists, teachers, etc.)*; ministry of healing *(workers of miracles, gifts of healing, etc.)*; ministry of leadership/administration *(helpers, administrators, etc.)*; and ministry to the congregation (tongues, interpretation of tongues, etc.).

Apostles. While it is important to recognize the whole ministry of the whole body, the place of the original apostles is unique (Rev 21:14). The Twelve were chosen, appointed, ordained, and sent by Jesus Christ himself. Matthias replaced Judas among the Twelve (Acts 1), and Paul became the apostle to the Gentiles through a gift of the Spirit given by the exalted Lord (Acts 9). So in a vital sense their ministry is that ministry which is necessary for the full ministry of the whole body. They are eyewitnesses of the resurrection and/or exaltation of Christ and they are the living foundations on which the church is built. It is their testimony that is the basis of the books of the New Testament. They were the gift of God to the church in its infancy and are irreplaceable.

Local Leadership. Apart from the apostles, prophets, and evangelists, we read of elders/presbyters, bishops, and deacons, who were settled in local congregations.

They facilitated the ministry of the whole church by being servants of Jesus Christ.

Elder/presbyter *presbuteros* [presbuvtero"] was the equivalent in the Christian congregation of the elder in the synagogue, with duties of oversight, supervision, and leadership.

(Acts 15:2; 20:17; 21:18; 1 Tim 3:1-7; 5:17; Titus 1:5-9; Heb 13:17). Therefore, in terms of what he did the elder was sometimes called the bishop or overseer (*episcopos*). That the elder is the bishop seems to be the natural meaning of Acts 20:17, 28; Philippians 1:1; 1 Timothy 3:4-5; 5:17-19; Titus 1:5-7; 1 Peter 5:2 (KJV). Apparently the elder was set in office by an act of ordination, but there are only minimal details of this in the New Testament (e.g., 1 Thess 4:14; 5:22; 2 Tim 1:6).

Within a short time of the apostolic age, when the church was separated from the synagogue, the distinction between the bishop and the presbyter (priest) developed. In the New Testament period the real distinction was among the itinerant apostles, evangelists, and prophets and the settled presbyters and deacons.

Diakonia [diakoniva] simply means "ministry" and "service" and so has reference to Christ and to all his servants. The noun *diakonos* [diavkono"] is often applied to the seven men who were set apart by prayer and the laying on of hands and appointed to serve tables by the apostles (Acts 6:1-6). Yet they are not called deacons. However, deacons are mentioned in Philippians 1:1 and in 1Timothy 3:8-13. Phoebe is called a deacon in Romans 16:1.

While the presbyterate may be said to originate within the synagogue, this cannot be said of the deaconate.

There is no parallel to it in Judaism. The main tasks of deacons, who were to be of sound character and with a firm hold on the faith, were administrative and financial.

Summary. Whether in the Old or New Testaments, ministry finds its meaning and expression in Jesus Christ. He is the Minister par excellence and the only source of ministry. The Old Testament looks forward to him while the New Testament looks both, up, and forward to him. In relation to Christ every member of Israel or the church has a ministry of serving the Lord by proclaiming the Word of God by word and deed both inside and outside the people of God.

In this sense all are royal priests. Further, in relation to Christ there are specific or particular forms of ministry within and for the sake of the church in its mission for God in his world. These are given only to a few and they include the callings of prophet, priest, and king in the Old Covenant and apostle, evangelist, presbyter, and deacon in the New Covenant. Though not strictly a biblical expression *"ordained ministry"* refers to persons who have received a gift of the Spirit and have been appointed by the church, through prayer and the laying on of hands, to specific offices within the church.

Peter Toon

Servant, Service

The words "servant," "service," and "serve," in various forms, occurs well over 1,100 times in the New International Version. People are servants of other human beings or servants of God. In the Old Testament, the Hebrew word for servant, *ebed*, contains at least two key ingredients: action (the servant as "worker") and obedience. Servants belonged to other people (Gen 24:35; Exod 21:21), and performed a variety of work.

Many persons in the Old Testament are called "servants," among them Abraham (Gen 26:24), Jacob (Gen 32:4), Joshua (Jos 24:29), Ruth (Ru 3:9), Hannah (1 Sam 1:11), Samuel (1 Sam 3:9), Jesse (1 Sam 17:58), Uriah the

Hittite (2 Sam 11:21), Joab (2 Sam 14:20), Isaiah (Isa 20:3), Daniel (Da 9:17), Ben-Hadad of Aram (1 Kings 20:32), and Nebuchadnezzar of Babylon (Jer 25:9). Moses is designated as such about forty times and David more than fifty.

During New Testament times the synagogue stood alongside the temple as an equivalent religious institution in Judaism. After the destruction of the second temple by the Romans in a.d. 70, the synagogue was considered a full substitute for the temple as the religious institution of Judaism.

Influence on Early Christian Worship. First-century Jewish Christianity rooted in the synagogue tradition had a considerable impact on the development of the early Christian church, specifically in the areas of church architecture, organization, and liturgy.

The influence of synagogue architecture and furnishings on the early Christian church may be seen in the use of the bema or raised platform, including an altar or table (replacing the ark of the Torah in the synagogue) and a pulpit or podium (much like the synagogue lectern used for the Scripture readings and sermon). In addition, seating the worship participants on the platform and arranging the congregation in rows of benches facing the platform are Christian adaptations of synagogue design and practice.

Similarities may also be identified in the functions of the ancient synagogue officers and the officers of the early Christian church.

For example, the Christian office of bishop or overseer combined some of the duties of the head of the synagogue (who presided over the worship service), the minister (who often functioned as the synagogue tutor), and the interpreter (who both translated and explained the Scripture lessons and sermon). The concept of spiritual patriarchs or elders in the synagogue congregation carried over into the early church as well. The first **deacons** of the Christian church were charged with the same commission of the almoners of the ancient Jewish synagogue; gathering and distributing charitable gifts to the needy in the congregation (cf. Acts 6:1-7).

Here are a few words I would like for you to study and get a full understanding of. They will assist you in having a overall scope of understanding. Look these words up in your bible help books, like commentaries, bible dictionaries, concordances and other helps that will give you a full understanding. Use whatever tools you need to obtain your information and gain the understating. I also like to use bible outlines for each book of the bible. It seems to give me a feel of having a overall grasp of the scriptures. Study until you have a understanding of the word, or its history in world and biblical history. Try some of these methods; it will help you understanding of God's word.

I chose words that have everything to do with being a true Levite. You'll find, the not only is the musician or the priest's Levites in the house of God. But all of us play the role of a Levite when you understand their purpose. They have every duty in the house of God.

Get these words in your spirit, heart and mind. This will increase your walk with God, which is real worship. Your everyday lifestyle before God!!!

Words to Study:

Submission:

Obedience:

Humility:

Charity:

Consistency:

Honesty:

Trustworthy:

Fear of God:

Spiritual Authority:

Delegated Authority:

Anointing:

Sacrifice:

Gift vs Talents (their differences of operation):

Accountability:

Pride:

Effects of Disobedience:

Sanctification:

Fasting:

Giving:

Holiness:

After you've done an in-depth study of these words, make yourself a journal of all the information. It will help you in your ministry and in your everyday walk as well.

Studying God's word is not only a vital part of your life, but a mainstay for your ministry. You can't minister a word if you don't know the word.

Master each word you studied, it will serve you well in your ministering. Preparation makes it easier for the anointing to flow not matter what part of the ministry you work in. This will also assist you in your everyday life; your job your home and marriage. Study to show yourselves approved in every area of your life, preparation is key. God will many times speak to you to prepare before He sends you to do a work. Prepare yourself so they when you minister you can prepare the people you're sent to.

Note Pad

Note Pad

Message to the Levites

Note Pad

Message to the Levites

Note Pad

Message to the Levites

Note Pad

Message to the Levites

Note Pad

Message to the Levites

Note Pad

Message to the Levites

Note Pad

Message to the Levites

Note Pad

Message to the Levites

Note Pad

Message to the Levites

Note Pad

Message to the Levites

Note Pad

Message to the Levites

Note Pad

Message to the Levites

Note Pad

Message to the Levites

Note Pad

Message to the Levites

Note Pad

Message to the Levites

Note Pad

Message to the Levites

Note Pad

Message to the Levites

Note Pad

Message to the Levites

Note Pad

The Aaronic Benediction to the Reader

The Lord bless thee and keep thee, the Lord make his face to shine upon thee, and be gracious unto thee: the Lord lift up his countenance upon thee, and give the peace. . . .

PAUL'S CONCLUSION TO THE CHURCH IN ROME

Now to him that is of power to stablish you according to my gospel, and the preaching of Jesus Christ, according to the revelation of the mystery, which was kept secret since the world began,

But now is made manifest, and by the scriptures of the prophets, according to the commandment of the everlasting God, made known to all nations for the obedience of faith: To God only wise, be glory through Jesus Christ for ever.
Amen. kjv

Romans 16:25-27

Bibliography

Bibliography R. de Vaux, *Ancient Israel*; M. Haran, "Temples and Temple Service in Ancient Israel"; C. L. Meyers, *HBD*, pp. 22-25.

Bibliography. B. Childs, "Old Testament Theology in a Canonical Context"; R. E. Clements, *God and Temple*; idem, *Wisdom for a Changing World*; R. H. Gundry, *Soma in Biblical Theology*; M. Haran, *Temples and Temple Service in Ancient Israel*; A. J. Heschel, *Quest for God*; A. F. Kirkpatrick, *The Book of Psalms*; M. E. Isaacs, *An Approach to the Theology of the Epistle to the Hebrews*; G. Josipovici, *The Book of God*; K. Koch, *The Prophets: The Assyrian Period*; C. Koester, *The Dwelling of God*; H. J. Kraus, *The Theology of the Psalms*; J. D. Levenson, *Sinai and Zion*; J. G. McConville, *Law and Theology in Deuteronomy*; W. McKane, *ZAW* 94 (1982): 251-66; D. H. Madvig, *NIDNTT*, 3; R. Mason, *Preaching the Tradition*; C. Meyers, *Ancient Israelite Religion*; R. W. L. Moberly, *The Old Testament of the Old Testament*; J. Neusner, *Wrong Ways and Right Ways in the Study of Formative Judaism*; W. Nowottny, *The Language Poets Use*; D. A. Renwick, *Paul, the Temple, and the Presence of God*; J. Z. Smith, *To Take Place*; W. R. Smith, *The Prophets of Israel and Their Place in History*; idem, *The Religion of the Semites*; J. Soskice, *Metaphor and Religious Language*; N. T. Wright, *The New Testament and the People of God*.

Bibliography. B. Childs, *Old Testament Theology in a Canonical Context*; R. E. Clements, *God and Temple*; idem, *Wisdom for a Changing World*; R. H. Gundry, *Soma in Biblical Theology*; M. Haran, *Temples and Temple Service in Ancient Israel*; A. J. Heschel, *Quest for God*; A. F. Kirkpatrick, *The Book of Psalms*; M. E. Isaacs, *An Approach to the Theology of the Epistle to the Hebrews*; G. Josipovici, *The Book of God*; K. Koch, *The Prophets: The Assyrian Period*; C. Koester, *The Dwelling of God*; H. J. Kraus, *The Theology of the Psalms*; J. D. Levenson, *Sinai and Zion*; J. G. McConville, *Law and Theology in Deuteronomy*; W. McKane, *ZAW* 94 (1982): 251-66; D. H. Madvig, *NIDNTT*, 3; R. Mason, *Preaching the Tradition*; C. Meyers, *Ancient Israelite Religion*; R. W. L. Moberly, *The Old Testament of the Old Testament*; J. Neusner, *Wrong Ways and Right Ways in the Study of Formative Judaism*; W. Nowottny, *The Language Poets*.

"These Are the Garments" A study of the Garments of the High Priest of Israel by Charles W. Slemming. Copyright Mrs. Hylda Slemming, Revised August 1955 First American Edition 1974. This printing 1992. All Rights Reserved.

"So what's the Difference?" Fritz Ridenour © Copyright 1967 by Regal Books. Revised Edition © 1979. All Rights Reserved.

Bibliography. R. E. Brown, *"The Churches the Apostles Left Behind"*; J. D. G. Dunn, *Unity and Diversity in the New Testament*; R. P. McBrien, *Ministry*; L. Morris, *Ministers of God*; E. Schweizer, *Church Order in the New Testament*.

Bibliography. J. Baehr, *NIDNTT*, 3:32-44; A. Cody, *A History of Old Testament Priesthood*; D. Guthrie, *New Testament Theology,* pp. 483-86; M. Haran, *Temples and Temple-Service in Ancient Israel*; R. A. Henshaw, *Female and Male, The Cultic Personnel: The Bible and the Rest of the Ancient Near East*; K. Koch, *"Sha'arei Talmon': Studies in the Bible, Qumran, and the Ancient Near East Presented to Shemaryahu Talmon,* pp. 105-10; J. Gordon McConville, *Law and Theology in Deuteronomy*; W. O. McCready, *ISBE,* 3:960-63; E. Merrill, *Bib Sac* 150 (1993):50-61; W. J. Moulder, *ISBE,* 3:963-65; *ABD,* 4:297-310; J. R. Spencer, *ABD,* 1:1-6; R. de Vaux, *Ancient Israel,* 2:345-405.

Bibliography. J. C. Beker, *Paul the Apostle: The Triumph of God in Life and Thought*; H. Bietenhard, *NIDNTT,* 2:789-800; L. Coenen, *NIDNTT,* 3:291-305; W. D. Davies, *Paul and Rabbinic Judaism*; R. G. Hammerton-Kelly, *Pre-Existence, Wisdom and the Son of Man: A Study of the Idea of Pre-Existence in the New Testament*; H. Küng, *The Church*; G. E. Ladd, *A Theology of the New Testament*; P. S. Minear, *Images of the Church in the New Testament*; R. L. Saucy, *The Church in God's Program*; K. L. Schmidt, *TDNT,* 3:501-36; R. Schnackenburg, *The Church in the New Testament*; A. J. M. Wedderburn, *Baptism and Resurrection: Studies in Pauline Theology against Its Graeco-Roman Background.*

Bibliography. *ABD* 6:973-79; M. J. Dawn, *Keeping the Sabbath Wholly: Ceasing, Resting, Embracing, Feasting*; W. Dyrness, *Themes in Old Testament Theology*; M. Eliade, *The Sacred and the Profane*; C. D. Erickson, *Participating in Worship: History, Theory, and Practice*; A. J. Heschel, *The Sabbath: Its Meaning for Modern Man*; A. E. Hill, *Enter His Courts with Praise!*; C. Jones, G. Wainwright, and E. Yarnold, *The Study of Liturgy*; R. P. Martin, *Worship in the Early Church*; A. Millgram, *Jewish Worship*; W. O. E. Oesterley, *The Jewish Background of Christian Liturgy*; D. Peterson, *Engaging with God: A Biblical Theology of Worship*; R. N. Schaper, *In His Presence*; M. H. Shepherd, *The Psalms for Christian Worship: A Practical Guide*; A. W. Tozer, *The Best of A. W. Tozer*; R. deVaux, *Ancient Israel: Religious Institutions*; R. E. Webber, *Worship Old and New*; idem, *Worship is a*

Verb; W. H. Willimon, *Word, Water, Wine and Bread*; J. F. White, *Introduction to Christian Worship.*

Bibliography. P. F. Kiene, *"The Tabernacle of God in the Wilderness of Sinai"*; M. Levine, *The Tabernacle: Its Structure and Utensils*; S. F. Olford, *The Tabernacle: Camping with God*; S. Ridout, *Lectures on the Tabernacle*; A. B. Simpson, *Christ in the Tabernacle.*

Nave, Orville J. "Nave's Topical Bible". By Crosswalk.com online studies. <http://bible.crosswalk.com/Concordances/NavesTopicalBible/ntb.cgi?Number=T3976>. 1896.

The Hebrew lexicon is Brown, Driver, Briggs, Gesenius Lexicon; this is keyed to the "Theological Word Book of the Old Testament." These files are considered public domain.

The New Testament Greek Lexicon based on Thayer's and Smith's Bible Dictionary plus others; this is keyed to the large Kittel and the "Theological Dictionary of the New Testament." These files are public domain.

The Old Testament Hebrew Lexicon is Brown, Driver, Briggs, Gesenius Lexicon; this is keyed to the "Theological Word Book of the Old Testament." These files are considered public domain.

Christian Classics Ethereal Library Website: www.ccel.org. by Mr. Doug Nicolet. The 1599 Geneva Study Bible.

Commentary Critical and Explanatory on the Whole Bible
This one volume commentary was prepared by Robert Jamieson, A. R. Fausset and David Brown and published in 1871.

M.G. Easton M.A., D.D., Illustrated Bible Dictionary, Third Edition, published by Thomas Nelson, 1897.

Johnson, Ashley S. "Entry for "The Worship," "Priesthood, Temple, Tabernacle." "Condensed Biblical Cyclopedia". <http://bible.crosswalk.com/Encyclopedias/CondensedBiblicalCyclopedia/
cbe.cgi? Number=T39>. 1896.

The Full Life Study Bible-King James Version
Copyright © 1992 by Life Publishers International
All rights reserved.
Library of Congress Catalog Card Number 92-060909

Published by Zondervan Publishing House

The Hebrew-Greek Key Study Bible
© COPYRIGHT 1984 AND 1991 SPIRO ZODHIATES
AND AMG INTERNATIONAL, INC. D/B/A AMG PUBLISHERS
Revised edition, June 1991 Hebrew-Greek Key Study Bible KJV.

Holman Illustrated Bible Dictionary
© 2003 by Holman Bible Publishers
Nashville, Tennessee
All rights Reserved
Some quotations were taken from the *Holman Christian Standard Bible®* Copyright © 1999, 2000, 2002, 2004 and *Holman Bible Dictionary.*

Some quotations were taken from the *Nelson's Bible Dictionary* Copyright © 1986 by Thomas Nelson Publishers. All Rights Reserved.
Published in Nashville, Tennessee, by Thomas Nelson, Inc., Publishers and distribution in Canada by Lawson falle, Ltd., Cambridge, Ontario.
Unless otherwise indicated, all Scripture quotations are from the New King James Version, copyright © 1982
by Thomas Nelson Inc., Publishers, All rights reserved.

Verses marked "NASB" are taken from the *New American Standard Bible*, copyright © 1960, 1962, 1963, 1968, 1971, 1972, 1973, 1975 by the Lockman Foundation.

Verses marked "RSV" are taken from the Holy Bible: *Revised Standard Version*, second edition,
Copyright © 1946, 1951, 1972 by the Division of Christian Education of the NCCCUSA.

Verses marked "NIV" are taken from the Holy Bible: *New International Version*, copyright   1978 by the
New York International Bible Society.

"*Nelson's Chapter-By-Chapter Bible Commentary.*" Warren W. Wiersbe
Thomas Nelson Publishers
Copyright © 1991 by Warren W. Wiersbe
All Rights Reserved.

"*Nelson's Bible Commentary*" Earl Radmacher, Ron Allen & H. Wayne House.
Copyright © 2004 by Thomas Nelson Inc.

"New International Bible Commentary"
Copyright © *1979* by Pickering & Inglis Ltd.
Formerly tittled *The International Bible Commentary*.
Based on the NIV. F.F. Bruce, General Editor
ZONDERVAN PUBLISHING HOUSE Grand Rapids, Michigan 49530.

"New International Encyclopedia of Bible Words" Copyright © 1985, 1991 by Zondervan Corporation
Formerly published under the tittle *Zondervan Expository Dictionary of Bible Words*.
The World Book Encyclopedia "M"
Copyright © 1976, U.S.A. by Field Enterprises Educational Corporation.

"Prophetic Training Manual" Copyright © 1999 by John A. Tetsola Ph. D. . . All Rights Reserved.
Published by END TIME WAVE PUBLICATIONS, P.O. Box 141, Bogota, New Jersey 07603-0141.

"The Complete Word Study Dictionary" {new testament} "A Deeper Understanding of the Word"
THE COMPLETE WORD STUDY DICTIONARY: © COPYRIGHT 1992 BY SPIROS ZODHIATES
AND AMG INTERNATIONAL, INC. D/B/A AMG PUBLISHERS
June 1992.

"THE COMPARATIVE STUDY BIBLE" a parallel bible. KJV, NIV, AB, NASB, ZONDERVAN.
The Comparative Study Bible Copyright © 1984 by Zondervan Corporation Grand Rapids, Mi. 49506 u.s.a.

"The Amplified Bible"
The amplified bible © 1965 by Zondervan Publishing House
The Amplified Old Testament (part one) © 1964 by Zondervan Publishing House
The Amplified Old Testament (part two) © 1962 by Zondervan Publishing House
The Amplified New Testament © 1958 by the Lockman Foundation
The Amplified Gospel of John © 1954 by the Lockman Foundation
All Rights Reserved.

"New American Standard Version"
New American Standard Version © copyright The Lockman Foundation 1960, 1962, 1963, 1968, 1971, 1972, 1973, 1975, 1977 All Rights Reserved.

"The New International Version"®

The Holy Bible, New International Version
Copyright © 1973, 1978, 1984 by the International Bible Society
All Rights Reserved.

"*The Nelson's Bible Reference*" concordance, topical index, dictionary. Copyright © 1982 by Thomas Nelson Publishers.
Originally released as *Guidepost Family Topical Concordance to the Bible* and published jointly by
Thomas Nelson Publishers and by Guideposts Associates, Inc.
All Rights Reserved.

Webster's "*New World*™ *Dictionary and Thesaurus*" Copyright © 1996 by Simon & Schuster, Inc.
All Rights Reserved.
Macmillan General Reference
A Simon & Schuster Macmillan Company 1633 Broadway New York, NY. 10019-6785

New College Edition. "*The American Heritage DICTIONARY of the English Language*" Houghton Mifflin.
HOUGHTON MIFFLIN COMPANY Boston/Atlanta/Dallas/Geneva, Illinois/Hopewell, New Jersey/Palo Alto William Morris, Editor. © 1969, 1970, 1971, 1973, 1975, 1976, 1978, 1979, 1980 by Houghton Mifflin
Company. All Rights Reserved under Bern and Pan-American Copyright Conventions.

"*The Illustrated Guide to World Religions*" Dean Halverson General Editor
Copyright © 1996
International Students, Inc.
This edition © 2003 Angus Hudson Ltd/ Tim Dowley & Peter Wyart trading as three's Company
Published by Bethany House Publishers 11400 Hampshire Avenue South Bloomington, Minnesota 55438
All Rights Reserved.

"*The Ministry Anointing of the PROPHET MINISTREL the Radical Renaissance*" David L. Brown. www.worship4him.com/ Apostle & Founder-The Davidic Company. President/CEO-Psalm of David Publishing Company, P.O. Box 760013, Southfield, MI. 48076 www.thedavidic.com. Copyright © 2003 by David L. Brown

"*Interpreting the Symbols and Types*" Kevin J. Conner revised and expanded version.

Bibliography

Published by City Bible Publishing 9200 NE Fremont Portland, Oregon 97220
Printed U.S.A.
Originally Published as *Interpreting the Symbols and Types* © Copyright 1980 by Kevin J. Conner
Interpreting the Symbols and Types Completely revised and expanded edition © Copyright 1992 by Bible
Temple Publishing.
All Rights Reserved.

"Singing In a Strange Land" C.L. Franklin, the Black Church, and the Transformation of America Copyright © 2005 by Nick Salvatore
Little Brown and Company
Time Warner Book Group
All Rights Reserved.

On-line PC Bible website
www.bible.crosswalk.com
bible.com
kingjamesbible.com
www.gospelcom.net The Lockman Foundation- Amplified Bible
www.html.biblesearch.com Bible Research/ Matthew Henry Commentary- HTML Bible.
http://www.johnhurt.com bible software developers.

Mathew Henry's Commentary on the whole Bible. Complete and Unabridged (HENDRICKSON) publishers.
Copyright © 1991 by Hendrickson Publishing, Inc.
ISBN: 0-943575-32-X fourteenth print version.

The Secret Symbols of the Dollar Bill. Copyright © 2004 by David Ovason
HarperCollins Publishers Inc., 10 East 53rd St., New York, NY 10022.

"THE PULPIT COMMENTARY," 23 volume set
Edited by H. D. M. Spence and Joseph S. Exell
Hedrickson Publishers P.O. BOX 3473
Peabody, Massachusetts 01961-3473.

Howard F. Vos 1925
Nelson's New Illustrated Bible Manners & Customs: how the people of the Bible really lived,
Howard F. Vos. Copyright © 1999 by Howard F. Vos.

"THE TRUTH BEHIND HIP HOP"DVD, on sex, drugs, crime, idolatry, violence. Copyright © 2004.
G. Craige Lewis All Rights Reserved.
EX Ministries Fort Worth, TX. 76103

"THE COMPLETE WORD STUDY DICTIONARY" Old Testament, word study series "A deeper understanding of The Word"
Copyright © 2003 by AMG Publishers 6815 Shallowford Rd. Chattanooga, TN. 37421
Warren Baker, D.R.E. Eugene Carpenter Ph.D.

"THE ANNALS of the WORLD" James Ussher's Classic Survey of World History. First printing: October 2003. Fourth printing: December 2004. Revised and updated by, Larry and Marion Pierce.
Copyright © 2003 by Larry and Marion Pierce. All rights reserved.
For Information write: Master Books, Inc., P.O. Box 726, Green Forest, AR. 72638. Bibliography. R. E. Brown, *"The Churches the Apostles Left Behind"*; J. D. G. Dunn, Unity and Diversity in the New Testament; R. P. McBrien, Ministry; L. Morris, Ministers of God; E. Schweizer, Church Order in the New Testament.

Shakespeare's *Hamlet's Soliloquies*
Bealey, Betty, ed. *Hamlet*. By William Shakespeare. Toronto: Academic Press Canada, 1963. Edwards, Philip, ed. *Hamlet*. By William Shakespeare. Cambridge: Cambridge UP, 1985.

Jenkins, Harold, ed. *Hamlet*. By William Shakespeare. London: Methuen, 1982. Kittredge, George, ed. *Hamlet*. By William Shakespeare. Toronto: Ginn and Company, 1967. Newell, Alex. *The Soliloquies of Hamlet*. London: Associated Unversity Presses, 1991.

Annette Bercut Lust *"THE ORIGINS AND DEVELOPMENT OF THE ART OF MIME"* ©1996-2006 the World of Mime Theatre. All rights reserved. This page last updated 01 January 2003. (No inserts from this book were taken, only used for informational purposes.)

GODDESS KALI Information/ www.hindunet.org/god/**Goddess**es/**kali**mata/ index www.geocities.com/Area51/Shadowlands/5229/**kali**/**kali**. http://en.wikipedia.org/wiki/Kali

"ADVENTURING THROUGH THE BIBLE" *A comprehensive guide to the entire bible.* Ray C. Stedman Copyright © 1997 Elaine Stedman. Discovery House Publishers is affiliated with RBC Ministries, Grand Rapids, Michigan 49512

Bibliography

"THE TABERNACLE OF ISRAEL" *"Its structure and symbolism Illustrated"* James Strong Published in 1987 by Kregal Publications, a division of Kregal, Inc., P.O. Box 2607, Grand Rapids, Mi. 49501.

"HE LEADETH ME" C.W.SLEMMING; *Shepard Life in Palestine-Psalms 23.* Christian Literature Crusade. United States P.O. Box 1449. Ft. Washington, PA. 19034.

"Exegeses Ready Research Bible" a literal translation and transliteration of Scripture, based on te Authorized King James Version and keyed to Strong's Concordance.
Second Edition, exegeses ready research Bible, © 1993. World Bible Publishers Iowa Falls IA 50126

"What does the bible say about. . . . .: The Ultimate Bible Answer Book. Copyright © 2005 by Brian Ridolfi. Published by AMG Publishers, 6815 Shallowford Rd. Chattanooga, Tenn. 37421

Copyright 1942 C.W. SLEMMING. First edition 1942, First North American addition 1965 and revised edition 1973. *"no part of this publication or translation were used in this book"* Only used as an informational tool for this work.

"THUS SHALT THOU SERVE" C.W. Slemming. *"An Exposition of the Offerings and the Feasts of Israel."by Charles W. Slemming d.d.*
CHRISTIAN LITERATURE CRUSADE, USA-P.O. Box 1449, Fort Washington, PA. 19034; BRITIAN- 51 the Dean, Alresford, Hants, SO24 9BJ.
Copyright © 1966 C.W. Slemming. New Revised Edition, August 1955 First American Edition 1974, this printing in 1994.

"Teaching of the Word" by Apostle Dr. Thomas H. Vinson. *"for the last 28 years"* Senior Pastor and Founder of Highpoint Christian Tabernacle, since 1984. *(mr)-**my** **r**ights* have been reserved to learn from this man of God. . .as of Nov. 1985.

"Drug-Facilitated Sexual Assault Resource Guide" *National* Drug Intelligence Center. George Mason University. May, 2003. 319 Washington St. – 5th floor – Johnstown, Pa. 15901-1622.
NDIC publications are available on the following websites: ADNET- http://ndicosa LEO- home.leo.gov/lesig/ndic RISS- ndic.riss.net INTERNET- www.usdoj.gov/ndic

Note:

If you go to the websites from the Drug-Facilitated Guide listed just above; you will find many of the drugs that are used in the Hip-Hop, Goth and Emo cultures. This is no joke; it's a serious problem with mainly the youth but adults also have a serious problem with drugs in America.

For more detailed information on these drugs and gang violence contact- John W. Williams at 678-457-1343 or email: shighwilli@aol.com.

CPSIA information can be obtained
at www.ICGtesting.com
Printed in the USA
LVOW04s0813051117
555072LV00010B/132/P